THE
LINDISFÄRNE
GOSPELS

Frontispiece. The Lindisfarne Gospels, fol. 210b, detail.

THE LINDISFÆRNE GOSPELS

JANET BACKHOUSE

Φ

To the memory of
Professor Dame Lillian Penson
(1896-1963)

Phaidon Press Limited, 140 Kensington Church Street, London W8 4BN
in association with the British Library

First published 1981
Paperback edition 1987, reprinted 1989, 1991, 1992, 1993
© 1981 by Phaidon Press Limited

British Library Cataloguing in Publication Data

Backhouse, Janet
The Lindisfarne Gospels.
1. Bible. New Testament. Gospels. *Latin.*
Lindisfarne Gospels – Criticism, interpretation, etc.
1. Title
226'.04'7   BS2552.L5

ISBN 0 7148 2461 5 p/b

Printed and bound in Singapore

CONTENTS

ACKNOWLEDGEMENTS

The Lindisfarne Gospels is one of the most cherished treasures of the British Library, and many members of the staff of the Manuscripts Department have given help, both practical and academic, during the preparation of this book. I am particularly grateful to the Keeper of Manuscripts, Daniel Waley, for his enthusiastic encouragement of the project. I am also grateful to Bernard Dod and Freda Quartley of the Phaidon Press, who made the practical arrangements run so smoothly, and to Bruce Barker-Benfield, who read through the typescript and helped to clarify a number of points.

Thanks are due to Leslie Webster, Andrew Oddy and Judy Rudoe of the British Museum; Professor Rosemary Cramp of Durham University; Dr George Salt of King's College, Cambridge; Canon A. N. Barnard of Lichfield; Canon R. L. Coppin of Durham; Revd. D. A. Bill of Holy Island and Revd. I. D. Bunting of Chester-le-Street, for information on particular points and for help in obtaining photographs. Sources of photographs are included in the captions; those for which no source is given were supplied by the British Library's photographic service.

Special thanks go to Lawrence Pordes, senior photographer in the British Library, for his skill and patience in making a new set of photographs of the manuscript, many of which are used here; and to Shelley Jones, who has been very much involved with the subject from the beginning, and with whom I visited the manuscript's three medieval homes, Saint Cuthbert's hermitage on Farne Island, and many other sites and monuments in Anglo-Saxon Northumbria.

1. LINDISFARNE AND SAINT CUTHBERT

The Lindisfarne Gospels (British Library, Cotton MS Nero D.iv), made in north-east England less than a century after the introduction there of Christianity and now rapidly approaching its 1,300th birthday, is one of the world's greatest masterpieces of manuscript painting. Fortunately for the many generations of scholars and art lovers who have studied and admired it, it is also one of the best documented. About the middle of the tenth century a priest called Aldred, who had added to it an Anglo-Saxon translation of the Latin text, wrote on the last leaf a colophon naming the four men who made it, including himself. Although the book was already some 250 years old, Aldred was certainly recording well-established tradition, and there is no reason to doubt his statement. In modern English the colophon reads:

> Eadfrith, Bishop of the Lindisfarne Church, originally wrote this book, for God and for Saint Cuthbert and — jointly — for all the saints whose relics are in the Island. And Ethelwald, Bishop of the Lindisfarne islanders, impressed it on the outside and covered it — as he well knew how to do. And Billfrith, the anchorite, forged the ornaments which are on it on the outside and adorned it with gold and with gems and also with gilded-over silver — pure metal. And Aldred, unworthy and most miserable priest, glossed it in English between the lines with the help of God and Saint Cuthbert....

The monastery of Lindisfarne, where Eadfrith and Ethelwald were bishops, was founded in or about AD 635 on a small outcrop of land, now known as Holy Island, lying among the sands about a mile and a half off the Northumberland coast and 12 miles south of Berwick-upon-Tweed (plate 1). The site is marked by the ruins of a later medieval priory, founded about 1083 as a dependency of Durham Cathedral Priory (plate 2). Today about 200 people live on Holy Island, most of them making a living either from fishing or through some aspect of the tourist trade, which every year brings thousands of visitors to their village. The modern causeway has a metalled surface, but until very recently residents and visitors alike were still obliged to follow a track across the sands, exactly as medieval pilgrims had done. Twice each day, for several hours at a time, the island is cut off from the mainland by the sea, which means that everyday matters such as postal deliveries and bus timetables are governed by the movements of the tide. To the members of the seventh-century monastic community the situation must have seemed ideal, the sea providing a visible barrier between them and the world (and at least a partial defence against attack from the land), without entirely hindering them in their comings and goings as missionaries and preachers in other parts of the kingdom of Northumbria.

The first Christian mission to the Anglo-Saxon population of Northumbria was undertaken by Saint Paulinus, one of a group of

men sent from Rome to England in 601 by Pope Gregory the Great to assist in the work of conversion already begun in Kent by Saint Augustine. Paulinus came north in 625 as chaplain to the Christian Princess Ethelberga of Kent, bride of King Edwin of Northumbria, and his preaching, supported by the conversion of the king, met with great success. However, Edwin's death in battle in 633 resulted in a resurgence of paganism, and Paulinus and Ethelberga fled back to the south. Two years later King Oswald, eager to re-establish the new faith, sent to the Irish monastery on Iona for priests. A fresh mission was led by Saint Aidan, and it was he who founded the monastery on Holy Island, conveniently close to his royal patron's stronghold on the rock of Bamburgh, which is clearly visible from Lindisfarne. Saint Aidan and his companions travelled the length and breadth of Northumbria, usually on foot, preaching and baptizing. By the time of Aidan's death in 651 the Christian faith was firmly established in the area and several further monastic communities had been founded.

Saint Cuthbert, in whose honour the Lindisfarne Gospels was to be made, was born about the time of the arrival of the missionaries from Iona. We know a great deal about him because, only a few years after his death, two detailed accounts of his life were written. The first was by an anonymous monk of the Lindisfarne community and the second, in part based upon it, was by the Venerable Bede, the 'father of English history', who died in 735. Both men were able to include material gathered from people still living who had known Saint Cuthbert well. He seems to have been a warm-hearted and practical person, and many of his miracles involve delightful animal stories.

Cuthbert entered the monastery of Melrose, in what is now lowland Scotland, soon after Saint Aidan's death, which he had seen in a vision while caring for sheep in the Lammermuir Hills. After a period of study under Boisil, the saintly prior of Melrose, he was ordained priest

2. The ruins of Lindisfarne Priory, built probably on the site of the Anglo-Saxon monastery. The Priory was founded about 1083 as a dependency of Durham Cathedral Priory, and the massive decorated columns of the ruined church are very similar to those in Durham Cathedral itself (*photo: the author*).

and began to journey about Northumbria, preaching and administering the sacraments, and rapidly acquiring a reputation for holiness and for the possession of miraculous powers. He spent a short period at Ripon, where he helped to found a new monastery, succeeded Boisil as prior of Melrose, and was eventually sent to Lindisfarne to reform the way of life of the community, as discipline there had become slack. At Lindisfarne Cuthbert found himself more and more attracted to the idea of a life of solitude. He began by withdrawing occasionally to a tiny islet only a few yards off the shore of the main island and, like it, accessible on foot at low tide. Later he moved to Farne Island, directly opposite Bamburgh, where he built himself a hermitage from which he could see nothing but the sky. There he lived alone for a number of years, visited not only by the monks of his own community but also by many people from far and near who had been attracted by his growing reputation for saintliness. In 684, after King Ecgfrith himself had visited the island to plead with him, Cuthbert bowed to pressure to accept election as a bishop, and the following Easter he was consecrated at York by Archbishop Theodore of Canterbury.

For the short space of two years Saint Cuthbert returned to his earlier itinerant life. Then, feeling that the end of his life was approaching, he returned to his hermitage on Farne Island. One of his last miracles, used by Bede to demonstrate the virtue of obedience, kept a group of monks from Lindisfarne imprisoned on the island by a storm for an entire week because they had neglected to obey his instructions to cook and eat a goose hanging ready in his little guest house (plate 3). He died on 20 March 687, attended at the last by a small group of his brethren, and his passing was signalled across the sea to Holy Island by the waving of torches.

Cuthbert himself realized that he would be venerated as a saint and that his tomb would quickly attract pilgrims. He would have preferred a simple grave on Farne Island, where he had a sarcophagus and a winding sheet in readiness, but he yielded to the wishes of the community and agreed that his body might be taken to Lindisfarne for burial. It was usual for the remains of a holy man to be left in the earth long enough for the soft parts of the body to disintegrate, and then for the bones to be raised, washed, wrapped in fine cloths, and placed in a casket above ground where they could be visited by the faithful. This 'elevation' of the relics amounted to a formal declaration of sainthood. Eleven years elapsed before Cuthbert's successor, Eadbert, gave his consent for the grave to be reopened. In the meantime a new roof of lead was placed on the monastery's wooden church, a carved oak chest was made to receive the relics, and, almost certainly also during this period, the Lindisfarne Gospels itself was written and illuminated. At last, in 698, on the anniversary of Cuthbert's death, the grave was opened to reveal a body miraculously undecayed, in further proof of holiness (plate 4). It was reverently placed in its casket and laid on the floor of the sanctuary. As Cuthbert had foreseen, pilgrims flocked to the shrine and miracles were soon recorded.

In 793, apparently without warning, Lindisfarne was raided and sacked by Vikings. Writing from the court of Charlemagne to King Ethelred of Northumbria, Alcuin of York exclaimed: '... never before has such terror appeared in Britain as we have now suffered from a pagan race, nor was it thought that such an inroad from the sea could be made.' Although the community soon returned to the island, it was

3. The miracle of the uncooked goose. An illustration from a copy of Bede's prose Life of Saint Cuthbert, written and decorated at Durham Cathedral Priory about 1100–20. University College, Oxford, MS 165, p. 98 (*Bodleian Library, Oxford*).

.xlii. in corp ipsi p undeci annos sine corrupcaone sic repται.

Uolens aut laō monſtrare diuina diſpenſacio quanta in głā uir ſēr p morċē uiueret. cui ance morċē uita ſullimī cre briſ eτā miraculoꝝ paτebat indiciuſ: cñs acciſ ſepulcure euſ anniſ undeci immiſic

4. The opening of Saint Cuthbert's grave in 698. The monks display their astonishment at finding his body miraculously undecayed. University College, Oxford, MS 165, p. 118 (*Bodleian Library, Oxford*).

with an increasing sense of unease as monastery after monastery suffered the same fate. At last, in 875, Bishop Eardulf took the relics of Saint Cuthbert and other treasures of the monastery, including the Lindisfarne Gospels and the bones of the two men who had made it, his predecessors Eadfrith and Ethelwald, and set off in search of a safer home. He was accompanied by all the inhabitants of the island, seven of whom were given special charge over the relics. Their wanderings, chronicled at the beginning of the twelfth century by Symeon of Durham, lasted about seven years. There was a time when it seemed that their final destination would be Ireland, but we are told that, as the bishop and his party tried to put out to sea, a terrible storm arose, three great waves swept over the ship and were turned to blood, and a copy of the Four Gospels, richly bound in gold and jewels, was swept overboard and lost. This was taken as a sign of the saint's displeasure, and the voyage was immediately abandoned. Saint Cuthbert then appeared in a dream to Hunred, one of the seven bearers, and told him where the manuscript could be found, washed up unharmed on the sands at a low tide. According to Symeon of Durham, the manuscript was the Lindisfarne Gospels.

Not long after this episode, the party settled at Chester-le-Street, in County Durham, where Saint Cuthbert's relics remained until 995, and it was there that Aldred the priest added his Anglo-Saxon gloss and colophon to the manuscript, probably during the third quarter of the tenth century.

2. THE MEN WHO MADE THE MANUSCRIPT

Four men are named in Aldred's colophon (plate 5) as contributors to the making of the Lindisfarne Gospels. The first is Bishop Eadfrith of Lindisfarne, who succeeded Bishop Eadbert in 698, shortly after Saint Cuthbert's elevation. He is said to have written the manuscript. The second, credited with binding it, is Bishop Ethelwald of Lindisfarne, who succeeded Eadfrith in 721. The third is Billfrith the Anchorite, who provided ornaments of gold, silver and jewels for its outer casing. The fourth is Aldred himself, who inserted the Anglo-Saxon translation or gloss.

Nothing is known of Eadfrith before he became bishop of Lindisfarne in May 698, except that he was apparently a member of the Lindisfarne monastic community. There are, however, several references to his activities after that date. Both the anonymous Life of Saint Cuthbert by one of the monks of Lindisfarne and the prose Life by the Venerable Bede are addressed to him. Eadfrith honoured Bede in return by promising that his name should be inscribed in the Lindisfarne *Liber Vitae* or *Book of Life* by Guthfrith the sacrist, and that he should be remembered in the prayers of the community. The original *Liber Vitae* kept by Guthfrith is no longer in existence, but a magnificent copy in letters of gold and silver was made about the middle of the ninth century. This is now in the British Library (Cotton MS Domitian A.vii) and Bede's name indeed appears in it, on folio 18b. In the prose Life, Bede refers to the restoration of Saint Cuthbert's hermitage on Farne Island by Eadfrith for Felgild, the saint's second successor there. From another eighth-century work, a Latin poem known as the *De Abbatibus*, by a monk called Ethelwulf, we learn that Eadfrith also gave advice and assistance in the foundation of Ethelwulf's own monastery, the history of which the poem recounts but the name of which unfortunately we do not know.

Ethelwald makes several appearances in Bede's *Ecclesiastical History* as well as in the Lives of Saint Cuthbert. As a young novice, he had been in personal attendance upon the saint, and he was witness to one of Cuthbert's miracles, when one of his own kinswomen was cured of an intolerable pain affecting her head and one side of her body. Soon after the elevation of the saint's relics in 698 he moved from Lindisfarne to Melrose, where he remained, first as prior and then as abbot, until shortly before he succeeded Eadfrith as bishop in 721. He died in or about 740 and was buried on Lindisfarne at the foot of a large stone cross which he himself had erected. This was later to be removed to Durham.

Of Billfrith's life nothing at all is known, except that he was an anchorite, or hermit, as Saint Cuthbert himself had been. He was also a priest. His name appears at the head of the second column on the page devoted to anchorites in the Lindisfarne *Liber Vitae* (folio 15), and its position in relation to other known names suggests that he probably

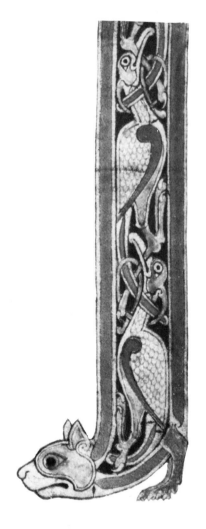

died during the latter part of the eighth century. The high regard in which anchorites were held is reflected in the fact that only two classes of people, both largely of royal blood, are placed before them in the *Liber Vitae*.

The wording of Aldred's colophon is not entirely unambiguous and there has been much discussion about its exact meaning. Some scholars have argued that Eadfrith and Ethelwald did not themselves make the manuscript but merely commissioned someone else to do so. However, Symeon of Durham, writing in the early twelfth century but with the full weight of local tradition behind him, says quite categorically that Eadfrith wrote the book with his own hand.

5. The Anglo-Saxon colophon added to the manuscript by Aldred in the mid-tenth century. It names Eadfrith, Ethelwald, Billfrith and Aldred himself as the four contributors to the making of the manuscript. A translation is given on p. 7 above. The Lindisfarne Gospels, folio 259 (detail).

The careful examination of the manuscript made when the facsimile edition was published 25 years ago showed clearly that, with the exception of the rubrics and some contemporary corrections and additions to the text, the whole of the Gospels had been written out by a single scribe. Furthermore, the decoration is so closely linked to the writing, particularly in one or two places where the original scheme was sketched out and then changed before the page was finished, that it must have been the work of the scribe himself. The examination also suggested that the book had been designed and made in a single campaign, without major interruption, and that it probably took at the very least two years to complete. This may be a considerable underestimate, as we do not have details about matters such as the weather. In 764 the Abbot of Wearmouth–Jarrow wrote to a friend, blaming an exceptionally cold winter for his scribe's inability to complete some books.

It seems unlikely that Eadfrith would have had the leisure to undertake a major artistic task of this kind after his election as bishop, when his life no doubt took on the strenuous pattern of travelling and preaching familiar from that of Saint Cuthbert. It is much more likely that he made the Gospels in the period immediately before the elevation of the relics in 698, when he was still only a senior member of the community, possibly head of the monastic scriptorium. Talented scribes and illuminators were held in very high esteem. Saint Columba, founder of Iona, was particularly noted for his activities as a scribe, and the *De Abbatibus* includes an account of an Irish monk called Ultan whose hand, 'once used to write the Lord's word', performed a miraculous cure as his bones were being raised from their original resting place. A senior monk who was also a talented scribe might well have been seen by his brethren as the most suitable candidate for election as bishop.

The known facts of Ethelwald's career also point to a date before 698 for the making of the Gospels. Immediately before the elevation he too was apparently only a senior member of the Lindisfarne community, but sometime between 699 and 705 he moved from the island to Melrose, not returning to Lindisfarne until 721. It thus seems sensible to suppose that he bound the manuscript before his departure, but the binding has long since disappeared. One single leather book binding made in Northumbria at this date has survived, the earliest European binding still associated with the manuscript for which it was made. This is the binding of the Saint Cuthbert Gospel, an exquisite little copy of the Gospel of Saint John which was found in Saint Cuthbert's coffin when his relics were translated to their new resting place in Durham Cathedral in 1104. The Gospel, which is at present on loan to the British Library, was copied in Bede's community of Wearmouth–Jarrow and may perhaps have been a gift to Lindisfarne in honour of the elevation. The binding is of crimson goatskin over beechwood boards, and the raised decoration on the front cover is moulded over cords (plate 6).

The exact form of Billfrith's contribution will never be known, for with Ethelwald's it disappeared centuries ago, probably at the Reformation. It was not uncommon for precious decoration to be added to the bindings of special Gospel books. Symeon of Durham's account of the Lindisfarne Gospels suggests that Billfrith's work was carried out at the request of Ethelwald whilst he was Bishop (721-40). No English jewelled binding of so early a date survives, but the silver plates added to Saint Cuthbert's portable altar presumably date from 698 and are therefore contemporary (plate 7).

6. The contemporary binding of the late seventh-century *Saint Cuthbert Gospel* (also known as the *Stonyhurst Gospel*), found in the coffin of Saint Cuthbert at the time of his translation in 1104, and at present on loan to the British Library (*by permission of the English Province of the Society of Jesus*).

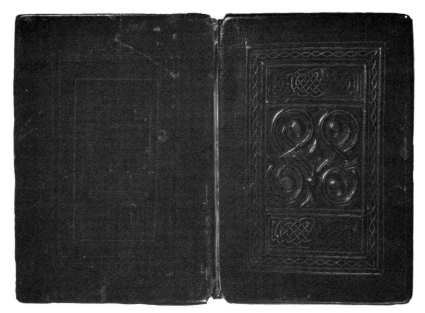

7. Fragments of silver ornaments from the back of Saint Cuthbert's portable altar. The fragments bearing foliate ornament probably date from the time of the elevation of the relics in 698. The decorated central patch is a ninth-century repair. The altar was found lying on Saint Cuthbert's breast when his tomb was opened in 1827 (*Durham Cathedral Library*).

Personal information about Aldred himself is also scanty. His father, according to a marginal note beside the colophon, was called Alfred. Two other manuscripts have additions which have been recognized as by his hand. One is the oldest surviving copy of Bede's Commentary on the Book of Proverbs (Bodleian Library, Oxford, MS Bodley 819; plate 12), written in the Wearmouth–Jarrow scriptorium in the second half of the eighth century and known to have been at Durham in the twelfth. The other, which reveals that Aldred advanced to be provost of Chester-le-Street, is the so-called Durham Ritual (MS A.IV.19 in Durham Cathedral Library), a collection of liturgical material probably written out in the south of England in the early tenth century, to which Aldred added (on page 167) four collects in honour of Saint Cuthbert. The collects are accompanied by a note recording that they were written out for Bishop Aelfsige by Aldred the Provost, at a place called Oakley, on a feast of Saint Lawrence which was also the fifth night of the moon. Aelfsige was bishop of Chester-le-Street between 968 and 990, and the feast of Saint Lawrence (10 August) coincided with the fifth night of the moon in 970. Oakley appears to be identifiable as a place in Wessex, on the road between Salisbury and Blandford. It seems likely that Aelfsige, accompanied by Aldred, was in attendance upon King Edgar at the appropriate time.

In the Lindisfarne Gospels colophon, which must be earlier than the note in the Durham Ritual because in it Aldred describes himself only as a priest, he goes on to tell us that each Gospel was glossed with a separate special intention. Matthew was for God and Saint Cuthbert, Mark for the bishop, Luke for the community (with the addition of eight 'ores' of silver for his induction), and John for the sake of his own soul (with four 'ores' of silver for God and Saint Cuthbert). This suggests that his work on the manuscript was intended to establish him in the community at Chester-le-Street. It probably dates from shortly after the middle of the tenth century.

3. THE TEXT OF THE GOSPELS

OVERLEAF:
8. A page from Saint Matthew's Gospel, including the beginning of the Sermon on the Mount (Matthew 4: 24–5: 10). Aldred's tenth-century gloss, a word for word translation of the Latin, is added between the lines and in the right-hand margin. The Lindisfarne Gospels, folio 34.

9. A page from the table of feast days preceding Saint John's Gospel. Aldred added little to this page, so the full beauty of Eadfrith's script can be appreciated without distraction. The headings are in a different hand, that of the rubricator. The Lindisfarne Gospels, folio 208.

The Lindisfarne Gospels contains not one but two versions of the Gospel texts. The first is the Latin copied out by Eadfrith and the second the Anglo-Saxon interlinear gloss added two and a half centuries later by Aldred. Aldred's gloss is of great interest to students of English because it represents the earliest surviving translation of the Four Gospels into any form of the English language. It is a literal translation, written word by word between the lines of the Latin text, with occasional passages in the margins (plate 8). There is no necessity to assume that Aldred himself composed it. His colophon quite probably implies that he copied it from some other source which has not come down to us. There is indeed a very similar gloss in the MacRegol Gospels, an early ninth-century Irish manuscript now in Oxford (Bodleian Library, MS Auct. D.2.19), and it is probably not much later in date than Aldred's work. A surprising quantity of Anglo-Saxon literature — original poetry and prose as well as translations of Latin texts — has survived in manuscript. Although a great deal more has doubtless disappeared, England can still boast the richest vernacular literature in Europe from so early a date. It is only necessary to recall that something as celebrated as the *Beowulf* poem is known only from a single copy (British Library, Cotton MS Vitellius A.xv), itself badly damaged as recently as 1731, when it was one of the casualties of the fire which destroyed a considerable portion of the Cotton library, to realize just how vulnerable such material can be.

We know of at least one eighth-century translation of the Gospel of Saint John, though it apparently has not survived. The Venerable Bede was working on it at the time of his death in May 735, and its final sentence was the last thing which he dictated to Wilberht, his young amanuensis.

The Latin Gospel text is that of Saint Jerome's Vulgate, a revision of the Latin Bible made in the late fourth century and subsequently the most widely adopted throughout the western world. In the Lindisfarne Gospels it is preceded by the text of Saint Jerome's letter to Pope Damasus, at whose command the revision had been carried out, by the prologue to Saint Jerome's commentary on Matthew, and by a series of Eusebian canon tables (see below, p. 41), prefaced by the explanatory letter of Eusebius to Carpianus. At the beginning of each of the Gospels is a short introduction ('argumentum'), a list of passages used as liturgical readings ('capitula lectionum') and a list of festivals on which passages from that particular Gospel should be read (plate 9). The last item has no practical value, as details of the passages concerned are not included in it. It is, however, of special interest, as references to Saint Januarius in the lists preceding Matthew and John, and to the dedication of a basilica of Saint Stephen before Matthew, reflect a connection with Naples, suggesting that Eadfrith's exemplar was a Gospel book imported into England from the south of Italy.

ABIIT OPINIO EIUS

IN TOTAM SYRIAM

ET OBTULERUNT EI OMNES

MALE HABENTES

UARIIS LANGUORIBUS

ET TORMENTIS

COMPREHENSOS

ET QUI DAEMONIA

HABEBANT ET LUNATICOS

COS ET PARALYTICOS

ET CURAUIT EOS

ET SECUTAE SUNT EUM

TURBAE MULTAE

DE GALILAEA ET DECAPO

LIM ET HIEROSOLIMIS

ET DE IUDAEA ET DE

TRANS IORDANEN

UIDENS AUTEM TURBAS

ASCENDIT IN MONTEM

ET CUM SEDISSET ACCESSE

RUNT AD EUM

DISCIPULI EIUS

ET APERIENS OS SUUM

DOCEBAT EOS DICENS

BEATI PAUPERES SPU

QUONIAM IPSORUM EST

REGNUM CAELORUM

BEATI MITES QUONIAM

IPSI POSSIDEBUNT

TERRAM

BEATI QUI LUGUNT

QUONIAM IPSI

CONSOLABUNTUR

BEATI QUI ESURIUNT

ET SITIUNT IUSTITIAM

QUONIAM IPSI

SATURABUNTUR

BEATI MISERICORDES

QUONIAM IPSI

MISERICORDIAM

CONSEQUENTUR

BEATI MUNDO CORDE

QUONIAM IPSI DM

UIDEBUNT

BEATI PACIFICI

QUONIAM IPSI FILII

DI UOCABUNTUR

BEATI QUI PERSECUTIO
NEM

þinda befeadande

TERTIO COMMENDANS
mid hræcing honda
EXTENSIONE MANUUM
tahte þ him for nodeð
SIGNIFICAT EI QUOD CRUCIS
deade ventoysand mid þroung
MORTE FORE MARTYRIO
sy isfertnad
CORONANDUS

quae lectio cum in natale
sci petri legitur.
a loco incoatur
quo ait
Dicit simoni
petro ihs simon
iohannis
diligis me plus his
usq: ad locum ubi dicit
significans qua morte
clarificaturus esset dm
cum uero innatale sci
iohannis euangelifte tu
choanda est a loco quo
ait dicat et hoc est dns
simoni petro sequere me
usq: ubi dicit et scimus
quia uerum est
testimonium eius

explicit secundum
iohannen

Sci iohannis
apostoli et
euangelista
post epiphania
dnica prima
post ephipania dnica
secunda
inuelanda
indedicatione sce mariae
Dnica ii. xlgisma paschae
post octabas dni in iha xpi
post iii dnicas de ephipania
de muliere famaritanae
De xlgisma feria iiii
in sci angeli et indedicatione
fontas
coucliana
innatale sci andreae
coucliana
post iii dnicas xlgisma
feria iiii
post iii dnica xlgisma feria
iiii

The most likely source for such a manuscript in seventh-century Northumbria is undoubtedly Wearmouth–Jarrow. The early Church in England did, however, have a long and consistent connection with Italy and the Mediterranean. The first missionaries to the Anglo-Saxons, Saint Augustine of Canterbury and his followers, came direct from Rome on the orders of Pope Gregory the Great. They brought books with them, and further books were subsequently dispatched from Rome with those who, like Saint Paulinus, were sent in later years to reinforce the mission. Books reputed to have belonged to Saint Augustine were preserved as relics at Canterbury in the later Middle Ages, and what is almost certainly one of these, an illuminated copy of the Four Gospels, is still in existence (Corpus Christi College, Cambridge, MS 286). It dates from the sixth century and was written and decorated in Italy. One of Saint Augustine's successors as archbishop of Canterbury was Theodore of Tarsus, who had been a monk in Rome before coming to England in 669. He was accompanied by another monk, Hadrian, who had been born in Africa but whose original monastery was in Campania, not far from Naples. Hadrian was appointed abbot in Canterbury. Both these were learned men who attracted many students and who had doubtless brought further manuscripts with them to England.

In Northumbria during the first decades after the conversion, in-spite of the initial Roman impetus of Saint Paulinus, the closest external links were with Ireland through Iona. However, after the Synod of Whitby in 664 had settled the disagreement over the calculation of the date of Easter in favour of Roman rather than of Irish custom, with the result that many Celtic diehards withdrew from Northumbrian communities, direct links between Northumbria and Italy grew stronger. One personality whose activities had considerable influence was Saint Wilfrid of York (634-709), who had already made one journey to Rome before appearing at Whitby to represent the Roman case. He was to go there twice more in the course of his long and turbulent episcopal career, and we know that he took a great interest in books and in learning.

Most significant of all in this context are the careers of Benedict Biscop, who founded the monastery of Saint Peter at Wearmouth in 674, and of his friend and successor Ceolfrith, to whom he entrusted the establishment of the sister house of Saint Paul at Jarrow in 681. It was at Jarrow that the Venerable Bede spent almost the whole of his life. Benedict Biscop, who came of a noble Northumbrian family, had already been more than once to Rome before he settled at Wearmouth. He made two further visits, one of them in Ceolfrith's company, in order to bring back books, relics and works of art for his twin foundations. Unfortunately, none of his acquisitions have survived, but we know that the books which he collected included fine texts written in Italy in the sixth century, outstanding amongst which were the Codex Grandior, a vast copy of the whole of the Bible, and some or all of the Novem Codices, a Bible in nine volumes, all of which had been made at Cassiodorus's monastery of Vivarium in the extreme south of Italy. The work of the scriptorium at Wearmouth–Jarrow was very much influenced by the script and appearance of these manuscripts, which were emulated there with great success.

Contact between Lindisfarne and Wearmouth–Jarrow, only 40 miles apart, seems to have been close during the late seventh and early eighth centuries. As we have already seen, Eadfrith, creator of the Lindisfarne Gospels itself, asked Bede to compose a Life of his own monastery's special saint, Cuthbert. The names of both Benedict

Biscop and Ceolfrith, like that of Bede, appear in the Lindisfarne *Liber Vitae* (on folios 17 and 15b respectively). The Gospel text which Eadfrith copied could well have been borrowed from Wearmouth–Jarrow and, indeed, textually the Lindisfarne Gospels has close relatives in the two most famous of the Wearmouth–Jarrow manuscripts, the Codex Amiatinus (Biblioteca Medicea-Laurenziana, Florence, MS Amiatinus I) and the Saint Cuthbert (or Stonyhurst) Gospel of Saint John. These are the three leading members of a distinct family of manuscripts, the so-called 'Italo-Northumbrian' group, which is one of the most important sources for the early form of the Vulgate text.

4. THE SCRIPT

Eadfrith chose to write the main text of his Gospels in the fine formal script known technically as insular majuscule (plates 8 and 9). The manuscript which he was making was intended not for the use of students in a library, but for ceremonial use in church, where it would be carried in procession and used for reading, perhaps not every day but certainly on special festivals. Its place would be with the altar vessels rather than with any other books that the monastery might possess. Every effort was therefore made to ensure that the final effect, both inside and out, should be in keeping with the status of a book enshrining the Word of God.

The insular majuscule script was developed in early Christian Ireland, whence it spread to Northumbria, through Iona and the Irish missionaries, and was subsequently adopted in other parts of England. As its name suggests, it was a speciality of the British Isles, but it is also found on the Continent, in areas influenced by Irish and English monastic foundations such as Bobbio, Sankt Gallen, Fulda and Echternach. Insular majuscule appears in a number of manuscripts earlier in date than the Lindisfarne Gospels, including the Book of Durrow (Trinity College, Dublin, MS 57; plate 53), but Eadfrith's interpretation of it is particularly stately, regular and disciplined. He wrote it with fairly broad nibs, cut to a remarkably consistent width throughout the execution of the text, and held parallel to the double guide lines which he ruled upon the page. The result is well-balanced and majestic, and was probably in some degree influenced by the appearance of Wearmouth–Jarrow books of the same date, even though these are not written in insular majuscule.

The script most characteristic of the Wearmouth–Jarrow scriptorium was uncial, a formal capitular hand developed in the Roman Empire during the fourth century and widely used for several centuries thereafter for writing out texts in book form. The manuscripts brought to England by Saint Augustine and his followers and those later collected by Benedict Biscop and Ceolfrith provided English scribes with many fine models for this script. So brilliantly did the scribes of Bede's community learn to execute it that the surviving masterpiece from Wearmouth–Jarrow, the huge one-volume Bible known as the Codex Amiatinus, now in Florence, was only recognized as English work within the last century, after much disagreement among scholars. Some of them, while eventually accepting that the book had been made in Northumbria, still refused to believe that it was not the work of immigrant Italian scribes. Only in recent years has the special flavour of 'English uncial' come to be discerned more easily. The Codex Amiatinus, like the Lindisfarne Gospels, is, however, unusually well documented. The anonymous author of the *Historia Abbatum,* who tells the story of the early abbots of Wearmouth–Jarrow, relates how Abbot Ceolfrith ordered three great

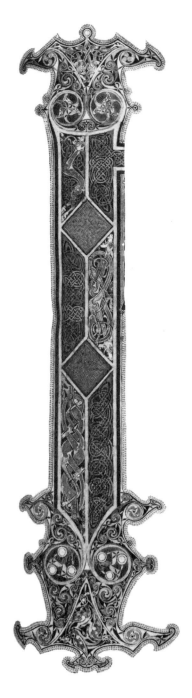

Bibles to be made, one for Wearmouth, one for Jarrow and the third to be presented to the Pope. The third copy he took with him when he left Northumbria to make a final pilgrimage to Rome in 716. He died on the journey and we do not know exactly what then became of the manuscript, but it is identifiable beyond doubt as the Codex Amiatinus because Ceolfrith's dedicatory inscription to the Pope, quoted in the *Historia Abbatum*, is still to be seen in it. The book reached Florence in 1787, when the monastery of Monte Amiata was suppressed and its library removed. Fragments of one of the other Ceolfrith Bibles have been discovered, re-used as wrappers for volumes of estate papers, and these are now in the British Library (Additional MS 37777 (plate 10), and Additional MS 45025).

The layout of the Ceolfrith Bibles' leaves and the layout of Eadfrith's text pages are certainly similar (though the Bibles are much larger), and it seems reasonable to suppose that Eadfrith decided to write his Gospels in two columns because he had seen earlier Italian books and their Wearmouth–Jarrow counterparts. His is not the only insular Gospel book to be laid out in this way. The virtually contemporary Echternach Gospels (Bibliothèque Nationale, Paris, MS lat. 9389; see plate 54 and pp. 36–9 below) is among other examples, and it is particularly interesting to note that it too has evidence of an Italian textual connection in the form of a colophon (folio 222b) copied from the exemplar, which records that the text was corrected in 558 from a manuscript which had belonged to Saint Jerome himself. The Durham Gospels (Durham Cathedral Library, MS A.II.17; plate 13 and p. 36 below), which is now attributed to the same scribe as the Echternach Gospels, although in it he is writing a different form of script, much closer to the insular majuscule practised by Eadfrith, is written in single columns.

Mention should be made of a third script characteristic of Anglo-Saxon England. This is insular minuscule, roughly speaking a cursive and time-saving form of the majuscule and, like it, developed in Ireland. This script is not used for any part of the original text of the Lindisfarne Gospels, but a later version was adopted by Aldred for the writing of his gloss. Minuscule was often used for business and legal documents and for transcribing less formal books, especially those written in the Anglo-Saxon language. Three special letter forms no longer in use in modern English are included in its alphabet for the vernacular language. These represent a 'w' and two 'th' sounds, and the two latter are still current in present-day Icelandic. One of the two persisted for several centuries in English and, because it looks very much like the modern 'y', has given rise to the spurious article 'ye' (for 'the'), very popular in 'olde worlde' contexts.

The earliest known copy of Bede's Latin *Ecclesiastical History* (University Library, Cambridge, MS Kk.5.16; plate 11) is written in minuscule. This manuscript, which is attributed to the Wearmouth–Jarrow scriptorium, was probably begun before Bede's death in 735. It is an unpretentious library copy, laid out so that no part of the vellum, which is not of the very best quality, should be wasted. Its pages contrast sharply with the spacious elegance of Eadfrith's pages. A later and more calligraphic example of minuscule, written in the second half of the eighth century and also probably from Wearmouth–Jarrow, is a copy of Bede's Commentary on the Book of Proverbs (Bodleian Library, Oxford, Bodley MS 819; plate 12), already mentioned because it contains glosses added by Aldred. This is the earliest surviving copy of the Commentary, though it must have been well-known and widely circulated in the eighth century. Saint

OVERLEAF:
10. The Greenwell Leaf. A single leaf from one of the three great Bibles written in the scriptorium of Wearmouth–Jarrow in the time of Abbot Ceolfrith. This is a particularly magnificent example of English uncial. The text is part of the Third Book of Kings. British Library, Additional MS 37777, verso.

dita morte eius reuersus est.
de aegypto
miseruntq. et uocauerunt eum
uenit ergo hieroboam et omnis
multitudo israhel,
et locuti sunt ad roboam dicentes
pater tuus durissimum iugum
inposuit nobis
tu itaq. nunc inminue paululu
de imperio patris tui durissimo
et de iugo grauissimo quod in
posuit nobis et seruiemus tibi
qui ait eis
ite usq. ad tertium diem
et reuertimini ad me
cumq. abisset populus init
consilium rex roboam
cum senibus
qui adsistebant coram salomone
patre eius dum adhuc uiueret
et ait quod mihi datis consilium
ut respondeam populo
qui dixerant ei
si hodie oboedieris populo huic
et seruieris
et petitioni eorum cesseris
locutusq. pueris ad eos uerba lenia
erunt tibi serui cunctis diebus
qui dereliquit consilium senum
quod dederant ei
et adhibuit adulescentes qui
nutriti fuerant cum eo
et adsistebant illi
dixitq. ad eos quod mihi datis
consilium ut respondeam
populo huic
qui dixerunt mihi leuius fac
iugum quod inposuit pater
tuus super nos
et dixerant ei iuuenes qui
nutriti fuerant cum eo
sic loqueris populo huic qui
locuti sunt ad te dicentes
pater tuus adgrauauit iugum

nostrum tu releuanos
sic loqueris ad eos
minimus dictus meus grossior
est dorso patris mei
et nunc pater meus posuit
super uos iugum graue
ego autem addam super iugum
uestrum
pater meus cecidit uos flagellis
ego autem caedam uos
scorpionibus
Uenit ergo hieroboam et omnis
populus ad roboam die tertia
sicut locutus fuerat rex dicens
reuertimini ad me die tertia
responditq. rex populo dura
derelicto consilio seniorum
quod ei dederant
et locutus est eis secundum
consilium iuuenum dicens
pater meus adgrauauit
iugum uestrum
ego autem addam iugo uestro
pater meus cecidit uos flagellis
et ego caedam scorpionibus
et non adquieuit rex populo
quoniam auersatus eum
fuerat dns
ut suscitaret uerbum suum
quod locutus fuerat in manu
ahiae silonitas ad hieroboam
filium nabat
Uidens itaq. populus quod noluis
set eos audire rex
respondit ei dicens
quae nobis pars in dauid
uel quae hereditas in filio isai
in tabernacula tua israhel
nunc uide domum tuam dauid
et abiit israhel in tabernacula sua
super filios autem israhel
quicumq. habitabant in ciui
tatibus iuda regnauit roboam
Misit igitur rex roboam

11. The Moore Bede. The upper part of a page from the oldest surviving copy of Bede's most famous work, *The Ecclesiastical History of the English People*. The manuscript, which is written in insular minuscule, was apparently made at Wearmouth–Jarrow between 734 and 737. As Bede himself lived until 735, it may thus have been begun within his lifetime. University Library, Cambridge, MS Kk.5 16, folio 97b (*by permission of the Syndics of Cambridge University Library*).

BELOW:

12. Bede's Commentary on the Book of Proverbs. Part of a page from a copy made in the second half of the eighth century and attributed to Wearmouth–Jarrow. Uncial is used for headings and insular minuscule for the body of the text. Aldred, glossator of the Lindisfarne Gospels, has added one or two words between the lines. Bodley MS 819, folio 29 (*Bodleian Library, Oxford*).

Boniface, the English apostle of Germany, wrote to ask Archbishop Egbert of York to procure him a copy of it, some time between 747 and 751.

Although he wrote out the whole body of the Gospel text himself, and designed and executed the great decorated pages, it seems that Eadfrith entrusted the writing of the rubrics (or titles) to another, somewhat less talented member of the Lindisfarne scriptorium. This man also helped to make final corrections to the text, some of which amount to several lines of writing in the upper or lower margin of a page. One or two smaller corrections were added by a third hand, also contemporary, and these are of particular interest because the same hand has now been identified making corrections to the Durham Gospels, which adds to the accumulation of evidence linking this fine, but badly worn and damaged, manuscript with the monastery on Holy Island.

13. The Durham Gospels. Part of a page from a manuscript written by a contemporary of Eadfrith, who was probably also a member of the Lindisfarne scriptorium. The script is insular majuscule. Durham Cathedral MS A.II.17, folio 39 (*Durham Cathedral Library*).

5. HOW THE MANUSCRIPT WAS MADE

For our knowledge of the techniques and equipment involved in making early manuscripts such as the Lindisfarne Gospels, we are dependent upon three main types of evidence. First and most important is what can be gathered from close scrutiny of the manuscripts themselves. Second is evidence from archaeological sites such as Whitby and Jarrow, where writing implements have been found (plate 18). Third is evidence from written sources, some historical and some literary. Particularly revealing in this last group are some of the Latin and Anglo-Saxon riddles describing everyday objects, one of which, from the tenth-century collection known as the Exeter Book (now in the library of Exeter Cathedral), actually describes the making of a Gospel book, from the preparation of the vellum to the application of golden ornaments to its binding:

> An enemy ended my life, deprived me of my physical strength: then he dipped me in water and drew me out again, and put me in the sun, where I soon shed all my hair. After that, the knife's sharp edge bit into me and all my blemishes were scraped away; fingers folded me and the bird's feather often moved over my brown surface, sprinkling meaningful marks; it swallowed more wood-dye and again travelled over me leaving black tracks. Then a man bound me, he stretched skin over me and adorned me with gold; thus I am enriched by the wondrous work of smiths, wound about with shining metal.

Such riddles were very popular, and surviving collections include relevant examples by such contemporaries of Eadfrith as Aldhelm, abbot of Malmesbury and bishop of Sherborne (*c*. 640-709), Tatwine, archbishop of Canterbury (d. 734) and 'Eusebius', who was probably Hwaetberht, abbot of Wearmouth and a friend of Bede (*c*. 680-747).

Books written in northern Europe during almost the whole of the Middle Ages were made of vellum. This was prepared from the skins of sheep or of calves and was therefore a costly commodity. It is not at all easy to distinguish between the two types of skin, but one or two stiff brown hairs have been found still clinging to pages of the Lindisfarne Gospels, which suggests that its vellum is made from calfskin.

In the Lindisfarne Gospels the pages are arranged for the most part in gatherings of eight, which is to say that four large sheets of vellum, each large enough for two pages, were placed one above the other and folded in two down the middle to make eight leaves. The manuscript contains 258 leaves, for which at least 129 large pieces of vellum, each measuring rather more than two feet by fifteen inches, were required. Close examination of the pages shows that the spines of the animals run horizontally across the book. We do not know the age or size of the calves involved, but it may well be that each large sheet represents one animal, which means that the number and value of the animals involved was very substantial. Both flesh and hair sides have been most expertly prepared to form a good and stable writing surface, very white in colour, and it is extremely hard to distinguish one from the other.

Once the sheets had been folded together to make a group of pages, the uppermost page was carefully measured out and the framework of the writing area marked by pricking. This was done sometimes with a sharp round stylus and sometimes with the point of a small knife, the latter leaving a tiny wedge-shaped rather than a round hole. These holes were pricked right through the entire gathering of eight leaves, then each individual text leaf was separately ruled for writing with a hard, dry point, very lightly so as to be as unobtrusive as possible. Each of the two text columns on a page is bounded by a double vertical line on the left and a single one on the right. The small initials at the beginnings of verses are governed by the left-hand rulings (plate 14). The horizontal lines on which the text is written are ruled between guiding prick marks lying on the extreme right-hand and extreme left-hand vertical lines. A pair of parallel rulings is provided for each of the 24 or 25 written lines in each column and, as each pair is of exactly the same width in spite of the fact that only the lower of the two lines is guided by a prick mark, we must assume that Eadfrith had a double-pointed instrument with which to make them.

The text of the Gospels is written in a dense, dark brown ink, often almost black, which contains particles of carbon from soot or lamp black. The pens used by Eadfrith may have been cut either from quills or from reeds. No direct evidence for either can be expected to emerge from archaeological investigation, as neither would be likely to survive in the soil. More than one of the riddles, including the one quoted above, apparently refers to the quill pen, but both reeds and quills are likely to have been readily available on or near Holy Island in Eadfrith's day. Today Holy Island is a celebrated bird sanctuary, its seasonal visitors including several sorts of goose, whose feathers are particularly well-suited for use as pens. It will be remembered that one of Saint Cuthbert's own miracles involved the cooking of a goose, implying their presence locally. Suitable reeds are also to be found in the area today, and could certainly have been obtained on the mainland if not on the island itself in Eadfrith's day.

When preparing his pages for writing, Eadfrith took immense pains not to allow his rulings to mar the smooth surface on leaves intended for pure decoration. Three of the five cross-carpet pages, those preceding Matthew, Luke and John, are not part of the basic gathering in which they appear but have been inserted separately. The Mark carpet is painted on the final verso of an irregular gathering devoted only to the prefatory material for that Gospel. The astonishingly complex designs on these pages are painstakingly built up over a measured geometric framework, traces of the construction work for which can be seen on the blank rectos of the leaves in the form of prick marks, compass holes, rulings and grid lines (plates 14-17). It appears that, within this mathematical framework, the more subtle curves were then drawn purely by eye. It has been suggested that templates were used in the execution of some seventh- and eighth-century manuscripts, and there certainly seems to be evidence that templates were part of a pre-Conquest stone-carver's equipment. In the decoration of the Lindisfarne Gospels there is nothing which immediately suggests the use of such an aid. Some of the outlines for the decoration were drawn with a dry point, and it is occasionally possible to see, under oblique light, places where the illuminator changed his mind. For

OPPOSITE ABOVE:
14. Enlarged detail showing the prickings and rulings which govern the arrangement of the script and minor initials. The Lindisfarne Gospels, folio 152b.

OPPOSITE BELOW:
15. Enlarged detail showing prickings and rulings on the reverse side of the central roundel of the cross-carpet page preceding Saint Mark's Gospel. The Lindisfarne Gospels, folio 94.

ċ peccatoribꝰ

⁊ ꝗⁱᵉ dp in cai

caꝉꝰ a b i b ꞇ a s

⁊ on d pⁱ un u de

xl
n
ꞇ m lxxni
ꞇ m xxnii

ⓒRespondens

cuoed   ꞇo hm

dⁱxⁱꞇ ad illos

ne doꝛed   dub

̄s non ege̅ꞇ quis

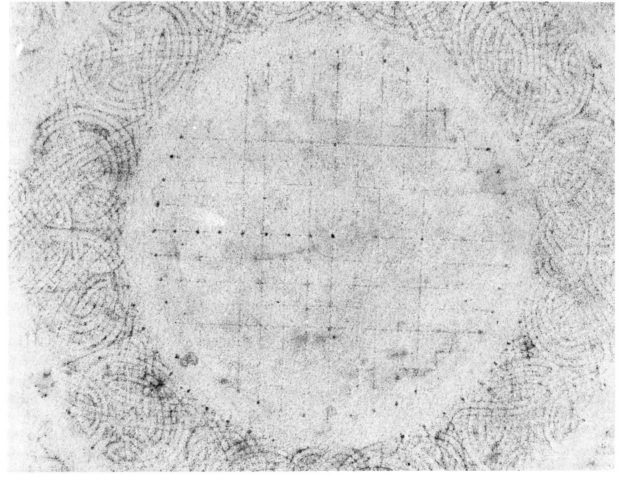

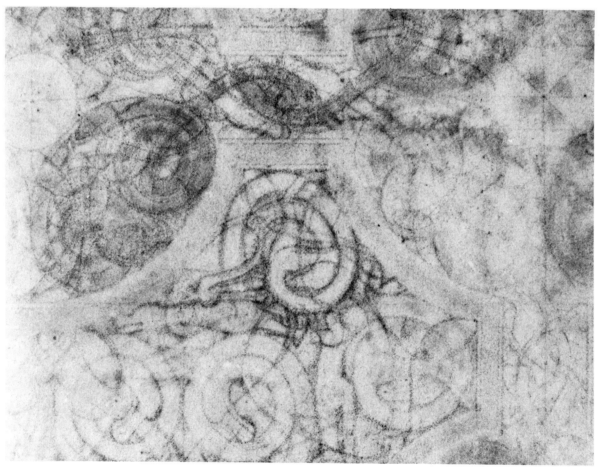

30

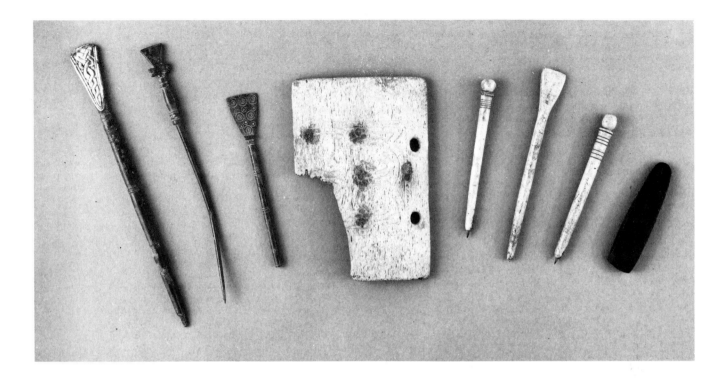

18. Anglo-Saxon writing implements. The largest stylus is about 5½ inches long. The carved bone tablet in the middle of the picture is hollowed on the other side to receive a wax writing surface. The styli to its left are made of bronze, those to its right of bone. The object on the extreme right is a miniature whetstone, used for sharpening a small knife. With the exception of the tablet, which was found at Blythburgh, all these objects were discovered during excavations at Whitby in the 1920s (*British Museum, Department of Medieval and Later Antiquities*).

OPPOSITE ABOVE:
16. Enlarged detail showing some of the construction marks on the reverse side of the major initial at the beginning of Saint John's Gospel. The Lindisfarne Gospels, folio 211b.

OPPOSITE BELOW:
17. Enlarged detail of a section of the 'pencil' sketch marks on the reverse side of the cross-carpet page preceding Saint Matthew's Gospel. The Lindisfarne Gospels, folio 26.

example, the decorative corner pieces on the frame around the miniature of Saint Matthew (plate 23) were originally to be much larger and heavier than in the final version. There are also traces of the use of a substance approximating to modern pencil, especially on the reverse sides of the decorated and major initial pages (plate 17).

It seems necessary to assume that some sketches preceded the execution of the finished pages, an equivalent to the carved bone 'trial pieces' associated with metalwork and found on pre-Conquest sites. These sketches, like the pens, have vanished without trace, and indeed there is a conspicuous lack of all such material for the whole of the Middle Ages. Costly sheets of vellum would not have been used in quantity for such a purpose. Rough preliminary designs could perhaps have been made on wax tablets, which were a common personal accessory during the period under discussion. Only one specimen has as yet been found in England (plate 18), but there is considerable written evidence for their existence. They were among the items of everyday equipment which the fifth-century Rule of Saint Benedict lists as essential for a monk. Wax tablets were made of wood or bone, with one or both surfaces hollowed out to receive a shallow layer of wax, on which it was possible to write or draw with the point of a stylus (plate 18). When the notes or sketches had served their purpose, the wax surface, perhaps slightly warmed, could be smoothed out with a spatula, usually provided at the other end of the writing implement. Two or more tablets might be joined together with thongs to form a little notebook. One of Aldhelm's riddles describes a wax tablet:

Of honey-laden bees I first was born, but in the forest grew my outer coat; my tough backs came from shoes [the leather thongs]. An iron point in artful windings cuts a fair design, and leaves long twisted furrows, like a plough.

A specific and relevant use of wax tablets in the planning of a book is recorded by Adamnan, abbot of Iona 679-704. Adamnan wrote an account of the Holy Places in Palestine, based on the pilgrimage experiences of a Frankish bishop called Arculf, who was blown off course to Iona on his return home. Adamnan tells us in his preface that he wrote down Arculf's story on tablets, as he told it, and then persuaded his guest to make sketch plans on the wax of the places he had seen, especially the Church of the Holy Sepulchre. From these sketches, the diagrams for the finished book were prepared.

A large and subtle range of colours is used in the decoration of the Lindisfarne Gospels, and these have been examined in some detail. It is not, of course, feasible to remove specimens from a medieval master-piece for scientific analysis, so microscopic examination under various types of light was employed. Pigments prepared in accordance with various later medieval recipes were painted onto vellum for compari-sons to be made. Results suggested that the binding medium used for most of Eadfrith's colours was simple white of egg, though in one or two cases it might have been fish glue. Recognized sources of indi-vidual colours include red and white lead, verdigris, yellow ochre, yellow arsenic sulphide (orpiment), kermes (a red colouring obtained from insects living on evergreen oak trees in lands bordering the Mediterranean), gall, and indigo (from an oriental plant) or woad (from a plant cultivated in northern Europe). A fine range of pinks and purples comes from folium, prepared from the fruit and flowers of the turnsole plant and treated with varying amounts of alkalines. Perhaps the most exotic source of colour is blue lapis lazuli, the only contemporary source of which was Badakshan, in the foothills of the Himalayas, far beyond Eadfrith's personal knowledge and ex-perience. It must have passed through many hands before reaching the monastery in Northumbria. Gold, in paint form and not in the raised, burnished form familiar in later manuscripts, is used only for one or two tiny patches on the major initial pages to Matthew and Luke (plates 25 and 32) and for the 'title' at the head of each Gospel. It was in general not a feature of early insular manuscripts, though both gold and silver are used quite extensively in the Codex Amiatinus, to emulate an earlier book from Italy. This was no doubt a matter of insular taste rather than a lack of raw materials, as gold was used lavishly in jewellery and was, as we have seen, added to the binding of the Lindisfarne Gospels later in the eighth century. All Eadfrith's colours are applied with great skill and accuracy but, as with the script, we have no means of knowing exactly what implements he used.

6. THE GREAT DECORATED PAGES

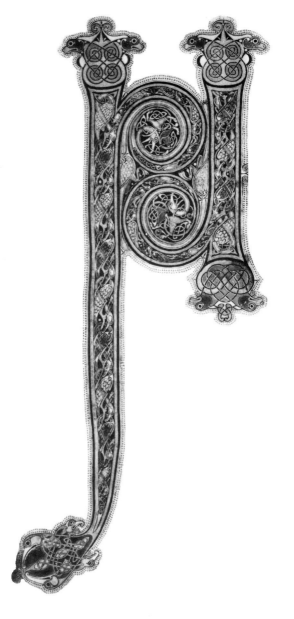

There are 15 elaborate fully decorated pages in the Lindisfarne Gospels. Each of the four Gospels is preceded by an illustration depicting its author with his symbol, and is introduced by a cross-carpet page and a major initial page. A second major initial page occurs in Matthew (1:18), to mark the beginning of the story of the Incarnation. There is a further cross-carpet page and a major initial page at the very beginning of the manuscript, introducing Saint Jerome's letter to Pope Damasus. There are also 16 pages of decorated Eusebian canon tables, enclosed within decorated arcades. The 15 main decorated pages, together with two examples from the sequence of canon tables, are all reproduced within this chapter, following the exact order and arrangement in which they appear in the manuscript.

A manuscript such as the Lindisfarne Gospels, richly decorated both inside and out and obviously intended for ceremonial use, played a symbolic as well as practical role in the life of the Church during the early centuries of conversion. It visibly represented the Word of God which the missionaries had carried to their converts. The early clergy were by no means unaware of the profound impression which a splendid book could make upon their often very primitive congregations. In 735 or 736 Saint Boniface asked his friend Abbess Eadburga of Minster-in-Thanet to make for him a copy of the Epistle of Saint Peter in letters of gold, so that its appearance would help to secure honour and reverence for Holy Scripture every time he used it. Every new church must have needed some form of Gospel book to supply a text for liturgical readings, and the provision of a new and more splendid Gospels is among the activities attributed to the benefactors of the ideal church described in the *De Abbatibus* of Ethelwulf. Such a gift is described by Eddius Stephanus, the biographer of Saint Wilfrid of York, probably writing shortly after his subject's death in 709. In the 670s Wilfrid built and equipped the church at Ripon, where he had taken over the monastery originally established by Saint Cuthbert and his companions from Melrose. To the church he gave 'a marvel of great beauty hitherto unheard of in our times. For he had ordered, for the good of his soul, the four Gospels to be written out in letters of purest gold on purpled parchment and illuminated. He also ordered jewellers to construct for the book a case made all of purest gold and set with most precious gems.' This manuscript, alas, has not come down to us. From the description it sounds as though Wilfrid may have procured it on his continental travels rather than from an English scriptorium. Books written in gold and silver on purpled parchment were well known to Saint Jerome in the fourth century, who regarded their opulent splendour with distaste and dubbed them 'burdens, not books'.

The Lindisfarne Gospels is not the only insular Gospel book to have survived from the seventh and eighth centuries, but it is the best-

OVERLEAF:

19. Cross-carpet page introducing Saint Jerome's letter to Pope Damasus. The Lindisfarne Gospels, folio 2b.

20. Major decorated initial page at the beginning of Saint Jerome's letter to Pope Damasus. The Lindisfarne Gospels, folio 3.

34

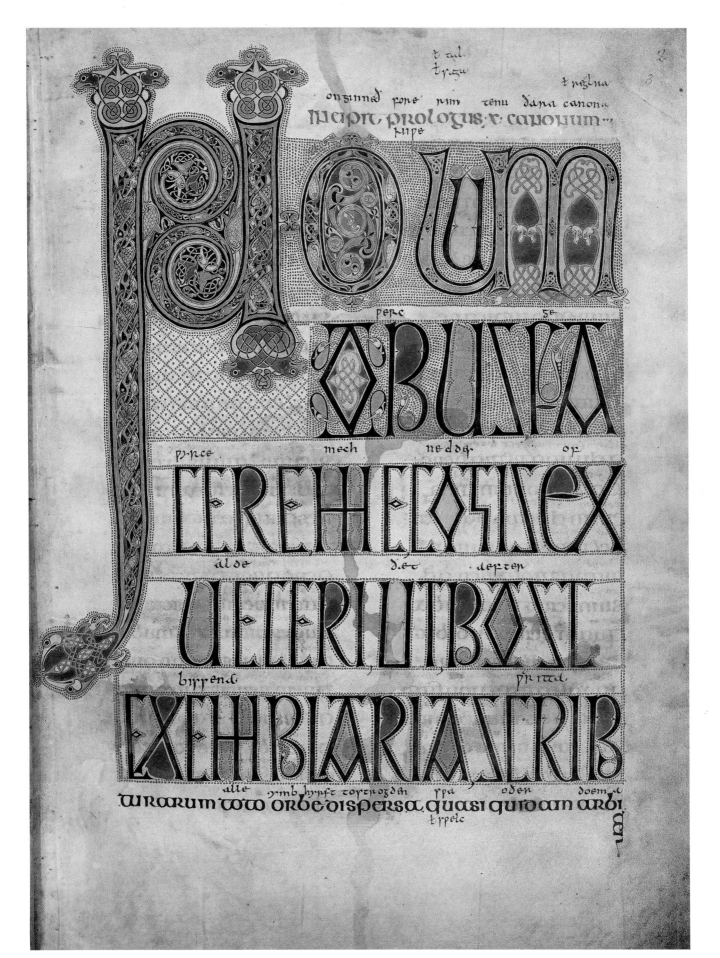

t tal
tryu

t reglna

onzinned pone rim tenu dana canona

INCIPIT PROLOGUS X CANONUM

rupe

NOum

perc   ge

TABUNFA

pynce   mech   neddq.   op

EEREHEROSINEX

alde   dæt   depten

UETERITBOXI

bippend   pr ital

EXEHBLARIANSERIB

alle   ymb hypft toptenogdn   ypa   oden   doem a

TURARUM TOTO ORBE DISPERSA QUASI QUIDAM ARDI

t ypele

uem

documented and also the most complete, having apparently lost neither text nor decoration during the thirteen centuries of its existence. Four or five other manuscripts of similar date may be compared with it. All contain major illuminated pages and must in their time have been extremely splendid, though all have suffered from time and use, some much more than others.

The earliest of these comparable books is the Book of Durrow (Trinity College, Dublin, MS A.4.5(57); plate 53), which was written and illuminated probably about 675, some 20 years earlier than the Lindisfarne Gospels. It takes its name from the Irish monastery of Durrow, in County Meath, where it certainly was in the late eleventh or early twelfth century. It was somewhere in Ireland even earlier than this, because we know that a 'cumdach' (a shrine-like book casket), now lost but known in the seventeenth century, was provided for it by King Flann, who died in 916. There has been much disagreement over the original provenance of this manuscript. Some scholars insist that it was unquestionably made in Ireland, others argue for Northumbria as a more likely place of origin. A request for prayers for Columba the scribe (folio 247b) is often taken as a reference to Saint Columba of Iona (d. 597), who numbered Durrow itself among his many monastic foundations in Ireland. Columba was noted for his prowess as a scribe, personally copying out books needed by the many churches in his care, and it is possible that the scribe of the Book of Durrow used one of these as an exemplar. It is also possible either that the seventh-century scribe's own name was Columba or that his inscription was merely a pious addition. If, however, a reference to Saint Columba is intended, the monastery of Iona is itself a third possible place of origin for the manuscript.

The Book of Durrow contains six decorative carpet pages, five major initial pages and five pages depicting the symbols of the four Evangelists, the man, the lion, the calf and the eagle. The four symbols appear together on one page at the beginning of the book. There is a carpet page at the end of the volume as well as at the beginning, and it seems that a seventh carpet, which should precede Matthew, is lacking. The Eusebian canon tables are written out on five pages, distinguished by simple rectangular frames containing plaitwork. The general arrangement of the manuscript's decoration is very similar to that of the Lindisfarne Gospels, but its design is far less complex and the range of colours employed by the illuminator is very limited. The manuscript shows signs of hard wear over a long period of time.

Apparently more nearly contemporary with the Lindisfarne Gospels is an incomplete and badly damaged Gospels in the library of Durham Cathedral (MS A.II.17; plate 45). This must once have been a book of great magnificence. The surviving decoration comprises a major initial page to Saint John's Gospel and a miniature of the Crucifixion, placed at the end of Matthew. The structure of the gatherings suggests that there were once either carpet pages or Evangelist/Evangelist symbol miniatures, as well as major initial pages, at the beginning of each Gospel, and that there may also have been a miniature at the end of each. There are strong reasons for connecting this manuscript with the Lindisfarne scriptorium because, as we have already seen, the hand of the author of minor corrections in the Lindisfarne Gospels itself has recently been recognized in it. In addition to this, it is known to have been with the other Lindisfarne treasures at Chester-le-Street in the tenth century.

To the scribe of the Durham Gospels is now attributed the famous Echternach Gospels (Bibliothèque Nationale, Paris, MS lat. 9389;

21. The third in Eadfrith's sixteen-page sequence of arcaded canon tables. In this example interlaced birds fill the columns and the arch, while a fairly simple ribbon knotwork design is used for the bases and capitals. The Lindisfarne Gospels, folio 11.

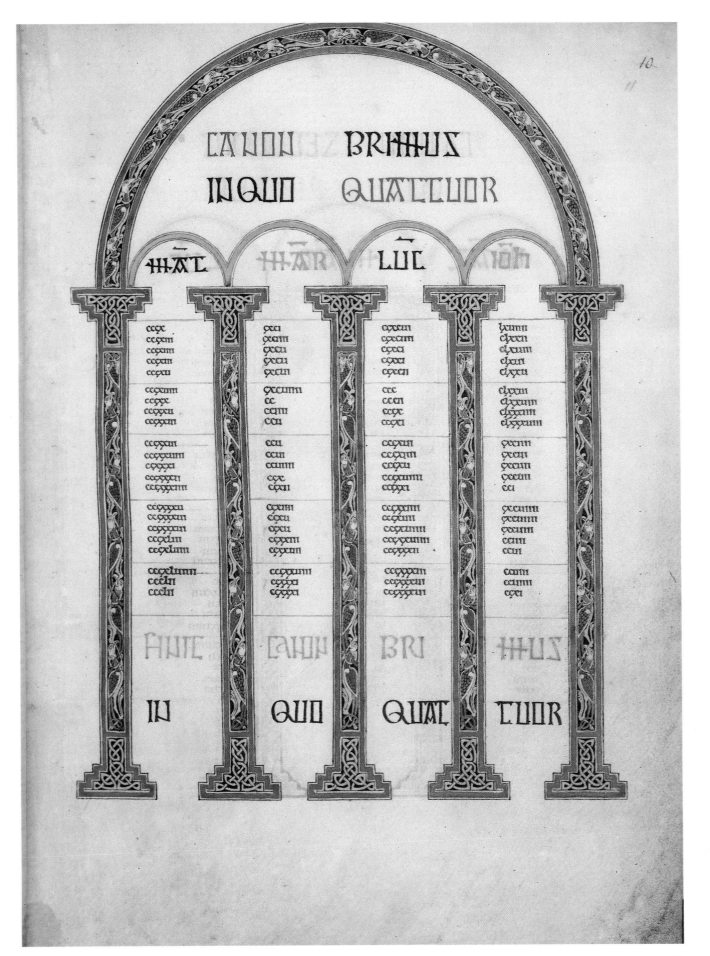

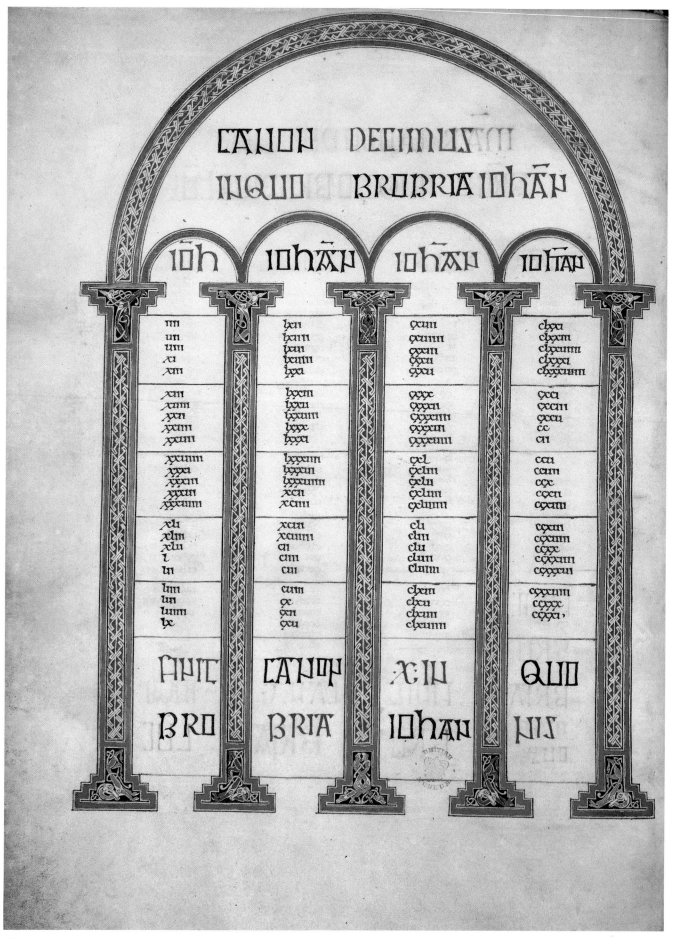

plate 54). This is ornamented with full-page pictures of the symbols of the four Evangelists, decorative initials on a fairly modest scale at the beginning of each Gospel, and canon tables within simple, coloured rectangular frames. There are no elaborate carpet pages, but in other ways the decoration of this manuscript suggests a distinct family relationship to the Book of Durrow. It has in the past been variously attributed to Ireland and also to the monastery of Echternach, where it certainly was in the fifteenth century. However, historical as well as palaeographical evidence can be used to support an attribution to Lindisfarne. The community at Echternach was established in or about 698, the year of Saint Cuthbert's elevation, by Saint Willibrord, the apostle of the Frisians. Willibrord was born in Northumbria and had gone as a missionary to Frisia in 690. His efforts met with much success and, probably in 695, he went to Rome to be consecrated archbishop for the new see of Utrecht, which was set up in the following year. By May 706 monastery buildings had been erected at Echternach, and the community was under the protection of Pepin, King of the Franks, the saint's special patron. It was Willibrord's own favourite foundation, and he was buried there when he died in 739. The town of Echternach still celebrates his festival with a dancing pilgrimage through the streets to his tomb in the basilica.

It is clear from the Life of Saint Willibrord, written by Alcuin of York, that he maintained close contact with Northumbria throughout his career. A member of his household was actually at Lindisfarne shortly after the elevation of Saint Cuthbert's relics, and was miraculously cured of a sudden illness by a painful visit to the saint's new resting place. A fine copy of the Gospels would have been considered a most fitting fraternal gift, either for Willibrord's new monastery or for his new cathedral. The very fluid, almost cursive, appearance of the script in the Echternach Gospels, and the simple but arresting design of its decorated pages lend support to the idea that the manuscript was produced in a short space of time for some particular reason, perhaps to be ready for presentation to mark a significant date such as a dedication ceremony, or perhaps to meet a deadline imposed by the availability of a suitable courier. Whatever the circumstances, the events of Willibrord's life suggest that a date very close to the date of the Lindisfarne Gospels is likely.

Parallels for the Echternach Evangelist symbol pages are found in a now fragmentary and divided Northumbrian Gospel book of which there are 36 leaves in the library of Corpus Christi College, Cambridge (MS 197 B, folios 1-36) and a collection of fire-distorted fragments in the British Library (Cotton MS Otho C.v). The Cotton fragments were unfortunately damaged beyond repair in the Ashburnham House fire of 1731, from which the Lindisfarne Gospels was mercifully saved. However, the figure of a leaping lion, very like the one in the Echternach Gospels, can still be distinguished among them, as can an introductory initial page for Saint Mark's Gospel. The leaves in Cambridge include an illustration of Saint John's eagle and an accompanying initial page. There is no trace of decorative carpet pages. However, it is possible that a set of arcaded canon table pages, now represented only by some shadowy offsets in British Library, Royal MS 7 C.xii (folios 2, 3), was once part of this manuscript. These are the only known arcaded canon tables of so early a date with distinctly insular decoration, apart from the ones in the Lindisfarne Gospels.

The Gospels of Saint Chad, in the library of Lichfield Cathedral, displays the most striking resemblances of all to the Lindisfarne Gospels. This manuscript, which must originally have been of quite

22. The last of the canon table pages. Here animal motifs are ingeniously induced to fit bases and capitals, the columns and arch being decorated with a diagonal fret pattern. The Lindisfarne Gospels, folio 17b.

outstanding beauty, is now very much damaged and worn. There are no clues to its place of origin, but it probably dates from the early eighth century. A number of documents copied onto its pages about the beginning of the ninth century reveal that it was by then in Wales, where it was offered on the altar of Saint Teilo (at Llandeilo-fawr, in South Wales) by Gelhi, son of Arihtuid, who had exchanged his best horse for it. It was quite common for legal documents, often concerned with grants of property to a monastery or church, to be copied for safe-keeping into a Gospel book, sacrosanct because of its associations. The Saint Chad Gospels apparently reached Lichfield some time in the tenth century and has ever since been associated with the name of Lichfield's patron, Saint Chad (who, interestingly enough, was educated at Lindisfarne), though he died in 672, far too early to have any connection with the manuscript. The sequence of decorated pages at the beginning of Saint Luke's Gospel is still complete and consists of a miniature of the Evangelist, a page with the four Evangelist symbols, a cross-carpet page and a major initial page (plate 42). There are three further major initial pages still in the book, two in Matthew and one in Mark, and a miniature of Saint Mark (plate 60). Most of the text of Luke and the whole of John are missing. It is likely that each Gospel was originally preceded by a series of decorated pages equivalent to those which remain before Luke, and there may also have been decorated canon table pages. The surviving carpet page and the initial pages are very closely related in design to similar pages in the Lindisfarne Gospels, so closely indeed that it seems necessary to assume that their artist had seen Eadfrith's work.

Mention must also be made of the Book of Kells (Trinity College, Dublin, MS A.1.6(58)), the decorative scheme of which has much in common with that of various of the insular Gospel books with which we have been dealing. It seems, however, to be considerably later in date than the Lindisfarne Gospels, and the questions of style and origin which it inspires are so very complicated that little is to be gained by introducing it into the present discussion.

The principal decorated pages of the Lindisfarne Gospels relate in some degree to decorated pages in each of the manuscripts just described, but they also display some marked differences. In particular the canon table pages, and the miniatures of the four Evangelists with their symbols, are treated very differently from those in other books.

Canon tables were devised early in the fourth century by Eusebius, bishop of Caesarea, to provide a system whereby parallel passages in the four Gospels could readily be located. Their long and visually unattractive columns of figures (corresponding to figures added in the margins beside the Gospel texts, examples of which can be seen in plates 8 and 14) offered considerable scope to the enterprising decorator, and in many early medieval copies of Gospels some of the finest illumination will be found associated with them. The total number of pages used could be varied in accordance with the degree of luxury of the manuscript. Two of the insular Gospel books described above still have their canon tables, but in neither does the decoration approach the complexity of Eadfrith's work. In the Book of Durrow the five pages of tables are given ornamented borders. In the Echternach Gospels they are simply framed in plain coloured bands. Only in the faint offsets possibly once a part of the book now divided between Cambridge and London do we see traces of arcaded canon tables with insular ornament applied to their architectural framework. There is one other contemporary series of arcaded canon tables in an insular manuscript, preceding the New Testament in the Codex

23. Full-page miniature of the Evangelist Saint Matthew, accompanied by his symbol, a winged man blowing a trumpet and carrying a book ('imago hominis'), and by a mysterious figure which may perhaps be intended to represent Christ. The Lindisfarne Gospels, folio 25b.

OVERLEAF:
24. Cross-carpet page introducing the Gospel according to Saint Matthew. The Lindisfarne Gospels, folio 26b.

25. Major decorated initial page at the beginning of the Gospel according to Saint Matthew. The Lindisfarne Gospels, folio 27.

42

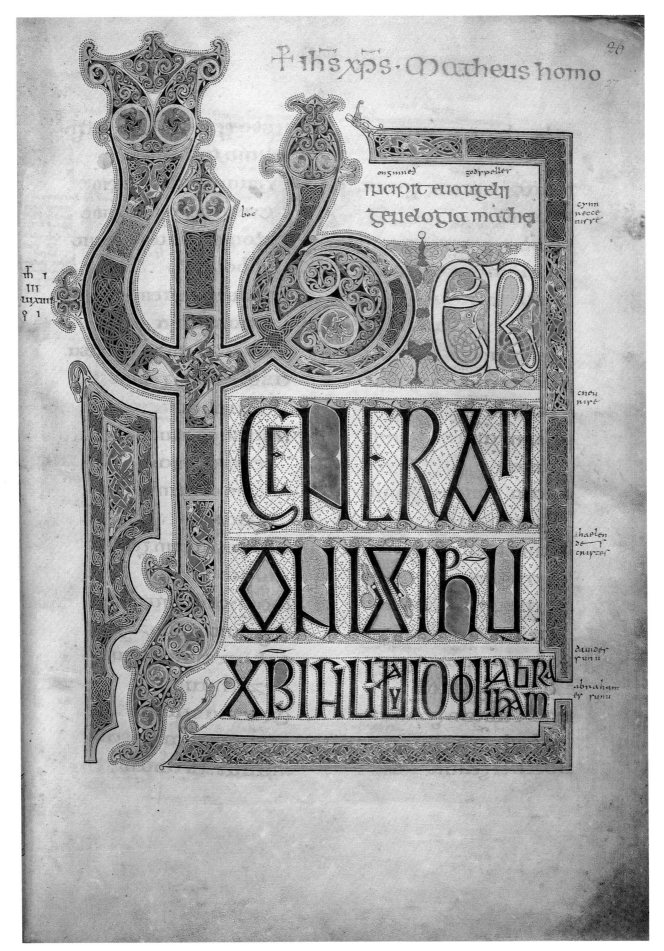

43

Amiatinus, but the decoration of these follows their late antique model.

Eadfrith's canon tables (plates 21 and 22) occupy a sequence of 16 pages, making up a complete gathering of eight vellum leaves. They are set within architectural arcades, the pillars and main arches of which are filled with varied and elaborate interlace designs. The first and last pages of the series are of individual design, but the remainder are in matching pairs, one pair to each opening of the book. The scheme as a whole must certainly have been inspired by knowledge of a set of arcaded canon tables in one of the manuscripts brought to England from Italy, where similar pages were certainly familiar. It would not have been beyond Eadfrith's powers of invention to adapt the Codex Amiatinus set, presumably based upon those in the Codex Grandior, although they are laid out to appear in the context of far larger pages than those which he was designing. A more likely source is the other Cassiodoran Biblical manuscript at Wearmouth–Jarrow, the Novem Codices. The seventh volume of this, containing the Gospels, would certainly have included canon tables, in a format closer to that of the Lindisfarne Gospels.

The decoration of Eadfrith's arcades is unmistakably insular, though it is possible that his decision to make such extensive use of bird motifs was inspired by the appearance of bird processions in his model, as these are quite commonly used in Mediterranean art. However, all the motifs which appear in the canon tables will be seen again in the decoration of the cross-carpet and major initial pages of the manuscript. He made no attempt to persuade his arcades to take on the appearance of marble, though this common antique device was to be enthusiastically adopted by later illuminators, as well as by the artist of the Codex Amiatinus. The arcades of the Lindisfarne Gospels are filled with long flat ribbons of entwined birds or straightforward interlace; bases and capitals enclose contorted beasts or knots cleverly moulded to fit an awkward space, and the whole relies successfully upon the alternation of animal and simple interlace ornament and upon some striking variations of colour for its lively effect.

Eadfrith's miniatures of the four Evangelists are very different from representations of the human figure in other insular Gospel books. From the clothing and accessories of the four seated figures (plates 23, 27, 30 and 33) it is at once clear that the inspiration lying behind them was, as in the case of the canon tables, the decoration of a late antique manuscript imported from the Mediterranean. Although the artist's love of pattern is in each case reflected in the addition of an overall network of folds picked out in a colour contrasting with that of the garment, his figures are still convincingly clothed in a fabric and not protected by a chequered tabard (as in Saint Matthew's man symbol in the Book of Durrow) or hung about with pneumatic loops (as in the Evangelist pictures of the Saint Chad Gospels; plate 60). All four Evangelists wear classical sandals, though these appear merely as very slender thongs, the soles having been omitted. Faces and hair are reduced, like the garments, to a very strong linear pattern but without losing their essential realism. Each Evangelist is accompanied by his symbol, those of Mark and Luke seen virtually in entirety, those of Matthew and John partially obscured by the haloes of their respective saints. The Matthew and Mark symbols are blowing trumpets, and all four have wings. Saint Matthew is also accompanied by a mysterious haloed figure with a book peeping out from behind a curtain. The arrangement is very reminiscent of that in later manuscripts of the *Registrum Gregorii* (the collected letters of Pope Gregory the Great),

26. Second major decorated initial page from the Gospel according to Saint Matthew, marking the beginning of the Christmas story. The Lindisfarne Gospels, folio 29.

onginned godspell ept matheus

Incipit euangeli um secundum mattheu∴

crister

uutedlice
ruel per
enister ends
per to

godlice

cynn pcccnire t cnenperiu ruel dur per mid ზ.

per bi poeddeſ t beboden t bepeuytnud t betahe

rogemanne
naller to hab
banne t ƥpis

moder hir

abiachan
de aldopmon
per indem
tid inhicru
ralem ƥone
bircob. he be
beod mania
iorepht to
ზemenne ɉ
tobezɉeong
annt mid
claennyre∴

pelta

trumpets

spiral

step

fret

key

fret

simple plait
and knot
interlace

Some patterns used in the decoration
in the Lindisfarne Gospels

where the attendant deacon manages an illicit glimpse of Pope Gregory the Great while he is being inspired by the Holy Dove. This figure has caused much discussion, and may possibly represent Christ.

Although Eadfrith's distinctive style has imposed upon the Evangelist pages the appearance of a coherent series, they are apparently not derived from a single set of Evangelist pictures. The close relationship of the first miniature, that of Saint Matthew, to the miniature of Ezra in the Codex Amiatinus (plate 59) has long been recognized. The Ezra picture must have been taken from one of the Cassiodoran manuscripts at Wearmouth–Jarrow, and the inclusion in it of a cupboard containing a Bible in nine volumes, appropriately labelled to represent the Novem Codices, strongly suggests that the model behind it, and therefore also behind Eadfrith's Saint Matthew, was a frontispiece to the Novem Codices themselves. The seventh volume of the same set of manuscripts, containing the Gospels, is a likely source for the other three Evangelists, as it was for the canon tables, but this can never be proved one way or the other as the book has long since disappeared. The Cassiodoran Evangelists are unlikely to have been accompanied by their symbols and, if the model for Matthew has been correctly identified, we know that it, of course, was not. The symbols must therefore have been added by Eadfrith from some other source and are closest to those seen on the exactly contemporary oak coffin made to receive Saint Cuthbert's relics in 698 (plate 61) and to those on the Maiestas page of the Codex Amiatinus, though the latter, while winged, have neither trumpets nor books. The use of two separate sources for the Evangelists and their symbols is probably underlined by the use of Latin for the inscriptions identifying the symbols and of the Greek 'O agios' preceding the names of the Evangelists.

The 11 other major decorated pages of the manuscript are all composed of pure ornament, each based either on a cross shape or on an initial followed by a sequence of letters. The ornament of these cross and initial pages is of amazing intricacy. Eadfrith had a highly developed sense of form and design which enabled him to fill even the most awkwardly shaped segments of his field with fluid arrangements of various types of decoration. Every one of the cross-carpet and initial pages calls for detailed examination, section by section, preferably with the aid of a magnifying glass, to bring out the full richness of its contents. The decoration is of several different types, woven and interwoven into a coherent whole, representing the high-water mark of the preoccupation with pattern which is a characteristic of early Anglo-Saxon art in all media.

Many of the patterns used by Eadfrith and his contemporaries go back far beyond the Christian period. Prominent are curvilinear motifs such as those which fill the bows of the letters on the Incarnation page (plate 26) and on the opening page of Luke (plate 32). The spiral, the trumpet and the pelta are all familar in Celtic art of the Iron Age. There are many varieties of plait and knot work, woven from 'flat' bands of colour or from simple lines, sometimes used in alternating areas of contrasting colour. Step, fret and key patterns are also among the purely linear elements. Most characteristic of all is the zoomorphic interlace, adopted from Germanic art and distinguished in the Lindisfarne Gospels by the extensive introduction of interlaced birds in addition to the more usual interlaced quadrupeds. The latter often have elongated, almost serpentine bodies, and legs, ears and tails are all stretched out to form part of the pattern. These animals tend, for the sake of convenience, to be described as dogs, though most of

48

49

them are entirely fanciful. However, one seems quite certainly intended for a cat, creeping down the side of the Saint Luke initial-page (plate 32) in search of further prey to add to the eight birds already entwined within her.

Eadfrith's birds have excited much scientific discussion, largely inspired by the suggestion that he had some specific local fowl in mind, since Holy Island and its surroundings are so very rich in wildlife. Informed ornithological opinion has discounted the attractive theory that the birds are meant for cormorants or for their cousins, the shags, both of which nest today in colonies on the Farne Islands. Certainly Eadfrith's birds cannot be regarded as accurate, scientific drawings, and their sinuous feet, with long, cruel talons, are not the feet of water birds. Nevertheless it is hard not to see in them some reflection of the cormorant family, seated in characteristic attitude on the rocks with necks and beaks proudly extended and with the sun striking the gleaming irridescence of their feathers.

One further very distinctive form of ornament is used to more striking effect in the Lindisfarne Gospels than in any other insular manuscript. This is the technique of applying tiny drops of red lead to the page, forming backgrounds, outlines or patterns as the space dictates. Red dots appear in the earliest Irish manuscripts, generally employed to enhance the outlines of otherwise simple initial letters. In the Lindisfarne Gospels too they are associated with letters, both on text pages and on the great initial pages, and never contribute to pages of pure ornament. On the most thickly dotted page, the initial page at the beginning of Luke (plate 32), approximately 10,600 red dots have been counted. They are very carefully applied and experiment suggests that a rate of 30 dots per minute might be achieved. Application of the dots on the Saint Luke page would thus have taken a basic minimum of six hours' hard work.

The first pair of decorated pages (plates 19 and 20), standing at the very beginning of the manuscript and introducing Saint Jerome's letter to Pope Damasus, is much the least complex of the series in the manuscript. The cross formation of the carpet page is clearly defined against a ground of fairly simple interlace, now somewhat discoloured through the interaction of the red lead pigment and the sulphur content of the adjacent yellow. The marginal procession of birds is drawn on a large scale. The initial page lacks the sense of overall design seen later in the manuscript, largely because it has no decorative bounding panels. Its text reads: 'Novum opus facere me cogis ex veteri ut post exemplaria scripturarum toto orbe dispersa quasi quidam arbiter [sediam]...' (You asked me to make a new work out of the old, so that following the copies of the scriptures scattered about the world, I might set myself up as a judge [where they vary, to decide which of them agrees best with the Greek truth.])

The Matthew carpet page (plate 24) is also based on a very clearly defined cross. Examination of the back of the page shows that the design is built up on a complex grid radiating largely from the 'jewels' in the centre of each segment of the cross. Both the ground of the page and the body of the cross are filled with what at first sight appears to be zoomorphic interlace, though closer examination reveals that only the former includes the heads and legs of birds. The Matthew initial page (plate 25) is bound together into a pattern by the use of marginal bounding panels of pure ornament, keyed into the shape of the principal monogram. The lettering reads: 'Liber generationis Iesu Christi filii David filii Abraham' (The book of the generation of Jesus Christ, the son of David, the son of Abraham).

30. Full-page miniature of the Evangelist Saint Luke, accompanied by his symbol, a winged calf carrying a book ('imago vituli'). The Lindisfarne Gospels, folio 137b.

OVERLEAF:
31. Cross-carpet page introducing the Gospel according to Saint Luke. The Lindisfarne Gospels, folio 138b.

32. Major decorated initial page at the beginning of the Gospel according to Saint Luke. The Lindisfarne Gospels, folio 139.

✝ lucas urtulus ⁊

on gynnet god spell
Incipit euangelium

æc lucas
secundum lucam⋯

f on ðon

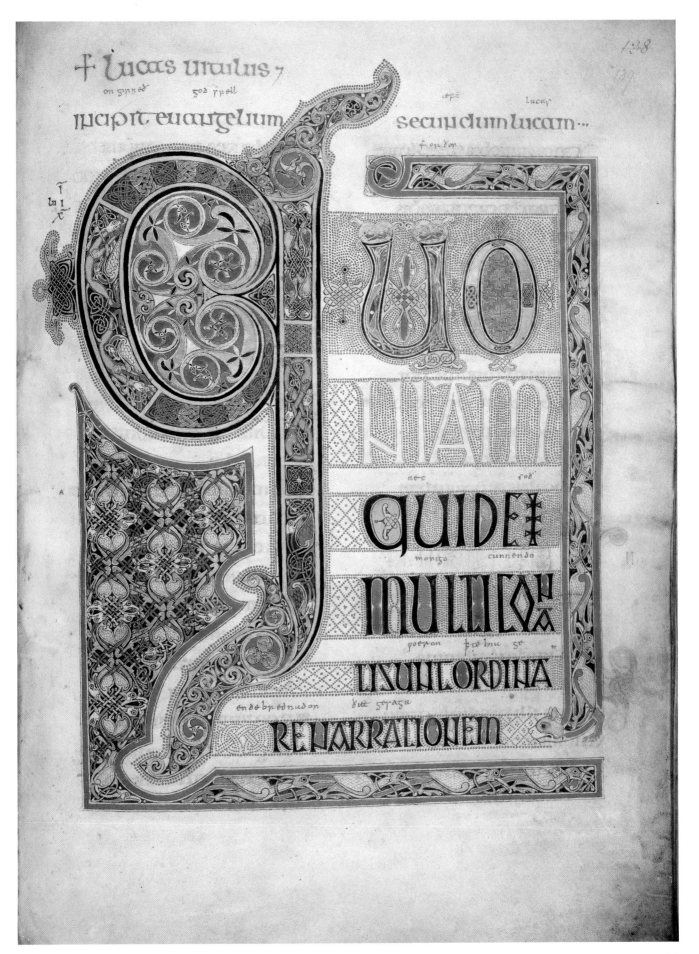

QVO
NIAM
æcc rob
QVIDE✝
moriʒo cunnendo
MVLTICOᴺᴴᴬ
poɽɽon ɽɽebɲu ʒᵗ
TISVNTORDINA
endebɲednudon ðut ʒoɽaʒa
RENARRATIONEM

ᴛ
ʟᴜ
ɪ
х

The second initial page in Matthew (plate 26) provides an especially fine example of the use of curvilinear ornament. Its text reads: 'Christi autem generatio sic erat cum esset desponsata mater eius Maria Joseph...' (Now the birth of Jesus Christ was on this wise: When as his mother Mary was espoused to Joseph...).

The range of colours used for the cross-carpet page at the beginning of Mark (plate 28) is fairly restricted, with the emphasis on blue, red and yellow. This gives a deceptive impression of simplicity, though in fact the number of different types of ornament introduced is extensive. The initial page (plate 29) is rather more rubbed than any of the others, this opening having been a favourite for display. It reads: 'Initium evangelii Iesu Christi fili(i) d(e)i sicut scriptum est in Esaia propheta...' (the beginning of the Gospel of Jesus Christ, the Son of God; as it is written in Isaiah the prophet...).

The decorated pages at the beginning of Saint Luke's Gospel (plates 31 and 32) form the most satisfying combination in the manuscript. This is largely due to the success of Eadfrith's design for the initial page, with its great curving letter 'Q' and the almost unbelievably intricate, textile-like panel which follows the contours of its tail. The text of this page reads: 'Quoniam quidem multi conati sunt ordinare narrationem...' (Forasmuch as many have taken in hand to set forth in order...). The range of motifs included in the carpet page is, as in the corresponding page of Mark, extensive, and here gives a more complex impression because of the tiny scale of the basically very simple key pattern with which the ground is filled.

The carpet page to Saint John (plate 34) is full of movement. Its ground is made up of a seething maelstrom of multicoloured birds, against which the almost microscopic interlace which fills the shape of the cross stands out very sharply. The initial page (plate 35) is also extremely complex, and the lines of decorated letters include a number of additional ornaments, one of which, on the second line, is a drawing of a human face, unique in the manuscript except for the Evangelist miniatures. The text on this page reads: 'In principio erat verbum et verbum erat apud d(eu)m et d(eu)s [erat verbum]' (In the beginning was the word and the word was with God and God [was the word]).

Eadfrith had one small idiosyncracy which is apparent on several of the major decorated pages of the Lindisfarne Gospels and which has not been satisfactorily explained. Apparently deliberately, he several times either left a small part of the design unfinished or introduced into it a detail at odds with the remainder of the page. On the first cross-carpet page (plate 19) two small patches of the interlace above the cross, which should be red, are left uncoloured. On the cross-carpet page preceding Matthew (plate 24) one of the birds in the lower right-hand quarter of the design has a spiral joint, though all the others are simply coloured. The Matthew initial page (plate 25) is incomplete, the 'er' of the first line being only partially painted. On the cross-carpet before John (plate 34), a bird in the top left-hand quarter has wings striped blue and pink, whereas all the others have had these stripes broken down into scales. These gaps and discrepancies are so small that it seems unlikely that they were the results of major interruptions to the work. It seems more feasible to suppose that Eadfrith was practising the humility of avoiding absolute perfection in the mammoth task which he had undertaken.

33. Full-page miniature of the Evangelist Saint John, accompanied by his symbol, an eagle carrying a book ('imago aequilae'). Alone of Eadfrith's Four Evangelists, Saint John is seated facing the reader. The Lindisfarne Gospels, folio 209b.

OVERLEAF:
34. Cross-carpet page introducing the Gospel according to Saint John. The Lindisfarne Gospels, folio 210b.

35. Major decorated initial page at the beginning of the Gospel according to Saint John. The Lindisfarne Gospels, folio 211.

56

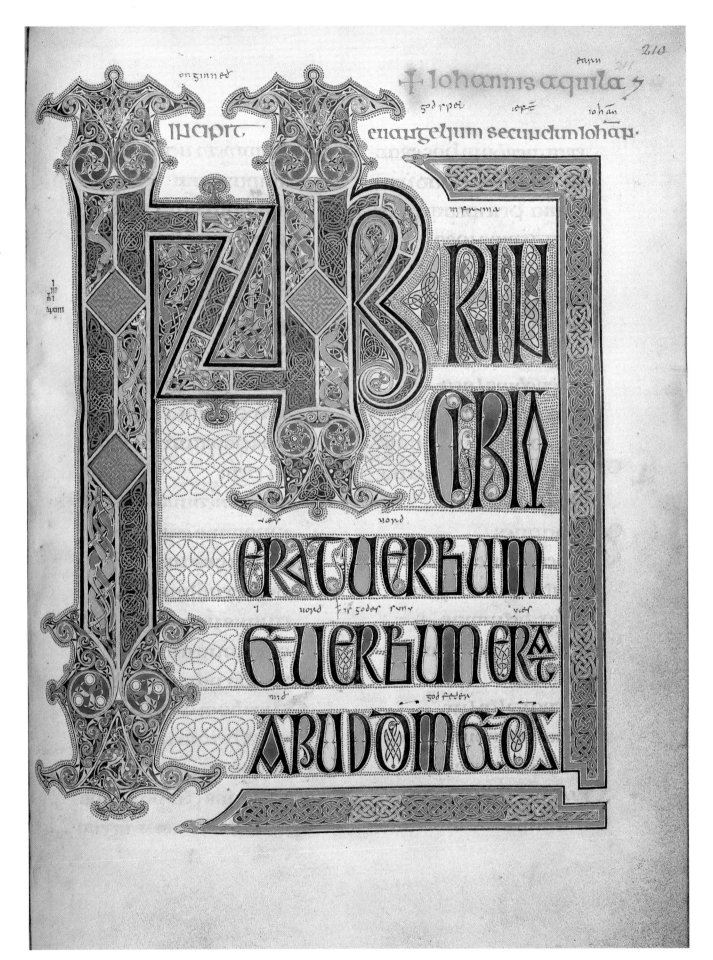

57

7. THE SMALLER INITIALS

In addition to its sequence of great illuminated pages, the Lindisfarne Gospels contains a hierarchy of lesser decorated initials. These appear on the text pages throughout the manuscript and are graded in accordance with the significance of the material which they introduce.

The simplest initials are merely the initial letters appropriate to Eadfrith's insular majuscule script, enhanced on occasion by additional ink contour lines. They are picked out by patches of colour, usually green or yellow, and are often outlined in the characteristic red dots. Some of this work may have been entrusted to an assistant. The red dots certainly seem to be associated with the work of the rubricator, who added the headings written in red (see p. 26). Good examples of these little initials appear on the beatitudes page of Saint Matthew's Gospel (folio 34; plate 8).

More ambitious in design are the initials used to introduce particularly important sections in the lists of liturgical readings. The most attractive of these, both on the same page, occur among the introductory material preceding Saint John's Gospel (folio 208; plate 9). These two initials, particularly the 'D' in the left-hand column, are very delicately drawn and coloured, the pigments being purple, yellow and green, surrounded by the inevitable red dots.

The largest and most splendid of the minor initials are reserved for the the prologue to Saint Jerome's commentary on Matthew and the letter of Eusebius to Carpianus, both at the beginning of the book, and for the 'argumentum' and 'capitula lectionum' preceding each of the Gospels (see above, p. 17). These are expanded to the height of several lines of the text and are followed by lesser decorated capitals, just as the great initial at the beginning of each Gospel is followed by a page full of decorated words, but on a smaller scale.

In designing these initials, Eadfrith made use of the same ornamental vocabulary as in the major decorated pages. The spirals, the ribbon interlace, the birds and the animals are all in their turn introduced. The red dots, which are to be expected in connection with initial letters in an insular manuscript, are used not just to outline his letter forms but to provide a background of soft colouring against which those forms stand out. Because they are overshadowed by the cross-carpets and the grand initial pages at the beginning of each Gospel, these smaller examples of Eadfrith's work tend to be overlooked. Of the four specimens reproduced here only one, the third, has previously been published in colour, and that is included in the facsimile edition of 1956.

The first of our four specimen initials is the 'P' which precedes Saint Jerome's preface to the commentary on Matthew (plate 36). It is succeeded by the remainder of his opening word, 'plures', with a bird's head introduced into the following capitals as well as into the initial itself.

36. Initial P at the beginning of Saint Jerome's Preface to the Four Gospels (actual size). The Lindisfarne Gospels, folio 5b (detail).

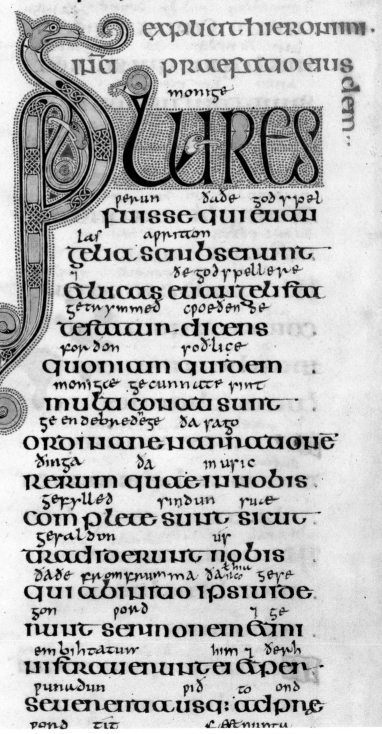

du ʒetreoppeafuir ʒemyndʒu
ualeas amemineris

minra papu du eudʒu
mei papa beatissime

explicit hieronimi

siua praefatio eius

moniʒe
PLURES

perun dade ʒodyrpel
fuisse qui euan

lar apprʒaon
ʒelia scribserunt

⁊ de ʒodyrpellore
qlucas euanʒelista

ʒetnymmed cpoeden de
testatur dicens

rop don rodlice
quoniam quidem

moniʒe ʒecunnure pint
multa conati sunt

ʒe en debnedeʒe da raro
ordinare narrationem

dinʒa da muric
rerum quae in nobis

ʒefylled rindun rute
completae sunt sicut

ʒepaldun ur
tradiderunt nobis

dade fromfnumma danico ʒeye
qui abinitio ipsiude

ʒon pond ⁊ ʒe
runt sermonem mini

embihtatur him ⁊ deph
niistrauerunt ei apen

punudun pid to ond
seuerentia usq: adpne

pond tit c. Athnunu

The second is a monogram rather than an initial, comprising the 'MA' of 'Mattheus' at the beginning of the 'argumentum' to Saint Matthew (plate 37). The main letter is made up of two great bows, and five animal heads are introduced, two of them combined at the foot of the monogram to form a single face.

The third initial is again an 'M', opening the 'argumentum' to Mark with the word 'Marcus' (plate 38). The form of this 'M' is quite different from the earlier one and its design is much more elaborate, for there are elongated animal forms, painted in very delicate colours, inside the outlines of the letter as well as on the ground which it

37. Monogram MA at the beginning of the 'argumentum' to Saint Matthew's Gospel (actual size). The Lindisfarne Gospels, folio 18b (detail).

38. Initial M at the beginning of the 'argumentum' to Saint Mark's Gospel (actual size). The Lindisfarne Gospels, folio 90 (detail).

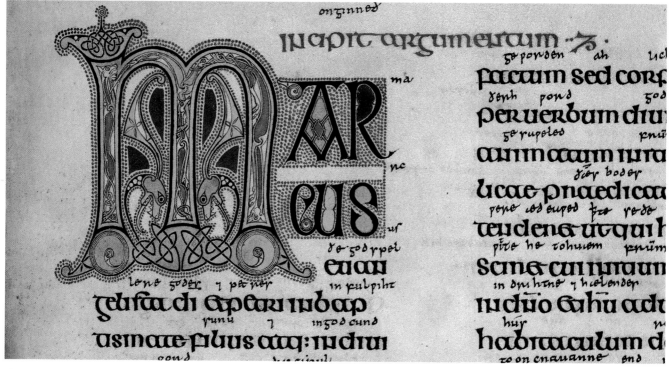

39. Initial E at the beginning of the 'capitula lectionum' to Saint Mark's Gospel (actual size). The Lindisfarne Gospels, folio 91 (detail).

encloses. The remaining five letters of Saint Mark's name are, like those on the major initial pages, enhanced with patches of colour against their background of red dots.

The last of our four initials is the 'E' with which the 'capitula lectionum' to Mark begins (plate 39). The main letter, like the 'M' of 'Marcus', has delicately painted animal forms within its outlines. Two bird heads as well as patches of colour are used to decorate the following letters, which complete the word 'Esaiae' (Isaiah). In the left-hand margin is a decorative motif very like those which occur on the frames of the cross-carpet pages, and this provides two fine specimens of one of Eadfrith's more distinctly legendary-looking creatures, an almost duck-like head with long rows of predatory teeth.

Of the insular Gospel books described in the previous chapter, only one, the Durham Gospels, has minor initials approaching the beauty of those in the Lindisfarne Gospels (plate 13). One other contemporary manuscript, a collection of canons apparently written and decorated in Northumbria, though it was in Cologne as early as the eighth century (Dombibliothek, Köln, cod. 213), is also comparable. Eadfrith stands at the beginning of the development of the highly decorated text initial, an aspect of manuscript illumination which was to become one of the great strengths of English book-painting. About half a century after the making of the Lindisfarne Gospels one of Eadfrith's Northumbrian countrymen took a very significant step forward, when he produced what has a good claim to be the earliest historiated initial (that is, an initial enclosing an illustration relating to the text) in European illumination. This initial, made up of a decorated outline filled with interlace which would be quite at home beside Eadfrith's own work, contains a 'portrait' of Pope Gregory the Great, who sent Saint Augustine to preach the Gospel to the heathen English in 596, and occurs in the second oldest surviving copy of Bede's *Ecclesiastical History*, made at Wearmouth–Jarrow in or about 746 (Leningrad, State Public Library, Q.V.I. 18, fol. 26).

8. SOME COMPARISONS

The creator of the Lindisfarne Gospels was not an isolated genius, producing his great masterpiece in an otherwise dark age. The seventh and eighth centuries were among the most artistically productive in the whole of English history, especially in Northumbria, where the two or three decades on either side of the year 700 were truly a golden age. From this period we still have many surviving examples of book painting, jewellery, metalwork, sculpture and building in stone. There is also a literature, both in Latin and in Anglo-Saxon, and ample evidence of outstanding scholarship, especially in the works of the Venerable Bede.

. Events and personalities of the time are familiar from Bede's *Ecclesiastical History of the English People*, which he completed in 731 and for which he had sought material from friends and correspondents all over England and from as far afield as the papal archives in Rome. He provides a detailed account of the years which produced the Lindisfarne Gospels and was, as we have already seen, personally acquainted with Eadfrith himself. Other historical material is preserved in contemporary lives of local saints, in accounts of the Anglo-Saxon missions to the pagan parts of Europe during the eighth century, and in the collected correspondence of individual personalities, particularly that of Saint Boniface, martyred for the faith in Frisia in 755.

In recent years the written evidence has been increasingly supplemented by evidence from archaeological excavations, and particularly from finds on two sites, both of them well known from the pages of the *Ecclesiastical History*. The first of these is Yeavering (Bede's 'Gefrin'), the Northumbrian royal village at the foot of the Cheviot Hills, about 12 miles south-west from the coast opposite Holy Island. It was at Yeavering that Northumbria's first Christian missionary, Saint Augustine's companion Paulinus, baptized converts in the River Glen for a period of 36 days in 626. Outlines of buildings on the site were identified from crop marks revealed by aerial photography. Excavation uncovered traces of a large complex of wooden buildings, including an extraordinary wedge-shaped grandstand, which must have looked like a section cut from a Roman ampitheatre and which may have been intended as a meeting place for the Northumbrian moot. The second outstandingly important site is the monastery at Jarrow, Bede's own home for almost the whole of his life, where it has proved possible to reconstruct the appearance of the stone-built monastery much as it was in Bede's time.

In the south of England all other discoveries have been overshadowed by the treasures from the ship burial at Sutton Hoo in Suffolk, which was totally unsuspected before the summer of 1939. These are now in the British Museum, and are still today in the process of full-scale publication and evaluation. The jewellery and other items recovered from the site, which is thought to mark the burial place of an

East Anglian king, probably Raedwald, who died about 625, have shed an entirely new light on the artistic achievement and capabilities of early seventh-century England.

Northumbria was by no means cut off from the rest of Britain, nor from Europe. The establishment of Christianity in the kingdom immediately introduced two very strong strains of outside influence into the area, both of which we have already recognized as contributing to the textual and artistic contents of the Lindisfarne Gospels. One strain came from the Mediterranean, firstly through Saint Paulinus and later by means of the close, direct contacts with Rome itself which were fostered by Saint Wilfrid and by Benedict Biscop and Ceolfrith of Wearmouth–Jarrow. The major results of this influence can be identified in contemporary Northumbrian art and scholarship, its outstanding achievement being the Codex Amiatinus, so long believed to be of Italian origin. The other strain came from Ireland through the Iona mission of Saint Aidan in 635, and relations between the two countries remained extremely close, even after the Synod of Whitby in 664 had diminished direct Irish influence on the Northumbrian Church.

There are many recorded instances of influential Northumbrians, both churchmen and members of the ruling family, visiting Iona or Ireland for periods of study. The outstanding example of a man educated in Ireland but at the same time ready and eager to take advantage of the new books and learning brought in from the Continent is Aldfrith, who was king of Northumbria from 685 to 705, his reign thus spanning an appreciable part of the careers of both Eadfrith and Bede. Aldfrith was the illegitimate son of King Oswiu and an Irish princess. While in exile in Ireland during the reign of his half-brother Ecgfrith, the patron of Wearmouth and Jarrow, he had received an Irish education and even spoke the Irish language. When he succeeded to the throne on Ecgfrith's death in battle at Nechtansmere, he rapidly showed himself to be fully appreciative of the new learning imported from Italy, but at the same time maintained contact with his old teachers. It was to Aldfrith that Adamnan of Iona presented his account of the Holy Places in Palestine, and the king soon circulated copies of this 'for lesser folk to read', to the great delight of Bede and his contemporaries.

Both England and Ireland drew on the same Celtic artistic legacy, into which they assimilated the Germanic motifs brought by the Anglo-Saxon settlers, and constant interchange produced such similar results that it is extremely hard, in the absence of written corroborative evidence, to distinguish the Irish from the Northumbrian, particularly in book painting and in metalwork. This subject arouses strong passions among partisan scholars, but the cautious tend to adopt some suitably ambiguous blanket description such as 'insular' or 'Hiberno-Saxon' when dealing with it. The histories of the Lichfield Gospels of Saint Chad, which had migrated to South Wales from its as yet unidentified birthplace by the early ninth century, and of the Lindisfarne Gospels itself, which could very well have been taken across to Ireland at the end of the ninth century, supply ample evidence of the way in which objects could be moved from place to place, even quite early in their existence.

In the eighth century it was Northumbria that provided, through the activities of the missionaries on the Continent, a strong strain of artistic and cultural influence on others. By the time the Vikings made their first raid on Lindisfarne in 793, one of the greatest of these English emigrants, Alcuin of York, a pupil of Archbishop Egbert who

OVERLEAF:
40. Enlarged detail from the cross-carpet page introducing Saint Matthew's Gospel. The area shown lies in the lower right-hand quarter of the page. The highlight which runs across the top of the picture marks the line of the spine of the animal from which the vellum came. The Lindisfarne Gospels, folio 26b.

41. The Gospels of Saint Chad. Enlarged detail from the cross-carpet page (p. 220) which introduces Saint Luke's Gospel. An area similar to that in the most closely related of the Lindisfarne Gospels cross-carpet pages (previous plate) is shown. Delicate shades of lilac and lavender are especially characteristic of the work of the Saint Chad artist. These appear too pink in this plate because the pigment used does not reproduce accurately on modern colour film. The same colours are similarly misrepresented on a number of the plates from the Lindisfarne Gospels itself (*Lichfield Cathedral, Chapter Library*).

64

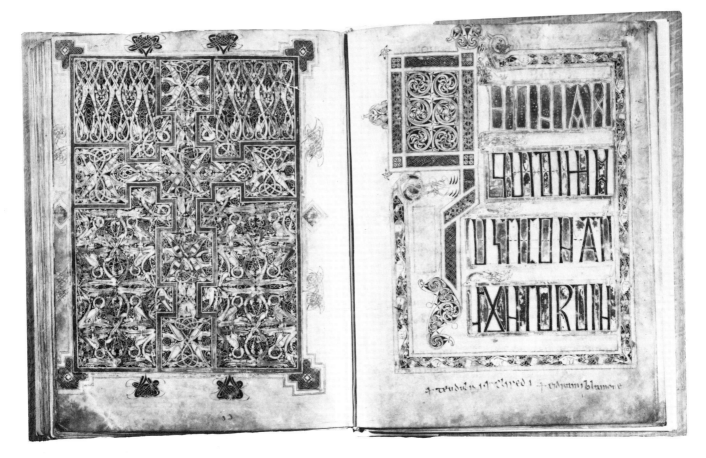

had, in his turn, been a disciple and friend of the Venerable Bede, had already for more than a decade been established at the court of Charlemagne. His position, first as tutor to the royal family and later as abbot of Saint Martin's of Tours, allowed him to play a leading role in the Carolingian renaissance.

Within the historical and artistic framework of the period, the Lindisfarne Gospels has a particularly important place. Firstly, it is a work of outstanding beauty and sophistication, displaying all the various elements which combine to make up the distinctive style current in seventh-century England. Secondly, thanks to Aldred's tenth-century colophon, we know exactly where, when and by whom it was made. It thus becomes a touchstone for the assessment of all other works of art of the period.

There can be no doubt of Eadfrith's technical mastery of the craft of book production, nor of his flair for subtle design. Even in their complete and undamaged state, none of the other Gospel books directly comparable with the Lindisfarne Gospels can have attained quite the same consistent perfection. It seems likely that the artist of the Gospels of Saint Chad, whose work is in several ways the closest, had actually seen and studied Eadfrith's great book. The outline of his surviving cross-carpet page (plate 42) is an amalgamation of the cross shapes in Eadfrith's first (plate 19) and second (plate 24) carpets, and his combination of animal and bird interlace is close in intention to Eadfrith's. But the very narrow and much more violently contorted tendrils between his individual birds and beasts are loosely woven, revealing larger areas of dark background than Eadfrith permitted (plates 40 and 41). The ornamental appendages to the frame, also derived directly from Eadfrith's Matthew carpet page, are more numerous and far fussier (plate 42). On the 'Quoniam' page he has abandoned the fluid, sweeping curves of Eadfrith's initial (plate 32), to which the curves of border and panels are fitted. Instead he pro-

42. The Gospels of Saint Chad. The cross-carpet page and major initial page (pp. 220–221) at the beginning of Saint Luke's Gospel. These should be compared with the cross-carpet pages preceding Saint Jerome's letter (plate 19) and Saint Matthew's Gospel (plate 24), and with the major initial page at the beginning of Saint Luke's Gospel (plate 32) in the Lindisfarne Gospels (*Lichfield Cathedral, Chapter Library*).

duces a very geometrical design (plate 42), with hard corners even within the stem of the initial 'Q', surrounded by a heavy, four-square border. Although this border too begins and ends with the head, feet and tail of a bird-filled beast, it entirely lacks the charm of Eadfrith's hunting cat. Where Eadfrith has varied his decorated capitals from large at the top of the page to relatively small on the sixth and lowest line, at the same time trying to ensure that their shapes make it possible for the words to be read, the Saint Chad artist has produced four lines of letters of exactly similar proportions and with a minimum of individual characteristics. The overall impression given by reproductions of the decorated pages of the Lichfield manuscript is one of heaviness, though in the original this is somewhat mitigated by the very delightful colouring, in which lilac and lavender play a leading part.

In many ways most closely related to the design and execution of the ornament in the Lindisfarne Gospels is the design and ornament of the Tara Brooch, now in the National Museum of Ireland in Dublin (plate 44). Unfortunately we have no direct indication of the date or place of origin of this marvellous piece of jewellery. It was found in 1850 on the seashore in County Meath, not very far from ancient Tara, though its· name was the invention of the Dublin jeweller who acquired it and sold replicas of it in London at the Great Exhibition in 1851. It is quite small, about 3 inches in diameter, but both back and front are heavily encrusted with the most intricate and delicately executed ornament, which conveys a richly polychrome effect, not merely because of the introduction of coloured studs but also through the interplay of areas of gold, silver and copper. The back of the Tara Brooch is particularly related to the Lindisfarne Gospels. On it appear panels of simple and of animal interlace, a long border filled with curvilinear patterns, two three-sided panels of curvilinear motifs, and a further border enclosing a procession of interlaced birds, very close indeed to those painted by Eadfrith. The three-sided panels and the bird border are shown in more detail in an enlarged photograph (plate 46), taken when the brooch was undergoing restoration in the British Museum research laboratory in the early 1960s.

The one surviving major (though badly rubbed) decorated page in the Durham Gospels (plate 45), which may be slightly earlier than the Lindisfarne Gospels or is possibly the work of an artist of an older generation, makes very little use of curvilinear patterns. A few tiny examples occur at the very base of the initial, but even there the slightly larger circular areas which we might expect to see treated in this way are actually filled with arrangements of birds' heads. It seems at first sight that birds are the mainstay of the Durham Gospels illuminator, as the entire framework of his great monogram is filled in with interlaced creatures possessed of prominent beaks. However, closer scrutiny reveals that these creatures have four limbs, extensions of which are used for the very open interlace which fills the spaces between them. They are very definitely the invention of an artist and convey nothing of the feeling for nature, however much it is adapted for its purpose, that comes through strongly in Eadfrith's work.

The curvilinear patterns found in the manuscripts have another important parallel in metalwork. Very similar designs are found on the decorative enamel escutcheons (small ornamental plaques) of hanging bowls. These bowls, while they are apparently of Celtic workmanship, are usually found in the context of pagan Anglo-Saxon graves. About 70 examples are known, and they have been recovered in conjunction with other materials ranging in date from the fifth to the seventh

OVERLEAF:
43. Enlarged detail from the second major initial page in Saint Matthew's Gospel, showing the curvilinear ornament in the bow of the main letter. The Lindisfarne Gospels, folio 29.

44. The Tara Brooch, reverse side (*National Museum of Ireland, Dublin*).

godspell   apt

euarrgeli   um secudoum m

                enister

                god lice

46. The Tara Brooch, National Museum of Ireland, Dublin. Enlarged detail from the reverse side, showing curvilinear ornament and interlaced birds (*photo: British Museum Research Laboratory*).

OPPOSITE:
45. The Durham Gospels. Major initial page at the beginning of Saint John's Gospel. This may be compared with the corresponding page in the Lindisfarne Gospels (plate 35) and with a similar page in the Book of Durrow (plate 53). Durham Cathedral MS A.II.17, folio 2 (*Durham Cathedral Library*).

OVERLEAF:
47. Enlarged detail from the major initial page at the beginning of Saint Luke's Gospel. The curvilinear ornament in the tail of the main letter and part of the adjacent panel of bird interlace are shown. The Lindisfarne Gospels, folio 139.

48. The Sutton Hoo ship burial. Enlargement of one of the escutcheons from the large hanging bowl, showing curvilinear ornament applied to enamelwork. The motif immediately below the enamelled area is also reminiscent of manuscript work, similar decorations often being used to break the straight lines of the border on cross-carpet pages (*British Museum, Department of Medieval and Later Antiquities*).

century. No one has as yet produced an entirely convincing explanation of their function, though it has been suggested that they were hanging lamps or containers for water, possibly holy water. It does, however, seem likely that they were part of the trappings of Christian churches in the Celtic west of the British Isles and that the Anglo-Saxon invaders acquired them as loot. The very finest hanging bowl yet found was among the treasures recovered from the Sutton Hoo ship burial. It has six escutcheons on the outer surface, three of them square and purely decorative and the other three round and attached to the rings by which the bowl would be hung (plate 48). They are decorated with coloured enamels and with insets of millefiori glass. Inside the base of the bowl is another round escutcheon from which rises a little movable fish on a pedestal. The Sutton Hoo bowl must have been a much cherished treasure, for it was provided with a decorated silver patch after it came into Anglo-Saxon hands.

In metalwork the red dots used by Eadfrith and his contemporaries to emphasize the outlines of their initial letters become tiny punch marks on an otherwise smooth ground. The technique is seen used to great effect on the Ardagh Chalice, a superb example of the jeweller's craft, which was found among a hoard of lesser items in County Limerick in 1874. It is now in the National Museum of Ireland. Its restrained yet sophisticated decoration, which includes coloured studs and little panels of gold filigree work, has much in common with the work seen on the Tara Brooch. The overall effect is, however, much less blatantly rich because of the large areas of plain silver against which the decoration appears. On the bowl of the chalice the names of the twelve apostles are written against a background of tiny indentations (plate 50), the result bearing a very strong resemblance to the work on some of the major initial pages in the Lindisfarne Gospels (plate 49). The general relationship of the Ardagh Chalice to Northumbrian craftsmanship from the years around 700 is recognized by pro-Irish and pro-English scholars alike, and it is unlikely — and perhaps unnecessary — that we shall ever be entirely certain on which side of the Irish Sea the man who made it lived.

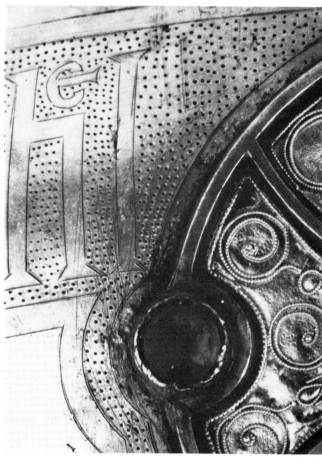

Scholars writing about early insular manuscripts in the years before 1939 were unable to draw attention to one of the most spectacular works of art which can be compared with them. This is the superb pair of gold and garnet shoulder clasps from Sutton Hoo, part of an assemblage of jewelled trappings and personal ornaments entirely without parallel from any other site. So rich are the objects found in the ship burial that it can only have been the resting place of one of the kings of East Anglia. Coins found in association with a jewelled purse lid suggest a date of about 625 for the deposit, and a mixture of pagan and Christian objects amongst the grave goods points to a similar date. The best candidate to be the man honoured with so sumptuous a burial is Raedwald, the powerful East Anglian king who died in or about 625. Raedwald had accepted the Christian faith early in his reign, under the influence of King Ethelbert of Kent, who had received Saint Augustine and his companions in 597. However, he subsequently returned to his old religion, and Bede tells us that he went so far as to set up altars to Christ and to the heathen gods under the same roof. East Anglia was re-converted by his successor, and the interesting suggestion has recently been made that the apparent absence of a body in the Sutton Hoo grave could be due to the removal of Raedwald's remains from their pagan resting place to a consecrated site, better befitting a king who had once been a baptized Christian.

Each of the Sutton Hoo shoulder clasps is made of two pieces, the main rectangular field of each filled with a colourful stepped design of garnets and millefiori glass surrounded by a border of animal interlace (plate 52). The very thin slices of garnet are laid over patterned gold foil, adding to the intricacy of the design. The resemblance to a decorated carpet page is very clear, both in detail and in general conception. A multicoloured stepped design, its cells seemingly di-

ABOVE LEFT:

49. Enlarged detail of the major initial page at the beginning of Saint John's Gospel, showing red dots used to emphasize the outlines of lesser decorated letters. The Lindisfarne Gospels, folio 211.

ABOVE RIGHT:

50. The Ardagh Chalice, National Museum of Ireland, Dublin. Enlarged detail from the bowl of the chalice, showing punch marks used to emphasize the outlines of the inscription (*photo: British Museum Research Laboratory*).

vided by walls of metal, is used as a centrepiece for the cross-carpet page at the beginning of Saint Mark in the Lindisfarne Gospels (plate 51). The simpler carpet pages in the Book of Durrow, with their bold, large-scale motifs and wide borders, underline the relationship. A further link with the Book of Durrow may be found in the border of animal interlace surrounding the central panel, whose long-nosed, almost beaked animals are first cousins to the long-snouted creatures on the Saint John carpet page of the manuscript.

The Book of Durrow is much simpler than the Lindisfarne Gospels and seems to represent an earlier stage in the development of insular book decoration, in which most of the elements are already present but are not yet thoroughly mingled (plate 53). A different kind of simplicity is displayed in the Echternach Gospels (plate 54), which seems to have been deliberately planned for speed of execution rather than to represent an early stage of development. Although only one full page of decoration precedes each of the Gospels in this book, its artist has contrived to combine in them not only a representation of the appropriate Evangelist through his symbol but also the feeling of a cross-carpet page, implied in the simple coloured bars which break up the background into a variety of different shapes and sizes of uncoloured vellum.

In Eadfrith's work the panels of different shapes and sizes which appear both on the fully decorated pages and within the outlines of the great initial letters are almost always filled with one or another variety of ornament. He showed enormous skill in adapting his motifs to fill the oddest of shapes. Panels of ornament in a totally different medium, but in design often closely resembling manuscript work, are found in the decoration of carved stone crosses, many of them apparently dating from the late seventh and the eighth centuries. Most of the crosses are entirely undocumented, their purpose and origin forgotten. Some of them may have been raised to commemorate important people and events. We know from Bede that the sainted King Oswald of Northumbria raised a great cross of wood to mark the place where he was about to engage in battle with the heathen at 'Heavenfield', near Hexham, in 634, and that he and his army knelt in prayer before it before the battle began. Other crosses may have marked traditional meeting places, used in the early days of Christianity as sites for the celebration of Mass, where an itinerant bishop or priest such as Saint Cuthbert would have consecrated the bread and wine on his portable altar. The cross in the churchyard at Bewcastle in Cumberland, some miles north of Hadrian's Wall, seems to indicate such a spot. Although the church and the handful of houses adjoining it are isolated in desolate country, they stand on the site of a Roman fort which was probably a notable landmark in Bede's day. This cross, which includes a long inscription in runes and some figure carvings now very much eroded by centuries of exposure to the weather, has panels of simple ribbon interlace exactly parallel to several of those used by Eadfrith (plate 57). A fragment of a cross from Aberlady, on the southern shore of the Firth of Forth, retains a panel of interlaced birds closely akin to those in the Lindisfarne Gospels, below which is the remains of a panel of the type of key pattern seen in the background to the cross-carpet page preceding the Gospel of Saint Luke (plate 55).

Stone carvings on a large scale have survived where carvings on a smaller scale and in more vulnerable materials have not. A unique relic from the early Christian period in Northumbria is the Franks Casket, a small box made up of panels of whalebone carved with scenes from a mixture of pagan and Christian stories, reminding us

OVERLEAF:
51. Enlarged detail from the cross-carpet page introducing Saint Mark's Gospel, showing Eadfrith's use of a cellular step pattern in the central roundel (for the reverse side of which, see plate 15). The Lindisfarne Gospels, folio 94b.

52. The Sutton Hoo ship burial. Enlargement of part of one of the gold, garnet and millefiori shoulder clasps. The overall design of this ornament is strongly reminiscent of a manuscript carpet page (*British Museum, Department of Medieval and Later Antiquities*).

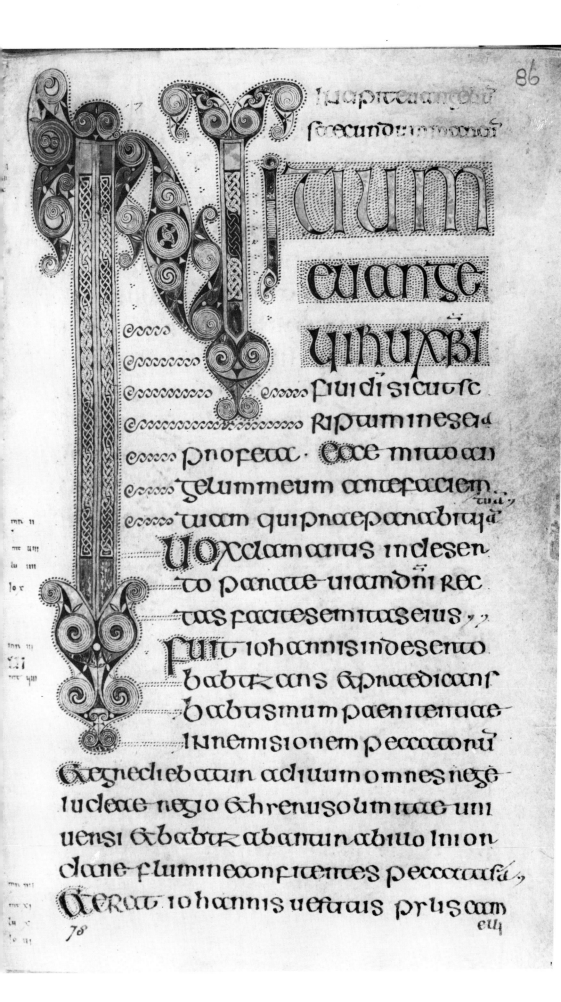

53. The Book of Durrow. Cross-carpet page and major initial page at the beginning of Saint Mark's Gospel. Trinity College, Dublin, MS A. 4. 5. (57), folios 85b–86 (*Trinity College, Dublin*).

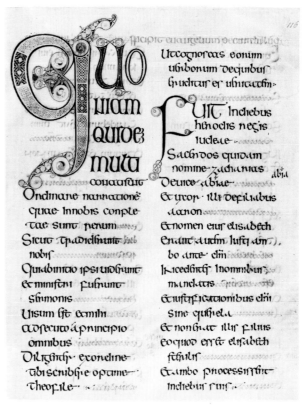

once again how little time had elapsed between the conversion of the Anglo-Saxons and the period with which we are concerned. On the front panel of this casket (plate 58) is shown, on the left, the legendary Wayland the Smith, a familiar figure in Norse mythology, fashioning into a goblet the skull of a boy whom he had slain in order to revenge himself upon the boy's father. On the right is a more familiar scene, the Adoration of the Magi. Both are accompanied by runic inscriptions. The style in which the figures are portrayed, with deeply marked drapery folds and features reduced almost to a formal pattern, is reminiscent of the Celtic rather than the Mediterranean strain in book decoration, though the lines on the two cloaks in the Wayland scene are not at all unlike the lines applied to the garments of Eadfrith's Evangelists. Two interesting features of this particular panel of the casket are the archway under which the Virgin is seated, which could well be adapted for use in a canon table arcade, and the fine collection of blacksmith's tools being used by Wayland, all quite clearly recognizable.

The miniature of Ezra from the Codex Amiatinus (plate 59) also includes tools, this time the tools of the scribe. Not only is Ezra shown writing, but he also has a stylus, dividers, ink pots, and a strange triangular object, which could just conceivably be a template for drawing curves, all scattered on the floor about his feet. Although we know that this picture was painted by an Anglo-Saxon artist, it is so clearly taken from an imported original that we must be wary of reading too much into the evidence which it offers. It is nevertheless sobering to remember how little writing implements changed in all the centuries between Eadfrith's time and that of our own great-grandparents. Only the development of the steel pen nib in Victorian times ousted the natural quill.

We have already seen that the miniature of Saint Matthew in the Lindisfarne Gospels (plate 23) is very closely related to the Ezra miniature, though Eadfrith adapted the basic figure to suit his own

54. The Echternach Gospels. Cross-carpet page and major initial page at the beginning of Saint Luke's Gospel. Bibliothèque Nationale, Paris, MS lat. 9389, folios 115b–116 (*Bibliothèque Nationale, Paris*).

55. The Aberlady Cross. Panels of bird interlace and of diagonal key pattern sculpted in stone (*National Museum of Antiquities, Edbinburgh*).

OPPOSITE:

56. Enlarged detail from the major initial page at the beginning of Saint John's Gospel, showing the outline of the main letters divided into clearly defined panels, filled alternately with animal ornament and with knotwork. The Lindisfarne Gospels, folio 211.

personal style and added to it the Evangelist's symbol and the mysterious figure peeping round the curtain. It is interesting to compare
the Ezra and the Matthew, both of which have recognizably descended from an Italian model, with one of the two surviving Evangelist pictures in the Lichfield Gospels of Saint Chad, that of Saint Mark
(plate 60). This figure has some features suggesting a classical model
(particularly in the form of the costume, although this has been
reduced to a linear pattern), and its feet are every bit as naturalistic as
those drawn by Eadfrith himself, but the general impression given by
the page is nevertheless barbaric rather than classical. This impression
is very much enhanced by the extraordinary 'throne' behind the
figure, which looks more like the iron frame from the Belgic burials at
Welwyn (now in the British Museum) than the simple footstool of the
other two miniatures. The lion symbol above the saint's head is,
however, recognizable for what it is, though in appearance it is closer
to the Echternach painter's interpretation than to that of Eadfrith. It
also lacks the wings and trumpet seen in the Lindisfarne Gospels.

The most directly relevant set of Evangelist symbols is that on the lid
of Saint Cuthbert's coffin, which is preserved at Durham Cathedral
with other relics from the grave. The coffin is a carved chest, made out
of oak, which was prepared to receive the saint's remains at the time of
the elevation in 698. Although by the time the tomb was investigated
during the nineteenth century, the coffin had disintegrated into a series
of broken and distorted lumps of wood, enough was recovered for the
whole of the decoration to be reconstructed and studied. The carving
consists of very simple incised lines. On one long side of the coffin and
at the head are figures of the archangels, on the other side figures of the
twelve Apostles. On the panel at the foot is a seated figure of the
Virgin, holding the Christ Child. On the lid is a figure of Christ,
surrounded by the symbols of the four Evangelists, those of Matthew
and Mark over his head and these those of Luke and John beneath his
feet (plate 61). Their resemblance to the symbols painted into the

83

84

Lindisfarne Gospels, which must have been in the making at the same time as the coffin, is very striking, although the medium and technique are so different.

So much fine material has survived the twelve or thirteen intervening centuries that we are at least able to make some assessment of the skill and artistry of Anglo-Saxon craftsmen working in many different fields. How much more has been lost we shall never know. The Viking raids, which began in the late eighth century and gradually affected the whole of England, hit Northumbria very hard and were to leave the most famous of her monasteries derelict, Lindisfarne and Jarrow among them. Had Eardulf and his community neglected to remove the body of their saint and all the treasures of their monastery to safety, a high proportion of the works of art described in this book, including the Lindisfarne Gospels itself, might very well have been lost to us.

61. Saint Cuthbert's coffin. Part of the lid, showing the outlines of the symbols of Saint Luke and Saint John, the calf and the eagle, incised in the wood (*Durham Cathedral Library*).

9. THE LATER HISTORY OF THE MANUSCRIPT

The relics of Saint Cuthbert, together with the other treasures of Lindisfarne, including the Gospels, came to rest at Chester-le-Street in 883, some seven years after Bishop Eardulf and his community had fled from Holy Island. Chester-le-Street, which is about six miles north of the City of Durham, was built within the ruins of a Roman camp, no doubt much more obvious in the ninth century than it is today. The medieval parish church, dedicated to the Virgin Mary and Saint Cuthbert, apparently occupies what was once the site of the Roman headquarters building. Saint Cuthbert's community remained there for more than a century until, in 995, news of fresh Viking incursions uncomfortably close at hand seemed to necessitate a further move, this time southwards to Ripon. A few months later, on the return journey, the saint miraculously indicated that he wished a new home to be established for him at Durham.

The old city of Durham stands on steeply sloping ground, almost encircled by a loop of the river Wear. It is, like Holy Island, a natural stronghold. The body of Saint Cuthbert has remained there until the present day, except for a very brief period in 1069-70 when the last Saxon bishop, Ethelwine, fled with the relics back to Lindisfarne in fear of the punitive expedition to the north led by the new Norman king, William the Conqueror (plate 62). The second Norman bishop of Durham, William of Saint Calais (Carilef) in 1083 replaced with Benedictine monks the by then largely secular community which he had found attending the cathedral and shrine, and a dependent priory was established on Holy Island. In 1093 he laid the foundation stone of the immense Romanesque cathedral which stands to this day (plate 64). In 1104, in the time of his successor, Bishop Ranulph Flambard, the building of the cathedral was far enough advanced for Saint Cuthbert's relics to be solemnly translated to their new setting at the high altar, where the shrine became the focal point of the church for pilgrims. During the translation the coffin was again opened and the saint's body seen still to be undecayed. It is clear from the account given by Symeon of Durham, who wrote shortly after the event, that at this time the Lindisfarne Gospels was still among the treasures associated with the saint.

There is no certain reference to the history of the manuscript during the remainder of the Middle Ages. What could be a description of it, as 'the book of Saint Cuthbert which fell into the sea', occurs in a list of the few books at Lindisfarne Priory in 1367, suggesting at least a temporary visit to its former home, but it is also possibly identifiable with an item in the Durham Cathedral relic list of 1383. When the Reformation came, the priory on Holy Island was dissolved in 1537 and the cathedral priory itself suffered the same fate about two years later. Henry VIII's commissioners seized the treasures of Saint Cuthbert's shrine, and the body of the saint, yet again seen to be intact,

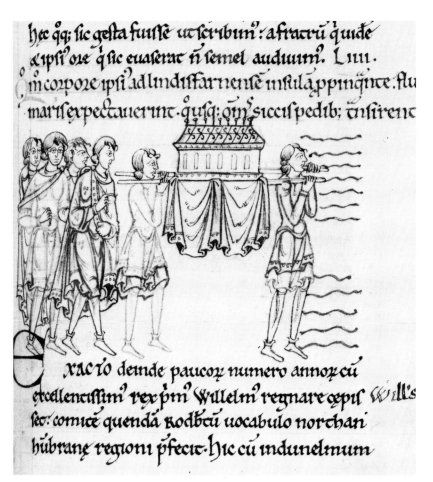

hæc qq; sic gesta fuisse ut scribun': a fratrū quide
& ipsi ore q sic euaserat ñ semel audiuim'. Liiii.
ȝin corpore ipsi ad lindisfarnense insula appingnce. flu
maris expectauerint. qusq; oms siccis pedib; transirent

Xacto deinde paucor numero annor cū
excellentissim' rex prim' Willelm' regnare cæpit Will's
secō comice quendā Rodbtū uocabulo norchan
hūbrane regioni pfecit. Hic cū indunelmum

62. The relics of Saint Cuthbert being carried
back across the sands to Holy Island in 1069, to
escape the wrath of William the Conqueror. An
illustration to the continuation of Bede's *Life of
Saint Cuthbert*, University College, Oxford, MS
165, p. 159 (*Bodleian Library, Oxford*).

was reburied beneath the pavement behind the high altar (though
there is a persistent tradition that the body reburied was not that of the
saint, which was spirited away to a secret resting place revealed only to
two Benedictine monks in each generation). We are not told speci-
fically what became of the Gospels, but it is likely that the manuscript
was dispatched to London with the rest of the treasures, for the sake of
its jewelled golden binding.

It is next heard of in 1567, when Aldred's gloss was one of the
sources used in the compilation of Laurence Nowell's *Vocabularium
Saxonicum*, the first ever dictionary of the Anglo-Saxon language (now
MS Selden Supra 63 in the Bodleian Library, Oxford). Nowell had
access to manuscripts owned by William Bowyer, Keeper of the
Records at the Tower, and Bowyer may well have acquired the
Gospels in consequence of his official position, as the Tower Jewel
House had been the destination of the confiscated monastic treasures.
The book certainly belonged to Bowyer's son, Robert, who succeeded
his father as Keeper of the Records and whose name is inscribed on its
second folio. It was from Robert Bowyer that Sir Robert Cotton
acquired the Gospels in the early years of the seventeenth century.
Cotton's magnificent library was housed in a series of bookcases
surmounted by busts of the Roman emperors, and the Lindisfarne
Gospels, as the fourth manuscript on the fourth shelf under Nero,
received the pressmark 'Nero D. iv', which it still bears. Since then the
history of the Gospels has been the same as that of the Cotton collection, which was made over to the nation in 1703 by Sir Robert's heirs
and incorporated into the British Museum as one of the foundation
collections in 1753.

A long list of published references to and reproductions of the
Gospels, one of the earliest being an engraving in Thomas Astle's

OPPOSITE:
63. The present binding of the Lindisfarne
Gospels, decorated with silver and gems, made
by Smith, Nicholson and Co. of Lincolns Inn
Fields in 1852–3. All the motifs used were
chosen from the decoration inside the
manuscript.

Origin and development of handwriting in 1784, leaves no doubt of the importance of the Lindisfarne Gospels as one of the outstanding works of art to have survived from the early Middle Ages. However, this particular book has never been regarded merely as a museum curiosity, of interest only to scholars and connoisseurs, but has kept something of the mystique of a holy relic, even into the twentieth century. Strong antiquarian interest during the nineteenth century inspired two investigations of Saint Cuthbert's tomb. The first, in 1827, was particularly concerned to show that the incorruptibility of Saint Cuthbert was a papist myth, 'invented for interested purposes in a supertstitious age'. The second (rather more scientifically conducted) took place in 1899. Fragments of the original oaken coffin of 698, together with such personal possessions as the saint's portable altar, pectoral cross and ritual comb, were recovered and may nowadays be seen in the cathedral treasury at Durham. During the same period Durham did not forget the Gospels. In March 1852 the octogenarian bishop, Edward Maltby, wrote to the British Museum and offered 60 guineas to pay for a new and more fitting binding for Saint Cuthbert's book. It is possible that he had seen and admired replicas of the Tara brooch, on sale at the Great Exhibition in the previous year. The offer was accepted and the work placed in the hands of Smith, Nicholson and Co., silversmiths in Lincolns Inn Fields, who endeavoured, with some success, to produce a design based upon motifs found in Eadfrith's own work. The result (plate 63), which has apparently never been published and which is invisible to visitors because the Gospels is always open in its exhibition case, is a magnificent piece of Victorian archaeological revival metalwork. However, Sir Frederic Madden, who was Keeper of Manuscripts in 1852 and who viewed the

64. The west front of Durham Cathedral, final resting place of the relics of Saint Cuthbert and one-time home of the Lindisfarne Gospels (*photo: the author*).

In the stained glass window, the following inscriptions appear:

BISHOP·EADFRITH·WRITES·THE·LINDISFARNE·GOSPELS

✠·ST·JOHN·WRITES·THE·GOSPEL·✠·✠

✠·ALDRED·THE·PRIEST·WRITES·THE·SAXON·GLOSS·✠

BISHOP·ETHILWALD·&·BILLFRITH·ORNAMENT·THE·GOSPELS

HUNDRED·THE·MONK·RECOVERS·THE·GOSPELS·

BISHOP·ALDUNE·FLEES·FROM·CHESTER·A.D.995

✠·✠·TO·THE·GLORY·OF·GOD·✠

IN·MEMORY·OF·EMMA·BARRETT·WOOD

BORN·OCT·20·1848·DIED·MAY·4·1891·

entire project with great disfavour, thought it '. . . a complete failure . . . The binding is hideous, as it now stands, and the effect wretched enough to bring us into ridicule.'

In more recent years the parish churches of both Chester-le-Street and Holy Island have marked their association with the Lindisfarne Gospels. In the north aisle at Chester-le-Street is a remarkable stained glass window (plate 65), installed in memory of Emma Barrett Wood, who died in 1891. This imaginatively re-creates scenes of Eadfrith and Aldred writing the manuscript, Ethelwald and Billfrith creating the covers, Hunred rescuing it from the sea, and Bishop Aldhune leading

65. Memorial window in the parish church at Chester-le-Street, installed soon after 1891, showing Eadfrith and Aldred writing their contributions to the Lindisfarne Gospels, Ethelwald and Billfrith at work on the binding, Hunred miraculously recovering the manuscript from the sea, and Bishop Aldhune urging his brethren on to their last flight from the Danes in 995 (*photo: Canuck Studios, Chester-le-Street*).

the flight from Chester-le-Street in 995. In the thirteenth-century church on Holy Island, which is separated from the site of the Anglo-Saxon monastery and the ruins of the later medieval priory by little more than the width of a footpath, the sanctuary is adorned with a large and sumptuous embroidered carpet, copied in detail from the cross-carpet page which precedes Saint Mark's Gospel in Eadfrith's manuscript. This was made by a group of 18 local ladies (plate 66), who devoted two years to the task. It was dedicated in June 1970.

Although it is certain that the Lindisfarne Gospels has not been seen on Holy Island since the end of the Middle Ages, and quite probable that its last appearance there was in 1069, when Bishop Ethelwine and his followers took flight from William the Conqueror, local awareness of the connection with this great treasure is still very much alive. A copy of the facsimile edition of 1956, a gift from the Rockford College Community, Illinois, U.S.A., lies in a glass case in the church, only a few yards from the place where Eadfrith and Ethelwald created it 'for God and for Saint Cuthbert and — jointly — for all the saints whose relics are in the island', almost thirteen centuries ago.

66. Miss Kathleen Parbury with four of the eighteen embroidresses who created the Lindisfarne Gospels carpet for the sanctuary of the parish church of Holy Island (*photo by permission of the vicar of Holy Island*).

BIBLIOGRAPHY

A. SUMMARY DESCRIPTION OF THE MANUSCRIPT

Cotton MS Nero D.iv: The Lindisfarne Gospels

Vellum; ff. 259. 340 × 250 mm. ($13\frac{1}{2}$ × $9\frac{3}{4}$ inches). Gatherings mainly of eight leaves (for full details the introductory volume to the facsimile edition of 1956, cited below, should be consulted). Latin (about AD 698) with an Anglo-Saxon gloss (mid-10th century). Bound in red velvet, lavishly ornamented with silver and gemstones, 1852-3.

Contents: (1) List of contents in the hand of Sir Robert Cotton's librarian, 17th century, f. 1. (2) Epistle of Saint Jerome to Damasus, ff. 3-5b. (3) Prologue to the Four Gospels, ff. 5b-8. (4) Epistle of Eusebius to Carpianus, ff. 8-9. (5) Eusebian canon tables, ff. 10-17b. (6) Preface ('argumentum') to Matthew, ff. 18b-19. (7) Table of chapters ('capitula lectionum') to Matthew, ff. 19-23b. (8) Table of feast days for lessons from Matthew, ff. 24-24b. (9) The Gospel according to Saint Matthew, ff. 27-89b. (10) Preface to Mark, ff. 90-90b. (11) Table of chapters to Mark, ff. 91-93. (12) Table of feast days for lessons from Mark, f. 93. (13) The Gospel according to Saint Mark, ff. 95-130. (14) Table of feast days for lessons from Luke, ff. 130-130b. (15) Preface to Luke, ff. 131-131b. (16) Table of chapters to Luke, ff. 131-137. (17) The Gospel according to Saint Luke, ff. 139-203. (18) Preface to John, ff. 203b-204. (19) Table of chapters to John, ff. 204-208. (20) Table of feast days for lessons from John, ff. 208-208b. (21) The Gospel according to Saint John, ff. 211-259. (22) Colophon recording the names of those who made the manuscript, in the hand of Aldred the glossator, mid-10th century, f. 259.

Decoration: (1) 16 pages of Eusebian canon tables, ff. 10-17b. (2) Miniatures of the Four Evangelists, ff. 25b, 93b, 137b and 209b. (3) 5 decorative cross-carpet pages, ff. 2b, 26b, 94b, 138b and 210b. (4) 6 major initial pages, ff. 3, 27, 29, 95, 139 and 211. (5) Lesser initials for prefaces etc., ff. 5b, 8, 18b, 19, 24, 90, 91, 93, 95b, 130, 131, 131b, 136b, 137, 139b, 203b, 204, 208 and 211b.

B. SUGGESTIONS FOR FURTHER READING

The Lindisfarne Gospels has been the subject of two major studies. The more recent of these is a facsimile edition, *Evangelium Quattuor Codex Lindisfarnensis*, Urs Graf Verlag, 2 volumes; full facsimile, 1956, and commentary (with contributions by T. D. Kendrick, T. J. Brown, R. L. S. Bruce-Mitford, H. Roosen-Runge, A. S. C. Ross, E. G. Stanley and A. E. A. Werner), 1960. This is still the most detailed published examination of any single manuscript. Fewer than 700 copies were printed, and the book is seldom available outside major academic libraries. Still valuable, and certainly more readily accessible, is E. G. Millar, *The Lindisfarne Gospels*, British Museum, 1923. A list of other references to the Gospels, and full bibliographies for the other illuminated manuscripts mentioned in this book, will be found in J. J. G. Alexander, *Insular Manuscripts, Sixth to Ninth Century* (A Survey of Manuscripts Illuminated in the British Isles, vol. I), Harvey Miller, 1978.

A lively and extremely readable general introduction to the history of the period, both social and political, is provided by Peter Hunter-Blair, *Northumbria in the Days of*

Bede, Victor Gollancz, 1976. More specialized information will be found in H. Mayr-Harting, *The Coming of Christianity to Anglo-Saxon England*, Batsford, 1972; *Saint Wilfrid at Hexham*, ed. D. P. Kirby, Oriel Press, 1974; and W. Levison, *England and the Continent in the Eighth Century*, Oxford University Press, 1946.

English translations of many of the original sources for the period are collected in *English Historical Documents, vol. I: c. 500-1042*, ed. Dorothy Whitelock, Eyre Methuen, 1955, second edition, 1979. There are several popular editions of English translations of the most important single source, Bede's *Ecclesiastical History*. A recent and particularly useful one, in which Latin and English are printed on parallel pages, is *Bede's Ecclesiastical History of the English People*, ed. Bertram Colgrave and R. A. B. Mynors, Clarendon Press, 1969. English editions of other major sources mentioned are Bertram Colgrave, *The Life of Bishop Wilfrid by Eddius Stephanus*, Cambridge University Press, 1927, and *Two Lives of Saint Cuthbert*, Cambridge University Press, 1940; C. H. Talbot, *The Anglo-Saxon Missionaries in Germany*, Sheed and Ward, 1954; A. Campbell, *Æthelwulf: De Abbatibus*, Clarendon Press, 1967; and D. Meehan, *Adamnan's De Locis Sanctis* (Scriptores Latini Hiberniae, vol. III), Dublin Institute for Advanced Studies, 1958.

The two riddles cited are taken respectively from Kevin Crossley-Holland, *Storm and Other Old English Riddles*, Macmillan, 1970; and J. H. Pitman, *The Riddles of Aldhelm* (Yale Studies in English, vol. LXVII), Yale University Press and Oxford University Press, 1925. All the riddles of the Exeter Book, in Anglo-Saxon and in modern English, will be found in *The Exeter Book: part II*, ed. W. S. Mackie (Early English Text Society, original series no. 194), Oxford University Press, 1934.

A recent survey of the archaeology of the period is *The Archaeology of Anglo-Saxon England*, ed. D. M. Wilson, Methuen, 1976. Individual objects and discoveries are described and illustrated in *The Relics of Saint Cuthbert*, ed. C. F. Battiscombe, Oxford University Press, 1956; R. L. S. Bruce-Mitford, *The Sutton Hoo Ship Burial: a Handbook*, British Museum Publications, third edition, 1979; and *Treasures of Irish Art 1500 BC – 1500 AD* (the catalogue of an exhibition at the Metropolitan Museum of Art, New York, etc., with contributions by G. F. Mitchell, P. Harbison, L. de Paor, M. de Paor, and R. A. Stalley), Metropolitan Museum of Art and Alfred A. Knopf, 1977.

Most of these books give further bibliography. Recent publications concerning every aspect of Anglo-Saxon history and culture are listed each year in the annual *Anglo-Saxon England*, Cambridge University Press, 1972 etc.

Finally, an unusual practical insight into the type of decoration seen in the Lindisfarne Gospels is offered by George Bain, *Celtic Art: the Methods of Construction*, William Maclellan, 1951 (paperback edition by Constable, 1977). Many of the methods described can actually be seen in use in Eadfrith's work.

INDEX

endorsed by
edexcel

EDEXCEL
GCSE
ADDITIONAL
SCIENCE

**CHRIS CONOLEY, MARY JONES
and DAVID SANG**

Hodder Murray
THE HODDER HEADLINE GROUP

This high quality material is endorsed by Edexcel and has been through a rigorous quality assurance programme to ensure that it is a suitable companion to the specification for both learners and teachers. This does not mean that its contents will be used verbatim when setting examinations nor is it to be read as being the official specification – a copy of which is available at www.edexcel.org.uk

Although every effort has been made to ensure that website addresses are correct at time of going to press, Hodder Murray cannot be held responsible for the content of any website mentioned in this book. It is sometimes possible to find a relocated web page by typing in the address of the home page for a website in the URL window of your browser.

Hachette's policy is to use papers that are natural, renewable and recyclable products and made from wood grown in sustainable forests. The logging and manufacturing processes are expected to conform to the environmental regulations of the country of origin.

Orders: please contact Bookpoint Ltd, 130 Milton Park, Abingdon, Oxon OX14 4SB. Telephone: (44) 01235 827720. Fax: (44) 01235 400454. Lines are open 9.00 – 5.00, Monday to Saturday, with a 24-hour message answering service. Visit our website at www.hoddereducation.co.uk

© Chris Conoley, Mary Jones, David Sang 2007
First published in 2007 by
Hodder Murray, an imprint of Hodder Education,
an Hachette Livre UK company
338 Euston Road
London NW1 3BH

Impression number   5 4 3 2
Year   2011 2010 2009 2008 2007

Illustrations by Oxford Designers and Illustrators Ltd
Typeset in 11.5/14pt Goudy by Stephen Rowling/Springworks
Printed and bound in Italy

A catalogue record for this title is available from the British Library

ISBN: 978 0 340 90730 6

Contents

1 Inside living cells

A DNA and protein synthesis

Woolly mammoths lived in Europe up until only 6000 years ago. Our ancestors hunted them and drew pictures of them on the walls of caves. We're not sure exactly why mammoths became extinct, but it was probably a combination of climate change (getting warmer after the Ice Age) and hunting by humans.

Several mammoth bodies have been found frozen in the ground in northern Europe. Some of them have been well enough preserved for scientists to extract DNA from their cells. If we can do this, might we be able to recreate a mammoth, using the instructions in the DNA?

Unfortunately, the DNA that has been found so far has been broken up into lots of little pieces and, although some lengths have been matched up and stuck together in order, we don't have *all* the DNA that would have been in a mammoth's cells. And even if we did, we probably couldn't recreate a mammoth from it, because to do this we would have to know how to switch on different genes in different parts of the body. But who knows – it might one day be possible.

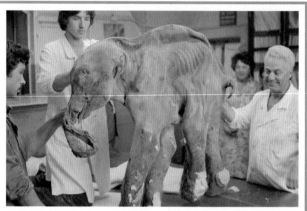

Figure 1.1 This young mammoth was preserved in the frozen ground in northern Russia for about 10 000 years. Its body was discovered and excavated in 1977

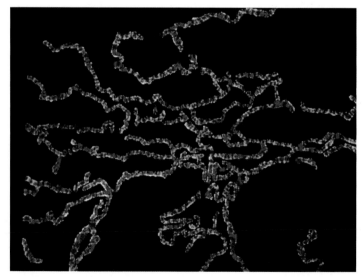

Figure 1.2 DNA molecules from a human cell, seen using an extremely powerful electron microscope

The total length of all the DNA in a human cell is about 3 m.

● The structure of DNA

DNA is the chemical that chromosomes are made of. Each chromosome is a very long molecule of DNA. DNA molecules are simply enormous compared with most molecules. For example, the DNA molecule in human chromosome 13 (which isn't the longest chromosome) is thought to be about 3.5 cm long. All the same, these molecules are still really difficult to see, because they are so thin. Figure 1.2 is a photograph taken with a very powerful electron microscope, and this is about the best view we can get of a DNA molecule.

Figure 1.3 shows the structure of a DNA molecule. You can see why it is often called a 'double helix'.

Each DNA molecule is made up two long strands, like the side pieces of a ladder.

Don't confuse thymine with thiamine (which you might have seen on the side of a cereal packet). Thiamine is a vitamin.

Attached to each of these strands, like the rungs of the ladder, are four different kinds of **bases**. The bases are called **adenine**, **cytosine**, **guanine** and **thymine**. The bases on one strand link to the bases on the other strand. They always do this in the same pairs – adenine with thymine, and guanine with cytosine. The whole molecule coils round like a helter-skelter.

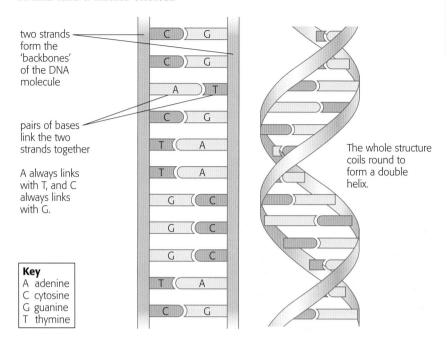

two strands form the 'backbones' of the DNA molecule

pairs of bases link the two strands together

A always links with T, and C always links with G.

The whole structure coils round to form a double helix.

Key
A adenine
C cytosine
G guanine
T thymine

Figure 1.3 The structure of a DNA molecule

● **What DNA does**

DNA carries instructions that tell the cell what kind of proteins to make. Many proteins are enzymes, and other proteins have other extremely important roles to play. The kind of proteins that a cell makes determines what the cell looks like and what it does. So DNA controls almost everything about how the cells in your body develop, which in turn has a big influence on the structure and shape of your body, and even some of the things that happen in your brain cells.

You may remember that proteins are made up of amino acids. The amino acids are linked together in long chains. There are 20 different kinds of amino acids. These are linked together in a different order in different proteins (Figure 1.4).

Figure 1.4 Amino acids and protein molecules

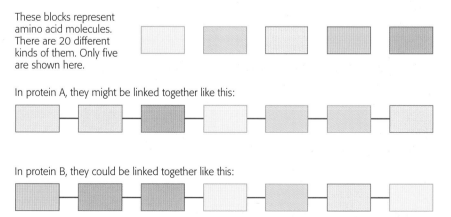

These blocks represent amino acid molecules. There are 20 different kinds of them. Only five are shown here.

In protein A, they might be linked together like this:

In protein B, they could be linked together like this:

DNA decides in what order the amino acids will be linked together. This is how DNA determines the kind of proteins that will be made.

How does it do this? It involves a kind of code, called the **genetic code**. The code is the sequence of bases in the DNA molecule. The sequence of bases determines the sequence of amino acids in the protein that the cell will make.

It's easiest to understand this if you think about a particular example. Say, for example, that the sequence of bases in part of the DNA molecule is:

AAG TGT CCC TAA

The bases are written here in groups of three because this is how the code works. Each group of three is called a **triplet** of bases. Each triplet stands for a particular amino acid. AAG stands for an amino acid called phenylalanine; TGT stands for threonine; CCC stands for glycine and TAA stands for isoleucine.

So this tiny length of DNA says: 'Make a protein molecule by linking four amino acids in this order: phenylalanine, threonine, glycine and isoleucine.'

● How proteins are made

The manufacture of proteins, or protein synthesis, in a cell involves several different organelles (structures inside the cell). What happens is as follows:

- In the nucleus, a molecule called **messenger RNA** (mRNA for short) is built up against one strand of a DNA molecule, copying its sequence of bases.
- The mRNA travels out of the nucleus, and finds a **ribosome** in the cytoplasm. Ribosomes are tiny roundish structures that look like little dark spots in photographs of cells (Figure 1.5). They are often attached to a network of membranes in the cell, called the **endoplasmic reticulum**.
- The mRNA attaches itself to the ribosome. Another kind of RNA brings amino acids to the ribosome.
- The amino acids are joined together in the sequence determined by the code carried on the mRNA.
- The chain of amino acids is called a polypeptide, and this will become part of a protein molecule (Figure 1.6).

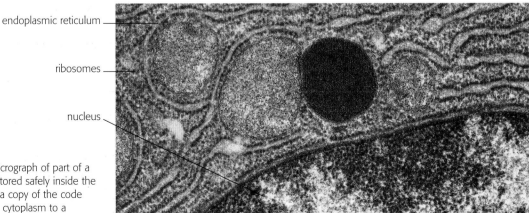

endoplasmic reticulum

ribosomes

nucleus

Figure 1.5 Electron micrograph of part of a body cell. The DNA is stored safely inside the nucleus. mRNA makes a copy of the code and travels out into the cytoplasm to a ribosome on the endoplasmic reticulum

Figure 1.6 The manufacture of proteins

1 In the nucleus, a length of DNA unzips and unwinds.

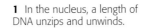

2 A molecule of mRNA builds up against one strand. The base sequence in the mRNA matches the base sequence in the DNA.

mRNA

3 The mRNA goes out of the nucleus and finds a ribosome.

4 Amino acids are brought to the ribosome and linked together in the sequence determined by the bases on the mRNA.

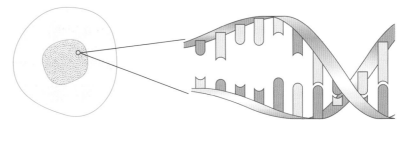

amino acid

mRNA

ribosome

When a virus infects one of your cells, it hijacks the machinery for making proteins, forcing the cell to make more viral proteins instead of its own proteins.

5 A long chain of amino acids, called a polypeptide, is made. The polypeptide will become part of a protein molecule.

Summary

- Chromosomes contain DNA. DNA molecules are made up of two twisted strands. The strands are held together by pairs of bases.
- Adenine always pairs with thymine, and cytosine always pairs with guanine.
- The sequence of bases in the DNA molecule determines which proteins are made in the cell. It does this by deciding the order of amino acids in the protein.
- Ribosomes, often attached to the endoplasmic reticulum, are the organelles where protein synthesis takes place.
- The code on the DNA in the nucleus is copied onto a molecule called messenger RNA (mRNA).
- The mRNA molecule travels out into the cytoplasm and attaches to a ribosome.
- Amino acids are brought to the ribosome, and linked together in the sequence determined by the base sequence on the mRNA.
- The chain of amino acids is called a polypeptide, and this will become part of a protein molecule.

Questions

1.1 Name the part of the cell where each of these processes takes place. Choose from:

> cell membrane   nucleus   ribosome

a A molecule of mRNA is made, copying the code on part of a DNA molecule.

b A polypeptide is made by joining amino acids together, following the code on the mRNA.

1.2 There is something wrong with each of these statements. Decide what is wrong, and then rewrite the statement correctly.

a A DNA molecule is made of one long strand twisted into a spiral.

b DNA is made of a long chain of RNA.

c The sequence of amino acids in a protein is determined by the sequence of amino acids in part of a DNA molecule.

d Protein synthesis happens in the nucleus of a cell.

1.3 These statements summarise the way that proteins are synthesised in cells. Write them down in the correct order.

- Amino acids are brought to the ribosome.
- A mRNA molecule is constructed with a copy of the code on one of the DNA strands.
- The amino acids are linked together to make a polypeptide.
- The sequence of bases on the mRNA is determined by the sequence of bases on the DNA strand.
- Part of a DNA molecule unzips and unwinds.
- The mRNA molecule attaches to a ribosome.
- The amino acids are in a sequence determined by the base sequence on the mRNA.
- The mRNA molecule travels out of the nucleus.

B Using microorganisms

If you go into a health food shop, you can find packets of something called Spirulina on the shelves. And if you do a Google search for Spirulina, you will be pointed towards pages and pages of websites telling you all the amazing things that Spirulina can do for you, and trying to get you to buy some.

Spirulina isn't new. It has been eaten by humans for thousands of years. It is a microorganism, related to bacteria, and it grows in ponds and lakes where the water is quite alkaline. It is made up of long filaments, which curl into a spiral shape (hence its name). It contains a blue–green pigment that absorbs sunlight, and it feeds by photosynthesis.

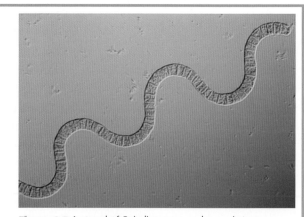

Figure 1.7 A strand of Spirulina seen under a microscope

We know that Spirulina was being harvested in the early 16th century in South America. One author, who had been shopping in a market in 1521, in what is now Mexico, found '…small cakes made of a mud-like algae, which has a cheese-like flavour, and that natives took out of the lake to make bread.' People in Africa have also eaten it for hundreds of years, where it is sometimes called 'dihé'.

Now Spirulina has been rediscovered. It is farmed in many different parts of the world. Some of the companies that market health foods claim that it can stop you getting HIV/AIDS, reduce your risk of getting cancer, reduce your cholesterol level, and have a host of other astoundingly good effects on your health. Many of these claims are at least partly supported by controlled experiments, so it is a shame that some of the claims have gone a bit too far, stating benefits for which there is no evidence. In reality, Spirulina is genuinely an excellent food. It is high in protein, essential fatty acids, vitamins and iron. It is cheap to produce and there is little waste. It really has been shown to help to reduce cholesterol levels, and may really help to boost the immune system and increase resistance to infection.

Figure 1.8 Cans of dried Spirulina produced in India

● Making genetically modified (GM) insulin

Eating microorganisms, such as Spirulina, is not the only use we make of them. In the late 20th century we discovered how we could alter the DNA of certain microorganisms and make them produce important proteins for us.

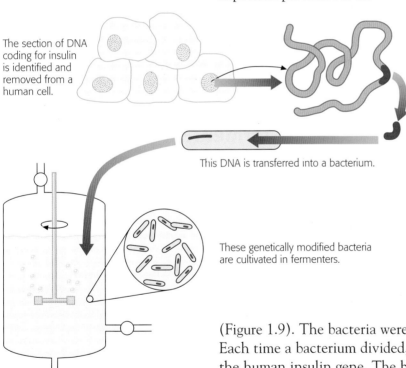

The section of DNA coding for insulin is identified and removed from a human cell.

This DNA is transferred into a bacterium.

These genetically modified bacteria are cultivated in fermenters.

The insulin they make is collected and purified.

Figure 1.9 The production of GM insulin

Insulin is a hormone that is used for treating people who have diabetes. Until the 1980s, all the insulin came from the pancreases of pigs or cattle. Now, as we saw in *GCSE Science* (page 55), it is obtained from bacteria. The bacteria used are a species called *Escherichia coli*.

Insulin is a protein. In the 1970s, scientists were able to work out which part of the DNA in human cells contained the instructions for making insulin. They were able to snip out some insulin genes from human cells, and insert them into the bacteria (Figure 1.9). The bacteria were then grown in a large container. Each time a bacterium divided, the new bacteria also got copies of the human insulin gene. The bacteria's cells followed the instructions on the gene and made human insulin.

Now these genetically modified (GM) bacteria are grown on a huge scale. They churn out human insulin, which is extracted and purified.

● Other uses of microorganisms

Spirulina is not the only microorganism that we use for food. You may have eaten something made from Quorn™, which consists of a fungus.

The fungus, like most fungi, is made of long threads, called **hyphae**. The hyphae are very rich in protein, and can be pressed together to provide a fibrous texture a bit like meat. This is marketed as Quorn™, and is sometimes called **mycoprotein**. ('Myco' means 'fungus'.)

We don't always eat the microorganism itself. We may just want something that it makes. For example, the microscopic fungus **yeast** is used to make bread, and also alcohol such as beers and wines. Other microorganisms can also produce alcohol. In Brazil, bacteria are used to turn sugar into alcohol which is used as a fuel in cars. It is called **bioethanol**.

We use bacteria to turn milk into yoghurt. The bacteria change a sugar called lactose, which is found in milk, into **lactic acid**. The lactic acid is what gives yoghurt its sharp taste.

Yet another use of microorganisms is to make **antibiotics**. For example, the antibiotic penicillin is made by a fungus called *Penicillium*.

Figure 1.10 Meat alternatives for vegetarians, made from Quorn™

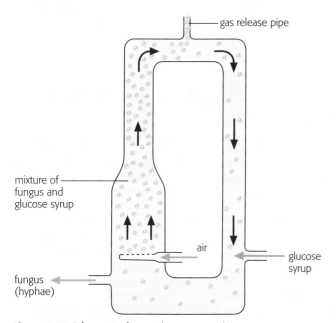

Figure 1.11 A fermenter for growing mycoprotein

A medium is just something that microorganisms grow in, and get their nutrients from. Agar jelly in a Petri dish is another kind of medium.

● Growing microorganisms in fermenters

All of these useful microorganisms need to be provided with the right conditions, so that they grow fast and produce large quantities of the product that we need. They are grown in large containers called **fermenters** (Figure 1.11).

The microorganisms grow in a liquid called a **medium**, which contains food for the microorganisms. As the microorganisms use the food source, they alter some of the substances in the medium, making new substances. This process is called **fermentation**.

For example, the bacteria that are used to make bioethanol are grown in a medium containing sugar (often obtained from sugar cane or maize). They change the sugar into ethanol.

The conditions in the fermenter can be carefully controlled, so that the microorganisms produce as much of the desired product as possible, in a short time. This involves:

) making sure that no unwanted microorganisms get into the fermenter. This is done by sterilising the fermenter before use, and also sterilising everything that is added to it. This is known as taking **aseptic** precautions.
) providing the right kinds of nutrients, in the right proportions and the right concentrations.

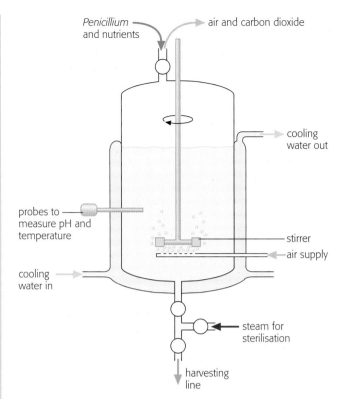

Penicillium and nutrients

air and carbon dioxide

cooling water out

probes to measure pH and temperature

stirrer

air supply

cooling water in

steam for sterilisation

harvesting line

Figure 1.12 Controlling conditions in a fermenter for producing penicillin

▸ keeping the medium in the fermenter at just the right temperature and pH – the optimum conditions for the enzymes in the microorganisms to work.

▸ ensuring the right amount of oxygen is provided. Sometimes, the microorganisms are not given any oxygen at all, because we want them to work anaerobically. This is done when we want yeast to change sugars into alcohol. Sometimes, they are given plenty of air, because we want them to work aerobically. This is done when we want *Penicillium* to make penicillin.

▸ ensuring the right amount of stirring or agitation is done. Usually, the medium is stirred, so that everything is thoroughly mixed up. However, this would not be a good idea for growing mycoprotein, because it would break up the long, thread-like hyphae so we would lose the fibrous texture in the food that is made.

● Advantages of using microorganisms for food production

In the 1950s and 1960s, there was huge enthusiasm for developing new foods that could be produced by growing microorganisms. It was thought that these could help to feed the world.

Unlike conventional crops, microorganisms do not need big areas of land, because they can be grown in fermenters. And they can be grown in any part of the world, so long as the conditions in the fermenters can be controlled to give them the right temperature and other factors that allow them to grow. They are also easy to handle – much easier than large farm animals.

Microorganisms grow quickly, so you can get more food in a shorter period of time. They can often be grown in a medium containing waste products that would otherwise just be thrown away. For example, fungi can grow on waste material left over from making flour, cheese, or paper.

Unfortunately, this revolution in food production never took place. Most people simply did not want to eat these foods. Quorn™ is one of the very few that ever made it into large-scale production for human consumption. Some others are still used, but mostly for feeding farm animals, such as cattle.

> In times of famine in China, some people have grown a green microorganism called *Chlorella* in containers of their own urine, then harvested and eaten it. It reportedly tasted vile, but did at least provide some nourishment.

Summary

- Sections of DNA coding for specific proteins can be put into microorganisms, which will then produce the protein, for example human insulin.
- Other microorganisms can be used as food, for example hyphae in mycoprotein, or in the process of making food, for example yeast in bread and alcohol, or to produce antibiotics such as penicillin.
- Microorganisms are cultivated in fermenters.

9

- Microorganisms use a food source in a medium to provide energy, changing substances in the medium. This is called fermentation.
- The conditions in a fermenter are carefully controlled. This includes using aseptic precautions, providing the right nutrients, keeping the temperature and pH at an optimum, either providing oxygen or keeping oxygen out, and either stirring (agitating) or not.
- Potential advantages of growing microorganisms for food include their rapid population growth, the ability to grow them no matter what the climate, the ease of handling them, and the use of waste products from other industrial processes as a medium.

Questions

1.4 Copy and complete the following sentences about making GM insulin. Use some of these words. You will need to use one of them twice.

bacteria   DNA   fermenters   high   liver
low   mice   pancreas   Petri dishes   protein

Insulin is a hormone made by the .... It is secreted when blood glucose levels get too ....
People with diabetes may need injections of insulin. Most insulin is now made by genetically modified .... The length of .... that codes for making insulin has been taken from a human cell and inserted into the .... These are grown in large .... The insulin that they make is extracted and purified.

1.5 Look at Figure 1.11 on page 8. It shows how a fungus is grown in a fermenter.
   a   Why is glucose syrup being piped into the fermenter?
   b   The fungus grown in the fermenter is collected and used as food. How is the fungus being collected from the fermenter?
   c   Many fermenters contain paddles that stir the contents to keep them mixed up together.
     i Suggest why this is not done in the fermenter in Figure 1.11.
     ii How are the contents being mixed in this fermenter?
   d   Fungi, just like all living organisms, respire.
     i Why is air being piped into the fermenter?
     ii What gases do you think might be released through the gas release pipe?

1.6 Look at Figure 1.12 on page 9. It shows a fermenter being used to grow the fungus *Penicillium*.
   a   What is the desired product of this fermentation?
   b   Describe how the contents of the fermenter are kept cool. Why is this necessary?
   c   Suggest what nutrients are added to the medium through the inlet at the top left.
   d   Explain why there are probes to measure the pH and the temperature.
   e   Suggest how the pH could be altered if necessary.

C Energy for cells

On 2 July 1951, a neighbour decided to drop in on her friend, 67-year old Mary Reeser. She was puzzled to find that the front door was rather hot, and worried when Mary did not answer the door. She asked two men who were working nearby if they could get the door open.

Mystery of Spontaneous Human Combustion

When the three of them went into the flat, they were shocked to see Mary's burnt dead body sitting in her armchair. Most of Mary's body was burnt to cinders, but her left foot wasn't burnt at all. But what completely amazed them was that there were no signs of burning anywhere in her flat, except for a small circle of singed carpet around her chair. The fire seemed to have started in Mary's body.

'Spontaneous human combustion!' cried the newspapers.

This was not the first case of mysteries where people have apparently just burst into flames. Does it really happen? And if it does, what is causing it?

Some people think that spontaneous combustion could maybe happen when reactions inside cells go wrong. In respiration, fuels such as glucose are combined with oxygen inside our cells, releasing energy. What if this reaction got out of control, so the glucose burned furiously? Could this explain the cases of a person's body burning all by itself, with no other apparent source of flame?

Forensic scientists who have examined the bodies of so-called spontaneous human combustion cases, or who have looked carefully at the records of incidents going back as far as the 16th century, don't think we need such alarming explanations. In every case, they say, there could be a more sensible reason for what happened. In Mary's case, it's possible that she dropped a lighted cigarette onto her flammable nightdress. Still, not everyone is completely convinced by such explanations. Maybe there is something happening that we cannot yet explain.

Don't confuse respiration with breathing. Respiration is a metabolic reaction that takes place in every living cell. Breathing is making movements that draw air into the lungs and push it out again. Every living thing respires, but not every living thing breathes.

● Aerobic respiration

All of the energy that our cells use comes from **respiration**. Respiration is a chemical reaction – a **metabolic reaction** – that happens inside all living cells. It releases energy from glucose and other nutrients by oxidising them.

Most of the time, our cells respire **aerobically**. The equation for aerobic respiration is:

glucose + oxygen ➔ carbon dioxide + water

In this reaction, the chemical energy stored in the glucose is released in a form that the cell can use to do work. This 'work' could involve activities such as:

- a muscle cell contracting
- a nerve cell sending an impulse from one end of itself to the other
- a skin cell joining amino acids together to make a protein molecule.

Providing the reactants for aerobic respiration

The two substances needed for aerobic respiration are glucose and oxygen. Both of these are brought to respiring cells by the blood. Oxygen is carried combined with haemoglobin in red blood cells. Glucose is carried in solution in the blood plasma.

Figure 1.13 shows how oxygen and glucose move from the blood and into a respiring cell. This happens by **diffusion**.

11

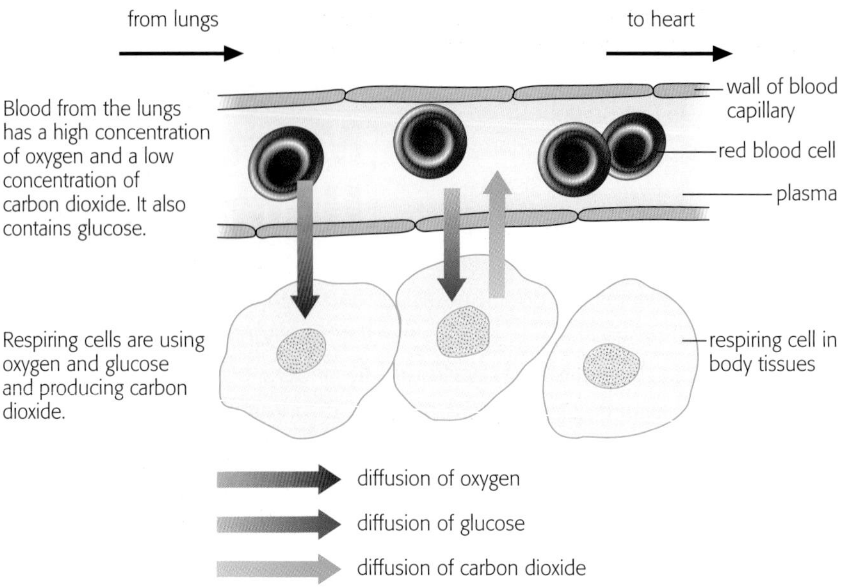

from lungs → to heart →

wall of blood capillary

red blood cell

plasma

Blood from the lungs has a high concentration of oxygen and a low concentration of carbon dioxide. It also contains glucose.

respiring cell in body tissues

Respiring cells are using oxygen and glucose and producing carbon dioxide.

diffusion of oxygen

diffusion of glucose

diffusion of carbon dioxide

Figure 1.13 Exchanges between blood and cells

You'll remember that particles of a substance are in constant motion. In liquids, such as the blood, particles can move around freely. As they move randomly about, bumping into each other and changing direction, they tend to spread themselves out evenly. This is how diffusion happens. Diffusion is a result of the random movement of particles. The particles move in all directions, but, over time, they will tend to end up distributed roughly evenly in the area within which they can move. We can define diffusion as:

> the net movement of particles from an area of high concentration to an area of low concentration, as a result of their random movement

We sometimes say that the substance moves 'down its concentration gradient'.

The cells in Figure 1.13 are respiring, so they are using up oxygen and glucose. This is reducing the concentration of these two substances inside the cells. So the concentration of both oxygen and glucose in the blood is greater than the concentration in the cells. As a result, oxygen and glucose diffuse from the blood into the cells, down their concentration gradients.

The faster the cell is respiring, the faster it uses up oxygen and glucose, and the lower their concentrations are inside the cell. This increases the concentration gradients for both oxygen and glucose between the blood and cell. So oxygen and glucose diffuse even more rapidly from the blood and into the respiring cell.

Where do the oxygen and glucose come from? Let's look at each of these in turn.

Oxygen gets into the blood in the lungs. Air, containing oxygen, is breathed into the lungs and reaches the millions of tiny alveoli (air sacs) inside them. Each alveolus has a blood capillary tightly pressed against it. The blood inside the capillary has been brought to the lungs after travelling around the body, so most of the oxygen it was carrying has been used up by the body cells. So there is a concentration gradient for oxygen from the alveoli into the blood capillary, and the oxygen diffuses down this gradient.

It's important to remember that diffusion is a 'passive' process. That means the cells just let it happen – the molecules of glucose and oxygen move around randomly.

H

Oxygen is carried inside the red blood cells, combined with the red pigment haemoglobin.

Figure 1.14 Parts of the body where oxygen and glucose enter the blood and where carbon dioxide leaves the blood

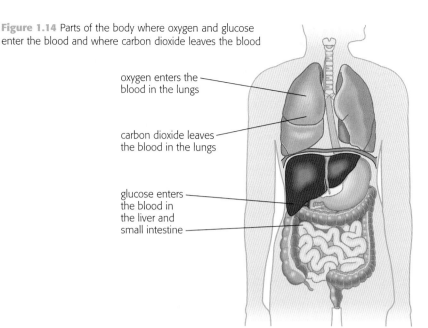

oxygen enters the blood in the lungs

carbon dioxide leaves the blood in the lungs

glucose enters the blood in the liver and small intestine

Glucose gets into the blood from the small intestine and the liver. When you eat food containing carbohydrates, these are broken down to glucose which diffuses into the blood in the wall of the small intestine. You will also have some glucose stored in the liver, and this can be released into the blood if your blood glucose levels are low.

Removing the products of respiration

Respiration in a cell produces water and carbon dioxide. The water is not usually a problem – there is already a lot of water in the body and this just adds to it. If there is too much water, then it is lost in the urine.

Carbon dioxide, however, needs to be got rid of quite rapidly. It diffuses out of the respiring cell and into the blood in a capillary. The blood transports the carbon dioxide to the lungs, where it diffuses into the alveoli down its concentration gradient.

When a person's cells are working hard, they will be respiring faster, using more oxygen and producing more carbon dioxide. So the blood arriving at the alveoli contains less oxygen and more carbon dioxide than usual. This increases the concentration gradient for both of these substances. As a result, oxygen diffuses more rapidly into the blood, and carbon dioxide diffuses more rapidly out of it.

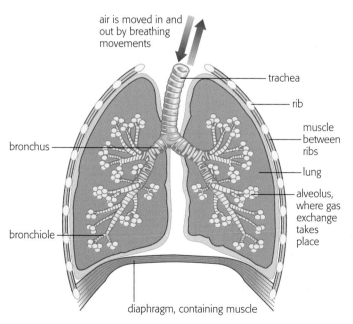

air is moved in and out by breathing movements

trachea

rib

muscle between ribs

lung

alveolus, where gas exchange takes place

bronchus

bronchiole

diaphragm, containing muscle

Figure 1.15 a Structure of the lungs

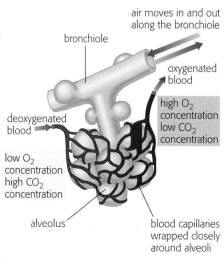

air moves in and out along the bronchiole

bronchiole

oxygenated blood

high O_2 concentration low CO_2 concentration

deoxygenated blood

low O_2 concentration high CO_2 concentration

alveolus

blood capillaries wrapped closely around alveoli

b Gas exchange in the alveoli

13

● The effect of exercise on heart rate and breathing rate

When you do exercise, you are making your muscles work hard. Muscles work by contracting (getting shorter) and they need energy to do this. Like every cell, muscle cells get their energy by respiration.

So, when you exercise, you need to supply your muscles with extra oxygen and remove the extra carbon dioxide they produce. This is done by increasing your **breathing rate** and your **heart rate**.

By increasing your breathing rate, you are moving air into and out of your lungs faster than usual. You probably increase both *how fast* you breathe (the number of breaths per minute) and *how deeply* you breathe (the volume of air moved in and out with one breath). As a result, the air inside the alveoli is constantly replaced with fresh air. As carbon dioxide diffuses into it from the blood, the carbon dioxide-rich air is quickly breathed out. More air, rich in oxygen, is breathed in, allowing oxygen to diffuse from it into the blood, which then transports it to the exercising muscles (Figure 1.16).

By increasing your heart rate, you are moving blood more quickly around the body. Oxygenated blood travels more rapidly than usual from your lungs to your muscles, supplying them with the oxygen they are demanding. And deoxygenated blood, rich in carbon dioxide, travels more rapidly from your muscles to the lungs where the carbon dioxide diffuses into the alveoli and is breathed out.

Figure 1.16 Transport of oxygen and carbon dioxide around the body

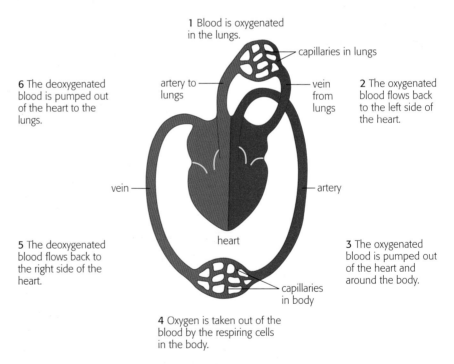

1 Blood is oxygenated in the lungs.

capillaries in lungs

6 The deoxygenated blood is pumped out of the heart to the lungs.

artery to lungs

vein from lungs

2 The oxygenated blood flows back to the left side of the heart.

vein

artery

5 The deoxygenated blood flows back to the right side of the heart.

heart

3 The oxygenated blood is pumped out of the heart and around the body.

capillaries in body

4 Oxygen is taken out of the blood by the respiring cells in the body.

● Anaerobic respiration

Sometimes, no matter how much your heart rate and breathing rate increase, you still cannot supply oxygen to your muscles as quickly as they need it. If this happens, and you still ask your muscles to work hard, they will have to supplement their energy supply by carrying out **anaerobic respiration**.

Anaerobic respiration is a last-ditch resort for getting energy out of glucose when there is no oxygen available to combine with it. The equation for anaerobic respiration is:

glucose ➜ lactic acid

The energy that is released from the glucose is much, much less than in aerobic respiration.

Anaerobic respiration does not get all of the energy out of the glucose. There is still a lot of energy left in the lactic acid. Lactic acid is not a good thing to have in your body in too great a concentration. If it builds up in your muscles, it causes cramp. The lactic acid diffuses out of the muscle cells and into the blood, which carries it to the liver. After you have finished exercising, and once more have enough oxygen in your blood to supply your cells' needs, the liver will get rid of the lactic acid by combining it with oxygen. To do this, it needs more oxygen than your normal breathing rate and heart rate would supply. So you go on breathing faster and having a high heart rate for some time after you have finished exercising. You are providing your liver with extra oxygen to pay off your 'oxygen debt'.

Figure 1.17 This athlete is trying to get enough oxygen into his lungs, but he won't be supplying as much as his muscles need

One way of measuring fitness is to measure the time taken for heart rate and breathing rate to return to normal after exercise.

● Monitoring heart rate and breathing rate

People who are interested in their fitness may want to measure their heart rate and breathing rate when they are exercising.

As you get fitter, your heart becomes stronger. If you exercise regularly, the size and strength of the heart muscle increase. For each beat, it pumps out more blood, so it does not need to beat so fast to move the same amount of blood around the body. Your resting heart rate is therefore slower than in someone who is unfit. Also, your heart becomes capable of working harder and faster, so your maximum possible heart rate increases, meaning that you can exercise harder.

Similar changes occur in breathing rate as you get fitter. Your resting breathing rate gets lower, and you become able to move more air into and out of the lungs with one breath.

You can measure your heart rate by taking a pulse – holding a finger against the skin where an artery runs close to the surface. You can feel the artery being pushed out as the heart muscle contracts and forces blood along it, then recoiling inwards as the heart relaxes.

Figure 1.18 Using a heart rate monitor

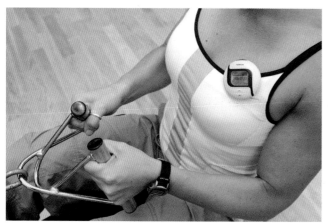

So one pulse represents one heart beat. Nurses usually count the number of beats in 30 seconds and then multiply by two to work out the heart rate in beats per minute.

Heart rate can also be measured using a heart rate monitor. This is a small device that you attach to your body – many of them look like wrist watches – and it gives you a read-out of your pulse rate. It can do this over a long period of time, so you can get a more reliable reading than a one-off pulse count over 30 seconds. Heart rate monitors can calculate various things for you, such as how

15

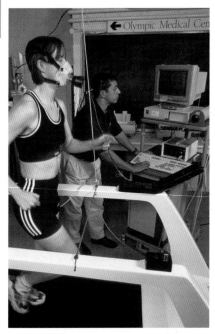

Figure 1.19 Using a breathing rate monitor

long you maintained a particular heart rate for, what your maximum heart rate was while you exercised, and how long it took for your heart rate to go back to normal once your exercise stopped.

Breathing rate monitors are less common, but these can sometimes be used if you are exercising in a gym where it is easy to hook you up to a machine that measures not only the frequency of your breaths but also how deep they are. Once again, this has the advantage of being carried out over a longer period of time than if someone is just counting your breaths for you, so you get a more reliable reading.

● How to keep healthy

Is exercising really good for you? What kind of exercise is best? How often should you exercise? What is a good resting heart rate to have? What should you eat? What shouldn't you eat?

If you listened to all the advice in the media about having a healthy lifestyle, you might think you should be eating nothing but wheat grass, drinking nothing but water and walking for 20 000 steps every day. The problem with giving advice on exercise, diet and health is that it is really, really difficult to get reliable data on how your lifestyle affects your health.

For example, we can't do very long-term controlled experiments with people to investigate how diet affects health. To start with, it would not be ethical – you can't feed people on a diet you think might be unhealthy for a long period of time and then compare their health with another group. Experiments like this have been done, but only over relatively short time periods. Usually, researchers rely on collecting information about what people eat and then trying to find relationships between their diets and their health. Numerous studies like this have been done, but their results often don't agree with one another. This is probably because there are all sorts of variables that cannot be measured or have not been controlled. For example, people's genes are likely to be different, and they would have been given different food while they were babies.

This results in great uncertainty about the best way to keep healthy. In general, most people agree that we should take regular exercise, preferably aerobic exercise (which makes you breathe faster) such as walking, cycling or dancing. We should eat a varied diet, not one that contains similar foods every day (for example burgers and chips), and that contains plenty of fresh fruit and vegetables (to provide vitamins, minerals and antioxidants that reduce the risk of cancer).

Summary

- All cells get their energy by respiration. Respiration is a metabolic reaction in which energy is released from glucose.
- Usually, respiration involves combining oxygen with glucose. This is aerobic respiration.
- Oxygen and glucose diffuse down their concentration gradients from blood capillaries into respiring cells. Carbon dioxide diffuses in the opposite direction.
- In the lungs, oxygen diffuses from the air in the alveoli into the blood, and carbon dioxide diffuses out of the blood and into the alveoli.

- During exercise, when muscle cells are respiring very rapidly, heart rate and breathing rate increase, so that oxygen is transported to the muscle cells more quickly.
- During exercise, the concentration gradients for oxygen and carbon dioxide in the lungs are greater than usual, so diffusion occurs more rapidly.
- When working muscles do not get enough oxygen, they respire anaerobically. This involves breaking glucose down without using oxygen. Lactic acid is produced and a small amount of energy is released.
- After exercise has finished, the lactic acid is broken down in the liver by combining it with oxygen. The extra oxygen needed to do this is called the oxygen debt.
- Measuring heart rate and breathing rate can help to determine how fit you are. Digital monitors are more reliable than traditional methods, and can also give more detailed information over longer periods of time.
- Determining what is the best diet to eat is really difficult, because we cannot do long-term experiments on it. Scientific research continues to find new links between certain types of diet and health, but often the results of the research are unclear or conflict with other research.

Questions

1.7 a Write down a definition of respiration.

b Explain the differences between aerobic respiration and anaerobic respiration.

1.8 This table shows the heart rate of a person before, during and after exercise.

Time (minutes)	0	2	4	6	8	10	12	14	16	18	20	22	24
Heart rate (beats per minute)	71	72	73	82	96	164	171	152	124	96	84	80	75

a Draw a graph to display these results.

b Use your graph to suggest:

  i when the person began exercising

  ii when the person stopped exercising.

c Explain why the heart rate increases during exercise.

d What other change would you expect to happen during exercise? Explain your answer.

e Do you think the person's heart rate had returned to normal by the end of the experiment? Explain your answer.

f Explain why the heart rate did not return to normal immediately after exercise finished.

2 Divide and develop

A Cell division

Every year, a baby that is born can expect to live longer than a baby born in the previous year. Since records began in 1950, the average life expectancy of people all over the world has been increasing. There are some exceptions – for example, in some African countries where HIV/AIDS has taken an enormous toll – but on the whole our improved health, diet and living conditions seem to be steadily stretching out our lives.

Ageing is a topic of great interest to researchers. Why do we age? What stops us living forever? Some scientists are predicting that new anti-ageing drugs could lead to it being normal for people in wealthy countries to live until they are 100 or more. If this happens, it will bring economic problems. In 2006 in Britain, there were 1.5 pensioners for every one person in work. Already, we are facing a problem of finding enough money to pay a decent pension to everyone over working age. At the moment, the age at which a person gets the state pension is 65. In 2006, the Government announced that from 2044 this will be raised to 68. Some economists think that, by the middle of the century, we may need to ask people to carry on working until they are 85 years old.

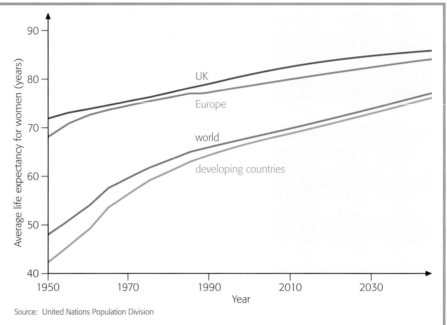

Source: United Nations Population Division

Figure 2.1 How average life expectancy for women has increased since 1950, and how it is predicted to increase further (yellow area). The trends for men are the same but at slightly lower ages

● The Hayflick limit

One theory to explain why we do not live forever is that our cells cannot keep on and on dividing. In 1961, researchers Leonard Hayflick and Paul Moorhead published a paper in which they described how human cells they had been studying seemed to have a pre-programmed limit on the number of times they could divide. For example, they found that lung cells could divide about 50 times. After that, they may begin to die and cannot be replaced. This maximum number of cell divisions was named the **Hayflick limit**.

Hayflick and Moorhead tried the same experiments with cells taken from other animals. They found that in animals that tend to live for a long time, cells seemed to be able to divide more times than in short-lived animals. For example, Galapagos tortoise cells could divide around 110 times, while mouse cells managed only 15 divisions.

Could this be a simple explanation of why we age and die? Do our cells just run out of dividing ability? Do we have to wait helplessly while our cellular 'clock' runs down?

More recent research has confirmed Hayflick and Moorhead's findings. Now, however, scientists are trying to find out exactly what it is that limits the number of times our cells can divide. They now know that changes and damage to a cell's chromosomes can build up; the more times it divides, the more bits of damage are caused to the chromosomes. They have also found other changes occurring in the cytoplasm of cells, all of which can help to explain their inability to live forever.

It seems that, when a sperm and an egg fuse together, a 'restart from fresh' switch is flipped on. All of the accumulated damage in the parents' own, 'old' cells is wiped out, and the new zygote starts with a clean slate.

We are still a long way from understanding why this happens. We do, though, know quite a lot about how cells divide, both to form new cells for our own bodies and also to form sperm and egg cells that might start off the life of a new person.

● Mitosis

In some parts of your body, cells are dividing all the time. For example, new cells are being formed in the inside layers of your skin, replacing old ones that have been rubbed off. Growth of the body, and repair of damaged parts, is a result of old cells dividing to form new ones.

The kind of cell division that is used for growth and repair is called **mitosis**. In mitosis (Figure 2.2), a cell produces two new cells that are genetically identical to itself. This is done by:

▸ making exact copies of every one of the 46 chromosomes in the cell nucleus
▸ sharing these chromosomes out equally into two new nuclei, so that each nucleus gets a copy of each of the 46 chromosomes
▸ dividing the cytoplasm into two, producing two new cells.

In a human embryo, it takes about 24 hours for a cell to divide and for the two new cells to be ready to divide again.

1 This cell has two sets of chromosomes – a 'red' set and a 'green' set. For simplicity we consider only two chromosomes per set – a long one and a short one.

2 When the cell gets ready to divide, a perfect copy is made of each chromosome. The two copies are held together.

3 The chromosomes line up in the middle of the cell. (The nuclear membrane has gone now, so it's easier for the chromosomes to move around.)

4 The copies of each chromosome now split apart, and move to opposite ends of the cell.

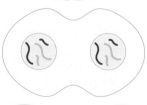

5 Now new nuclear membranes form around each group of chromosomes. The cytoplasm starts to divide.

6 The end result is two new cells, each genetically identical to the parent cell.

Figure 2.2 How mitosis happens

● **Meiosis**

When **gametes** – sperm and egg cells – are being made, a different kind of cell division is used. It is called **meiosis**.

Each of your cells contains two complete sets of chromosomes. They are therefore said to be **diploid cells**. There are 23 in each set, making 46 chromosomes in all.

In meiosis, these chromosomes are shared out in the new nuclei. Each nucleus gets one complete set, that is 23 chromosomes. These nuclei become part of gametes – either **eggs** or **sperm**. Gametes are **haploid cells**.

You already know why this is important. At fertilisation, two gametes fuse together to produce a **zygote**. The zygote gets one set of chromosomes from the sperm and one set from the egg, so it ends up with two complete sets. It is a diploid cell (Figure 2.3).

As the zygote develops, it divides repeatedly by mitosis, gradually producing all of the cells in the new person's body.

> When a girl is born, cells in her ovaries have already nearly completed meiosis to form egg cells.

Figure 2.3 The importance of meiosis

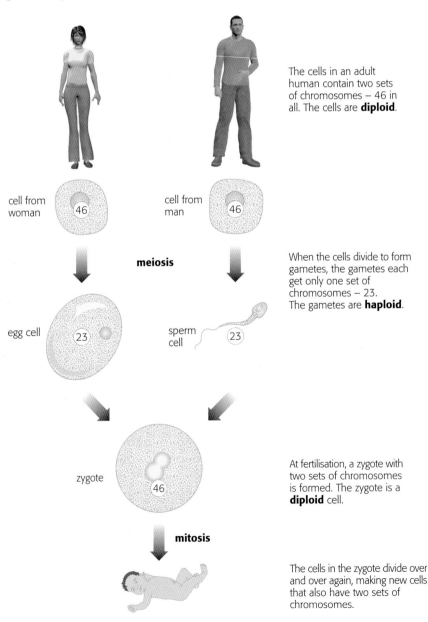

The cells in an adult human contain two sets of chromosomes – 46 in all. The cells are **diploid**.

cell from woman — 46

cell from man — 46

meiosis

When the cells divide to form gametes, the gametes each get only one set of chromosomes – 23. The gametes are **haploid**.

egg cell — 23

sperm cell — 23

zygote — 46

At fertilisation, a zygote with two sets of chromosomes is formed. The zygote is a **diploid** cell.

mitosis

The cells in the zygote divide over and over again, making new cells that also have two sets of chromosomes.

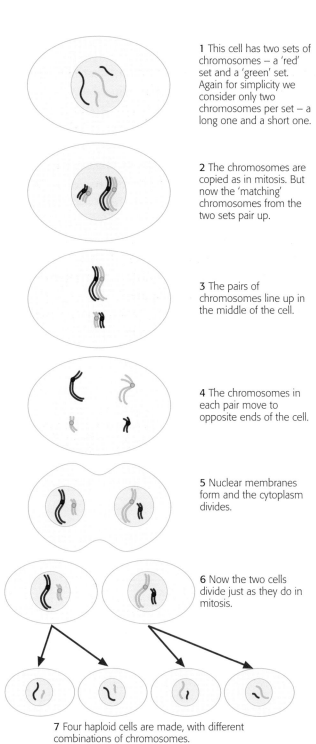

1 This cell has two sets of chromosomes – a 'red' set and a 'green' set. Again for simplicity we consider only two chromosomes per set – a long one and a short one.

2 The chromosomes are copied as in mitosis. But now the 'matching' chromosomes from the two sets pair up.

3 The pairs of chromosomes line up in the middle of the cell.

4 The chromosomes in each pair move to opposite ends of the cell.

5 Nuclear membranes form and the cytoplasm divides.

6 Now the two cells divide just as they do in mitosis.

7 Four haploid cells are made, with different combinations of chromosomes.

Figure 2.4 How meiosis happens

Figure 2.4 shows what happens to the chromosomes during meiosis. Note that four 'daughter' cells are produced from one original cell. Each of these has just one set of chromosomes (a mixture of the original two sets) – it is haploid.

So meiosis is a kind of cell division that produces four haploid cells from one diploid cell. It is essential in sexual reproduction. A very important feature of meiosis is that it produces gametes with different mixes of chromosomes (Figure 2.5). The cells produced by meiosis are therefore genetically different from one another.

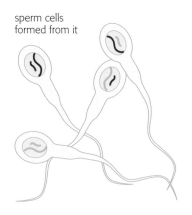

sperm cells formed from it

original cell

This body cell has two sets of chromosomes. The 'red' ones came from the father and the 'green' ones from the mother.

We consider here only two chromosomes per set – a long one and a short one.

Sperm cells formed from the body cell each have one set of chromosomes – one long chromosome and one short one.

There are four possible combinations of the two chromosomes, so each sperm is genetically different.

Figure 2.5 Meiosis and variation

Summary

- There seems to be a limit to the number of times cells can divide. This is known as the Hayflick limit and may explain why we don't live forever.
- Cells divide by mitosis to produce new cells for growth or for repair. The new cells that are produced are genetically identical.
- Cells divide by meiosis to produce gametes. Meiosis halves the chromosome number, so a diploid cell produces four haploid cells. The cells produced by meiosis are genetically different from each other.

Questions

2.1 Cells covering the inside of the intestines are always getting rubbed off as food moves through. New ones have to be made all the time, to replace them.

   a What is the name for the kind of cell division that will be used?

   b The cells that divide have 46 chromosomes each. How many chromosomes will each of the new cells have?

   c Suggest some other parts of the body where cells might be dividing, and explain why.

2.2 For most of the cells in our body, there is a limited number of times that they can divide. But sometimes cells mutate and begin to behave as if they had no Hayflick limit. They can form cancer cells.

   a Explain what is meant by the statement that cancer cells have no Hayflick limit.

   b Why is this dangerous?

2.3 Make a copy of this table, and then complete it to compare mitosis and meiosis.

	Mitosis	**Meiosis**
Why does it happen?	to produce new cells for growth and repair	
Where does it happen?		
How many cell divisions does it involve?		
How many sets of chromosomes does each new cell receive?		
Are the new cells genetically identical?		

2.4 In the third stage of Figure 2.4, the pairs of chromosomes have lined up with one of the 'red' chromosomes on the left, and the other on the right. Imagine they lined up with both of the 'red' chromosomes on the left. What combinations of chromosomes would the four 'daughter' cells have? Draw the possibilities.

B Growth and development

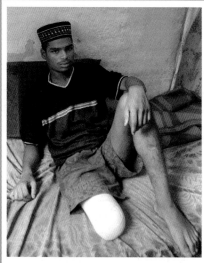

The boy in the photograph had a leg amputated after he was attacked by a shark. His leg will never regrow. He will probably have an artificial leg to help him to get around.

Figure 2.7

Figure 2.6

The gecko (a kind of lizard) lost its tail when a predator attacked it. It also lost a chunk of skin. The gecko will regrow its tail and the missing skin.

Other animals can do even better. If a salamander loses a leg, it can regrow a whole new leg, with all the bones, muscles, tendons, blood vessels, nerves and skin in all the right places. Researchers are trying to find out the secret of doing this. Salamanders are amphibians, so they, like us, are vertebrates. If they can do it, why can't we?

Perhaps one day we *will* be able to. It may be possible to find drugs that can persuade cells to divide and develop to regrow missing limbs or other body parts. Success will hinge on persuading specialised cells near the wound to 'unspecialise' – to go back to behaving as they would in a tiny embryo, dividing and then taking up different specialisations to produce all the different tissues in the new body part.

● **What is growth?**

Growth means getting bigger. We can define growth as 'an increase in size'. Usually, we mean a *permanent* increase in size. So getting fatter because you ate too much for a week or so wouldn't normally be considered to be growth, because once you go back to eating normally again you are likely to lose the excess weight you temporarily put on.

There are different things that we can measure when we want to determine how much an organism is growing.

Increase in height or length

One of the easiest things to measure is how tall or how long something is. For humans, we often measure height. The big advantage of this is that it is really easy to do. If we want to keep track of how quickly a child is growing, we can measure the child's height once a month, and perhaps plot the results on a graph. Figure 2.8 shows how the height of a girl changed between the ages of 2 and 20 years old.

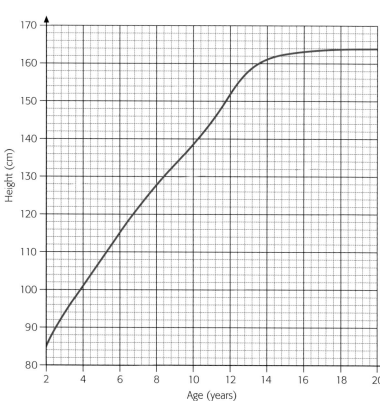

Figure 2.8 Typical growth in height for a girl

Measuring height is also quite a good way of measuring the growth of a plant, again because it is really quick and easy to do. However, it doesn't, of course, take into account the growth of the root underground, or any 'sideways' growth that the plant makes.

Increase in weight

We can also measure a person's growth by measuring changes in their weight. This is almost as easy to do as measuring height. In some ways it is better, because it takes into account the whole of the person's body, including 'sideways' growth. On the down side, people can get fatter and then thinner again, so an increase in weight may not always be growth in the sense of a *permanent* increase in size.

Weight can also be used to measure the growth of a plant. However, here things become more difficult, because to weigh a plant we have to uproot it, and that will probably kill it. So if we want to use this method, we have to grow a lot of similar plants. You could, for example, sow 100 seeds. Each day (or each week) you could uproot five seedlings and weigh them, after washing any soil off the roots. You could then calculate the mean (average) weight of one plant, and record this. With 100 seedlings, you would be able to make 20 readings.

The weight we are measuring when we stand on the bathroom scales, or when we weigh a recently uprooted plant, is the **wet weight**. This doesn't mean that you or the plant are wet. It means that the weight includes all the water within your body. This can vary considerably at different times of day or in different weather conditions. If we want to get rid of this variable, and get a better idea of how much new living tissue has been produced, we need to measure **dry weight** instead. Figure 2.9 explains how you could do this for plants. It obviously isn't something you would want to do to measure the growth of an animal or yourself!

Try weighing yourself before you have a bath, and when you have just got out. The water on your body surface can weigh as much as half a kilogram.

Figure 2.9 Using dry weight to measure plant growth

1 One seed is placed in each of 100 identical pots of compost, and left in identical conditions.

2 Each week five seedlings are taken and washed to remove soil from their roots.

3 The five seedlings are placed in a Petri dish which is put in a warm oven and they are left to dry.

4 The dried seedlings are weighed. Then they are put back into the oven for a little longer. Then they are weighed again, until two consecutive weighings give the same reading. (That means *all* the water in them has been driven off.)

This is repeated over the next 19 weeks.

● How tall will you be?

People normally grow until they are somewhere between 18 and 21 years old. What is it that determines how tall a person grows?

There are three main influences on your height.

▸ The **genes** you received from your parents have a big part to play in determining how tall you will grow. There are lots of different genes, on several different chromosomes, that are involved in affecting height. As you get a mix of genes from both your parents, it is possible to be tall even if your parents are short, and vice versa. But, in general, tall parents tend to have tall children and short parents tend to have short children.

▸ Your **environment** also affects how tall you will grow, especially the diet you have as you grow up. Children who get very little to eat, or who have a diet that is deficient in protein, won't grow very tall. In Britain, the average height of an adult man has increased from about 1.65 metres in the 17th century to about 1.75 metres today. We think that change is because our nutrition is so much better now.

▸ Several **hormones** that are secreted in your body help to decide your height. The main one is called human growth hormone, or HGH for short. This hormone is secreted by the pituitary gland. The quantity of the hormone that your body secretes is affected by your genes and by your environment. Some people have a faulty gene that means they do not secrete enough of this hormone, and would not grow properly if they weren't treated. A child with a deficiency of HGH can be given this hormone as they grow up, which will help them to grow to a normal size.

Because so many different factors influence a person's height, there is a wide range of heights that a person can be (Figure 2.10). Within that range, a person can be absolutely any height. We say that height is a **continuous variable**.

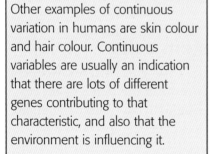

Other examples of continuous variation in humans are skin colour and hair colour. Continuous variables are usually an indication that there are lots of different genes contributing to that characteristic, and also that the environment is influencing it.

Figure 2.10 Continuous variation in human height

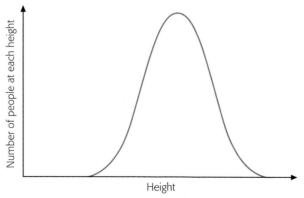

● Misuse of growth hormones

We've seen that human growth hormone, HGH, is needed to make sure that a person's body grows normally. This hormone is also very helpful to people with AIDS, because it helps to stop the muscles wasting away as the disease progresses.

In the past, HGH for medical treatment was obtained from the pituitary glands of dead people. Now, it is made by genetically

Figure 2.11 Some body builders have used HGH to make their muscles grow abnormally large

Hormones are broken down by the liver and their remains are excreted in the urine. So testing urine can often detect the intake of hormones by a sportsperson.

modified bacteria (see page 7). In many countries, it is freely available for anyone to buy and use.

Unfortunately, some competitive sportsmen and sportswomen have misused HGH to make their bodies grow larger and stronger, in order to do better in their sport. Many competitive body builders, for example, have used it. Most sports now ban the use of HGH, not only because it may give a competitor an unfair advantage but also because it can be very damaging to health. It can cause abnormal growth of tissues in different parts of the body and high blood pressure.

Other hormones that are sometimes misused by sportspeople are called **anabolic steroids**. 'Anabolic' means 'building up', and these hormones also help muscles to grow larger and stronger than normal. Testosterone is an example of an anabolic steroid. These hormones not only help to increase size and strength, but they can also increase aggression – which can increase competitiveness in some sports – and enable athletes to train harder and for longer. But, over time, they can decrease the body's own production of steroid hormones, which could be very harmful. They can cause liver damage and decrease the activity of the immune system.

Most sports ban the use of these hormones. The governing bodies of many sports, such as the International Association of Athletics Federations, carry out random tests on athletes before, during and after they compete in events. Anyone found to have taken anabolic steroids faces the risk of a lifetime ban from taking part in top-level competitions.

● **Differentiation and stem cells**

As we grow, we don't simply get bigger. During the first few weeks of its life, a human embryo gradually develops all the different organs within its body. Its cells, which were originally all exactly the same, become different from each other, as they become specialised for different functions. So, for example, some of the cells in what will become the brain become nerve cells. Some of the cells in the newly forming stomach become specialised for secreting enzymes, while others become muscle cells. This process is called **differentiation**, because the cells are becoming 'different' from one another.

A cell that is able to differentiate into a specialised cell is called a **stem cell**. All the cells in a very young embryo are stem cells. But once a cell has differentiated, it will normally stay specialised for the rest of your life. Nerve cells can't change into muscle cells; bone cells can't change into stomach cells.

We have some stem cells in our bodies even when we are fully grown. For example, there are stem cells in our bone marrow, which are always dividing to produce new cells that differentiate into red blood cells and white blood cells. If a person has a disease that affects their red or white blood cells, they can sometimes be treated by giving them a bone marrow transplant. The transplant contains bone marrow stem cells, which can make new blood cells in the patient's body.

But the stem cells in our adult bodies aren't usually able to produce *any* kind of cell. All the ones that have so far been discovered appear to have a limited range of specialised cells that they can produce. For example, the stem cells in the bone marrow can only produce red blood cells and white blood cells. They can't produce muscle cells or nerve cells.

Stem cells have recently become the focus of some very exciting research. Stem cells appear to have no Hayflick limit. They can go on dividing over and over again. So, in theory, we could get stem cells to keep on dividing and producing different kinds of specialised cells (Figure 2.12). Stem cells might be able to be used to treat and even cure many diseases and illnesses that are now untreatable.

For example, an accident could badly damage someone's spinal cord in their neck. There is then no way that nerve impulses can get between the brain and body organs below the neck. The person becomes paralysed from the neck down. At the moment, we cannot cure these injuries. But if we could somehow get some stem cells into the damaged part of the spinal cord, maybe these cells could divide and produce new nerve cells. Perhaps it might one day be possible for a person with this kind of damage to walk again.

Here is another example of what stem cells might do for us. In an illness called Parkinson's disease, some of the cells in a particular part of the brain begin to die, and the person gradually loses the ability to move. If we could put stem cells into the brain, perhaps they could divide and make new cells to replace the dead ones.

Figure 2.12 Division and differentiation of stem cells

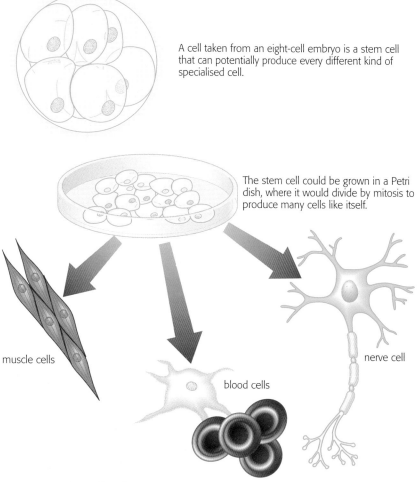

A cell taken from an eight-cell embryo is a stem cell that can potentially produce every different kind of specialised cell.

The stem cell could be grown in a Petri dish, where it would divide by mitosis to produce many cells like itself.

muscle cells

blood cells

nerve cell

By adding different growth factors to the stem cells, we could persuade them to differentiate into many different kinds of cells.

Figure 2.13 These are stem cells taken from a very young human embryo. They have formed themselves into a ball. If growth factors are given to the cells, they will begin to differentiate into specialised cells

Scientists are particularly interested in the possibility of using stem cells from human embryos to treat such diseases. This is because the cells in a newly formed embryo are able to differentiate into any kind of cell. Researchers think that, if we could use stem cells from an early embryo (Figure 2.13), we might be able to treat many different unpleasant or life-threatening diseases. But is it right to take cells from an early embryo? So far, research suggests that, if this is done when the embryo is so new that it only contains eight cells, we can take away one of these cells without affecting the embryo in any harmful way. Other scientists aren't so sure about this. At the moment, anyone wanting to carry out research using embryonic stem cells has to apply to the Human Fertility and Embryology Authority for a licence to be allowed to do it.

There are also stem cells in the umbilical cord. Some people are having stem cells collected from the blood in the umbilical cord of their baby, and having them frozen in case they might be able to be used to cure a disease later in the child's life.

● Regeneration

On page 23, we saw that lizards are able to regrow their tail if they lose it, and that salamanders can even regrow legs if they are bitten off by a predator. Spiders, which shed their skins as they grow, are also able to regenerate lost legs (Figure 2.14). Earthworms can regenerate their bodies if cut into two.

How do these animals manage this? We think that this happens because specialised cells near the wound are able to go back to being stem cells. Interestingly, if a crayfish loses just part of its leg, it usually has to cast off the rest of it before regrowth will begin. It seems that only the cells in a particular place, near to where the limb grows out of the rest of the body, are able to turn into stem cells that can produce all the bone, skin, muscle, nerve and other cells that are needed to make a new leg.

These animals, though, are exceptions to the rule. We, and most other animals, cannot produce stem cells that can help to regenerate missing body parts. But some researchers think that, if they could only find the right mix of chemicals, they might one day be able to persuade human cells to behave like the cells near the stump of a missing salamander leg, and become stem cells that could regenerate a complete human leg.

Figure 2.14
a This female tarantula has lost her rear right leg   b After her next moult, she has a new leg

Summary

- Growth can be defined as a permanent increase in size.
- Growth can be measured by taking measurements of length or height, wet weight or dry weight, over a period of time.
- Growth in humans is influenced by several different genes, by hormones and by environment, especially nutrition.
- Humans can be any height within a range, so height is said to be a continuous variable.
- Some people use hormones to enhance their performance in sport.
- A cell that can divide and produce one or more kinds of specialised cells is called a stem cell.
- As an embryo grows and matures, its stem cells become differentiated and lose their ability to form other specialised cells.
- Stem cells may one day be widely used to treat or even cure many different kinds of diseases and injuries.

Questions

2.5 Copy and complete this table about some different ways of measuring growth. You may be able to think of several advantages and disadvantages for each one.

Method	Advantages	Disadvantages
measuring length or height		
measuring wet weight		
measuring dry weight		

2.6 Look at Figure 2.8 on page 23.

  a By how many centimetres did the girl grow between the ages of 2 and 10?

  b Calculate her average growth per year between the ages of 2 and 10.

  c Between which ages did she grow most rapidly?

  d Had she finished growing when she was 20? Explain your answer.

2.7 a List the *three* main factors that influence how tall a person grows.

  b The average height for a Dutch man is about 1.78 metres. The average height for a British man is about 1.75 metres. Which of the three factors you have listed in **a** do you think is most likely to account for this difference? Explain your answer.

  c The size range for pygmy shrews is 43–64 mm long, and the size range for common shrews is 58–87 mm long (Figure 2.15). What do you think causes this difference in size range? Explain your answer.

  d The size of a pygmy shrew is a continuous variable. Explain what this means.

  e Discuss whether you could use length as a way of deciding whether a shrew is a pygmy shrew or a common shrew.

2.8 Explain each of these statements.

  a Stem cells might one day be used to cure people with Parkinson's disease.

  b Stem cells have no Hayflick limit.

  c Embryonic stem cells could be more useful in medicine than stem cells from an adult person.

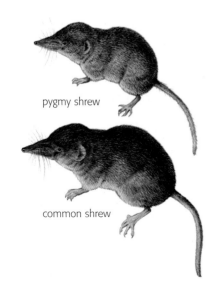

pygmy shrew

common shrew

Figure 2.15

C Plant growth

What is the oldest living thing in the world?

There isn't complete agreement about the answer to this question, but many people think it may be one of the ancient bristle-cone pine trees that grow in the western parts of the USA.

Each year, a tree gets a little bit wider as its trunk grows sideways. We can see this growth as rings in the wood. By counting the rings, we can calculate how old the tree is. One bristle-cone pine tree has more than 4800 growth rings.

Archaeologists can use tree rings to find out the age of wooden structures that they have found. In a 'bad' year – when perhaps there isn't much rain, or it is very cold – trees don't grow as much as in a good year, so the ring in the wood is narrower. The pattern of thick and thin rings in the wood is likely to be very similar in all the trees growing in that place at that time.

Figure 2.16 This bristle-cone pine tree, growing in Nevada in the USA, is thought to be more than 3000 years old

Figure 2.17 This wood is from the trunk of a Douglas fir tree. You can see that the growth rings vary a lot in thickness

A dendrochronologist – a person who is an expert at using tree rings to date wooden structures – can match up the pattern in a sample of wood of unknown date with the patterns in other wood samples whose date is known. This can give a very precise date to the unknown sample. Sometimes, the dendrochronologist can even tell whether the tree was cut down in the spring, summer, autumn or winter.

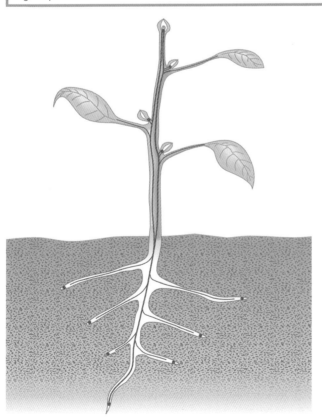

● How plants grow

Like animals, plants grow as their cells divide to form more and more cells. However, there are some differences between plant and animal growth.

- Most animals grow to a certain size and then stop growing. Most plants carry on growing continuously.
- In an animal, growth usually takes place all over the body. In plants, cell division tends to take place in just a few areas. Figure 2.18 shows where these regions of cell division are found.

Roots grow downwards, into the soil. The part of a root where the cells are dividing is just behind the tip. If you look at this part of the root under a microscope, you can see that the cells are very small – which is what you would expect if they've just divided and haven't yet had time to grow. And if the root has been stained with a dye that makes

Figure 2.18 Parts of a growing plant where cells divide. Regions of cell division are shown in red

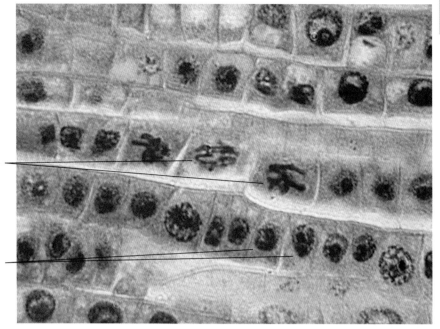

These cells are in the middle of mitosis. You can see the chromosomes inside the cells.

These cells have just finished dividing. You can see that they are very small, as they haven't had time to grow yet.

Figure 2.19 Photomicrograph showing dividing cells near a root tip of a plant

the chromosomes show up, you can also see mitosis happening in some of the cells (Figure 2.19).

Some of the cells that have divided just grow a bit and then divide again. But some of them carry on growing, getting longer and longer. This makes the root grow longer.

As these cells grow, some of them differentiate into specialised cells. For example, some of them become phloem sieve tubes, which will be used for transporting sucrose around the plant. Some of them get longer and longer and then die, forming xylem vessels that will carry water through the plant.

Figure 2.20 Growth in a plant root

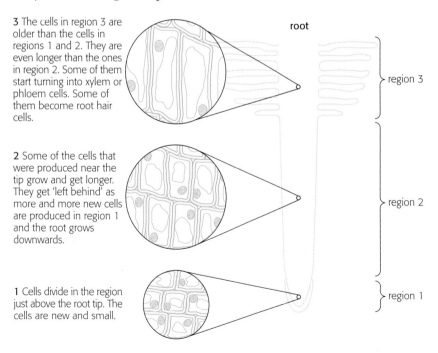

3 The cells in region 3 are older than the cells in regions 1 and 2. They are even longer than the ones in region 2. Some of them start turning into xylem or phloem cells. Some of them become root hair cells.

root

region 3

2 Some of the cells that were produced near the tip grow and get longer. They get 'left behind' as more and more new cells are produced in region 1 and the root grows downwards.

region 2

1 Cells divide in the region just above the root tip. The cells are new and small.

region 1

The very tip of the root is called the root cap. It is made up a tough layer that protects the rest of the root as it pushes through the soil.

The shoot of the plant grows in a similar way. Just behind the tip of the shoot, there is a region of cell division. The newly formed cells elongate and differentiate, so the shoot grows taller and develops different tissues such as xylem and phloem.

Factors affecting plant growth

In order to make new cells, a plant must make new materials that it can use for building them. It does this by first making glucose in photosynthesis, and then using the glucose to make other substances such as proteins and carbohydrates (especially cellulose for the new cell walls). So anything that affects the rate of photosynthesis is likely to affect the rate of growth of the plant. All of the following factors are important:

> **light** Plants tend to grow faster when light intensity is higher, so growth tends to be faster in summer than in winter. They are also affected by day length – the longer the day, the more light they get. Once again, this means that growth is likely to be greater in summer than in winter. We can see this in tree rings, where there is usually a wide 'spring and summer growth' ring alternating with a narrower 'autumn and winter growth' ring.

> **temperature** Most species of plants tend to grow fastest in a particular range of temperature, which depends on the optimum temperatures of their enzymes. The temperature range is different for different types of plant, varying according to the conditions that the plants are adapted for. For example, a plant that has evolved to grow in the tropics may need temperatures around 25 to 30 °C for good growth, while a plant that has evolved in the Arctic may grow best at around 15 °C. Some plants are able to survive freezing, while others are killed if the temperature drops below 0 °C. In Britain, most plants hardly grow at all in winter if it is very cold, doing most of their growth in spring and summer as temperature increases and days lengthen.

> **carbon dioxide concentration** Carbon dioxide is needed for photosynthesis, so higher carbon dioxide concentration in the environment means faster growth. The carbon dioxide concentration in the air is only 0.04%, and this low concentration limits the rate at which plants can photosynthesise. If they are given more carbon dioxide, they will grow faster. Growers sometimes add carbon dioxide to glasshouses, to increase the yields they get from crops such as tomatoes.

> **nutrients** Plants need a variety of inorganic ions (minerals) from the soil in order to grow well. For example, they need ammonium ions and nitrate ions for making amino acids and proteins. The minerals are absorbed from the soil, into the roots. If there is a shortage of nitrate ions in the soil, this can limit the rate of growth of the plant. Farmers often add ammonium nitrate to the soil as a fertiliser, which gives them higher yields from their crop plants.

> **oxygen** Plants, like all living organisms, respire. Respiration requires oxygen. Plant cells in parts where photosynthesis is happening usually get plenty of oxygen, because photosynthesis produces it as a waste product, and also because these parts are usually in the air, where there is plenty of oxygen available. But underground parts of plants can run short of oxygen. Roots rely on getting oxygen from the air spaces in the soil. If these air spaces fill

Burning paraffin in a greenhouse helps plants to photosynthesise and grow faster, for two reasons. It increases the temperature and it provides extra carbon dioxide.

up with water – that is, the soil becomes waterlogged – then they may not be able to get enough oxygen. The cells in the root therefore cannot respire and they die.

● The distribution of plants

Figure 2.21 Ferns can grow in shadier places than most other plants

Plants can only grow where all the things that they require for growth are present. They all need light, a suitable temperature, oxygen, carbon dioxide, mineral ions, and of course water. But different species of plants are adapted to live in different conditions – that is, with different levels of these essentials.

No plant can grow where there is no light at all, for example deep in the sea or inside a dark cave. But some plants *are* able to grow in shady places, where others cannot. For example, ferns grow well in the shade (Figure 2.21). Here, they are free from competition with other plants that need full sun.

We've seen that some plants grow well where it is cold, while others require higher temperatures. So certain plants may be able to grow high up a mountain where it is cold, while others grow best down in the valley. Some may grow only in tropical regions, while others grow best much further north or south.

Look at Figures 2.22, 2.23 and 2.24 to see some other examples of plant adaptation to different conditions.

Figure 2.22

a In Iceland, where it is very cold a lot of the time, most plants are small and grow close to the ground

b In the hot, wet conditions of the tropics, dense rainforest with huge trees can grow

33

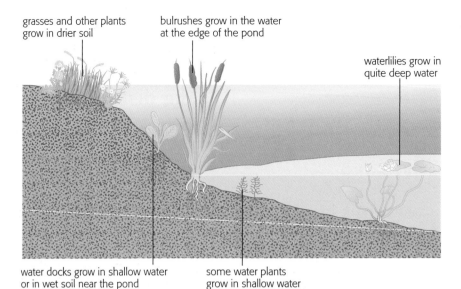

Figure 2.23 Distribution of plants around a pond

grasses and other plants grow in drier soil

bulrushes grow in the water at the edge of the pond

waterlilies grow in quite deep water

water docks grow in shallow water or in wet soil near the pond

some water plants grow in shallow water

Figure 2.24

a These sundews are growing in a very thin layer of wet, poor soil. They supplement their nutrition by getting nitrogen from insects that they catch

b The sundews are growing on the almost bare rocks in the foreground. Why do you think trees are able to grow further back?

● Plant hormones

Like animals, plants produce hormones that help to coordinate the activities of different parts of their bodies. The hormones are chemicals that are made in one part of the plant and move around it to other parts, where they affect the activity of cells. Plants don't have blood to transport their hormones around, so the hormones usually travel in the xylem or phloem tubes, or just diffuse from one cell to the next.

There are several different hormones that affect the growth of a plant. One of these is called **auxin**. Auxin is made by the cells in the dividing regions of the shoots. It diffuses down the shoot, and stimulates the cells in the elongating region to get longer.

> Unlike animal hormones, plant hormones are not made in glands.

> Auxin is also known as indoleacetic acid, or IAA.

Another hormone that affects growth is called **gibberellin**. Most plants make gibberellin in their seeds, young leaves and roots. Some mutant varieties of plants don't make much gibberellin, and they become dwarfs. If gibberellin is sprayed onto them, they will grow tall (Figure 2.25).

Figure 2.25 These two plants are genetically identical and are growing in the same compost. The one on the left has been sprayed with gibberellin

Using plant hormones

Plant growers can sometimes make use of hormones to give them bigger and better yields from their crops.

Figure 2.26 shows how fruit is formed on a plant. The flower has to be pollinated. Then the male gametes in the pollen grains travel down to the female gametes in the ovules, and fertilise them. The zygote that is formed becomes an embryo, and the ovules become seeds inside a fruit.

Figure 2.26 How seeds and fruit are formed

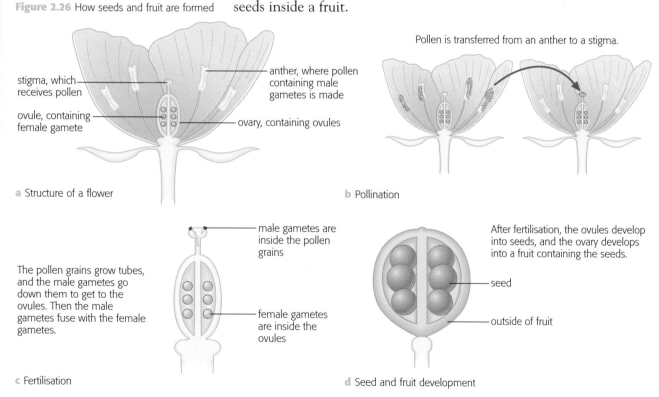

stigma, which receives pollen

ovule, containing female gamete

anther, where pollen containing male gametes is made

ovary, containing ovules

a Structure of a flower

Pollen is transferred from an anther to a stigma.

b Pollination

The pollen grains grow tubes, and the male gametes go down them to get to the ovules. Then the male gametes fuse with the female gametes.

male gametes are inside the pollen grains

female gametes are inside the ovules

c Fertilisation

After fertilisation, the ovules develop into seeds, and the ovary develops into a fruit containing the seeds.

seed

outside of fruit

d Seed and fruit development

Plants that always produce seedless fruits have to be propagated asexually, for example by taking cuttings.

Tomatoes are actually fruits – you can tell because they have seeds inside them.

With some plants, growers can bypass all of this, by using hormones. Grape growers, for example, may dip the bunches of flowers on the grape vines into a solution of gibberellin. The fruits then start growing, even though fertilisation hasn't taken place. This can give the grower a crop more quickly than if he just lets it happen naturally. Better still, the grapes don't have any seeds in them. And they tend to grow larger, and make bigger bunches, because the gibberellin also stimulates the fruit stalks to grow longer.

Today, however, most seedless grapes – such as Thompson's grapes – come from varieties that have a mutated gene that prevents them from producing seeds.

Auxin is also used to help fruits to grow. Some tomato growers use auxin. The flowers are sprayed with auxin, or dipped into it. Although this takes time and costs money, the fruit growers get more tomatoes and bigger tomatoes than if they just let bees pollinate the flowers. In addition, the tomatoes tend to ripen all at the same time, making it easier for the grower to pick and transport them efficiently.

Figure 2.27 Spraying tomato flowers with auxin stimulates the plants to produce better fruit yields

Summary

- Most plants grow continuously throughout their lives.
- Cell division and cell elongation take place near the tips of roots and shoots.
- Cell differentiation takes place as the cells grow.
- Light, temperature, carbon dioxide, oxygen and nutrients (minerals) all affect the growth of plants.
- Each species of plant has a particular range of conditions in which it can grow well, so these varying conditions affect the distribution of plants.
- Plant hormones, such as auxin and gibberellin, help to control the growth of plants.
- Some fruit growers use hormones to initiate the growth of fruit from flowers, for example tomatoes.

H

Questions

2.9 Two students investigated the distribution of plants in a wood and in the field next to the wood. They stretched a 7 m long tape measure from inside the wood and out into the field. Then they put down quadrats every metre along the tape, and identified the plants they found inside the quadrats. These are their results.

Plant	Distance along the line (m)							
	0	1	2	3	4	5	6	7
bramble	✔	✔	✔	✔	✔			
moss	✔		✔					
fern	✔	✔	✔					
bluebell	✔	✔	✔	✔				
violet			✔	✔				
daisy					✔	✔		✔
buttercup						✔	✔	✔
grass					✔	✔	✔	✔
cowslip						✔	✔	✔

a   The first quadrat was placed inside the wood. From the results, suggest approximately how far along the line the edge of the wood was.

b   Which plants were found only in the wood?

c   Suggest one type of plant that grew in the wood but was not recorded in the students' quadrats. Why do you think this type of plant was not recorded?

d   Which plants appeared to grow best near the edge of the wood?

e   Suggest *two* environmental factors that would be different in the wood and in the field.

2.10 Explain the reasons for each of these facts about plant growth.

a   The rings that are produced in a tree trunk in spring and summer are wider than the rings produced in autumn and winter.

b   The cells just behind the tip of a growing root are much smaller than the cells further up the root.

c   Adding fertilisers containing ammonium nitrate to the soil can produce a higher yield of crops such as wheat.

d   Tomato growers may spray auxin onto the plants when they are flowering.

H

D Genetic modification

In the late 19th century, Alexander Graham Bell, the inventor of the telephone, took up a new hobby – breeding sheep. He thought that he would make more money from his sheep if they gave birth to more lambs, and if they managed to supply these lambs with enough milk to help them to grow well. So, in 1889, he let all the other sheep farmers in the area know that, if they had a sheep with more than the usual two teats (through which lambs suck milk), he would pay a good price for them.

He then bred only from these multi-teat sheep. By 1890, his sheep had an average of 2.5 teats; by 1921 the average was 5.39. Along with these changes in number of teats, there was an increase in the number of lambs born. In 1889 only 24 out of every 100 births were twin lambs, but by 1922 more than 50% of the births were of twins.

Bell died in 1922. His sheep were passed to a University Experimental Station, where his breeding programme was carried on. By 1938, almost 70% of the sheep had twins, and by 1939 this had risen to 80%.

Figure 2.28 Alexander Graham Bell with his grandson

Figure 2.29 A ewe with twin lambs

Figure 2.30 Modern 'dwarf' varieties of wheat (on the left) have much shorter stalks than 'normal' varieties (right)

● Selective breeding

In Chapter 1 of *GCSE Science* we looked briefly at how selective breeding is done. The breeder chooses the animals or plants that will breed together, rather than just leaving this to chance.

First, a desired feature is chosen. For example, the breeder – like Alexander Graham Bell – might want to produce a flock of sheep where most of the ewes (female sheep) give birth to two lambs rather than one lamb. Each year, after the ewes have given birth, he removes from the flock all the sheep that had only one lamb. He chooses a ram whose female offspring tend to give birth to two lambs, and allows that ram to mate with his chosen ewes. If he does this for several generations, he can end up with a flock of sheep where almost all of the ewes give birth to twins almost every year.

Almost all of the crops that we grow for food, and animals that we keep for meat, milk or wool, have been bred selectively for many generations. For example, dairy cattle have been bred to give high milk yields, or to give milk with higher or lower fat or protein content. Wheat has been bred to have shorter stems (Figure 2.30), so more of its energy can be put into making grain. This also helps it resist being knocked over by heavy rain or winds, and means the farmer has less straw to get rid of after harvest.

● Cloning mammals

While selective breeding has been going on for hundreds of years, it is only recently that we have understood how it works. We now know that organisms inherit characteristics from their parents because DNA is passed on from parents to offspring. This discovery, made in the middle of the 20th century, opened a whole new world of possibilities for humans to manipulate the characteristics of living things to suit our requirements. The technology allowing us to do this has advanced so rapidly that we haven't always had time to think about all of the ethical and health issues that arise.

For example, we now know how to clone mammals (Figure 2.31). Dolly the sheep was the first mammal to be cloned, but since then scientists have had success with several other species, including horses and dogs. As yet, no one has cloned a human. This is considered by most people to be unethical.

> Remember that cloning means producing genetically identical copies of an organism.

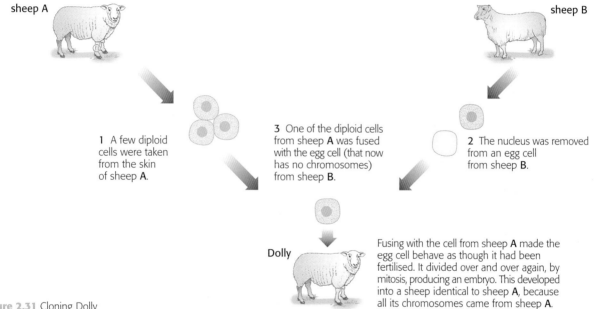

1 A few diploid cells were taken from the skin of sheep **A**.

3 One of the diploid cells from sheep **A** was fused with the egg cell (that now has no chromosomes) from sheep **B**.

2 The nucleus was removed from an egg cell from sheep **B**.

Fusing with the cell from sheep **A** made the egg cell behave as though it had been fertilised. It divided over and over again, by mitosis, producing an embryo. This developed into a sheep identical to sheep **A**, because all its chromosomes came from sheep **A**.

sheep A

sheep B

Dolly

Figure 2.31 Cloning Dolly

But there are still many aspects of cloning mammals that aren't fully understood. Only a tiny percentage of the cells that are produced actually develop into embryos. And most of those embryos die before they are born. Scientists don't fully understand why this is, but it is likely that it is to do with the embryo being developed from 'old' cells, rather than a 'new' one produced by fertilisation. This seems to adversely affect the health of the cells. Another problem is that cloned embryos often grow a lot bigger in the later stages of pregnancy than normally produced ones, with bigger organs. This can lead to problems with their circulatory and breathing systems. It also increases the risk to the mother, because she is carrying a bigger baby and may have more difficulty in giving birth.

● Genetic modification

Although the technology for cloning mammals hasn't yet reached the stage where we can do it easily and successfully, there has been a lot of success in producing genetically modified (GM) animals and plants. Table 2.1 lists some examples.

Organism	Genetic modification	Purpose
maize	gene for making an insect-killing toxin introduced	insects eating the maize are killed, so less of the crop gets eaten before harvest
soya beans	gene for resistance to a herbicide (weedkiller) introduced	farmers can destroy weeds growing in the crop without harming the soya plants
rice	genes for making vitamin A introduced	many people whose staple diet is rice don't get enough vitamin A and may suffer night blindness; eating this rice improves their diet
bananas	genes for making a protein from the virus that causes hepatitis introduced	a person eating the bananas gets a dose of this protein, as though they were being vaccinated, and becomes immune to hepatitis
bacteria	gene for making human insulin introduced	the bacteria are bred in huge vats, and make insulin which is used for treating people with diabetes
sheep	gene for making a human protein called alpha-1-antitrypsin introduced	the sheep's milk contains this protein, which could be used to treat cystic fibrosis

Table 2.1 Some examples of genetically modified organisms

In each of the examples in Table 2.1, there is an obvious possible benefit to humans. But what about the other side of the coin? What questions should we be asking about the possible health risks, environmental risks and ethics of genetically modifying organisms to suit our needs? Here are a few of them:

- **safety for humans** Do the GM organisms pose any safety risks for humans? For example, could the insect toxin in the GM maize plants harm us when we eat the maize? Should people have the choice of being able to buy food that is absolutely guaranteed not to contain any GM material?
- **safety for the environment** Could the herbicide-resistant gene in the GM soya plants somehow get into wild plants growing near by, which might then become 'super-weeds'?
- **ethical issues** Do we have the right to produce genetically modified animals? Might they suffer in some way? Or is genetic modification really no different from selective breeding?

● Gene therapy

We can in some cases genetically modify ourselves, but this is usually referred to as gene therapy.

Many people have diseases that are caused by faulty genes. For example, a person with cystic fibrosis has inherited two copies of a faulty gene from their parents. If we could replace these genes with normal ones, we could cure the disease. The way this might be done for cystic fibrosis is described on page 26 of GCSE Science. At the moment, there are still many hurdles to get over before success can be achieved, but there is certainly hope for the future. Treatment through gene therapy could make an enormous difference to the life of someone with cystic fibrosis.

Cancer is also caused by faulty genes, but in this case the genes have become faulty in just one cell in the body, which multiplies uncontrollably and makes thousands of copies of itself. Although gene therapy might be helpful in some cases of cancer, it will probably prove easier to find better ways of getting rid of the cancer cells, rather than trying to modify the genes in them.

Currently, it is forbidden for gene therapy to be carried out on cells that could be passed on to the next generation. So, for example, it is not allowable to introduce genes into a fertilised egg. If that was done, then the introduced genes would be copied into every cell in the baby's body. When the child was grown up and able to have children, his or her sperm or eggs would also contain these genes, so the genes would be passed on to the next generation.

Carrying out gene therapy on a child or an adult, though, would not result in the genes being passed on, because the introduced genes would only be in a small part of the body, not in the ovaries or testes.

> Cells that contain genes which could be passed on to the next generation, such as cells that will divide to form eggs or sperm, are said to belong to the 'germ line'. Altering these cells is called germ line therapy, and it is currently forbidden.

Summary

- Selective breeding has been used to improve the quality of milk from cattle, increase the number of offspring in sheep and increase the yield from wheat.
- Some limited success has been achieved with cloning mammals, but there are still many problems to be overcome.
- Genetic modification of animals, bacteria and crop plants can have considerable benefits, but we also need to look carefully at the risks and ethical dilemmas that this may pose.
- Gene therapy may one day be used to reduce the symptoms of diseases such as cystic fibrosis.
- It is currently forbidden to carry out gene therapy on cells that might be passed on to the next generation.

Questions

2.11 a One day, it may be possible to treat cystic fibrosis using gene therapy. Explain what is meant by gene therapy.

b Why might gene therapy be a better way of treating cystic fibrosis than giving a person medicines or other treatment?

c Could a person who has had gene therapy for cystic fibrosis pass on the disease to their children? Explain your answer.

2.12 Imagine that you are a scientist working on genetic modification of a crop plant or an animal. Think of a new genetic modification you might be interested in making in a named plant or animal.

a Describe what the genetic modification would be, and suggest how it might be useful.

b What risks or ethical problems might there be if your idea was carried out?

c Write a paragraph, or draw a labelled picture, as though you were the scientist and were trying to persuade people to take up your idea.

d Write another paragraph, or draw another picture, as though you were a person opposed to this idea and you want to stop the genetic modification being carried out. Try to justify your point of view.

Biology

3 Energy flow

A Plants

Many plants contain poisons in their flowers, leaves, seeds or roots. It's thought that the poisons probably help to stop animals from eating them. Some of these poisons are quite well known. For example, hemlock, which comes from a plant looking like cow parsley, is deadly. It often makes an appearance in detective stories. Sophocles, a Greek philosopher, famously killed himself by drinking a liquid made from hemlock. Deadly nightshade, which grows in rough ground and hedgerows, lives up to its name, and people have died from eating just a single one of its black berries. In the past, women used it to make their pupils wide to make their eyes look more attractive – and this has given it its Latin name of *Belladonna*, meaning 'beautiful woman'. Heroin and opium, from opium poppies, have destroyed the lives of many people, although if carefully used they can have an important role in medicine for the relief of severe pain.

Even some of the plants that we eat as vegetables or fruits can be poisonous. We eat the red stalks of rhubarb, but its leaves contain a substance called oxalate, which can cause intense burning sensations and swelling in the mouth and throat and – in large doses – permanent liver and kidney damage. We eat potato tubers, but potato leaves contain a poison called solanine, which can give you a really severe headache and has been known to cause coma and even death when large amounts have been eaten.

Figure 3.1 Foxgloves provide the heart drug, digitalin

Because poisons affect our metabolism, if carefully used they can help to treat illness. For example, the foxglove plant is grown to provide drugs called digitalin and digitoxin. These drugs affect the heart, and they are commonly used to treat heart disease. They slow down the heartbeat but increase its force, and can make an irregular heartbeat become more regular.

There must be many more plants that could provide medicines for us, some of which we don't even know exist. Researchers are studying the uses that native people make of plants that grow in rainforests and other environments – a subject called ethnobotany – and then investigating these plants to see if chemicals that they contain could become useful drugs.

● Using plants

We've always used plants. The most obvious use is as food. Plants are producers, using energy in sunlight to make glucose and other substances. Plants are at the beginning of almost every food chain.

There are many other uses that we make of plants. These include:

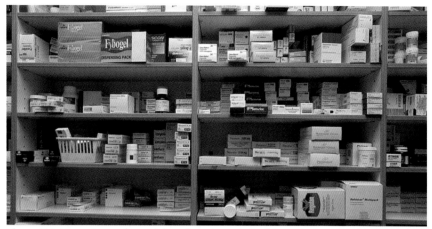

Figure 3.2 Many commonly used drugs have been derived from plants

medicines We have seen that foxgloves are the source of the heart drug, digitalin. Other examples are aspirin from willow bark, vincristine (used to treat childhood leukaemia) from the rosy periwinkle, and quinine (used to treat malaria) from the bark of the cinchona tree. Altogether, there are around 7000 different medicinal drugs that come from plants.

buildings and furniture Houses and other buildings usually contain wood, and we use wood for making furniture and other useful objects. Furniture can also be made from tropical climbing plants called rattan, or from tall woody grasses called bamboos.

Figure 3.3 Despite all the new materials we could now use, most houses are still built using wood

Figure 3.4 The seed heads of cotton plants provide fibres that are used for making cloth

Other fibres, such as viscose, are made from wood. Wood is also used for making paper.

clothing Cotton comes from the seed heads of cotton plants. Linen comes from flax plants.

fuel In many parts of the world, wood is the major source of fuel for cooking and heating. Now there is a move towards growing plants for fuel in the UK. For example, the giant grass *Miscanthus* is being grown for burning in power stations in several parts of the country.

Figure 3.5 *Miscanthus* growing in Somerset

Figure 3.6 Many people enjoy spending leisure time in a natural environment where there are trees and other plants

recreation and relaxation People enjoy being in places where plants are growing. Woods and forests, flower-rich downland, meadows and parks are enjoyed for picnics and walking. Many people enjoy gardening, which they find relaxing and rewarding.

● **Plant cells and photosynthesis**

Figures 3.7 and 3.8 show the structure of an animal cell and a plant cell.

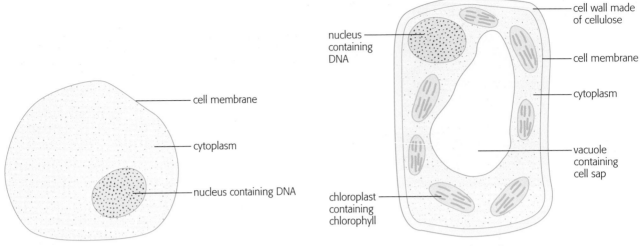

Figure 3.7 The structure of an animal cell

Figure 3.8 The structure of a plant cell

> Don't confuse cell membranes and cell walls. All cells have cell membranes. But animal cells don't have cell walls.

Plant cells differ from animal cells in that they always have a cell wall, made of **cellulose**. Another difference is that plant cells usually have a large, permanent **vacuole** that contains a liquid called cell sap – a solution of sugars and other substances in water.

Some plant cells also contain organelles called **chloroplasts**, as shown in Figure 3.8. Chloroplasts contain a green pigment called **chlorophyll**, which absorbs energy from sunlight. This energy is then used to produce glucose, by reacting carbon dioxide with water. The reaction is called **photosynthesis**, meaning 'making with light'.

carbon dioxide + water ➜ glucose + oxygen

$$6CO_2 + 6H_2O \rightarrow C_6H_{12}O_6 + 6O_2$$

The plant then uses the glucose to make many other substances, including:

▹ other carbohydrates, especially starch for energy storage, cellulose for building cell walls, and sucrose for transport
▹ fats and lipids for energy storage and for making new cells
▹ proteins for making new cells and for use as enzymes.

Factors affecting photosynthesis

What affects how fast a plant can make food? Growers of fruit, vegetables and other crops are very interested in this, because if they can make their plants photosynthesise faster they can get higher yields from them. The more a plant photosynthesises, the more glucose it makes, and therefore the more growth it can put on.

Amount of light

Light supplies the energy that is needed for photosynthesis. The more light shining on the plant, the more energy it receives, so the faster photosynthesis takes place. Figure 3.9 shows apparatus that you could use to investigate this.

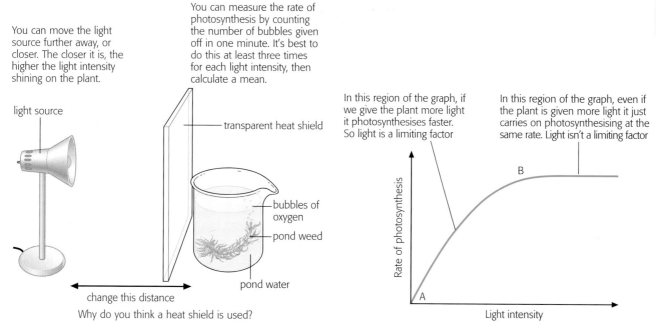

You can move the light source further away, or closer. The closer it is, the higher the light intensity shining on the plant.

You can measure the rate of photosynthesis by counting the number of bubbles given off in one minute. It's best to do this at least three times for each light intensity, then calculate a mean.

light source

transparent heat shield

bubbles of oxygen

pond weed

pond water

change this distance

Why do you think a heat shield is used?

Figure 3.9 Investigating the effect of light intensity on photosynthesis

In this region of the graph, if we give the plant more light it photosynthesises faster. So light is a limiting factor

In this region of the graph, even if the plant is given more light it just carries on photosynthesising at the same rate. Light isn't a limiting factor

Rate of photosynthesis

Light intensity

B

A

Figure 3.10 The effect of light intensity on the rate of photosynthesis

Figure 3.10 shows the relationship between light intensity and the rate of photosynthesis.

At low light intensities (A), the plant's rate of photosynthesis is low, because it isn't getting much light. Light is a **limiting factor** – it is limiting the rate at which the plant can photosynthesise. If we give the plant more light, it will photosynthesise faster.

But when we get to point B on the graph, the plant seems to be photosynthesising as fast as it can. No matter how much more light we give it, it still goes on photosynthesising at the same rate. At these high light intensities, light is *not* a limiting factor.

Amount of carbon dioxide

Carbon dioxide is one of the reactants for photosynthesis. The more carbon dioxide in the environment around the plant, the faster photosynthesis takes place. Figure 3.11 shows the relationship between carbon dioxide concentration and the rate of photosynthesis.

The pattern is the same as for light intensity. At low carbon dioxide concentrations, carbon dioxide is a limiting factor. We can see that because, if we give the plant more carbon dioxide, it can photosynthesise faster. But once we get to a carbon dioxide concentration of about 600 parts per million, the plant is photosynthesising as fast as it can. Giving it more carbon dioxide has no effect. Carbon dioxide is no longer a limiting factor.

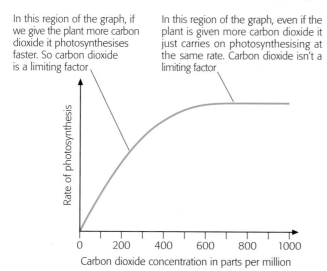

In this region of the graph, if we give the plant more carbon dioxide it photosynthesises faster. So carbon dioxide is a limiting factor

In this region of the graph, even if the plant is given more carbon dioxide it just carries on photosynthesising at the same rate. Carbon dioxide isn't a limiting factor

Rate of photosynthesis

Carbon dioxide concentration in parts per million

Figure 3.11 The effect of carbon dioxide concentration on the rate of photosynthesis

Only about 0.04% of the air is carbon dioxide. This is a very low concentration, so carbon dioxide is often a limiting factor for photosynthesis.

● **How plants absorb mineral salts**

Photosynthesis makes glucose. Glucose is a carbohydrate, with the formula $C_6H_{12}O_6$. In order to make proteins, another element is needed – **nitrogen**.

Plants absorb nitrogen in the form of **nitrate ions** or **ammonium ions**, from the soil into their roots. The roots also absorb any other mineral salts that the plant needs, including **magnesium**, which it uses for making chlorophyll.

Just behind the tip of a root is a region where there are thousands of **root hairs** (Figure 3.12). These are extensions of cells covering the outside of the root. There are so many of them, and they are so long and thin, that they provide a huge surface area.

Soil is made up of particles of clay, sand and other substances, with spaces in between them. The spaces contain air, with a film of water covering the soil particles (Figure 3.13). This is where the plant gets its water from. It absorbs the water by osmosis, into its root hairs.

It has been estimated that a young wheat plant has root hairs with a total surface area of almost 400 m².

Figure 3.12 Root hairs increase the surface area for absorption

Figure 3.13 Root hairs absorb water from around the soil particles

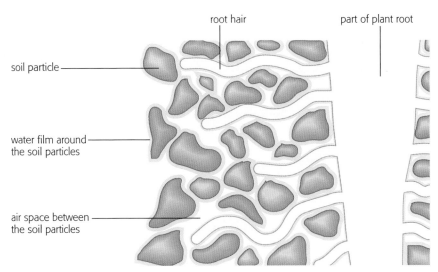

There are many different ions dissolved in the water film, including nitrate ions. However, these ions are often at a lower concentration in the soil than they are inside the root hair cells. Left to their own devices, they would diffuse *out* of the root hairs, down their concentration gradients, into the soil.

But this is not what happens. In the surface membranes of the root hair cells are special proteins, called **transporter proteins**. They have slots in them that perfectly fit nitrate ions. When a nitrate ion bumps into one, the transporter protein grabs the nitrate ion, changes shape and flips the nitrate ion through the cell surface membrane and into the cell (Figure 3.14).

This needs energy. The energy comes from respiration inside the cell. The process is called **active transport**, because the cell is actively moving the ions into itself. Active transport can be defined as the movement of a substance across a cell membrane against its concentration gradient, using energy supplied by the cell.

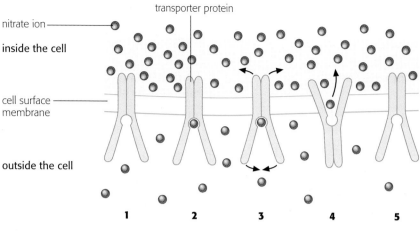

transporter protein

nitrate ion

inside the cell

cell surface membrane

outside the cell

1   2   3   4   5

1 The transporter protein sits in the cell surface membrane. It has a slot exactly the right size and shape for a nitrate ion.
2 As the nitrate ions move around randomly, one moves into the slot in the protein.

3 The protein changes shape.
4 The nitrate ion is flipped into the cell.
5 The protein goes back to its original shape, ready to capture and transport another nitrate ion.

Figure 3.14 Active transport of nitrate ions

Summary

- Humans exploit plants as a food source, for medicines, for building, for fibres, for fuel and for recreation.
- Plant cells differ from animal cells in having a cellulose cell wall, a large vacuole containing cell sap and, often, chloroplasts containing chlorophyll.
- The reactants in photosynthesis are carbon dioxide and water. The products are glucose and oxygen.
- Light intensity and carbon dioxide concentration can be limiting factors for photosynthesis.
- Mineral salts, such as nitrate ions, are taken into roots by active transport, using energy from respiration.

Questions

3.1 a Name *three* structures that are found in both animal cells and plant cells.

   b List *three* differences between the structure of animal cells and plant cells.

3.2 a From memory, write down the word equation for photosynthesis.

   b What are the reactants in photosynthesis?

   c What are the products of photosynthesis?

3.3 Figure 3.15 shows the effect of light intensity on the rate of photosynthesis.

   a What is the limiting factor between points A and B?

   b Explain why light intensity affects photosynthesis in this way.

   c Figure 3.16 shows how light intensity affects the rate of photosynthesis at two different carbon dioxide concentrations.
   What is limiting the rate of photosynthesis in region X? Explain why you think this.

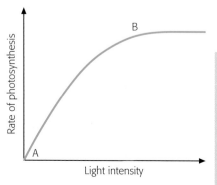

Figure 3.15

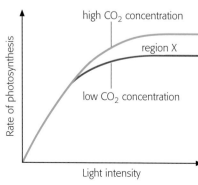

Figure 3.16

3.4 a Define the term *active transport*.

b The table shows the concentrations of three different mineral ions inside a root hair cell and in the soil outside.

Mineral ion	Concentration inside the root hair cell (arbitrary units)	Concentration outside the root hair cell (arbitrary units)
X	12	4
Y	9	9
Z	6	11

i Which mineral ion could be entering or leaving the root hair cell by diffusion? Explain your answer.

ii Which mineral ion could be moving into the root hair cell by active transport? Explain your answer.

iii Which mineral ion could be moving out of the root hair cell by active transport? Explain your answer.

iv Suggest what mineral ion X might be. Why does the plant need this mineral ion?

B Nutrient cycles

It may sound like science fiction, but it is probable that one day we really *will* colonise Mars. If and when we do, we will need plants to come with us.

Neither we nor the plants will have an easy time. Temperatures on Mars are around −7 °C on a nice summer's day, but the average is around −60 °C. There is probably no available water. Light intensity is much lower than on Earth, because Mars is further away from the Sun. The Martian atmosphere is very thin, and made up mostly of carbon dioxide – which might be good for plants, but certainly not for us.

We and the plants will need to have a special, enclosed space in which to live. Here, we could control the temperature and atmospheric composition.

Figure 3.17 A colony on Mars might look like this. Buildings would be sealed to protect people from the cold and the lack of oxygen. Plants would be needed to recycle carbon dioxide into oxygen, to recycle water and to provide food

We'll need oxygen. Where could that come from? In a space satellite, it can be made by breaking down water by electrolysis. But if there isn't water on Mars, we will need to find another source. Plants produce oxygen when they photosynthesise, so perhaps that could be made use of. But again, this oxygen actually comes from water that the plants take in and break apart. There's no getting away from the need for water.

So we'll need to conserve every drop of water and recycle it. The plants can also help with this. Waste water from humans, called 'grey water', could be used to water the plants. The plants will produce 'clean' water when they respire, which if collected would be safe to drink.

People could eat the plants. The faeces and urine from the people will contain mineral ions and other nutrients that the plants could use for their growth.

The aim would be to produce a 'bioregenerative' system – an enclosed environment where all the living organisms would help each other out in some way, and that would keep going with the minimum inputs of materials from outside. Everything would be recycled and reused.

Is it a possibility? Yes, though we will need to keep on developing new technologies over the next few years before we can send people to Mars to live for any length of time.

● The carbon cycle

The bodies of all living organisms contain a lot of carbon. The element carbon, C, is part of every molecule of carbohydrate, fat, protein and DNA.

We get our carbon atoms from the food that we eat. But these carbon atoms originally came from carbon dioxide in the air. Plants take in the carbon dioxide and combine it with water to make glucose and other carbon-containing molecules.

All living things respire. They break down glucose and release carbon dioxide, which goes back into the air.

Combustion is another way in which carbon is returned to the air. When we burn wood, or fossil fuels that were formed from living organisms millions of years ago, carbon dioxide is released.

Figure 3.18 shows how carbon is cycled through an ecosystem. The carbon atoms go from one organism to another, and eventually back to the air.

> If a plant is growing, it must be photosynthesising faster than it is respiring – so it is taking in more carbon dioxide than it is giving out.

Figure 3.18 The carbon cycle

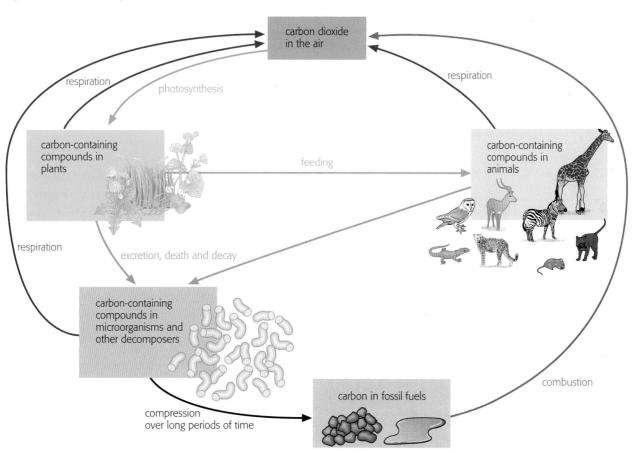

Human activities and the carbon cycle

Today, the concentration of carbon dioxide in the air is greater than it has been for the past 30 million years. And it is at least partly our fault. On page 20 and in Chapter 7 of *GCSE Science*, we saw how the burning of fossil fuels has added to the carbon dioxide in the air. Not only this, but the destruction of forests – **deforestation** – has reduced the amount of photosynthesis taking place in some parts of the world, so less carbon dioxide is being taken out of the air.

Figure 3.19 Deforestation contributes to an increase in carbon dioxide levels in the atmosphere

The increased concentration of carbon dioxide in the air is causing the Earth's temperature to increase. This is called **global warming**. There is absolutely no doubt that it is happening. It is likely to cause very large environmental changes. For example, weather patterns will change, bringing extreme storms to some places and drought to others. Sea level will rise, bringing flooding.

Other effects of deforestation

As the population of humans on Earth keeps growing, we are using more and more of the Earth's resources. If we use them at a rate faster than they can be replaced, then we are using them **unsustainably**.

For example, in many parts of the world forests are being cut down faster than new trees can grow. We've already seen how this contributes to global warming, but deforestation has other harmful effects:

> Soil is made from weathered rock particles and the remains of decayed plants and animals. It takes thousands of years to form, so if it is washed away it takes a really long time to replace it.

Figure 3.20 Illegal logging in Borneo has led to severe soil erosion. Once trees have been removed from a slope, there is nothing to hold the soil in place

▶ **soil erosion** Tree roots help to hold the soil in place. If a forest is growing on a slope, then when the trees have gone the soil can slide down the slope into the valleys or rivers below. Then there is no soil left for other plants to grow in, so the forest cannot regrow. Trees usually help to intercept raindrops as they fall to the ground, so if the trees aren't there the rain hits the soil harder. In tropical regions it can sometimes rain very heavily, with huge raindrops that can hit the ground with great force. This can increase soil erosion.

Figure 3.21 This squirrel-like rodent was newly discovered in 2005 in Laos

Figure 3.22 Orang-utans live only in Borneo and are in danger of extinction in the wild as their tropical rainforest habitat is destroyed

Notice that plants use nitrogen in an inorganic form, as nitrate or ammonium ions. We have to have nitrogen in an organic form, such as in proteins.

The manufacture of ammonia by combining nitrogen and hydrogen is called the Haber process.

Nitrogen fixation works best in well-aerated soil, so plants growing in water-logged soil may be short of nitrogen. Carnivorous plants can grow in wet soil as they get plenty of nitrogen from the insects they feed on.

» **flooding** The eroded soil can fall into rivers, blocking them and causing floods. Also, without the trees, a lot of the rainwater runs off the soil and straight down hillsides into streams and rivers. With the trees there, a lot of the water is taken up into their roots, so there is less run-off and less danger of flooding.

» **loss of habitat** A lot of plants and animals live in forests. It is their habitat, and they have adaptations that allow them to live there. If the forest is cut down, they have nowhere suitable to live. Many species are known to be in danger of extinction if nothing is done to conserve their forest habitats. And we are still finding new species of forest-dwelling animals. If we keep on cutting down forests, these could become extinct before we even know they exist.

» **climate change** Trees and other plants constantly lose water vapour to the air, through transpiration. This forms clouds, which eventually give rain – sometimes nearby, or sometimes hundreds of miles away. Without trees, there is less water vapour in the air, fewer clouds and less rain. In some parts of the world, this can lead to severe water shortages.

● The nitrogen cycle

Nitrogen is part of protein molecules, and also of DNA. As with carbon, we get our nitrogen from the food that we eat.

Almost 80% of the air is made up of nitrogen gas, N_2. This is very unreactive. We breathe in nitrogen with every breath that we take. It goes into our bloodstream, round the body and out again. It does nothing at all while it is inside us. It is completely useless to us.

The same is true for plants. Although they are surrounded by endless quantities of nitrogen gas, they cannot make any use of it. It is simply too unreactive.

We've already seen though that plants *can* use nitrogen in the form of **nitrate ions**, NO_3^-, which they obtain from the soil. They can also use **ammonium ions**, NH_4^+. Where do these ions come from?

» Air contains both nitrogen and oxygen. Each time lightning flashes through the air, the huge temperatures it generates make nitrogen and oxygen atoms combine with each other, forming compounds that fall to the ground in the rain and become nitrate ions in the soil.

» Farmers put fertilisers, containing ammonium nitrate, onto the soil. The fertilisers are made by the chemical industry, by making nitrogen and hydrogen react to produce ammonia.

» Decomposers in the soil break down dead organisms and their waste products. Bacteria in the soil then work on the nitrogen-containing substances that are produced. They produce first ammonium ions, then nitrate ions. These bacteria are called **nitrifying bacteria**.

Some plants have their own personal supply of useable nitrogen, provided by bacteria that live in little swellings on their roots. These bacteria are called **nitrogen-fixing bacteria**. They take nitrogen from the air spaces in the soil and use it to make ammonium ions. The plants can then use these to make proteins.

You can see all of these processes in the diagram of the nitrogen cycle in Figure 3.23. This diagram also shows the completion of the cycle – the return of nitrogen gas to the air. This is done by yet another kind of bacteria, called **denitrifying bacteria**.

Figure 3.23 The nitrogen cycle

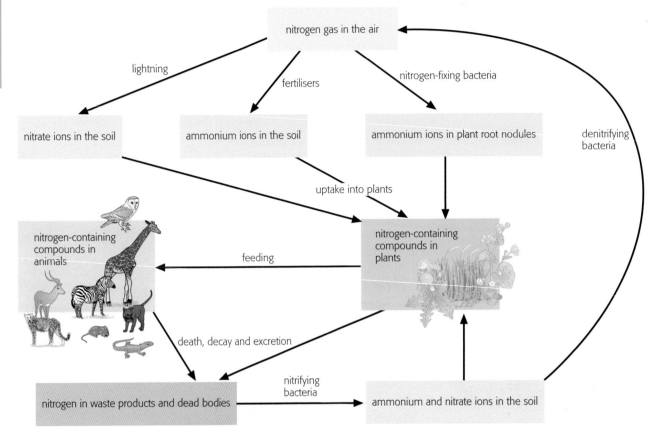

Fertilisers

In Britain each year, thousands of tonnes of fertiliser are added to the soil. A lot of this fertiliser contains nitrogen, in the form of nitrate ions or ammonium ions, or both.

Farmers add fertiliser to the soil to make their crops grow better, so that they get higher yields. In GCSE *Science*, you have seen that, during and after World War II, the Government became very worried that Britain was dependent on other countries to supply us with food, so they used grants and other incentives to persuade farmers to grow as much food as they possibly could on their land. In most cases, the soil did not contain as much nitrate or ammonium as the plants needed. Adding fertilisers, such as cattle manure or ammonium nitrate, meant that crops grew better, and more grain or other produce could be harvested.

Similar changes have occurred worldwide. As our population increases, so does fertiliser manufacture and usage (Figure 3.24).

Care has to be taken when using nitrogen-containing fertilisers, no matter whether they are inorganic ones such as ammonium nitrate, or organic ones such as cattle manure. If they are applied indiscriminately, they can harm the environment.

For example, old meadows where fertiliser has never been used tend to have a much greater biodiversity – more different species – than grassland where fertiliser has been used (Figure 3.25). With the

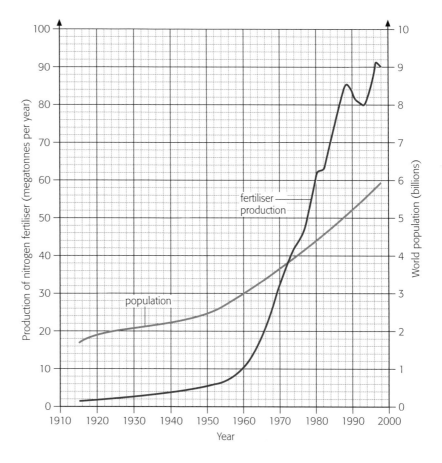

Figure 3.24 Change in nitrogen-containing fertiliser production with world population increase 1910–2000

Figure 3.25 The field on the right has been treated with fertiliser

extra supply of nutrients that fertiliser provides, grasses and other tall plants grow much bigger. They shade out many of the smaller plants, which cannot compete successfully and die.

Problems also occur if the fertilisers accidentally get into streams or ponds. This is most likely to happen if the fertiliser is applied just before it rains, or when there is no crop growing on the land. If the plants don't have time to take up the ammonium or nitrate ions before it rains, then these ions may get washed out of the soil and into the water. Here, they are used by algae and water plants, which grow much faster than usual and can quickly cover most of the water surface.

These fast-growing surface plants stop light from getting to plants underneath them. These plants die – and so, eventually, do many of those growing at the surface. Bacteria take advantage of this, feeding

> The rapid growth of algae is called an algal bloom. Some kinds of algae are toxic, and animals can die if they drink water from a pond where there is an algal bloom.

53

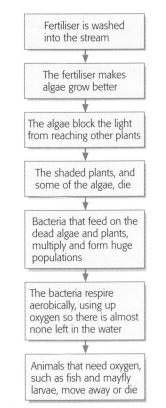

Fertiliser is washed into the stream

↓

The fertiliser makes algae grow better

↓

The algae block the light from reaching other plants

↓

The shaded plants, and some of the algae, die

↓

Bacteria that feed on the dead algae and plants, multiply and form huge populations

↓

The bacteria respire aerobically, using up oxygen so there is almost none left in the water

↓

Animals that need oxygen, such as fish and mayfly larvae, move away or die

Figure 3.26 How fertiliser run-off can cause eutrophication in a stream

Untreated sewage can also cause eutrophication.

on the dead plant matter and breaking it down. These bacteria respire aerobically, so they take oxygen out of the water. As they have so much food, they breed rapidly. Before long, there is so little oxygen in the water that animals such as fish and mayfly larvae cannot survive there. They either move away, or die. This process is called **eutrophication**.

There are several simple rules that farmers follow to try to make sure that this does not happen. They include:

‣ don't apply fertiliser close to a stream
‣ don't apply fertiliser just before it rains
‣ don't apply fertiliser to a crop that is not actively growing (for example, in winter)
‣ don't apply any more fertiliser than you know the plants will use straight away.

Figure 3.27 You may have seen an algal bloom like this one, caused by eutrophication

Summary

- Carbon is constantly recycled between organisms and the environment. Photosynthesis takes carbon dioxide from the air. All organisms, including plants and microorganisms, return carbon dioxide to the air in respiration. Combustion also returns carbon dioxide to the air.
- As our population increases, we add more carbon dioxide to the air by burning wood and fossil fuels. The increasing concentration of carbon dioxide in the atmosphere is causing global warming.
- The unsustainable use of forests – that is cutting them down faster than they regrow – reduces the amount of carbon dioxide that is removed from the air by photosynthesis, and has other harmful effects on the environment.
- Nitrogen is needed for making proteins. Plants get nitrogen in the form of nitrate ions and ammonium ions, and use them to make proteins. Animals get nitrogen in the form of proteins that they eat.
- Decomposers break down dead bodies, and then nitrifying bacteria produce nitrate ions and ammonium ions from their remains.
- Denitrifying bacteria break down nitrate ions and convert them to nitrogen gas which goes into the air.
- Nitrogen-fixing bacteria, many of which live in nodules in plant roots, convert nitrogen gas into ammonium ions, which plants can then use for making proteins.
- Nitrogen-containing fertilisers are added to crops to increase yields. If they get into waterways, they can cause eutrophication, in which respiring bacteria take so much oxygen out of the water that animals must move elsewhere or die.

H

Questions

3.5 Outline the roles of each of these in the carbon cycle:

   a plants

   b microorganisms

   c combustion.

3.6 a Name *one* type of compound in your body that contains nitrogen.

   b Explain how your body got the nitrogen that it contains.

   c Explain why our bodies cannot use the nitrogen in the air around us.

   d Describe how the nitrogen in your body could eventually get back into the air.

3.7 Explain how deforestation can contribute to each of these kinds of environmental damage:

   a global warming

   b soil erosion

   c animal extinctions.

C Food production

Kenya, in eastern Africa, has traditionally had a very successful agricultural industry. Although many Kenyan people are subsistence farmers, a lot of produce is also grown for export. If you look around a supermarket, you will find Kenyan green beans for sale, and Kenyan coffee. Three-quarters of Kenyans make their living by farming.

But in 2006, millions of people in Kenya were facing starvation. After two successive years of drought, farmers in some parts of the country were unable to grow enough crops to feed themselves, let alone others. Their cattle and other livestock died. More than 40 million people found themselves in danger of starvation.

Figure 3.28 Successful cultivation of green beans in Kenya (left) and the disastrous effects of the drought in 2004–6 (right)

● Hunger

Each year, there seems to be a new story of famine somewhere in the world. Sometimes the scale of the famine is so large that it becomes a big story in the media, and people are asked to give money to help out. Many people are very generous in these circumstances, and a lot of money can be raised by charities such as Oxfam, who will use it to help to get food to people who are starving.

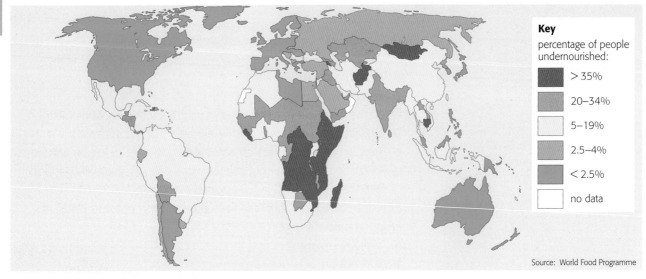

Figure 3.29 Where people go hungry in the World

Key
percentage of people undernourished:
> 35%
20–34%
5–19%
2.5–4%
< 2.5%
no data

Source: World Food Programme

While people in some parts of the world go hungry, others have too much food to eat. In America, it is estimated that around 300 000 people die each year as a result of their obesity.

Why does this happen? In Kenya, it is because drought has prevented people from growing crops. When it eventually rains, they won't have seeds to plant, because they will have eaten all the grain. Sometimes, flooding is to blame. Often, it is war which prevents farmers from sowing and harvesting their crops, or stops supplies getting to people who need them.

Yet there *is* enough food in the world to feed everyone. It is simply not in the right place at the right time. The United Nations' World Food Programme gets donations from countries all over the world, and uses these to try to provide food aid where it is needed, and to coordinate the activities of the charities and aid agencies that try to help. Often, though, the response of these food aid programmes is too slow, and many people die from starvation before help gets to them.

Even once the food is in the country, it still may not get to the people who need it. For example, in some parts of Kenya where people were starving in 2006, there was maize for sale in the markets. But it was too expensive for people to buy.

● Producing food

Until about 10 000 years ago, the people who lived in Britain got their food by hunting animals, digging up roots to eat and collecting berries and seeds. Gradually, they changed from being hunter-gatherers to farmers. Now, most of the food that we eat is produced by farmers or market gardeners.

In *GCSE Science*, on pages 3 to 5, we saw how we can make better use of the energy in the sunlight falling onto a field if we grow crops rather than rear farm animals. Each time energy is passed from one organism to another in a food chain, most of the energy is lost from the food chain. If we can maximise the efficiency of energy transfer along the chain, then we can produce more food. Two examples showing how this can be done are **fish farming** and **growing crops in greenhouses**.

Fat molecules are made up of glycerol and fatty acids combined together. Some kinds of fat (mostly from animals) are said to be saturated, and too much in our diet can increase the risk of heart disease. Plants and some fish generally produce unsaturated fats, which are much better for our health.

Figure 3.30 Fish farming is an example of intensive farming

Fish farming

Fish is an excellent health food. It is low in saturated fat, but high in the kinds of fatty acids that are good for us – especially 'omega-3' fatty acids. It contains a lot of protein and minerals. We are recommended to eat at least two portions of fish each week.

Most of our fish comes from the sea. But over-fishing has put many wild populations of fish in danger. Now, an increasing quantity of the fish on sale in shops and restaurants comes from fish farms.

Fish farming isn't new. In medieval times, most monasteries had their 'stew ponds', where fish such as carp were kept and fed. Now, though, it is done on a huge scale. Salmon, sea bass and trout are just three examples of fish that are farmed in Britain.

Salmon farming is an important industry in Scotland. The fish are kept in large, underwater pens in sheltered lochs containing seawater. They are mostly fed on pellets containing all the nutrients they need in exactly the right proportions. A food chain containing farmed salmon would be: pelleted food ➔ salmon ➔ human. You'll probably remember that the arrows in the food chain represent energy flow. At each transfer, energy is lost so the energy passed on to each level gets less and less (Figure 3.31).

Figure 3.31 Food chain at a salmon farm, showing energy losses

For farmed salmon, much less energy may be wasted than if we catch and eat wild salmon. The caged fish can't swim far or fast, so they don't use up very much energy in movement. They are given carefully calculated quantities of food, so they eat most of it and there isn't too much waste. And there are no (or few) predators, so we don't have to share the fish with any other animals.

H

Maximising production in a fish farm

Fish farmers want to produce the most fish they can, as quickly as possible, and to be able to sell them at a good price. So they want their fish to be healthy, grow rapidly and look good when they are on the fishmonger's stall.

There are several things that are done to improve the quantity and quality of fish that are produced, with the minimum wastage of energy:

▶ **provide optimum feeding conditions** The fish are fed on a very carefully calculated diet. For example, salmon are fed on pellets that contain about 50% protein, 20% fat and 10% carbohydrate. They may be fed on different pellets, with different proportions of nutrients, at different stages of their lives. Young fish, for example, may need more protein than older ones. The fish farmer has to work out how often to feed the fish, and how much to give them each time. He wants them to eat as much as possible (so they will grow faster) and to eat everything they are given – it is a waste of money if a lot of the feed just sinks to the bottom of the loch and gets eaten by something else. Generally, younger fish need feeding more often than older ones.

▶ **provide optimum growing conditions** The fish need to be kept in water that is clean and clear, and with enough space so that each fish can grow large.

▶ **control diseases** One of the big problems for fish farmers is trying to control diseases in the fish. Because a lot of fish are living close together in a confined space, it is really easy for disease-causing organisms (pathogens) to be transmitted from one fish to another. So most fish farmers use chemicals – pesticides – to kill pathogens. Others, in particular those practising organic methods, reduce the disease risk by not keeping too many fish in a particular area, giving lots of room for clean water to keep flowing through and reducing the chance that pathogens will be a serious problem.

▶ **control predators and parasites** Wild fish have many predators. Salmon, for example, might be eaten by seals, cormorants or other birds such as ospreys. On a fish farm it isn't easy for a predator to get to the fish, because the fish are inside cages. Some farmers have covers over the cages, to stop birds diving in and catching fish. But predators can still find their way in. Seals, for example, may learn how to push up through the net cages from below, biting fish through the net and eating chunks of their flesh. Long, thin predatory fish such as lampreys just slide through the mesh and into the cages, fixing themselves onto the salmon with their suckered mouth and biting them.

> Chemicals may be used on fish farms to kill parasites on the fish. These chemicals may harm other organisms living in the water near the fish farm.

Figure 3.32 An osprey with a freshly caught fish

Greenhouse crops

When we grow crops in greenhouses, we have much more control over them than if we grow them in an open field. We can control the temperature, the lighting and the carbon dioxide concentration, which means we can help the plants to photosynthesise as fast as possible (see page 45). We can provide the plants with exactly the right nutrients that they need. It is easier to stop animals eating the plants, and to control diseases.

The glass of a greenhouse lets in short-wave radiation from the Sun. This warms the contents of the greenhouse, and is radiated back as long-wave radiation which cannot get out through the glass – just as in the greenhouse effect in our atmosphere.

In Britain, most tomatoes are grown in greenhouses. The energy that the tomatoes use for photosynthesis comes from the sunlight that falls onto them. By planting the tomatoes at the right distance apart, and getting rid of any weeds, the grower can make sure that almost every scrap of sunlight falls onto a tomato plant leaf, rather than on the ground or onto weeds. That way, less of the energy in the sunlight is wasted.

By growing the plants in greenhouses, we also avoid loss of energy to animals that might eat the plants (instead of us eating them) or to fungi or other disease-causing organisms that might harm them. We can keep all of the energy in the tomatoes for ourselves.

vents in the roof open to allow hot air to escape, if the temperature gets too high

transparent glass lets as much light in as possible

heaters keep the temperature warm, even when the outside temperature is cold

In a big, commercial glasshouse, extra carbon dioxide is sometimes added to the air.

As the plants are growing in a confined space, pests can be stopped from getting in. If they *do* get in, it is relatively easy to destroy them.

exactly the right balance of mineral ions can be added to the soil in which the plants are growing

Figure 3.33 Controlling environmental factors in a greenhouse

Maximising production in a greenhouse

We've seen that both light and carbon dioxide concentration can be limiting factors, slowing down the rate of photosynthesis if they are in short supply. In a greenhouse, a grower can control the intensity of the light and the concentration of the carbon dioxide, finding levels of both that help the plants to photosynthesise as fast as they possibly can. And he can keep the plants at exactly the right temperature, so that they grow quickly.

In most commercial greenhouses, computers control the conditions inside. For tomato growing, the best conditions have been found to be:

- about 0.1% carbon dioxide concentration in the air
- a temperature of around 20 °C
- plenty of light.

On a really sunny day, it can get very hot in the greenhouse – even too hot for tomato plants. The greenhouses have 'windows' in the roof that open automatically when the temperature gets to a certain level. The warm air inside the greenhouse, being less dense than the cooler air outside, rises upwards and goes out of the greenhouse by convection, while cooler air drops in to replace it.

Summary

- There is more than enough food in the world to feed everyone, but while some countries have more than they need, others do not have enough.
- We can maximise energy transfer in food production by keeping plants or animals under controlled conditions so that less energy is wasted to the environment or to other animals.
- Farming fish and growing crops in greenhouses help to maximise energy transfer in food production.
- Optimum feeding and growing conditions, and control of diseases and predators in fish farms and in greenhouses can all help to increase food production.

Questions

3.8 a List *three* reasons why people in some countries do not get enough to eat.

  b There are many ways we could help to reduce the number of people who die from hunger each year. For example, we can:
  - ask people to give money for food aid when a famine strikes
  - keep a supply of staple foods such as wheat ready and waiting to be distributed when famine strikes
  - help people to move away from areas where they can no longer grow food, and set them up in new areas.

  Choose *one* of these ideas, and give *one* advantage and *one* disadvantage of it. Find out what other people in your class think about them.

  c Suggest *one* other way in which world hunger could be reduced.

3.9 a The pellets fed to farmed salmon are often made from fish that have been caught out at sea. Redraw the food chain in Figure 3.31 on page 57 to show this, including the original source of the energy in the food chain.

  b Draw a diagram to show the energy losses in a food chain involving tomatoes grown in a greenhouse.

  c Now draw a diagram like the one you drew in **b**, but this time show the extra losses of energy you might expect if the tomatoes were grown outside.

3.10 Tomatoes are an important commercial crop in Canada, where they are grown in greenhouses. The outside temperature is often cold, so growers heat the greenhouses. The recommended air temperatures in greenhouses being used for growing tomatoes are shown in the table.

	Temperature (°C)	
	days when light intensity is low	**days when light intensity is high**
at night	17	18
during the daytime	19	21

a The tomatoes would grow even faster if they were kept at slightly higher temperatures. Suggest why it would not be economical for the growers to heat their greenhouses to higher temperatures. (Think about the balance between their costs and what they get when they sell the crop.)

b Using what you know about temperature, photosynthesis and limiting factors, suggest why the recommended temperatures are higher during the daytime than at night.

c Suggest why the recommended temperatures are higher on sunny days than on dull days.

d Suggest *one* other way in which the growers could change the environment inside the greenhouse to increase the yields of tomatoes.

4 Interdependence

A Interrelationships

In the 1980s, the Great Barrier Reef off the east coast of Australia came under a severe threat. A normally uncommon starfish, called the crown-of-thorns, suddenly increased in numbers. Seemingly from nowhere, there were suddenly about 1.5 million of these starfish crawling over the reef.

Crown-of-thorns starfish feed on corals. They have stomachs that they can turn inside out. They push their inverted stomachs into the coral animals, secrete enzymes onto them and digest them alive. Then they pull their stomachs back inside themselves and move on to their next prey. The corals are fixed in place by their calcium carbonate skeletons, so they have absolutely no way of escape.

In some parts of the Great Barrier Reef, almost 90% of the corals were killed. Some people thought that the destruction would be permanent. But, 10 to 15 years later, a good recovery had been made. But it will take even longer for the corals on the reef to be as luxuriant and diverse as they were previous to the attack by the voracious starfish.

Figure 4.1 Crown-of-thorns starfish feeding on coral

Figure 4.2 A coral reef supports many species

● Coral reefs

Of all the different habitats in the seas and oceans, coral reefs have the highest **biodiversity**. They are the home for a huge number of species of brightly coloured fish, invertebrates such as prawns, worms, feather stars and sea urchins and, of course, the corals themselves.

Coral reefs are made by tiny animals called coral polyps. They are like miniature sea anemones – little animals with tentacles that trap food and push it into their mouths. Coral polyps make a hard skeleton around themselves, out of calcium carbonate. It is this skeleton that makes up the reef. The polyps in a piece of coral connect up with each other through channels in their skeletons.

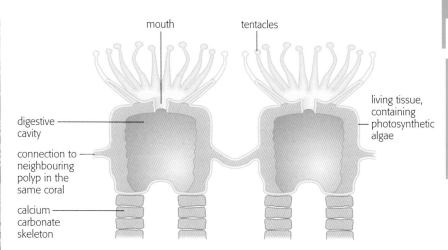

Figure 4.3 Coral polyps – living in a coral reef, and their structure (right)

Coral polyps are adapted to be able to live in a certain set of conditions. They have a close partnership with microscopic algae, which live inside their body tissues. The algae photosynthesise, providing the coral with a source of glucose and other substances that the polyps need in addition to the food they catch. The algae can only do this if they have plenty of light. So coral reefs are always found in clear water, no more than 70 metres below the surface and usually in water even shallower than this. The coral polyps and their algae also need to live where the water temperature never drops lower than 20 °C. The map in Figure 4.4 shows the areas of the world's oceans where coral reefs are found.

As global warming progresses and sea level rises, many coral reefs will die because not enough light will reach them.

Figure 4.4 The global distribution of coral reefs

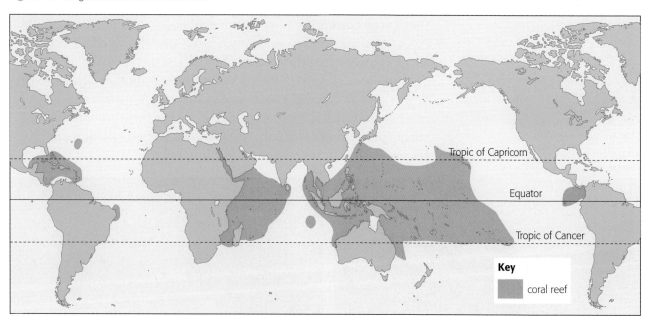

Competition on a coral reef

You may remember that there is **competition** when two or more organisms need the same thing, which is in short supply. On a coral reef, the coral polyps compete for space to attach themselves, for light and for food.

Figure 4.5 shows the cross section of a coral reef around an island. Different species of coral animals live in different parts of the reef.

Figure 4.5 The structure of a coral reef

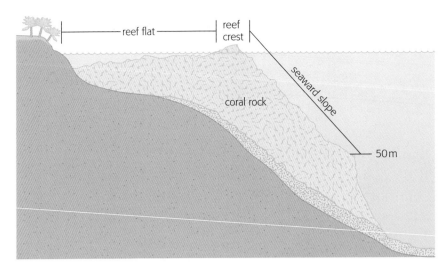

reef flat — reef crest

seaward slope

coral rock

50m

On the seaward slope of the reef, strong waves buffet the corals. Here, only corals that are adapted to survive these rough conditions can grow. Strong, stout, branching corals such as stagshorn or elkhorn coral (Figure 4.6) live here. Their large surface area helps them to capture as much sunlight as possible, so they can grow some way down the reef slope, deeper in the water than some other kinds of corals, where less light penetrates. Their branches can cover and shade other corals, which often kills them.

On the more sheltered parts of the reef (the reef flat), many different species of coral grow. Here there is plenty of light, and plenty of food brought in on the waves. There is great competition for space here. Corals may look peaceful and unmoving, but in fact they battle constantly with their neighbours.

The tentacles of the coral polyps have special cells that eject stinging barbs when they are touched. These are normally used for catching prey. But when a coral senses there is another coral growing nearby, it grows specially long 'sweeper tentacles', which may be as much as 20 times as long as normal. It sweeps these around itself, stinging any other coral polyps that it touches and killing them (Figure 4.7).

Figure 4.6 The branching shape of elkhorn coral helps it to absorb a lot of sunlight

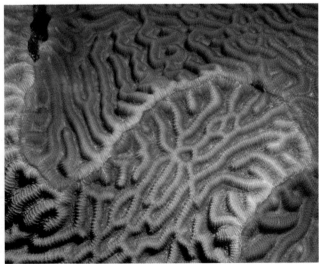

Figure 4.7 Corals that are competing for space reach out to their neighbours with long filaments, which attack and digest them. The coral at top right of the picture is silently battling with the one below it

Predation on a coral reef

We've seen how corals can be killed and eaten by crown-of-thorns starfish. Normally, these starfish are found only in low numbers. But every now and then their numbers can suddenly increase. There are several theories about why this happens, but at least some of the time it may be our fault. One idea is that run-off from the land into the sea may provide nutrients and stimulate an algal bloom (see page 54), which means there is a lot of food for the larvae of the starfish. Another possibility is that overfishing may remove most of the fish that would normally eat the starfish.

Whatever the reason, when there is a population boom in the crown-of-thorns starfish, the size of the coral population falls. The starfish seem to prefer to eat stagshorn corals, so these are often the first to suffer. Eventually, as the starfish run out of food, their population drops back to normal, and the corals begin to recover. This is a slow process. It can take 20 years for the corals to grow back to covering one-third of the area that they did previously.

Coral polyps aren't the only animals to be attacked by predators on a coral reef. Most of the reef fish are prey for predatory fish, either ones that live on the reef all the time, such as moray eels (Figure 4.8), or ones that swim in from the open ocean, such as sharks. All of the prey fish have adaptations that help to reduce the risk of being eaten. For example, they are often able to hide in crevices and tunnels inside the coral. Some have wonderful camouflage.

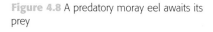

Figure 4.8 A predatory moray eel awaits its prey

Cooperation on a coral reef

Many different species of animals live on and around a coral reef. Competition between them for space and food is often intense, and prey species must be constantly on guard against their predators. But not every interaction between the different species is a battle. Sometimes two different species help each other out. When two different species live closely together and both of them benefit, their relationship is known as **mutualism**. One of the best examples of this is the relationship between the coral polyps and their photosynthetic algae, but there are many others to be found on the reef.

For example, the clown fish keeps safe amongst the poisonous tentacles of a sea anemone (Figure 4.9). The fish is protected from

Figure 4.9 A clownfish is safe from predators amongst an anemone's tentacles

Figure 4.10 A cleaner fish at work

the poisons in their stinging tentacles by a covering of special mucus. The anemone also benefits, because its resident fish protect it from being eaten by other fish species.

Some small fish work as cleaners, removing parasites from larger fish. Their colours advertise their profession to other fish, which will come specially to a 'cleaning station' and allow the cleaner fish to work over their body surfaces. Even predatory fish do this, and don't hurt the cleaners. In this relationship, the cleaners get food, and their customers have many of their parasites removed.

Summary

- In any habitat, the interrelationships between the organisms living there affect their distribution and population sizes.
- Each species of organism is adapted to live in a particular set of conditions. Its adaptations determine where it can live.
- Competition occurs when two organisms need the same resource, which is in short supply. On a coral reef, corals compete for space, light and food.
- Predation can affect the size of the population of the prey species. In turn, the size of the population of the prey species can affect the population of the predator.
- Sometimes organisms of different species live close together, cooperating in ways that help them both to survive.

Questions

4.1 Describe one example of each of these interactions on a coral reef. You could use examples from this book, or you could look for different ones on the internet.
  a competition
  b predation
  c mutualism

4.2 Look at the map in Figure 4.4 on page 63. Explain why coral reefs are found in these regions of the world, but not in places such as the north Atlantic Ocean.

4.3 Some people have suggested that infestations of crown-of-thorns starfish are natural events, and not caused by humans. They also say that the starfish feed on faster-growing corals and so can increase the biodiversity on the reef.
  a Explain what is meant by *biodiversity*.
  b Suggest how you could carry out an investigation to test one of these hypotheses:
    • Crown-of-thorns infestations are not always due to human activity.
    • A crown-of-thorns infestation can increase the biodiversity of corals on a coral reef.

B Extreme environments

In early January 1912, Robert Falcon Scott and his four companions struggled towards the South Pole, aiming to be the first people to reach it. The original plan had been to use ponies to pull the sledges that carried their supplies, but the ponies had not been able to cope with the cold and had had to be shot. So the team were pulling their own sledges. They had to haul them up steep slopes, manoeuvre them over crevasses and run behind them, hauling them back, as they slid down slopes.

The men were already weak. As they dragged their heavy sledges,

Figure 4.11 Scott and his team at the South Pole

they slipped and fell many times. Nevertheless, they did eventually reach the Pole on 17th January – only to find that the Norwegian explorer Roald Amundsen had got there one month before them.

Cold, hungry, exhausted and dispirited, the five men set out to trudge back to safety. One of the party regularly lagged behind the rest, and on 17th February he died. This was a tremendous blow to the rest of the party but they had no way out of their predicament other than to struggle on. No one could help them. On 17th March, another member of the party, Titus Oates, recognising that his weakness was holding the other three back, famously walked out of the tent into the cold and never returned.

By 11th March the remaining three were only 11 miles from a food depot, but they might as well have been 200 miles away. In atrocious weather conditions, they had to hole up in their tent. Running out of fuel and food, Scott continued to write in his diary until the end. His last entry was on 29th March.

● **The Antarctic climate**

The lowest temperature ever recorded on the surface of the Earth was at Vostok in Antarctica – it was −89 °C.

Temperatures in many parts of Antarctica rarely rise above 0 °C. Scott had expected temperatures of about −20 °C, but was unlucky to encounter freak weather with temperatures regularly dropping to −40 °C. For two months of the year, in the Antarctic winter, the sun scarcely rises above the horizon.

Antarctica is a windy place, and wind chill seriously affects the conditions there. For example, if the temperature is −20 °C and the wind is blowing at 30 km per hour, it will feel as though it is −30 °C.

Antarctica is a polar desert. It is the driest continent on Earth. Almost all the precipitation falls as snow rather than rain, and some parts receive only 50 mm a year.

In such conditions, you would think nothing would be able to survive for long. But there are a few organisms that do live, even in some of the coldest and driest areas. They have evolved remarkable adaptations that enable them to make a living in this harsh environment.

Figure 4.12 Weather conditions in Antarctica are extremely harsh

67

For example, some lichens actually live *inside* sandstone rocks. They grow in the tiny spaces between the sand grains that make up the rock. Lichens are strange organisms, consisting of a very close relationship between an alga and a fungus. These lichens live near the surface of the rocks, where just enough light gets to them for a few months in the year for them to be able to photosynthesise and stay alive.

In the seas around Antarctica, it is a different story. The water is very rich in nutrients, and in the summer – when it is light for almost 24 hours a day – tiny microscopic plants in the sea photosynthesise rapidly, allowing their populations to grow quickly. They form the start of a food web that supports huge numbers of marine animals (Figure 4.13).

Figure 4.13 A food web in the Antarctic Ocean

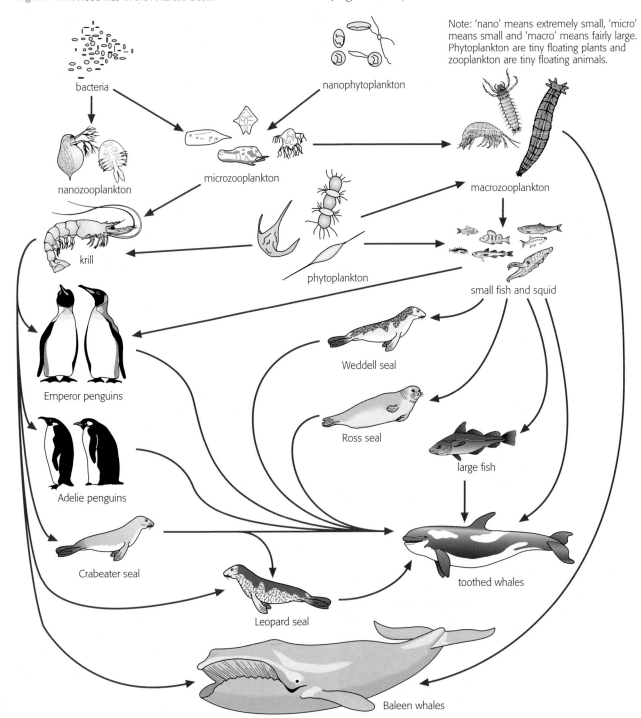

Note: 'nano' means extremely small, 'micro' means small and 'macro' means fairly large. Phytoplankton are tiny floating plants and zooplankton are tiny floating animals.

● Deep sea volcanic vents

While the Antarctic is the coldest environment on Earth where living things survive, deep sea volcanic vents are the hottest. Here, water at more than 370 °C pours out from fissures in the ocean floor, giving them their other name of 'hydrothermal vents'. These vents are found deep in the oceans, at places where two of the Earth's tectonic plates interact with each other. The water pouring out is seawater that has seeped down into the ocean bottom through cracks, come into contact with hot rocks and then spewed out again. It is full of dissolved minerals, including sulphur, iron and even gold. The hottest vents are called 'black smokers', because the iron and sulphur in them combine to form black iron sulphide.

At these depths, it is completely dark. There are no photosynthesising plants, and it is a long way from the surface where oxygen could dissolve into the water. So there is virtually no oxygen. Yet here, just as in Antarctica, some living organisms have become adapted to survive and thrive in extremely harsh conditions. The base of the food web is formed by bacteria that use the minerals as a source of energy. They effectively take the place of plants in the food chain. The bacteria are the food of giant tube worms (their tubes are up to 2.5 metres tall), giant clams and giant barnacles. The tube worms have no mouth, no digestive system and no anus. Instead, the bacteria live inside their cells. Somehow – we still don't understand exactly how – the tubeworm helps to provide the bacteria with the chemicals they need to make food, and then takes some of this food for itself.

Figure 4.14a Location of hydrothermal vents

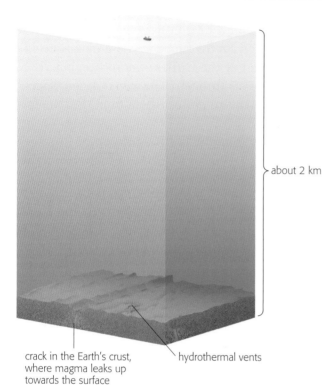

about 2 km

crack in the Earth's crust, where magma leaks up towards the surface

hydrothermal vents

Figure 4.14b A hydrothermal vent

the water can be as hot as 370 °C

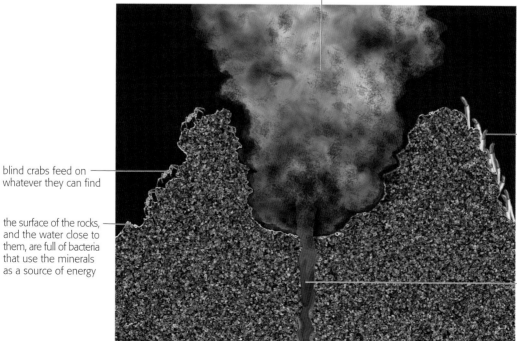

blind crabs feed on whatever they can find

the surface of the rocks, and the water close to them, are full of bacteria that use the minerals as a source of energy

giant tube worms use the bacteria as food

hot water, full of minerals, pours out through a fissure in the ocean floor; as it hits the cold ocean water its dissolved minerals come out of solution

69

Figure 4.15 Cushion plants high in the Andes, Peru

People who travel to high altitudes may experience altitude sickness, brought on by the low concentrations of oxygen. It can be fatal. The cure is to get the person down to a lower altitude as quickly as possible.

● High altitudes

Deep sea volcanic vents are found around 2000 metres below the ocean surface. At the other extreme, the highest mountains on Earth reach to 8850 metres above it.

Some of the difficult environmental conditions found in the high mountains are similar to those in the Antarctic. It can get very cold, and winds are often strong. Plants living at high altitude are usually very small, growing in low clumps close to the ground, where they get at least some shelter from the cold, drying winds. Some have leaves covered with silvery hairs, which help to trap a layer of moist air next to the leaf surface and prevent it from drying out.

Ultra-violet (UV) radiation from the Sun can cause mutations in living cells. It is partly absorbed by the Earth's atmosphere, but at high altitude more of the UV gets through. The silvery leaf surfaces of many high-altitude plants helps to protect them from the damage that the UV might do.

As you move upwards, away from the Earth's surface, the atmosphere becomes thinner. Organisms that live in high mountains have to be able to survive with a much lower concentration of oxygen in the air than if they were living at sea level. For example, llamas – camel-like mammals that live in the high Andes in South America – have a kind of haemoglobin that is better at picking up oxygen than our haemoglobin is. This enables them to get more oxygen from the thin air in their environment.

Summary

- In the Antarctic, temperatures are very low, there are strong winds and the air can be very dry. In winter, there is very little daylight.
- Around deep sea volcanic vents, hot water containing chemicals that would be toxic to most organisms flows out into the sea. There is no light here.
- At high altitudes, temperatures are low and wind speeds can be high. The thin atmosphere allows more ultra-violet through than at lower altitudes. Oxygen concentration in the air is low.
- Organisms have adapted to live in even these extreme environments.

Questions

4.4 Copy this table, and then complete it by placing a tick in each box that applies to each of the extreme environments listed.

Condition	Antarctic	Deep sea volcanic vents	High altitude
low temperatures			
high temperatures			
low oxygen concentration			
high ultra-violet radiation			
no light or low light levels			
drying winds			

H

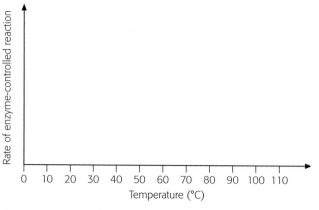

Figure 4.16

4.5 a Enzymes are affected by temperature. As the temperature increases up to about 40 °C, their activity increases. But at temperatures above 40 °C the enzyme molecules begin to lose their shape and don't work so well. At 60 °C they stop working completely. Copy the axes in Figure 4.16, and then sketch a curve showing how temperature affects the rate of an enzyme-controlled reaction.

b Organisms that can live in extreme environments are sometimes known as extremophiles. Some extremophile bacteria can live at temperatures of up to 100 °C or even more. On the same axes, sketch a curve to show how you predict that the activity of their enzymes would be affected by temperature.

c Suggest how enzymes from extremophiles could be useful to us.

C Pollution

The Norfolk Broads are an area of wetland with many interlinked shallow, open areas of water. More than one million visitors a year go there to fish, to laze around in a boat, or just to relax. But by the 1990s the Broads were becoming less attractive. Weeds were clogging up many of the channels, so boats could not use as much of the water as they had in the past. In places the water was becoming very smelly and dirty-looking. Fishermen were complaining that there were fewer fish to catch.

Analysis of the water showed that it in many places it was much, much richer in nutrients than it had been in the past. The nutrients, especially nitrates and phosphates, had been gradually increasing since the 1930s. The more people that visited the Broads, the worse it seemed to get. It looked like an increasingly common situation – lots of people visiting a beautiful place were destroying it just by being there.

Figure 4.17 The Norfolk Broads are one of the most popular holiday areas in Britain

● Water and air pollution

The Norfolk Broads (see the box above) were suffering from pollution. We can define pollution as the addition of something to the environment that causes harm to the organisms that live there.

Humans produce enormous quantities of waste products. We add all kinds of different things to the air, water and soil around us. Some of these can cause serious pollution. Air pollution by carbon dioxide has been explored on pages 19–21 and 125–131 in *GCSE Science*. Other air pollutants include sulphur dioxide, CFCs and carbon monoxide. In this book we have already seen, on pages 53–54, how nitrate ions can cause water pollution. Another serious water pollutant is phosphate.

Increasing levels of carbon dioxide in the atmosphere are causing global warming. The average global temperature has gone up by around 1 °C since 1900.

71

Phosphate pollution

On page 54 we saw how nitrates can cause eutrophication if they get into rivers and streams. They act as nutrients for algae, which are fed on by bacteria, which use up oxygen in the water. The water becomes cloudy and smelly, and short of oxygen.

This was part of the problem in the Norfolk Broads. But an even worse problem was caused by **phosphates**.

Phosphate ions are often added to detergents. They get into waste water from industries and from people's washing machines, and so may end up in streams and rivers in the outfall from sewage treatment works. Phosphates are also often included in fertilisers, because plants need them for healthy growth. Like nitrate ions, phosphate ions can be washed off the soil and into rivers. However, phosphate ions are much less soluble than nitrate ions. They tend to settle to the bottom and get trapped in the mud.

In the Broads, as eutrophication took place and the waters became cloudy, many of the fish that normally lived there moved away. Others, which are better adapted for living in these conditions, did well and their populations increased. Unfortunately, some of these species made matters worse. For example, a kind of fish called bream feed by poking around in the mud, churning it up and releasing even more phosphate ions back into the water. The propellers of some of the thousands of boats using the Broads had a similar effect.

In 1981, an attempt was made to solve the problem of water pollution by phosphates. New technology was introduced to remove all the phosphate from sewage, before it went into the rivers. Farmers followed a strict code about where and when they could apply fertilisers, greatly reducing the quantity of nitrate and phosphate ions that ran off farmland and into waterways. But this didn't seem to have any effect at all in the Broads.

Not until huge quantities of the phosphate-rich mud were pumped out, in 1995, did the water of the Broads begin to become clearer. Now most of the plant-clogged channels have been cleared and the fish have come back. Even the farmers have benefited – the phosphate-rich mud has been put onto farmland, where it makes an excellent fertiliser for growing crops.

Sulphur dioxide pollution

Most fossil fuels contain sulphur. Coal contains the most. When coal is burned, the sulphur in it combines with oxygen from the air, forming sulphur dioxide. Sulphur dioxide is an invisible gas. It is harmful to many different kinds of living things. People who already have a problem involving their respiratory system, such as asthma or bronchitis, may find it makes their illness worse.

Lichens are very sensitive to sulphur dioxide, and many lichen species are only able to grow where sulphur dioxide levels are below a certain value. They can be used to give a good idea of how bad the sulphur dioxide pollution is – you just count up the species that you find growing in an area, and check this against a scale to see what level of pollution this indicates (Figure 4.18).

Now that there are restrictions on burning coal in houses in towns and cities, there is much less sulphur dioxide in the air than in the past, and many more species of lichens can be found growing on walls, gravestones and trees.

Figure 4.18 The Hawksworth and Rose scale: lichen species are classified into 'zones' according to how much sulphur dioxide they can tolerate. If you find lichens that belong to zone 4, but not zone 5 or zone 6 lichens, then you know that the concentration of sulphur dioxide is probably about 70 micrograms per cubic metre

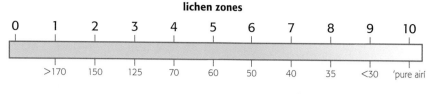

lichen zones

| 0 | 1 | 2 | 3 | 4 | 5 | 6 | 7 | 8 | 9 | 10 |

| >170 | 150 | 125 | 70 | 60 | 50 | 40 | 35 | <30 | 'pure air' |

mean winter SO₂ level (micrograms/m³)

Figure 4.19 Lichens

a This is a zone 2 lichen. It can grow where there is a lot of sulphur dioxide

b This is a zone 7 lichen. It is only found where the sulphur dioxide level is low

Sulphur dioxide in the atmosphere reacts with oxygen and water to form sulphuric acid. This dissolves in raindrops and falls to the ground as **acid rain**. All rain is slightly acidic, because it contains dissolved carbon dioxide. It has a pH of just below 6. But acid rain can have a much lower pH than this. Rain with a pH as low as 1.5 has been recorded in some places in the world.

Acid rain causes several different problems. These include:

- It increases the acidity of the soil. This can make it more difficult for trees and other plants to take the minerals that they need into their roots.
- It releases harmful heavy metal ions from the soil, which can then be washed into rivers. For example, aluminium ions can kill fish.

Most developing countries have now done a lot to reduce the production of sulphur dioxide and acid rain. For example, power stations that burn coal and other fossil fuels have installed 'scrubbers', which remove the sulphur dioxide from waste gases before they are released into the air.

CFC pollution

CFC stands for chloro-fluorocarbon. CFCs are chemicals that have been used in fridges and in aerosols. They are no longer used in European countries or in the USA, but some developing countries still use them.

High up in the atmosphere, between 20 km and 35 km above the ground, a gas called **ozone** collects. Ozone has the formula O₃. This

73

Don't confuse CFCs with carbon dioxide. Increasing carbon dioxide is causing global warming, but CFCs damage the ozone layer which doesn't affect the Earth's temperature.

Figure 4.20 How the ozone layer protects us

high-altitude ozone layer helps to protect us from the Sun's ultra-violet (UV) radiation. The ozone stops a large proportion of the UV from reaching the ground. This is good, because UV can cause skin cancers and damage eyes.

But CFCs are harming the ozone layer. CFCs released at ground level drift up through the atmosphere, eventually reaching the ozone layer. They react with the ozone, breaking it down. Less ozone means that more UV reaches the ground.

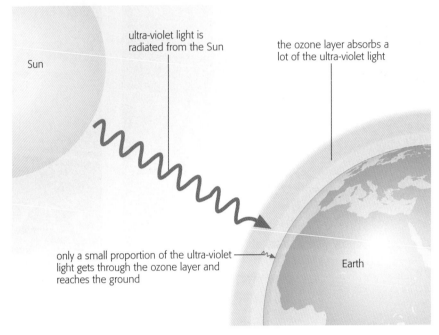

ultra-violet light is radiated from the Sun

the ozone layer absorbs a lot of the ultra-violet light

Sun

only a small proportion of the ultra-violet light gets through the ozone layer and reaches the ground

Earth

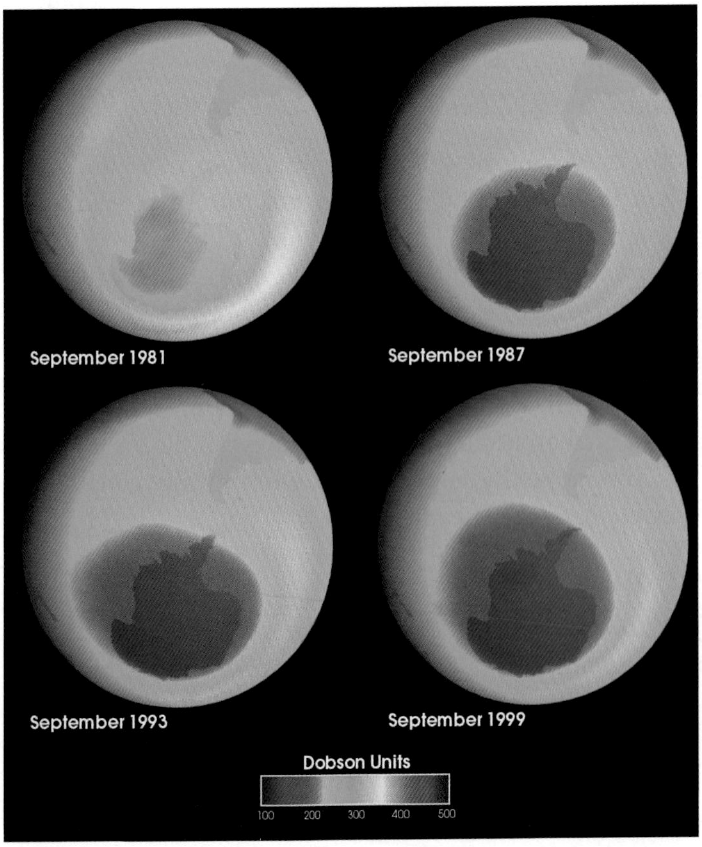

Figure 4.21 The ozone hole over the South Pole has been getting much bigger in recent decades

September 1981

September 1987

September 1993

September 1999

Dobson Units

100   200   300   400   500

The worst effects are over the South Pole. Here, the ozone layer has been so badly damaged that there is an 'ozone hole' – an area where the ozone layer is much thinner than it should be. This 'hole' has been getting bigger and bigger.

People living underneath the ozone hole are at an increased risk of getting skin cancer. Skin cancer happens when UV radiation damages the DNA in skin cells. The most dangerous kind of skin cancer is called melanoma. People with dark skins are not so much at risk as people with light skins, because the dark pigment in the skin absorbs the UV and protects the cells from harm. In Australia, which is close to the ozone hole, light-skinned people are at a high risk of getting melanoma if they do not protect their skins from sunlight. The number of cases of melanoma in Australia is very high compared with other countries (Figure 4.22).

Now that the use of CFCs has been banned, we would expect to see the ozone layer gradually recovering. But it will be a slow process, over several decades, because CFCs are very stable and remain in the atmosphere for a very long time.

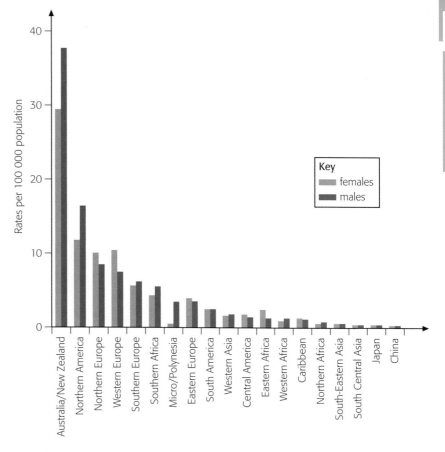

Figure 4.22 The incidence of melanoma in different countries in 2002

Carbon monoxide pollution

Carbon monoxide, CO, is produced by incomplete combustion (burning with insufficient oxygen). Carbon monoxide is present in the exhaust gases from cars and other road vehicles. However, most new vehicles are now fitted with catalytic converters, which cause the carbon monoxide to combine with oxygen and form carbon dioxide. Carbon monoxide is also found in cigarette smoke, so cigarette smokers breathe it into their lungs.

Carbon monoxide is a poisonous gas. It is quickly absorbed into the blood from the alveoli in the lungs. It combines with the haemoglobin inside the red blood cells, taking the place of the oxygen. Worse still, once it has combined, it tends to stay there for a long time. This means that the blood cannot carry as much oxygen as usual. Body cells don't get as much oxygen as they need for respiration, so they cannot release energy from food as efficiently as usual.

If a pregnant woman smokes, the carbon monoxide goes into her baby's blood. So the baby's cells don't get as much oxygen as they should. This can stunt the baby's growth. Women who smoke tend to have smaller babies than women who don't smoke.

Summary

- Water pollution by phosphates, nitrates and untreated sewage can cause algal blooms and eutrophication.
- Sulphur dioxide in the air is harmful to plants and animals, including humans. It can increase the severity of asthma and bronchitis. It also causes acid rain, which can damage plants and aquatic animals.

- Most lichens can only grow where there is little or no sulphur dioxide in the air, so they can be used to indicate how much sulphur dioxide pollution there is in a particular area.
- CFCs damage the ozone layer. This allows harmful ultra-violet radiation from the Sun to reach the ground. Ultra-violet radiation can cause skin cancer and cause damage to eyes.
- The incidence of skin cancer has increased, which is probably related to the loss of ozone in the high parts of the Earth's atmosphere.
- Carbon monoxide combines irreversibly with haemoglobin, reducing the oxygen-carrying capacity of the blood.

Questions

4.6 Copy and complete this table about pollution. If you have forgotten about nitrates and carbon dioxide, you will need to look back at pages 49–54.

Pollutant	Where it comes from	Some of its effects
untreated sewage	houses, factories	causes eutrophication in streams and rivers
nitrates		
phosphates		
carbon dioxide		
sulphur dioxide		
CFCs		
carbon monoxide		

4.7 a Explain how ultra-violet radiation can cause skin cancer.

b How does the high-altitude ozone layer help to protect us from getting skin cancer?

The graph below shows the number of diagnosed cases of skin cancer in Britain between 1975 and 2002.

c Describe the trend in the incidence of skin cancer in women between 1975 and 2002.

d Suggest *two* reasons for this trend.

Figure 4.23 Incidence of malignant melanoma in Britain

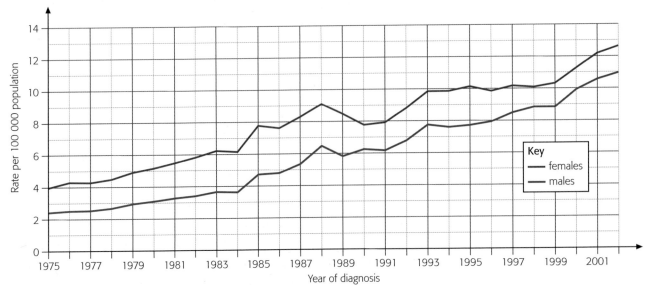

4.8 Explain each of these facts.
   a Lichens can be used to find out how much sulphur dioxide pollution there is.
   b Even if we stop releasing CFCs, the ozone layer won't be repaired for many years.
   c If a pregnant woman smokes cigarettes, her developing baby's blood cannot carry as much oxygen as it should.

D Conservation

Corncrakes are not very colourful birds and are not easily seen. Yet people in the places where they live – which is now mostly in Ireland or the north west of Scotland – have noticed that the birds have become more and more rare. In many places where there used to be corncrakes, they have now disappeared. For example, in Ireland there were tens of thousands of corncrakes around 1900. By 1960, it was estimated there were less than 8000, and by 1993 only about 300 corncrakes were living in Ireland.

Corncrakes live up to their name. They like to spend their time hidden in vegetation (though it doesn't have to be corn), and the males set up an almost incessant croaking in the breeding season. The sound has been compared to two cheese-graters rubbing together! They have become so rare because modern farming methods cut down the vegetation where they hide, feed and breed much earlier in the year than in the past.

Now a lot of work is being done to try to conserve corncrake populations and stop the birds from becoming extinct in Britain. In particular, farmers are being encouraged to leave grass to grow for longer before they cut it to make hay, and to leave more weedy patches in the corners of fields, where the corncrakes can hide in amongst nettles and other tall weeds. This is working. Slowly, slowly the corncrakes are making a comeback.

Figure 4.24 A corncrake

You can hear the sound of a corncrake at
http://avisoft.com/sounds.htm

● Protecting natural populations

There are a lot of us living on our planet. We share it with millions of other species of animals, plants, fungi and single-celled organisms such as bacteria. As our own population grows, we put more and more pressure on many of these other species. Many of them have already become extinct, or are in great danger of this happening, because of the harm we do to their habitats.

We've seen how pollution can kill living things. Another big problem is the loss of habitats – rainforests, wetlands, heathlands and many more. Most animals and plants are adapted to live in a very particular kind of habitat, and if this habitat is destroyed by humans then they have nowhere to live and may become extinct.

Conservation involves protecting natural populations and their habitats. Conservation tries to maintain the **biodiversity** in a habitat – the range of different species that live there. Sometimes it can even increase the biodiversity.

Why is this important? Many people think that conservation is important, but their reasons may not all be the same. For example, some people simply like the idea that they are caring for other species – for example corncrakes, badgers, bats or newts – and just enjoy seeing them around. Others are concerned about the impact on the environment if species are lost. If one species is lost, that can have a big effect on other species that interact with it. Yet another reason is the potential use we might one day make of some species, for example getting medicines from plants growing in rainforests. Overall, many people feel that the Earth will be a better, healthier place to live if we can make it possible for all the other species to live here, too.

The ecosystems with the highest biodiversity on Earth are coral reefs and tropical rainforests.

● Sustainable use of forests

In Britain, there are few if any places that have never been affected by humans. Yet there are still thousands of species of wild plants and animals that live here with us. Many of these species live in forests and woodlands.

People in Britain have been using trees for thousands of years, making tools, carts, boats, houses and furniture from their wood, or burning it for fuel. Trees are a valuable resource for us. It is possible to use trees without permanently damaging woodland habitats. There are several ways in which this can be done.

Reforestation

Where large areas of trees have been cut down in the past, the area can be replanted. Britain used to be covered with forests – mostly deciduous forests in the south, with many beech, oak, ash and lime trees, and coniferous forests in the north, with Scots pine trees. Over the centuries, much of this forest was cut down to make way for agriculture. Now, with more efficient farming methods, there is less need for us to use large areas of land to grow food, so some of these areas have been planted with trees again. Often, you don't even need to plant trees to get the forest back again; if the land is fenced off to keep rabbits and deer out, then tree seeds may just germinate and grow on their own.

Figure 4.25 This area of the Pennines is being reforested

Coppicing

In the past, deciduous woodland was regularly used to provide wood to make charcoal or for building homes or other things. The woodland was divided into several different areas, perhaps seven or eight. Each year, the trees in one section of the wood were cut down to just above ground level, and the wood harvested. Each stump left formed a **coppice stool**, which then gradually regrew. The next year, a different part of the wood was harvested in the same way. Coppicing is a really good way of using woodland in a sustainable way. The trees are never killed – they just regrow after they have

Figure 4.26 These sweet chestnut trees were coppiced a few years ago. They are regrowing from close to the ground, producing several long, straight poles that can be used to make fences

been cut down. And, because only part of the wood is harvested each year, animals and plants still have plenty of habitat to live in. Coppicing can actually *increase* biodiversity in the wood, because there are several different parts of the wood in different stages of regrowth. Where the trees have recently been coppiced, there is a lot of light reaching the woodland floor and plants such as primroses can grow. Where the trees are older, they form the perfect habitat for a different set of species of animals and plants.

Replacement planting

Conifers, unfortunately, do not regrow when they have been cut down. When conifer trees have been harvested, the trees die. If we want to keep the woodland, then new trees must be planted to replace the ones that have been cut down. As in a coppiced woodland, harvesting in conifer woods is least damaging to the habitat if only part of the woodland is felled each year. Animals that were living in the trees that were cut down can move to other parts of the wood – there is still a suitable habitat for them. The areas where the trees have been recently felled will provide a habitat for a different set of plants and animals. Once again, we can actually *increase* biodiversity if trees are harvested carefully.

● Recycling

Another way in which we can harm the habitats of living things is by extracting natural resources. We extract oil from the ground, and use it for fuel and to make plastics. We dig up metal ores and use them to make metals such as iron, steel and titanium. We mine slate and other rocks for building materials. We cut down trees and use the wood to make paper. The list goes on.

Figure 4.27 China clay mine in Cornwall

You may already have read about recycling on pages 133–136 in *GCSE Science*. In a consumer society such as ours, we use large quantities of products every day. The more we use, the more raw materials for them have to be extracted from the environment. Can we reduce this? Can we somehow cut down on the quantity of natural resources that we extract from the environment?

One possible way of doing this is by recycling. For example:

- **paper** can be re-pulped and made into paper again. This avoids having to burn it or allowing it to rot in the ground, and it could perhaps reduce the quantity of trees that are cut down to make paper. However, most of the trees used for making paper have been specially planted. They are used sustainably, so when trees are cut down new ones are planted to replace them. We also have to take into consideration the energy we use in collecting up the waste paper, delivering it to the recycling factory and processing it. The benefit to the environment of recycling paper is perhaps not quite as great as we might initially think.

- **plastics** can also be recycled – or at least some of them can. For example, bottles made from a type of plastic termed PET can be collected and used to make plastic sheeting, fleece garments and other fibres. Once again, we need to balance the costs of the energy used in transport and in the recycling process against the costs of making new plastics. Really, it would be much better if we simply reused the plastic items as they are, rather than making something different from them or just throwing them away.

- **metals**, too, can be recycled. For example, aluminium drink cans can be crushed and made into sheet aluminium that can be used to make other things. It is very expensive to get aluminium from its ore, because the process involves the use of a lot of electrical energy. So by recycling aluminium we not only reduce the damage to the Earth when aluminium ore is extracted from the ground, but also reduce the quantity of fossil fuel used to provide the energy to get it from its ore.

Figure 4.28 Bales of crushed aluminium cans stacked together at a recycling plant. Recycling used cans, used in vast quantities by the soft drink industry, reduces the industry's energy demands

If we don't recycle these materials, then we have to find ways of disposing of them. Much of our household waste goes to **landfill sites**, where it is buried or used to make a large mound to be covered over later. But there are limited amounts of land we can use for landfill, and this in itself can harm the environment.

Another method of waste disposal is **incineration**. Waste paper, plastics and most other waste materials are burned at a very high temperature. However, waste gases are given off by this process, some of which can be harmful.

So recycling not only reduces the quantity of resources that we extract from the Earth, but could also reduce the damage we do to the environment when we dispose of waste.

Summary

- Conservation aims to protect natural populations and to maintain or increase biodiversity.
- Sustainable use of forests can be achieved by management techniques such as coppicing, reforestation or replacement planting.
- Recycling paper, plastics and metals can reduce demand for resources and the problems associated with waste disposal. However, the energy costs of recycling must be balanced against the benefits.

Questions

4.9 Explain what is meant by:
  a biodiversity
  b conservation
  c sustainable use of a resource.

4.10 Explain each of the following.
  a Coppicing can increase biodiversity in a woodland.
  b Recycling paper may *not* reduce pressure on natural woodland habitats.
  c Recycling plastics may help our reserves of fossil fuels to last longer.

Chemistry

5 Synthesis

A Alkanes

Our modern world depends on crude oil, but how was it formed in the first place? The story of oil is thought to begin as far back as 400 million years ago. Billions of tiny plants and animals living in the sea would die each year and fall to the bottom. Here they would become covered in mud. This was important because it meant that oxygen could not reach the dead plants and animals, so bacteria decomposed them anaerobically (without oxygen). More and more layers of mud buried the decaying organisms. Over

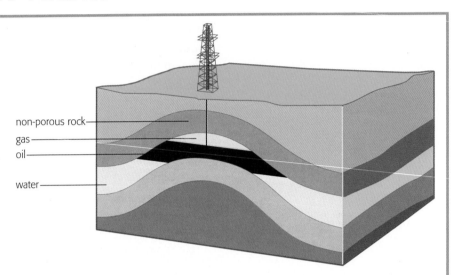

Figure 5.1 A layer of non-porous rock traps oil and gas. The rock looks dome-shaped because it has been folded this way when the Earth's plates have pushed together. This creates an oil reservoir but the oil is not an underground lake, as it is still trapped in the pores of rock

millions of years this mud was transformed into rock. The temperatures rose inside this rock, often to over 100 °C. The pressure was also very high and radioactive substances in the Earth's crust subjected the chemicals that were once sea organisms to radiation. This combination changed the chemicals into the mixture we know as crude oil. Natural gas was formed at the same time.

This mixture was pushed up through pores in the rock. In many cases the oil and gas were trapped by a layer of non-porous rock, waiting for the drill from an oil rig to eventually release it, millions of years later.

● Carbon: the basis of life

Carbon is very unusual because, out of all the elements that have so far been detected in the Universe, it can form strong bonds with itself, as well as with most other elements. Also, carbon forms four bonds, which means that a vast number of carbon compounds exist. More compounds on the Earth contain carbon than any other element. To date, almost nine million carbon compounds have been discovered. Scientists have even detected carbon compounds way out in space. It is carbon's ability to form bonds to itself that means that chains and rings of carbon atoms are possible. This has made carbon the element of life. The structure of the DNA in our genes (see page 3) relies on carbon's ability to form bonds to other carbon atoms. If life exists on other planets, that life will probably be based on carbon atoms.

The branch of chemistry that deals with carbon compounds is often called **organic chemistry**, as originally nearly all carbon compounds known were associated with organisms.

● Alkanes

Crude oil is a mixture of many **hydrocarbon** molecules. Natural gas is also made up of hydrocarbons, mostly methane. But what are these hydrocarbon molecules like? The simplest hydrocarbon is methane, CH_4. You should remember that this **formula** tells you that there are four hydrogen atoms bonded to one carbon atom. We can represent a molecule of methane by building a molecular model of it with balls to represent the atoms and sticks for the bonds (Figure 5.2).

If we had to draw this model of methane each time we talked about methane then it would take us ages. Instead, we change the three-dimensional model into one that is easier to draw on paper. Atoms are represented by element symbols and bonds are drawn as lines (Figure 5.3).

The bond that joins carbon to itself or other atoms is called a **covalent bond**. Covalent bonds usually join atoms of non-metals together.

Methane is a member of a family of chemicals called **alkanes**. The first four members of the alkane family are shown in Table 5.1.

Figure 5.2 A ball and stick model of methane

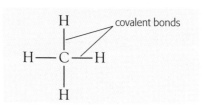

Figure 5.3 This is an easier way to draw a methane molecule

Alkane	Formula	Structure	Ball and stick model
methane	CH_4	H | H—C—H | H	
ethane	C_2H_6	H H | | H—C—C—H | | H H	
propane	C_3H_8	H H H | | | H—C—C—C—H | | | H H H	
butane	C_4H_{10}	H H H H | | | | H—C—C—C—C—H | | | | H H H H	

Table 5.1 The first four members of the alkane family

Table 5.1 on the previous page tells us several things about alkanes.

▸ In these molecules each carbon atom forms four covalent bonds. This is always the case for carbon.
▸ Alkanes are **hydrocarbon** molecules, because they contain only hydrogen and carbon atoms bonded together.
▸ We say that alkanes are **saturated** hydrocarbon molecules because all four covalent bonds are single bonds. The carbon atoms are bonded to the maximum possible number of hydrogen atoms. As you will see later, carbon can sometimes form double covalent bonds. When this occurs we say the molecule is **unsaturated**.

These four alkanes are not the only ones; crude oil can often contain alkane molecules with up to 70 carbon atoms.

> The term 'saturated hydrocarbon' comes from a time when chemists used to add hydrogen to organic molecules. Those molecules that did not react with any more hydrogen were called 'saturated'.

Summary

- Carbon forms more compounds than any other element because it forms strong covalent bonds to itself.
- Covalent bonds are formed between the atoms of non-metal elements.
- Carbon always forms four covalent bonds in compounds.
- Alkanes are saturated hydrocarbons. This means they contain only single covalent bonds in their molecules and the carbon atoms are bonded to the maximum possible number of hydrogen atoms.
- The first four members of the alkane family are:
  - methane, CH_4
  - ethane, C_2H_6
  - propane, C_3H_8
  - butane, C_4H_{10}
- The structures of the alkane molecules can be drawn using lines for the covalent bonds and element symbols for hydrogen and carbon:

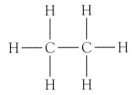

Questions

5.1 Propane is the main molecule in Calor gas. Give its formula and draw its structure.

5.2 Butane is an alkane. Explain what is meant by *alkane*.

5.3 Ethane and methane are both found in natural gas.
  a To what family of compounds do they belong?
  b Why are they called hydrocarbons?
  c Write the formulae of ethane and methane and draw their structures.
  d Methane is the main constituent of natural gas. Write the word equation and the balanced formulae equation for the combustion of methane.

5.4 Pentane and hexane are both alkanes that are found in petrol. Pentane, with the formula C_5H_{12}, is the next member of the alkane family after butane.
  a Draw the structure of pentane and label the covalent bonds.
  b Hexane has six carbon atoms. Predict the formula of hexane.

B Cracking hydrocarbons

Oil has been called *black gold*. This expression was used almost from the sinking of the first oil well in the United States in 1859 and it has perhaps never been more true as the price of a barrel of oil continues to rise. The world's economy has come to rely on this black, sticky liquid that is pumped from the ground. But how long will the oil last?

Until recently it has been rare for governments to discuss openly what will happen when oil production begins to decline. A scientist, Dr M. King Hubbert, produced one model to predict when oil production will start to fall, called Hubbert's Curve. So what is Hubbert's Curve and why is it important today?

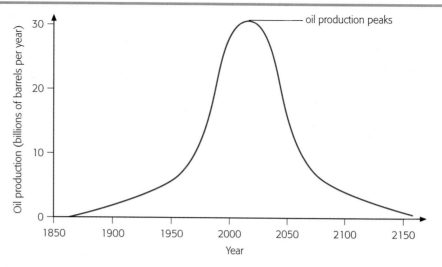

Figure 5.4 This bell-shaped curve was proposed by Dr Hubbert in 1956. Some scientists think his predicted peak in oil production will be reached around 2010

Hubbert's Curve is a graph that suggests there will be a peak in oil production and after this there will be a decline (Figure 5.4). This may seem rather obvious, but not all scientists agree with Hubbert's model. These other scientists suggest that there will continue to be a steady growth in oil production as new oil fields are discovered and new technologies are used to pump more oil out of existing oil fields. However, the worldwide demand for oil continues to increase as more countries, such as China and India, develop their own industries and older industrialised nations, such as the United States and Great Britain, fail to slow down their demand for oil.

The world used an average of 84.3 million barrels of oil a day in 2005. This works out as 976 barrels per second and, as a barrel contains 159 litres, this means that the world uses 155 000 litres of oil in one second. Oil reserves must have a limit, but the problem is that no one really knows exactly how much oil is left. Since 2004 we have not found enough new oil to match the amount we are taking out of the known reserves. Also, the new oil finds are becoming smaller and more difficult to extract. In Great Britain, North Sea oil production has been declining steadily since 1999.

So what of Hubbert's Curve? One thing we do know is that he used it to predict that oil production in the United States would peak in 1970, and he was correct. Other scientists are using Hubbert's Curve to suggest that the peak in world oil production is almost upon us. Once that peak is reached, and some say that will be by 2010, the future for the world is a lot less certain. We will look at some of the consequences of an oil shortage later in this chapter (page 90).

● Using all the fractions from crude oil

As much as 90% of the oil that comes out of the ground is burnt as fuel. The rest is used to make most of our everyday chemical products, from paint to medicines and from cosmetics to textiles. If we consider petrol, 30–40% of a barrel of oil goes to making this fuel for cars. However, when crude oil is fractionally distilled much less than this comes off in the petrol fraction (Figure 5.5, overleaf). This means that the supply of petrol from fractional distillation does not meet demand.

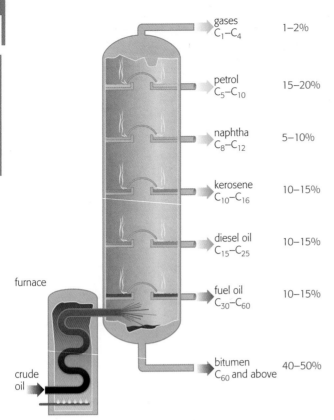

gases
C_1–C_4 1–2%

petrol
C_5–C_{10} 15–20%

naphtha
C_8–C_{12} 5–10%

kerosene
C_{10}–C_{16} 10–15%

diesel oil
C_{15}–C_{25} 10–15%

fuel oil
C_{30}–C_{60} 10–15%

bitumen
C_{60} and above   40–50%

furnace

crude oil

Figure 5.5 When oil is fractionally distilled in a fractionating column, there are not enough of some fractions, such as the petrol fraction, to meet demand

Petrol is made mostly from alkanes containing five to ten carbon atoms. This is where **cracking** comes in. Cracking is the breaking down of larger hydrocarbon molecules into smaller ones. We don't need all the larger hydrocarbon molecules in crude oil because the demand for these is much less than the supply. It is these larger molecules that can be cracked to produce the smaller molecules we burn as petrol.

Let's look at an alkane containing 12 carbon atoms. This can be broken down to make smaller molecules (Figure 5.6).

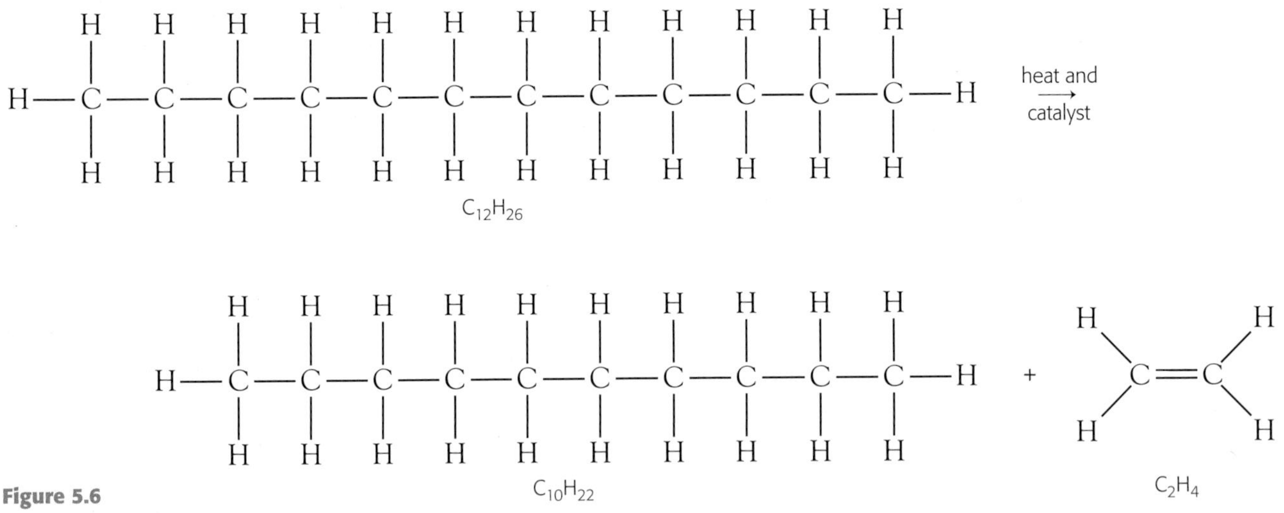

$C_{12}H_{26}$ heat and catalyst →

Figure 5.6 $C_{10}H_{22}$ + C_2H_4

Decane, $C_{10}H_{22}$, can now be used in petrol. However, look at the other molecule produced, C_2H_4. This has a *double* covalent bond, which makes it much more reactive and useful for making other chemicals. The molecule is called ethene (Figure 5.7).

Ethene, like decane, is a hydrocarbon, but decane is an alkane and all its bonds are single covalent bonds. Decane is therefore a saturated hydrocarbon. Ethene belongs to a different hydrocarbon family, called the **alkenes**, and because it has a double covalent bond it is an **unsaturated hydrocarbon**. When alkanes are cracked, mixtures of alkanes and alkenes are formed.

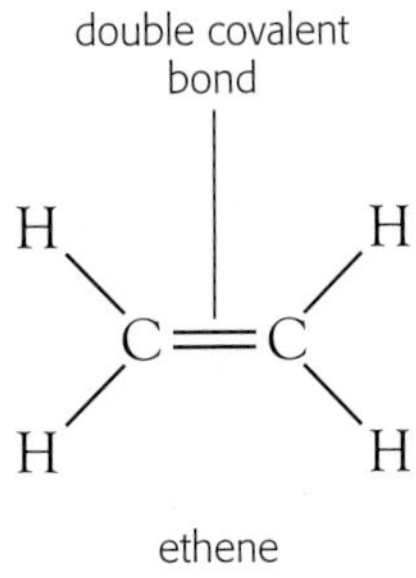

double covalent bond

ethene

Figure 5.7

Figure 5.8 Cracking alkanes in the laboratory

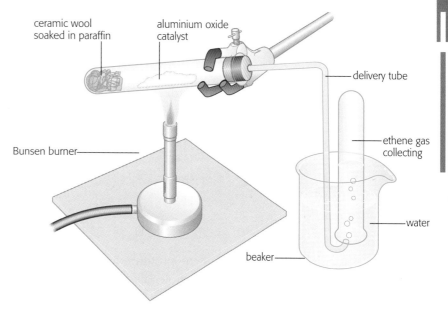

ceramic wool soaked in paraffin

aluminium oxide catalyst

delivery tube

ethene gas collecting

Bunsen burner

water

beaker

Figure 5.9 A cracker in an oil refinery

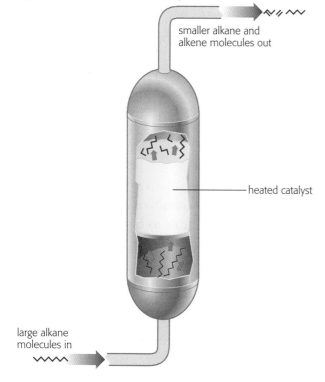

smaller alkane and alkene molecules out

heated catalyst

large alkane molecules in

We can crack hydrocarbons in the laboratory to produce smaller molecules using the apparatus in Figure 5.8 above. The catalyst we use here is aluminium oxide. **Catalysts** speed up chemical reactions. Paraffin is a mixture of larger alkanes and they are cracked to make smaller alkanes and alkenes. The gas that is produced is mainly ethene.

Cracking is a very important reaction at oil refineries, producing smaller, more useful alkanes for use as fuels and also producing alkenes (Figure 5.9).

● Alkenes

Ethene, C_2H_4, is the first member of the alkene family. The next member is also produced in cracking reactions. It is called propene, C_3H_6. Its structure is shown in Table 5.2 below.

Table 5.2 The first two alkenes

Alkene	Formula	Structure	Ball and stick model
ethene	C_2H_4		
propene	C_3H_6		

Figure 5.10 Bromine water has been used to test whether the gas in the jar is an alkene. The decolourisation, which is immediate, shows that it is

The state symbol for liquid is (l) and for solid is (s).

The phosphoric acid catalyst, the high temperature and the pressure of 60 atmospheres are all conditions chosen to speed up the reaction. See Chapter 8 for more about speeding up reactions.

It is the '**-ene**' part of prop**ene** and eth**ene** that tells you that there is a double bond. This is the reactive part of the molecule.

A way to tell if you have an alkane or an alkene is to use bromine water. Bromine water is yellow but if an alkene is present it turns colourless immediately. The bromine reacts with the double bond in the alkene. Alkanes will not turn bromine colourless.

$$C_2H_4 \quad + \quad Br_2 \quad \rightarrow \quad C_2H_4Br_2$$

If the bromine water turns colourless immediately, this means that the molecule being tested is unsaturated. Look at the equation above: when ethene reacts it becomes saturated, with every bond a single bond. This is called an **addition** reaction, because one molecule has added to another to make a single product.

Chemists often add **state symbols** to balanced formulae equations. These tell what state of matter each substance is in. Ethene is a gas so this is shown with (g). Bromine is dissolved in water and this means it is aqueous and is given the state symbol (aq). The product ($C_2H_4Br_2$) stays dissolved in the water so it is also aqueous. We can re-write the balanced formulae equation using these state symbols:

$$C_2H_4(g) + Br_2(aq) \rightarrow C_2H_4Br_2(aq)$$

The double bond in alkenes makes them reactive. It is this reactivity that is used by chemists to make the thousands of organic chemicals on which we rely. When we make chemicals using chemical reactions we often call the reactions **synthesis** reactions.

Making ethanol from ethene

We have already mentioned that cracking reactions produce alkanes and alkenes. It is the double bond in the alkenes that makes them such important molecules. One important synthesis reaction is the reaction to make ethanol from ethene using water (as steam). Ethanol is the alcohol that is found in alcoholic drinks but when it is made for industry it is usually made from ethene. It is a very useful solvent, and is found in many products, from cosmetics to printing inks. Ethanol is also used to make other very important organic chemicals.

$$C_2H_4 \quad + \quad H_2O \text{ (steam)} \xrightarrow[\text{60 atmospheres}]{\text{300 °C, phosphoric acid catalyst}} C_2H_5OH \text{ (ethanol)}$$

This is also an addition reaction because the molecules of ethene and water combine to produce a single product.

Hydrogenating vegetable oils

Vegetable oils are liquids. Olive oil, soya oil and sunflower oil are examples of vegetable oils. A vegetable oil molecule has *three* hydrocarbon chains in it. If there are no double bonds in the hydrocarbon chains then the oil is **saturated**. If there is one double bond then the oil is **monounsaturated**. If the chains contain two or more double bonds then the oil is **polyunsaturated**. The more double bonds in the oil molecules the runnier they are. Saturated oils are very **viscous** (thick, the opposite of runny). This is because the chains can lie straighter and there are more forces, holding the molecules together. The more double bonds there are the more uneven the shape of the molecules. This means that there is less force between the molecules, and so they are less viscous (more runny).

> The fewer the number of double bonds in the hydrocarbon chains of fats and oils, the higher the melting point. This is for the same reason that viscosity increases with fewer double bonds. The chains are less kinked and the molecules have more forces between them.

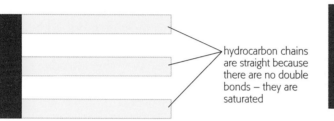

Figure 5.11 A saturated vegetable oil molecule has straight hydrocarbon chains so the forces between the molecules are strong

Figure 5.12 A polyunsaturated vegetable oil molecule has kinks in the hydrocarbon chains. The molecules cannot line up very well so there is less force between them

Changing oils into fats

Oils, as we have seen, are liquids. **Fats** have the same type of molecule in them but they are solids. Fats are usually saturated. Examples of fats are cheese and butter. Oils can often be changed into fats simply by removing some of their double bonds. This is done by the addition of hydrogen and the process is called **hydrogenation**.

We make **hydrogenated vegetable oil** (fat) by bubbling hydrogen into the vegetable oil. A catalyst, usually nickel, speeds up the hydrogenation reactions.

Figure 5.13 This reaction is the addition of hydrogen to a double bond in the hydrocarbon chain to produce hydrogenated vegetable oil or fat

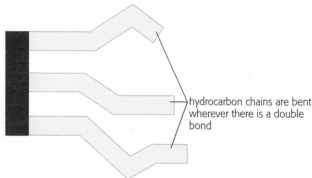

Why would we want hydrogenated vegetable oils and fats? If we go back in history to 1869, this was when vegetable oils were first made into margarine. We prefer to spread fat onto our bread rather than dip bread in liquid oil; we believe it tastes nicer and has a more pleasant texture. The problem was that many people were moving from the countryside to the towns and cities. It became more difficult to store and transport butter, so there was a butter shortage. The hydrogenation of vegetable oils to make margarine filled this gap.

Margarine also had a big advantage. It would last much longer than vegetable oils before it started to go rancid. The reason for this again lies with the double bond between the carbon atoms. These double bonds react with oxygen in the air causing the oils to turn rancid. If the double bonds are saturated with hydrogen the hydrocarbon chains are much less reactive. Food manufacturers have long used hydrogenated oils to extend the shelf-life of food products. Hydrogenated vegetable oils occur in many processed foods, such as ready meals, chocolate and pies.

Figure 5.14 This out-of-town shopping centre, The Metro Centre at Gateshead, is one of the largest in Europe. It is connected by rail and bus but most of the thousands who visit it each day come by car

● What will happen when oil begins to run out?

At the start of this section we talked about the production of oil reaching a peak (page 85). Many scientists believe we are now close to the peak in world oil production. If there is a peak this must be followed by a decline. So what will be the consequences when this happens? We have already said that our world depends on the supply of cheap energy that using oil offers. We have also become reliant on the many chemicals that we make from the alkenes produced from cracking.

Consider for a moment the UK – the way of life of most people revolves around the car. People travel to supermarkets that are often out of town, people often work long distances away from their homes and many families enjoy the freedom that owning a car provides. Petrol prices will continue to rise and the way of life we have become used to will become increasingly difficult to afford. So using our cars less will be one consequence of an oil shortage. We are dependent on oil in many other ways:

◗ Most of our food and other goods are transported to shops and supermarkets by lorries and vans, which are fuelled by diesel.
◗ If you think about agriculture, which supplies our food, we find that diesel is used to power the machines that plough the fields, plant the seeds and harvest the crops.
◗ The crops then have to be transported to where they are processed into the foods we buy.
◗ The very processing itself, whether it is the grinding of corn or the baking of bread, also relies on energy from fossil fuels.
◗ The fertilisers farmers use to increase crop production also depend on fossil fuels, such as oil, to provide the energy to make them.
◗ Then there are the many chemicals that we use, ranging from polymers in clothes to detergents, paints and medicines.
◗ The power to heat our homes and produce our electricity is often supplied by crude oil.

As a nation, we are almost totally dependent on the supply of cheap crude oil. But what about the rest of the world?

- Tensions between nations over dwindling oil supplies may spill out into wars.
- Less-developed countries will find it increasingly difficult to afford to buy the oil that richer countries can afford.

As you can see, the world clearly cannot **sustain** (keep going into the future) the way we are using oil at the moment. This is why people and governments are beginning to discuss and plan for **sustainable development**. 'Sustainable development' involves balancing the need for economic development, decent standards of living and respect for the environment, so that resources are available for future generations. A very famous French author, Saint-Expuréy, once wrote: 'We do not inherit the Earth from our parents, we borrow it from our children.' We have to search for alternative ways of living that preserve oil stocks, and do not contribute to global warming. We need to re-use products rather than use energy and the Earth's resources to make new products.

Summary

- Cracking is the breaking down of larger hydrocarbon molecules to make smaller, more useful ones.
- When alkanes are cracked, mixtures of alkanes and alkenes are formed.
- Alkenes are unsaturated hydrocarbons containing double covalent bonds, which make them very reactive.
- Ethene and propene

  are alkenes.
- Bromine water turns immediately from yellow to colourless with alkenes. This is a way of distinguishing alkenes from alkanes, as the bromine water remains yellow with alkanes.
- The reaction between bromine water and alkenes is an addition reaction, where two molecules join together to make a single product:

  $$C_2H_4 + Br_2 \rightarrow C_2H_4Br_2$$

- State symbols can be added to equations so that you know what state the reactants and products are in: (g) = gaseous, (aq) = aqueous (dissolved in water), (l) = liquid, (s) = solid. So the equation for the addition of bromine to ethene is:

  $$C_2H_4(g) + Br_2(aq) \rightarrow C_2H_4Br_2(aq)$$

- Ethene can be reacted with water, in the form of steam, to make ethanol. Ethanol is the alcohol found in alcoholic drinks, but it is also a very important industrial solvent:

  $$C_2H_4 + H_2O \xrightarrow[\text{60 atmospheres}]{\text{300 °C, phosphoric acid catalyst}} C_2H_5OH$$

- Saturated oils have no double bonds in their hydrocarbon chains; monounsaturated oils contain one double bond; polyunsaturated oils contain two or more double bonds.
- Polyunsaturated oils are less viscous than saturated ones because the double bonds in the hydrocarbon chains cause them to kink, so that they cannot line up beside other molecules. This means there are less forces between the molecules of polyunsaturated oils.
- Vegetable oils can be hydrogenated, by adding hydrogen molecules to the double bonds. Hydrogenated vegetable oils and fats (which are solids) have an increased shelf-life. They are used in many food products, from chocolate to pastry crusts.
- Our modern society depends on crude oil and its products. When the oil begins to run out our lives could change dramatically.
- Sustainable development involves balancing the need for economic development, decent standards of living and respect for the environment, so that resources are available for future generations.

Questions

5.5 There is never enough petrol in the petrol fraction to satisfy demand.

   a What process is used to produce smaller hydrocarbon molecules from larger ones?

   b One possible reaction involves breaking down the molecule dodecane, $C_{12}H_{26}$, in this reaction:

     i The molecule containing nine carbon atoms is called nonane. Why is this a saturated molecule?

     ii How many carbon atoms are there in the molecule that is not shown?

     iii Draw the structure of the missing molecule and name it.

     iv What chemical test could you use to tell the difference between these two molecules?

5.6 a Draw the structure of a molecule of ethene.

   b Why is ethene more reactive than ethane?

   c When ethene reacts with bromine water the reaction is called an addition reaction.

     i Explain what *addition reaction* means.

     ii Write the balanced formulae equation for this reaction. Include state symbols.

   d Explain how ethene can be reacted with water to make ethanol. Include in your answer a balanced formulae equation.

5.7 a Vegetable oils may be polyunsaturated. What does *polyunsaturated* mean?

b Why are polyunsaturated oils far less viscous than saturated ones?

c Sometimes vegetable oils are hydrogenated.
 i What does *hydrogenated* mean?
 ii Use the internet to research *one* use of hydrogenated vegetable oil in food manufacture.

5.8 Think about one day in your life. Now write about how this day would change when crude oil begins to run out.

C Polymers

One of the problems with many of the plastics that are made from oil is that they do not decompose in the ground like other organic molecules do. The molecules are just too big and the bonds between the atoms too strong for bacteria and other decomposing organisms to work on them and break them down. We say that these plastics are **non-biodegradable**. We make so many articles from plastics these days; most of the plastics we throw away end up in landfill sites and could take hundreds of years to break down.

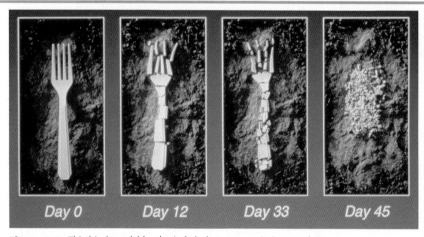

Figure 5.15 This biodegradable plastic fork decomposes in just 45 days

In 1990 a UK chemical manufacturer began making a biodegradable plastic, called Biopol. This plastic is actually made by a particular species of bacteria called *Alcaligenes eutrophus*. It makes globules of the plastic to store energy, in the same way that we make fat to store our energy from food. The food the bacterium uses in the manufacturing process is carbohydrates from wheat and the reactions take place in giant fermentation vats. Up to 80% of the dry weight of this bacterium is plastic.

For a time there was great interest in this product. Wella used it for some of their shampoo bottles and Greenpeace, the environmental group, used it for their affinity credit card. The issue, however, was price. Biopol was about five times more expensive to make than conventional plastics made from crude oil, so it did not take off in the way the manufacturer had hoped.

With the advent of genetic engineering, a biotechnology company decided to see if it could transfer the plastic-making gene into wheat plants and other

bacteria. This holds out the prospect of fields of growing plastic. However, opponents say that we can already produce biodegradable plastic with natural bacteria, so why use genetic manipulation to do the same job?

There is now another way to make this plastic. We throw away millions of tonnes of food each year from canteens and restaurants. Bacteria can be used to make this waste food into plastic in much the same way as Biopol was originally manufactured. The huge advantage is that most of this food would go into landfill sites, producing methane (a greenhouse gas) when it decomposes. Instead, this new process makes the food into a useful plastic. For every 100 tonnes of waste food that is processed in this way, 25 tonnes of plastic can be produced. It is also cheaper to manufacture than the original Biopol.

And what is produced when biodegradable plastic decomposes? Only carbon dioxide and water, and the carbon dioxide produced is no more than was originally used when the plants made the carbohydrates on which the bacteria feed.

Figure 5.16 This early 20th century kitchen didn't contain any plastics. Items of metal and wood were used instead

Figure 5.17 Thousands of small monomers bond together to make a polymer

'Poly-' means 'many'. 'Mono-' means 'one'. Polymers are made up of many monomers.

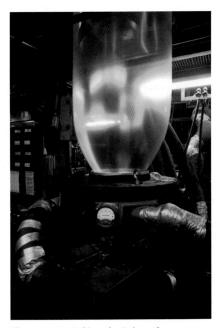

Figure 5.18 Making plastic bags from poly(ethene)

● What is a polymer?

If you could go back in time 100 years there would be no plastics in your home. The plastics that have revolutionised many of the products we take for granted were just not available. Just take a look around your kitchen and see how many items are made from plastic.

Plastics are made from very long molecules called **polymers**. Polymers are long-chain molecules made from hundreds of smaller molecules joined together. The small molecules that make up a polymer are called **monomers**. When monomers react together to form polymers the reaction is called **polymerisation**.

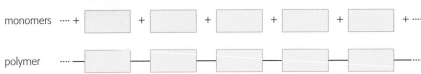

Ethene and poly(ethene)

Poly(ethene), or polythene as we usually call it, had a huge influence on the 20th century. To give just one example, it is the polymer that is used to make supermarket plastic bags.

The discovery of poly(ethene) occurred by accident way back in 1933. Two chemists, Eric Fawcett and Reginald Gibson, working for the UK chemical manufacturer ICI, were doing experiments with ethene when they discovered a white waxy solid. They had made poly(ethene). They tried to repeat the experiment they had been doing, but the mixture exploded. It was two years before they attempted the reaction again, this time with vessels that could withstand the high pressures of an explosion. Eventually a safe way to make poly(ethene) in bulk was found. The equation for the reaction is shown here:

ethene

high pressure

part of the poly(ethene) polymer

Notice the following:

- ethene is the monomer
- the reactive double bonds break to join the ethene monomers together
- this is an **addition polymerisation** because the monomers join (add) together to produce a single product
- we call poly(ethene) an **addition polymer**
- we can only show a small section of the polymer chain here – the dots at both ends show that this is only a part of a much longer molecule.

There is a more convenient way of writing this reaction:

$$n \quad \begin{matrix} H \\ \diagdown \\ C \end{matrix} = \begin{matrix} H \\ C \diagup \\ \end{matrix} \quad \longrightarrow \quad \left(\begin{matrix} H & H \\ | & | \\ C - C \\ | & | \\ H & H \end{matrix} \right)_n$$

'n' is used to show that a large number of monomers join together.

More addition polymers

To make an addition polymer, the monomer must have a carbon–carbon double bond, so it is called an **unsaturated monomer**.

Poly(ethene), made from ethene, was the first addition polymer to be discovered. Other unsaturated monomers can be used to make addition polymers. For example, propene can be used to make poly(propene):

$$\cdots + \begin{matrix} CH_3 \\ \diagdown \\ C \\ \diagup \\ H \end{matrix} = \begin{matrix} H \\ C \\ \diagdown \\ H \end{matrix} + \begin{matrix} CH_3 \\ \diagdown \\ C \\ \diagup \\ H \end{matrix} = \begin{matrix} H \\ C \\ \diagdown \\ H \end{matrix} + \begin{matrix} CH_3 \\ \diagdown \\ C \\ \diagup \\ H \end{matrix} = \begin{matrix} H \\ C \\ \diagdown \\ H \end{matrix} + \cdots$$

propene monomers

$$\longrightarrow \cdots - \begin{matrix} CH_3 & H & CH_3 & H & CH_3 & H \\ | & | & | & | & | & | \\ C - C - C - C - C - C \\ | & | & | & | & | & | \\ H & H & H & H & H & H \end{matrix} - \cdots$$

poly(propene)

$$n \quad \begin{matrix} CH_3 \\ \diagdown \\ C \end{matrix} = \begin{matrix} H \\ C \diagup \\ \end{matrix} \quad \longrightarrow \quad \left(\begin{matrix} CH_3 & H \\ | & | \\ C - C \\ | & | \\ H & H \end{matrix} \right)_n$$

Poly(propene) is stronger than poly(ethene). It is also more hard wearing and is used to make ropes, carpets, the plastic part of school chairs that you sit on, crates and bottles.

PVC is another addition monomer. 'Vinyl chloride' is the old name for the monomer and the polymer was called **poly(vinyl chloride)**, hence the name PVC, which we still use today.

An **addition polymer** is made when monomers join together to form one product – the long-chain polymer.

Remember: molecules containing carbon–carbon double bonds are called **unsaturated**. When all the bonds in the molecule are single bonds the molecule is called **saturated**.

We use 'CH$_3$' in the propene molecule as a shorthand way of drawing

$$\begin{matrix} H \\ | \\ H - C - H \end{matrix}$$

Figure 5.19 The plastic in these school chairs is poly(propene)

The addition reaction is:

chloroethene
(old name 'vinyl chloride')

poly(chloroethene),
better known as PVC

PVC is very hard-wearing and strong. It has a large number of uses.

- The electric cables in your home are probably covered with it, and it is also used in electric sockets and plugs.
- Any plastic curtain tracks you have will be made from it.
- If your windows and doors are plastic, these will also be PVC.
- Plastic guttering is made from PVC, and so is artificial leather.

Figure 5.20 PVC is used to make many parts of a modern house, such as doors, window frames and guttering

'Polystyrene' is another old name that has stuck. The monomer was originally called 'styrene'.

phenylethene
(old name 'styrene')

poly(phenylethene),
better known as
polystyrene

Polystyrene is used to make yoghurt pots and plant pots. If gas is blown into it then it is known as 'expanded polystyrene' and is used to make insulation and the soft white packaging used around fragile items.

These are only some of the monomers that can be used to make addition polymers. You will be expected to draw a section of polymer when given the structure of the monomer and vice versa. Chemists often need to work out the products of reactions given the reactants and products of similar reactions.

Once chemists knew how addition polymers were made, they set about making new ones by changing some of the hydrogen atoms on ethene for other atoms and groups of atoms (Figure 5.21).

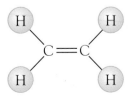

Figure 5.21 Any of these hydrogen atoms can be replaced by other atoms or groups of atoms to make a whole range of addition polymers

Thermoplastic and thermosetting polymers

The polymers we have so far discussed are **thermoplastic** polymers. This means that they can be melted and moulded again many times. The reason this can happen becomes clear when we look at the molecular structure of polymer chains (Figure 5.22).

Figure 5.22 Thermoplastic polymers have only weak forces holding their chains together

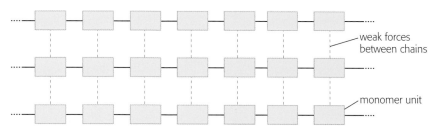

There are weak forces between these polymer chains, which keep them in the solid state. When heat is applied the chains can move over one another allowing the polymer to be moulded into something different.

The fact that these polymers can be melted and re-moulded into new articles means that they can be recycled. This is not true of **thermosetting** polymers, which can be moulded only when they are first produced. A thermosetting polymer has cross-links between the polymer chains. These cross-links are very strong (Figure 5.23) and heating will not allow the sheets to move over one another. The thermosetting polymer decomposes rather than melts.

Figure 5.23 Thermosetting polymers have strong cross-links between their chains

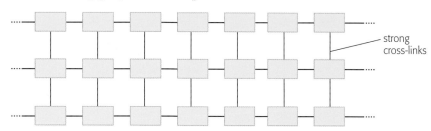

Changing the properties of polymers

We have already seen one way to change the properties of a polymer, which is to change the starting materials. Poly(ethene) is made up from ethene monomers. If one of the hydrogen atoms is swapped for a chlorine atom in the monomer then the plastic made is PVC (Figure 5.24).

Figure 5.24 Changing the starting material from ethene to chloroethene changes the properties of the polymer produced

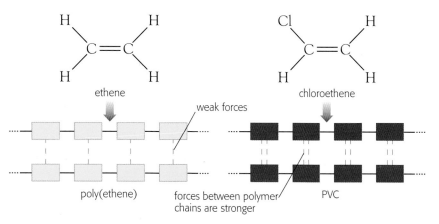

It is the chlorine atom that helps make PVC such a versatile polymer. For a start the chlorine atom makes the forces between the

polymer chains much stronger and this is what makes PVC so much stronger and harder than poly(ethene).

However, the presence of the chlorine atom also helps PVC to mix with various **additives**. Additives are substances that are added to plastics to alter their properties. **Plasticisers** are added to PVC to allow the polymer chains to move over each other more easily. This makes the plastic more flexible and so increases the range of uses of PVC, so that PVC is the second most produced plastic in the world each year after poly(ethene). The more plasticiser that is added the more flexible the PVC produced.

Plasticisers are not the only additives that are added to PVC. **Preservatives** can be added to lengthen its useful life. These might be antioxidants, which prevent oxygen in the air reacting with the polymer, or they might be stabilisers, which make PVC more resistant to being broken down by ultra-violet light or high temperatures.

Another additive that can be used is one that will form cross-links between the chains. This stops the chains moving over one another. This increases the melting point and often it produces a thermosetting plastic that can only be melted and moulded once.

There is another way to change the properties of some plastics and that is to alter the conditions of the reaction in which they are made. When poly(ethene) was first manufactured, the conditions of the reaction were very high pressure with a trace of oxygen. This produced polymer chains with lots of branches (Figure 5.26). The chains could therefore not lie close together, which gave the poly(ethene) particular properties.

▶ The density was low because the branching kept the chains apart.
▶ The melting point was fairly low, about 130 °C; the chains could not line up, so reducing the forces between them.
▶ It softened in boiling water; articles would go out of shape easily because the chains were able to move over one another at quite low temperatures.

This form of poly(ethene) is known as **low-density poly(ethene)**. Today it is used for supermarket carrier bags, dustbin liners and for electrical insulation.

By changing the reaction conditions, a German chemist called Karl Ziegler was able to make unbranched polymer chains that could line up next to each other (Figure 5.27). The conditions he used

Where strength and hardness are required, such as in plastic doors and window frames, uPVC is used. The 'u' stands for unplasticised.

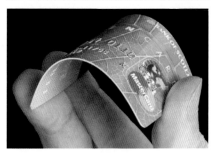

Figure 5.25 What makes this credit card flexible (bendy) is that it is made from PVC with added plasticiser

Figure 5.26 In low density poly(ethene) the chains are branched and so cannot line up close together

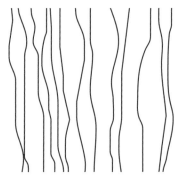

Figure 5.27 Unbranched chains can line up close together in high density poly(ethene)

> A catalyst speeds up chemical reactions.

were a catalyst and atmospheric pressure. The catalyst he used was a titanium compound. Because the chains could lie close together the properties of the poly(ethene) were changed.

▶ The polymer was harder.
▶ The melting point was higher.
▶ It did not soften in boiling water.

The polymer is called **high-density poly(ethene)**. It is used for food storage containers, buckets, washing-up bowls and car petrol tanks.

Disposing of plastics

At the start of this section we looked at Biopol, a polymer produced from bacteria. This is one of a number of **biopolymers** that have been developed. Biopolymers have two important characteristics.

▶ They are not manufactured from a fossil fuel that will one day run out.
▶ They are biodegradable, which means that they can be broken down in the environment by bacteria and other decomposer organisms.

The problem with plastics made from crude oil is that decomposer organisms cannot easily break them down – they are **non-biodegradable**. Most of them end up in landfill sites. So what are the alternatives?

▶ We could recycle them, but there are real issues here. It costs a lot of money to sort the different plastics from household waste. At the moment we just do not have the necessary technology to sort the different plastics easily and make recycling them an economic proposition.
▶ We could bury plastic waste separately. This would have the advantage that one day we might be easily able to sort the different plastics from the mixed plastic waste we started with.
▶ We could burn the plastics to provide energy to make electricity. The issue here is that burning some plastics gives off toxic gases such as hydrogen chloride.

There is another issue with leaving some plastics to degrade in the ground. Some of the chemicals that may be produced could be toxic, leaving us with yet another environmental problem to confront.

Summary

- Polymers are large molecules formed from many small molecules, called monomers, joining together.
- An addition polymer is made when unsaturated monomers join together to form one product, the long-chain polymer.
- A typical example of an addition polymer is poly(ethene):

$$n \quad \begin{array}{c} H \\ \diagdown \\ C = C \\ \diagup \\ H \end{array} \begin{array}{c} H \\ \diagup \\ \diagdown \\ H \end{array} \quad \longrightarrow \quad \left(\begin{array}{cc} H & H \\ | & | \\ C - C \\ | & | \\ H & H \end{array} \right)_n$$

'n' is used to show that a large number of monomers join together.

● Once you know how ethene reacts to make poly(ethene), it is possible to predict the products of similar reactions such as propene forming poly(propene):

$$n \quad \underset{H}{\overset{CH_3}{}} C = C \underset{H}{\overset{H}{}} \quad \longrightarrow \quad \left(\underset{H}{\overset{CH_3}{}} C - C \underset{H}{\overset{H}{}} \right)_n$$

● Thermoplastic polymers can be melted and re-moulded many times.
● Thermosetting polymers have cross-links between their chains, which means they can be melted and moulded only once.
● The properties of a polymer can be altered by:
 – changing the starting materials
 – changing the conditions of the reaction
 – mixing the polymer with additives such as plasticisers, preservatives and chemicals that form cross-links between the polymer chains.
● Most plastics are made from fossil fuels, particularly crude oil. They are usually non-biodegradable and some may break down into toxic products.
● It is not yet economic to separate out plastic waste from homes so most of this is either buried in landfill sites or incinerated (burnt) to provide electricity.

Questions

5.9 'Teflon' is the polymer used in non-stick frying pans. It was discovered by accident by Roy Plunkett in 1938.
 a What does *polymer* mean?
 b What properties would Teflon need to have to make it a useful polymer to choose for coating frying pans?
 c Another name for Teflon is PTFE. It is used in PTFE tape by plumbers to make joints in water pipes watertight. What properties would be necessary for this polymer to be useful for plumbers' tape?
 d A section of the PTFE polymer looks like this:

$$\cdots - \underset{F}{\overset{F}{C}} - \underset{F}{\overset{F}{C}} - \underset{F}{\overset{F}{C}} - \underset{F}{\overset{F}{C}} - \underset{F}{\overset{F}{C}} - \underset{F}{\overset{F}{C}} - \cdots$$

 What is the structure of the monomer?
 e Why is this monomer called unsaturated?
 f Teflon is a thermoplastic polymer. What does *thermoplastic* mean?
5.10 More poly(ethene) is made each year than any other polymer.
 a What is the name and formula of the monomer that produces poly(ethene)?
 b Draw a section of the polymer chain of poly(ethene) showing three repeating units.
 c Poly(ethene) is an addition polymer. Explain what is meant by *addition polymer*.

d There are two types of poly(ethene) that can be manufactured and they have different properties.

  i What are these two types of poly(ethene) called?

  ii Explain why the properties of these two types of poly(ethene) are different.

e Poly(ethene) is non-biodegradable.

  i What does *non-biodegradable* mean?

  ii Why is this an environmental problem?

5.11 PVC has many uses in the home.

  a Give *three* products in your home that are made from PVC.

  b The monomer for making PVC is

  Write a balanced formula equation for the manufacture of PVC.

  c The properties of PVC can be altered by using additives.

   i What does *additives* mean?

   ii One of the additives used is a plasticiser. What properties does the plasticiser give to PVC?

  d Use the internet to discover why some plasticisers in PVC have been banned by the European Union.

D Synthesising new substances

Drug test nightmare

Drug test man's brain on fire

Disaster in drug test

At 8a.m. on Monday 13 March 2006, six healthy men were injected with a drug. Within minutes they were screaming in agony and soon after their organs began to shut down. They were rushed to an intensive care ward in critical conditions. It was doubtful whether they would survive the night. In fact, all the volunteers survived their terrifying ordeal but why were these healthy men injected with a drug in the first place? When any new drug is developed it goes through a number of stages. One of these stages is to inject healthy volunteers with very dilute amounts of the drug to see if there are any serious side-effects. Before this happens the drugs are tested on animals to see if there are any dangerous reactions. No dangerous reactions with this drug were discovered in the laboratory animals, so it was considered safe to test it on human volunteers.

The drug in this trial was designed to help cure diseases such as leukaemia and rheumatoid arthritis. In both these diseases the body's immune system starts attacking its own tissue, destroying it. Finding a drug that stops this would have been a real breakthrough.

An investigation into this particular trial showed that the drug-testing procedure followed UK Government guidelines and that a reaction such as this was completely unexpected and extremely rare. The next stage after this would have been to go to large clinical trials, where hundreds of patients with these diseases would have been tested. Without the help of the healthy volunteers many more people may have been badly affected.

● Clinical trials

As you learnt from the box on the previous page, before a drug can be sold as an effective medicine to cure disease it has to go through a number of testing stages, called phases. When the drug is tested on humans the phases are called **clinical trials**.

- **Phase 1**: this is the phase that went so badly wrong in the trial discussed earlier. It involves using healthy people who volunteer to take part. They are paid to do this. What scientists look for is how the drug actually works in the body, how the body breaks it down and how the body eventually gets rid of it. They also look to see if the drug works better in some people than in others and if some people experience serious side-effects.
- **Phase 2**: if the drug is working the way scientists predicted that it would work and if there are no signs of serious side-effects, then 100 to 300 patients are asked to take part in trialling the drug. They will be suffering from the disease the drug is designed to cure. What scientists look for in this phase is that the drug is effective in curing the disease and that no serious side-effects are obvious. They also try to find out how much of the drug needs to be given in one dose.
- **Phase 3**: if the drug still looks promising, then this stage involves thousands of patients all over the world.

It can take years before it is proved that a drug is effective and, most importantly, safe. Only if these three phases are passed successfully will a drug be considered for sale to health services. It is only when a drug reaches the market, which means it can be sold, that the pharmaceutical company that developed it can start to get money back for all the costs incurred in testing it. The testing process costs millions of pounds.

● Synthesising a new drug

Before a drug reaches clinical trials it must be synthesised (made). But how do chemists know what chemical compounds will make effective drugs to cure diseases?

A drug works because of its shape and the way the atoms are arranged in its molecule. The drug must fit into a site on the molecules in the body that are associated with the disease. This site is called a **receptor**. It is like a key (the drug) fitting into a lock (the receptor).

These molecules in the body that have receptor sites are almost always proteins. Proteins are very important molecules in our bodies, controlling much of what we do. Our genes provide the information to make these proteins; genes are part of the chemical called DNA. Over the past few years, scientists have mapped out our genes in a huge research project called the Human Genome Project. This research is now having a huge impact on the development of drugs by pharmaceutical companies. Scientists are beginning to discover

'Synthesising' means 'making'. When chemicals are made using chemical reactions these are often called **synthesis** reactions.

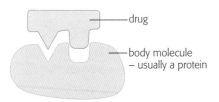

Figure 5.28 For a drug to work it must fit into a receptor site on the protein molecule that is associated with the disease

Nearly all drugs produced naturally, or synthesised by chemists, are organic chemicals (i.e. compounds containing carbon atoms).

Figure 5.29 Automated synthesis can produce and test a million new drugs in a few weeks

E, **F** and **G** are monomers; they are small molecules that will join together to build up a long-chain molecule.

E–F is not the same molecule as **F–E**. The order of the atoms in each molecule is different. The same applies to similar examples.

Another name for stage synthesis is 'split synthesis' because the molecules produced in each reaction vessel are mixed and divided (split) into equal portions.

that particular genes in our body might make us more susceptible to (more likely to get) a particular disease because of the proteins they produce. Once the gene is known, the protein this gene makes can be investigated to see if any molecule might fit a receptor site on it and perhaps cure a particular disease.

To find possible molecules that might fit the receptor sites and be effective as drugs used to be a very long process. Until a few years ago most drug molecules were natural products made by plants, animals or microorganisms. Pharmaceutical companies keep molecules that might be useful as drugs in huge collections called libraries. A library might contain over a million compounds. Now just imagine that you had to make each one of these compounds separately. It would take years and yet about 30 years ago this is what chemists did. It is also a very expensive process, because the company not only has to pay for the chemicals it uses to make potential drugs, it also has to pay for the chemists' time.

To make the search for an effective drug faster, thousands of different molecules can now be produced at one go. This is done automatically in stages using computer-controlled syringes (Figure 5.29).

Stage synthesis

'Stage synthesis' means that chemists synthesise the molecules they want for their libraries in stages. Each time the molecule they are designing gets larger. We will consider an example, illustrated in Figure 5.30 on the next page.

» **Stage 1**: there are three different compounds that react together. These are the building blocks for making larger molecules. We will call these compounds **E**, **F** and **G**. In this first stage these molecules are bonded to polystyrene beads. The advantage of having the compounds **E**, **F** and **G** stuck to the beads is that they can easily be washed at the end of each stage. This removes any remaining solutions of **E**, **F** and **G** which are not bonded to the beads.

» **Stage 2**: the polystyrene beads from stage 1 are mixed together and split into three equal sets. This means each set contains ⅓ beads with **E** attached, ⅓ beads with **F** attached and ⅓ with **G** attached. Each of these three sets are split into three again and then reacted with **E** or **F** or **G** in reaction vessels to give nine compounds:

E–E, F–E, G–E, E–F, F–F, G–F, E–G, F–G , G–G

The polystyrene beads are again washed to remove any reagent that has not reacted.

» **Stage 3**: the polystyrene beads from stage 2 are mixed together again and split into three equal sets so that the molecules are evenly divided between the three reaction vessels. They are reacted with compounds **E**, **F** and **G**, as before, to give 27 different compounds. The polystyrene beads, with their molecules attached, are washed, ready for stage 4.

Figure 5.30 An example of stage synthesis. At each stage the beads with their molecules are mixed and divided

You can see that this is a very quick way of producing a large number of compounds. There is only one molecule per bead but the beads are very small. One gram of beads may contain as many as one million beads. So there will be a large number of molecules of the 27 compounds produced. When the compound is needed the covalent bond that attaches it to the bead can be broken by a chemical reaction.

Chemists working for the pharmaceutical company can screen all the compounds they have made (their library) to see if any of them have activity with the proteins associated with a particular disease.

Calculating the number of possible products from a staged synthesis experiment

If you look at Figure 5.30 you can probably see a mathematical pattern to the number of compounds produced.

- **Stage 1** = the original three compounds (monomers)
- **Stage 2** = 3×3 compounds = 9 compounds or products
- **Stage 3** = $3 \times 3 \times 3$ compounds = 27 compounds or products
- So **Stage 4** would be $3 \times 3 \times 3 \times 3 = 81$ products (3^4)

The pattern is that the number of starting compounds (monomers), which we will call x, is raised to the power of the number of stages, n.

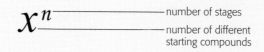

$$x^n$$

number of stages

number of different starting compounds

You will only have to calculate up to four stages in your examination. Let's do another example. Imagine you have four starting compounds and you do a three-stage synthesis. The number of possible products you will make is 4^3, which is $4 \times 4 \times 4 = 64$ compounds.

● Designing a large-scale synthesis

Once a potential drug compound has been discovered it needs to be synthesised. Chemists will have already made this compound, but only on a tiny scale. It now has to be synthesised on a much larger scale. To do this a number of factors have to be investigated.

▹ How much will the raw materials cost? This is important to produce the drug as cheaply as possible.
▹ How much product would be produced from the amount of reactants used? The amount of product made is called the **yield**. It is possible to calculate how much yield to expect from a certain mass of reactants from the balanced formulae equation (see the next page). This is called the **theoretical yield**. This is the maximum amount produced if all the reactants were converted into products. In practice, reactions very rarely produce the calculated theoretical yield. The amount of product actually made is called the **actual yield**. The closer the actual yield to the theoretical yield, the cheaper the reaction will be.

But these two factors are not the only considerations, as you can read below and on the next page.

▹ Are the raw materials from a renewable source? If they are not renewable then they are going to reduce raw materials available for future generations. The use of renewable raw materials where possible is important for **sustainable development**.
▹ How many of the atoms in the starting material end up in the final product? Ideally all the atoms that are in the reactants should end up in the product you want, which in this case is the drug. This concept is known as **atom economy**. A high atom economy means most of the reactants end up in the product. This is important for sustainable development because there is less waste, so there is less potential for environmental damage and fewer resources are used in the first place. Generally, the more steps there are in the synthesis the more waste products are produced and the lower the atom economy. Ideally, chemists should design a synthesis so that there is no waste at all.

Sustainable development involves balancing the need for economic development, standards of living and respect for the environment, so that resources are available for future generations.

For more information on atom economy see pages 112–113.

Toxic substances are poisonous and can cause death. You may remember that carbon monoxide produced by the incomplete combustion of fuels has a high toxicity.

Remember that **catalysts** speed up chemical reactions. They are also unchanged chemically at the end of the reaction, which means they can often be re-used many times.

Remember that state symbols tell you what state of matter each substance is in: (s) = solid; (l) = liquid; (g) = gas; (aq) = aqueous (dissolved in water to make a solution).

▶ Are the waste products harmful to the environment? If there have to be waste products, what is their level of **toxicity** to us and to the rest of the environment? 'Toxicity' means how poisonous a substance is. A high toxicity means that the substances can cause death even in very low concentrations.

▶ How much energy does the reaction require? To be really energy efficient a reaction should take place at room temperature and not therefore require any heating. The use of catalysts can often reduce the temperature required for a reaction.

▶ Does the reaction need a **solvent**? A solvent is something that dissolves the chemicals that react together. For one pill the volume of solvent used may be as high as 25 000 times the volume of the pill. Atoms in the solvent do not end up in the final product and they are often thrown away. If a solvent does have to be used it should be safe and not harmful to the environment.

▶ How safe is the synthesis? Where possible, chemicals should be chosen that are of low toxicity, with no risk of explosions.

Although these last six questions may seem obvious, many older chemical processes that synthesised chemicals were not set up with sustainable development in mind. These questions form part of the principles of **Green Chemistry**. These principles try and ensure that the synthesis of a chemical is not harmful to the environment and is sustainable.

● Working out how much reactant is needed

Balanced formulae equations

Before we start looking at the more complicated equations of drug synthesis, let's remind ourselves about chemical equations by looking at a simpler reaction.

Calcium oxide is made by heating limestone (calcium carbonate) and the other product is carbon dioxide. The word equation for this reaction is:

calcium carbonate ➔ calcium oxide + carbon dioxide

However, chemists find formulae equations give much more information. The formula of a compound tells you what elements are present and in what proportions. Often chemists will add **state symbols** to the equation.

$$CaCO_3(s) \rightarrow CaO(s) + CO_2(g)$$

In this case, the number of each different type of atom is the same on both sides of the equation. We say that this is a **balanced formulae equation**. Most formulae equations you come across will require balancing, because chemical reactions do not create or destroy atoms.

Here is another example, the manufacture of bromine from dissolved sodium bromide in seawater using chlorine gas.

1 Write the word equation.

   sodium bromide + chlorine ➜ sodium chloride + bromine

2 Change the words into formulae.

   $NaBr + Cl_2 ➜ NaCl + Br_2$

3 Balance the equation by making the number of atoms of each element the same on both sides.

   $2NaBr + Cl_2 ➜ 2NaCl + Br_2$

4 Add state symbols.

   $2NaBr(aq) + Cl_2(g) ➜ 2NaCl(aq) + Br_2(aq)$

> Remember: the formulae are fixed when balancing equations. You cannot change $NaBr$ to $NaBr_2$ because this would be a new compound. In fact, $NaBr_2$ does not exist.

Relative formula mass

The masses of atoms are very tiny. It is much more convenient to compare masses of atoms relative to one another using the **relative atomic mass** scale (Table 5.3). Hydrogen is given a relative atomic mass (A_r for short) of 1 because it is the lightest atom. Carbon has an A_r of 12. This means that one atom of carbon is twelve times heavier than one atom of hydrogen.

> The 'r' in A_r stands for 'relative'.

Table 5.3 The relative atomic masses of some elements

Element	Symbol	Relative atomic mass, A_r
hydrogen	H	1
carbon	C	12
nitrogen	N	14
oxygen	O	16
sodium	Na	23
sulphur	S	32
chlorine	Cl	35.5
calcium	Ca	40
iron	Fe	56
bromine	Br	80

> M_r is the symbol we give to relative formula mass. It is also known as relative molecular mass when referring to a molecule.

Once you know the A_r of the different elements that make up a formula, you can work out the **relative formula mass** (M_r).

The relative formula mass of calcium carbonate, $CaCO_3$

$$
\begin{aligned}
Ca &= 40 \times 1 = 40 \\
C &= 12 \times 1 = 12 \\
3O &= 16 \times 3 = \underline{48} \\
M_r &= 100
\end{aligned}
$$

Let's now look at two other compounds.

Worked example 1

The formula of ethanol is C_2H_5OH. What is its relative molecular mass?

Look up the A_r values in Table 5.3.

M_r C_2H_5OH = (A_r of C × 2) + (A_r of H × 5) + A_r of O + A_r of H
$= (12 \times 2) + (1 \times 5) + 16 + 1$
$= 46$

Worked example 2

What is the M_r of calcium hydroxide, $Ca(OH)_2$?

You will notice that this formula has brackets. The brackets tell you that there are two hydroxide ions. We will look in detail at ions in Chapter 6. Ions are charged particles. Metals always form positive ions in compounds and the hydroxide ions are negatively charged. The charges do not affect the A_r values.

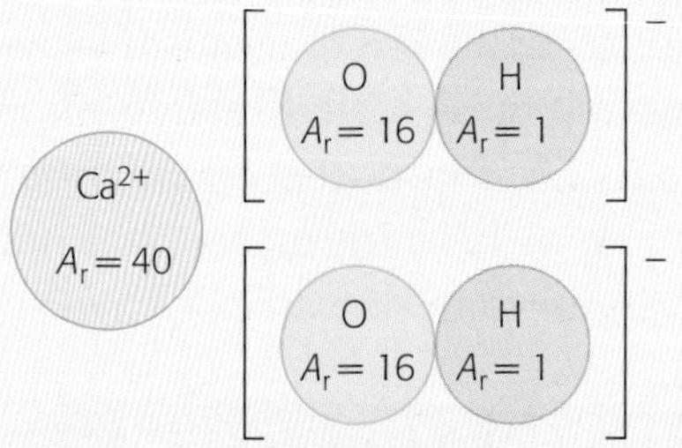

Figure 5.31 Diagram to show the parts of the formula $Ca(OH)_2$

M_r of $Ca(OH)_2$ = A_r of Ca + 2(A_r of O + A_r of H)
$= 40 + 2(16 + 1)$
$= 74$

Calculating the formulae of compounds

We have now seen that we can represent substances by formulae. When a pharmaceutical company makes a new compound it is very important to know its formula. Once the formula is known then chemists can set about finding the best way to synthesise it. So how do chemists find the formulae of compounds?

If the masses of the reactants that produce the compounds are known then it is possible to work out the formula of a new compound. Often the drugs we use have very complicated formulae that would be very difficult to work out. In the following worked examples we will show you how to work out formulae by calculating the formulae of some simple compounds.

Worked example 3

14 g of nitrogen reacts with 3 g of hydrogen to make ammonia. What is the formula of ammonia?

1 Find the **reacting masses** of the elements in the compound. These will usually be given to you and are found from experimental data.

The **reacting mass** means how much of the reactant reacts to form a compound.

	nitrogen	hydrogen
mass in grams	14 g	3 g

2 Find the relative atomic masses of the elements in the compound.

A_r	14	3

3 Divide the masses by the A_r values. This tells you how many A_r there are in the formulae.

Number of A_r	$\frac{14}{14} = 1$	$\frac{3}{1} = 3$

4 Work out the simplest whole number ratio of the atoms by dividing by the smallest. In this case the smallest number is 1.

Simplest whole number ratio	$\frac{1}{1} = 1$	$\frac{3}{1} = 3$

5 The formula is NH_3.

This gives you the simplest whole number ratio of atoms in the formula and this is called the **empirical formula**. This formula means that are three times as many atoms of hydrogen as there are of nitrogen. The actual formula unit could be NH_3 or N_2H_6 or N_3H_9 and so on. At the moment we haven't enough information to work out which one it is. But the empirical formula is very helpful.

Worked example 4

8 g of sulphur reacts with 8 g of oxygen. What is the empirical formula of this oxide of sulphur?

1 Find the **reacting masses** of the elements in the compound.

	sulphur	oxygen
mass in grams	8 g	8 g

2 Find the relative atomic masses of the elements in the compound.

A_r	32	16

3 Divide the masses by the A_r values. This tells you how many A_r there are in the formulae.

Number of A_r	$\frac{8}{32} = 0.25$	$\frac{8}{16} = 0.5$

4 Work out the simplest whole number ratio of the atoms by dividing by the smallest.

Simplest whole number ratio	$\frac{0.25}{0.25} = 1$	$\frac{0.5}{0.25} = 2$

The empirical formula is SO_2. This may not be the actual formula of this sulphur oxide. It could be S_2O_4, S_3O_6, etc. All we know is the ratio of atoms in the formula.

A chemist was calculating the empirical formula of iron oxide. When she got to Step 4 her ratio came to Fe = 0.5 : O = 1.5. This is not a whole number ratio. As you cannot have 0.5 of an atom the answer must be multiplied by 2, to give Fe_2O_3.

Remember: reactants are the chemicals that react together to make the products.

Using chemical equations in calculations

Whether a factory is manufacturing a drug on a large scale or making calcium oxide from limestone in a lime kiln, it is very important to know how much of the reactants it needs to use and how much product it can expect to produce. This is where knowing the balanced formulae equation is essential.

Let's look at the manufacture of calcium oxide from calcium carbonate (limestone). As we have already seen (page 106), the balanced formulae equation is:

$$CaCO_3(s) \rightarrow CaO(s) + CO_2(g)$$

We now need to work out the relative formula masses:

$$40 + 12 + (16 \times 3) \rightarrow 40 + 16 + 12 + (16 \times 2)$$
$$= 100 \qquad\qquad = 56 \qquad = 44$$

This tells us that for every 100 g of calcium carbonate we can produce 56 g of calcium oxide and 44 g of carbon dioxide. These are tiny quantities in industry, but the equation also tells us that 100 tonnes of calcium carbonate will produce 56 tonnes of calcium carbonate and 44 tonnes of carbon dioxide.

Suppose we had only 50 tonnes of calcium carbonate to start with. This is half the mass in the equation:

$$\frac{50}{100} = 0.5$$

so we would expect to produce half the mass of calcium oxide: $56 \times 0.5 = 23$ tonnes.

Now let's try another worked example.

Worked example 5

In the manufacture of bromine from seawater, what mass of chlorine is required to produce 80 tonnes of bromine?

1 Write down the balanced formulae equation:

$$2NaBr(aq) + Cl_2(g) \rightarrow 2NaCl(aq) + Br_2(l)$$

2 Work out the relevant relative masses in the equation.
   You only need to look at the relevant compounds, so we only require the formula masses of chlorine and bromine.

$$(35.5 \times 2) \rightarrow \qquad\qquad (80 \times 2)$$
$$71 \rightarrow \qquad\qquad 160$$
So, $\qquad 71 \text{ tonnes} \rightarrow \qquad\qquad 160 \text{ tonnes}$

3 Scale the masses above to the masses used or required.

   In this case the mass required is 80 tonnes of bromine: $\dfrac{80}{160} = 0.5$

   So we scale everything relevant in the equation by 0.5.

$$71 \times 0.5 \rightarrow \qquad\qquad 160 \times 0.5$$
$$35.5 \text{ tonnes} \rightarrow \qquad\qquad 80 \text{ tonnes}$$

So 35.5 tonnes of chlorine are required to produce 80 tonnes of bromine.

● **Theoretical yield and percentage yield**

If we look at how much calcium oxide we would produce from 100 tonnes of limestone, we can see from the previous page that this is 56 tonnes. Remember, the mass produced in a chemical reaction is called the yield. Now in practice, much less calcium oxide is actually produced in a lime kiln. There may be many reasons for this; perhaps other reactions take place in the kiln. The masses we calculate from a balanced formulae equation are known as the **theoretical yield**. This is the *maximum* amount we would produce if all the reactants were converted into products. In worked example 5, the theoretical yield from 35.5 tonnes of chlorine is 80 tonnes of bromine. Again, much less is actually produced in the industrial process.

The actual yield from a reaction can only be found by doing that reaction. The **percentage yield** tells you how close the actual yield is to the theoretical yield. The closer it is the cheaper the process, since less raw materials will be needed.

$$\text{percentage yield} = \frac{\text{actual yield}}{\text{theoretical yield}} \times 100$$

Organic reactions rarely produce their theoretical yield. Ethanol, as we have seen on page 88 of this chapter, can be produced from ethene:

$$C_2H_4 + H_2O \rightarrow C_2H_5OH$$

Worked example 6

If 23 tonnes of ethanol are produced from 28 tonnes of ethene, what is the percentage yield?

1 Write down the balanced equation.

$$C_2H_4 \qquad\qquad + H_2O \rightarrow C_2H_5OH$$

2 Work out the relative formula masses in the equation. Note: in this case we do not need to bother about the relative mass of the water.

$$(12 \times 2) + (4 \times 1) \qquad\rightarrow\qquad (12 \times 2) + (5 \times 1) + 16 + 1$$
$$= 28 \qquad\qquad\qquad = 46$$

3 Work out the theoretical yield.

$$28 \text{ tonnes} \qquad\qquad \rightarrow \qquad 46 \text{ tonnes}$$

4 Work out the percentage yield.

$$\text{percentage yield} = \frac{\text{actual yield}}{\text{theoretical yield}} \times 100$$

$$= \frac{23}{46} \times 100 = 50\%$$

So the percentage yield of ethanol = 50%

● Calculating the atom economy

Percentage yield is one way of measuring how efficient a reaction is. At first sight a reaction with 100% yield would seem to be perfect, but it isn't if it produces a lot of by-products that are wasted. This is where an understanding of atom economy comes in. We first met this term on page 105. To synthesise a drug often requires a number of steps, with each step usually producing by-products. The atoms that end up in the by-products cannot end up in the final product and are often wasted.

The hydration of ethene to produce alcohol has a 100% atom economy because there are no by-products in the reaction.

$$C_2H_4(g) + H_2O(g) \rightarrow C_2H_5OH(l)$$

We calculate atom economy using this equation:

$$\text{atom economy} = \frac{\text{mass of useful product}}{\text{total mass of product}} \times 100$$

> **Hydration is the addition of water.**

Worked example 7

What is the atom economy for heating calcium carbonate in a lime kiln to produce calcium oxide?

$$CaCO_3(s) \quad \rightarrow \quad CaO(s) \quad + \quad CO_2(g)$$

The theoretical yields for this reaction are:

$$100 \text{ tonnes} \quad \rightarrow \quad 56 \text{ tonnes} \quad + \quad 44 \text{ tonnes}$$

The useful product here is calcium oxide, so the atom economy is:

$$\text{atom economy} = \frac{\text{mass of useful product}}{\text{total mass of product}} \times 100$$

$$= \frac{56}{(56 + 44)} \times 100 = 56\%$$

This reaction has a poor atom economy and the waste product is carbon dioxide, which contributes to global warming.

Ibuprofen is a very common drug. It was developed by Boots and until the 1980s the company held the patent to manufacture it. It was manufactured in six steps. The first step in the Boots' synthetic route to its manufacture is:

$$C_{10}H_{14} + C_4H_6O_3 \rightarrow C_{12}H_{16}O + C_2H_4O_2$$

The atom economy of this step is found by working out the relative masses of the products in the equation:

useful product: $C_{12}H_{16}O = (12 \times 12) + (1 \times 16) + 16 = 176$

waste product: $C_2H_4O_2 = (12 \times 2) + (1 \times 4) + (16 \times 2) = 60$

total product = $176 + 60 = 236$

> Developing effective drugs is very expensive, as we have seen. A patent protects the company which developed the drug and gives it 20 years to manufacture the drug without competition from other drug companies.

Since the products are calculated as relative masses, they could be in tonnes or grams. It does not matter what unit you use if you are calculating the atom economy. However, the greater the mass of product the greater the mass of the waste.

$$\text{atom economy} = \frac{\text{mass of useful product}}{\text{total mass of product}} \times 100$$

$$= \frac{176}{236} \times 100 = 74.6\%$$

But this is only one step in the synthesis. There are six steps overall: the mass of the final useful product, ibuprofen, is 206 tonnes and the total mass of all the product is 514.5 tonnes.

$$\text{atom economy} = \frac{\text{mass of useful product}}{\text{total mass of product}} \times 100$$

$$= \frac{206}{514.5} \times 100 = 40\%$$

Since 3000 tonnes of ibuprofen are produced each year in the UK alone, using this synthetic route, there are 4500 tonnes of waste. Since the expiry of Boots' patent, an alternative manufacturing route for ibuprofen has been found involving only three steps, with an atom economy of 77%. For every 3000 tonnes of ibuprofen made, only 896 tonnes are wasted.

Summary

- Clinical trials are carried out to see if a drug that has been developed is effective and non-toxic to humans.
- In chemistry 'synthesis' means making chemicals.
- Stage methods of synthesis speed up the development of new drugs because thousands of compounds can be produced very quickly. These compounds make up a pharmaceutical company's library of potential drug molecules.
- The number of possible products from a staged synthesis experiment can be calculated using x^n, where 'x' is the number of different starting compounds (monomers) and 'n' is the number of stages.
- Once a potential drug has been discovered it needs to be synthesised on a large scale. The theoretical yield from the synthesis is calculated from the balanced formulae equation.
- The theoretical yield is the maximum mass obtainable if all the reactants are converted to products.
- In practice the actual yield is less than the theoretical yield. The more it differs the higher are the costs of the synthesis.
- One of the important questions for a drug manufacturer to ask when designing a synthesis is 'How high is the atom economy?' A high atom economy means most of the reactants end up in the desired product and not in unwanted by-products. This is important for sustainable development because there is less waste.
- Balanced formulae equations have the same number of atoms of each element on both sides of the equation. Often state symbols are added: (s) = solid; (l) = liquid; (g) = gas; (aq) = aqueous (dissolved in water).
- The masses of atoms are very tiny so we use the relative atomic mass (A_r) scale. Hydrogen is given a relative atomic mass of 1 because it is the lightest atom.

- The relative formula mass (M_r) is the total relative masses of all the atoms in the formula unit. If the formula unit is a molecule, M_r is the relative molecular mass.
- The empirical formulae of compounds can be calculated from reacting masses. Empirical formulae are formulae that have the simplest whole number ratio of atoms.
- Chemical equations can be used to calculate masses of reactants and products. The relative formula masses are calculated for each reactant and product in the balanced formula equation. If more than one formula unit of a reactant is present then the relative formula mass is multiplied by the number of formula units.
- $$\text{percentage yield} = \frac{\text{actual yield}}{\text{theoretical yield}} \times 100$$
- The atom economy is often more important than the percentage yield of a synthesis because it tells us how much of the reactants actually end up in the product:
$$\text{atom economy} = \frac{\text{mass of useful product}}{\text{total mass of product}} \times 100$$

Questions

Note: relative atomic masses can be found in Table 5.3, page 107.

5.12 **a** Before a drug reaches clinical trials it is tested on animals. Why is this done?

    b Animal testing is very controversial. Use the internet to find out *four* arguments which support animal testing and *four* arguments that oppose it.

5.13 Drug companies use stage methods of synthesis in their search for new drugs.

    a Explain what is meant by *stage methods of synthesis*. Your answer should include an explanation of what happens at stage 1 and stage 2.

    b Why are stage methods of synthesis important to drug companies?

    c When manufacturing a drug, the atom economy of the large-scale synthesis should be as high as possible.

      i What is the atom economy of a reaction?

      ii Why is it important for sustainable development to have a high atom economy in an industrial synthesis?

5.14 Five different starting compounds are used in a staged synthesis experiment. How many possible compounds will be made at the fourth stage?

5.15 Use Table 5.3 on page 107 to calculate the relative formula masses of the following compounds:

    a nitrogen monoxide (NO)

    b nitrogen dioxide (NO_2)

    c ethene (C_2H_4)

    d water (H_2O)

    e sodium nitrate ($NaNO_3$)

    f calcium hydroxide ($Ca(OH)_2$)

    g ethanoic acid (CH_3CO_2H)

    h calcium nitrate ($Ca(NO_3)_2$).

5.16 In a car engine nitrogen (N_2) reacts with oxygen to produce nitrogen monoxide (NO). The nitrogen monoxide reacts with more oxygen to produce nitrogen dioxide.
Write down the two balanced equations for these reactions and include state symbols.

5.17 a Explain what is meant by the term *empirical formula*.
b What is the empirical formula of ethene (C_2H_4)?
c A simple hydrocarbon is made from 24 g of carbon and 8 g hydrogen. What is the empirical formula of this compound?
d An iron compound contains 28 g iron and 80 g bromine. What is the empirical formula of this compound?

5.18 a One of the important reactions in the production of iron from iron oxide has the balanced formula equation:

$$Fe_2O_3(s) + 3CO(g) \rightarrow 2Fe(s) + 3CO_2(g)$$

i How many tonnes of iron will be produced from 320 tonnes of iron oxide?
ii How much carbon dioxide is given off into the atmosphere?
b Calculate the mass of carbon dioxide produced from 1.68 g of baking soda ($NaHCO_3$) when it is heated in a cake mixture.

$$2NaHCO_3(s) \rightarrow Na_2CO_3(s) + H_2O(l) + CO_2(g)$$

5.19 One way of synthesising aspirin ($C_9H_8O_4$) is shown in the balanced formulae equation:

$$C_7H_6O_3 + C_4H_6O_3 \rightarrow C_9H_8O_4 + C_2H_4O_2$$

a What is the atom economy of this reaction?
b If the reaction uses 552 kg $C_7H_6O_3$, what is the theoretical yield of aspirin?
c The actual yield produced from 552 kg $C_7H_6O_3$ is 576 kg. What is the percentage yield?
d In 'Green Chemistry' why is the atom economy more important than the percentage yield?

Chemistry

6 In your element

A Explaining the properties of metals

Nitinol is a mixture of two metals, nickel and titanium. Any mixture of a metal with other elements is called an alloy and you can read about alloys in this section. What's special about nitinol is that it can remember its shape, which is why it is called a 'shape memory alloy'.

The discovery of nitinol's remarkable properties happened by chance in 1962 in the USA. Research scientists were trying to make titanium less brittle by mixing it with nickel. To demonstrate that this alloy could be deformed many times without breaking, a thin wire was made into a zigzag shape and pulled and pushed many times. At a meeting the flexible nitinol was being demonstrated when someone decided to see if heating it with a cigarette lighter spoilt the flexibility. Immediately it was heated, the wire straightened to its original shape.

The temperature at which nitinol returns to its original shape can be set anywhere between −100 °C and +100 °C by altering the amount of nickel in the alloy. This opens up many possibilities. For example, in 2001, an Italian fashion designer made a shirt that would roll up its own sleeves when the temperature rose. He did this by incorporating nitinol fibres in the fabric of the sleeves. One reason you may never have seen anyone wearing the shirt is that each one cost £2500 to manufacture!

A more important use is in re-opening blocked arteries and strengthening artery walls inside peoples' bodies. Nitinol wire is coiled in a tube of the same diameter as the inside of the artery. The tube is heated, so that the coiled shape is remembered, and then cooled. The tube is made narrower to fit into the artery. When the blood warms it, the tube returns to its original remembered diameter – opening up a blocked artery or strengthening a weak artery wall.

Figure 6.1 Nitinol wire in a zigzag shape straightens out on heating

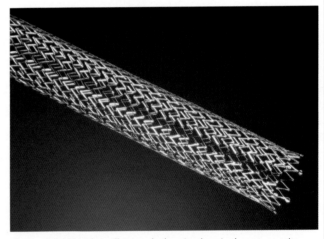

Figure 6.2 This tube will expand when in place in the artery as it warms. As well as re-opening blocked arteries, this nitinol-reinforced tubing can strengthen sections of artery

Physical properties are those you can observe without changing the metal chemically.

● The physical properties of metals

This will not be the first time that you have considered the physical properties of metals. Just take a few moments to look at different metals around your home or your classroom. Think what properties of metals make them suitable for the various ways they are used.

a Steel is used in this radiator because it is hard and strong, as well as being a good conductor of heat with a high melting point. The copper pipe that carries the hot water to the radiator is easy to bend but it is softer than iron, which is why it is not used to make the actual radiator

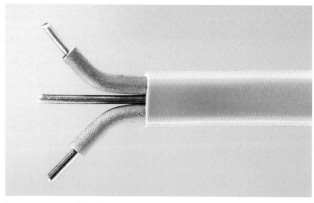

b Copper is used in the electric cables that carry the electric current around your home because it is a good conductor of electricity and it can be drawn into wires (it is ductile)

c Hard, strong and shiny, this stainless steel cutlery looks attractive and is ideally suited to its use

d The strength, high density and hardness of this steel girder will keep this roof structure safe

Figure 6.3 Metals in everyday use

Metals have the following physical properties. They are:

▶ solids at room temperature because they have high melting and boiling points (although you may be able to think of an exception)
▶ hard and dense
▶ shiny
▶ good conductors of heat and electricity
▶ **malleable** – this means they can be hammered into shape without breaking
▶ **ductile** – this means that they can be drawn into wires without breaking.

Explaining the physical properties of metals

Metals are elements, which means they are made up of only one type of atom. But what is it that holds these atoms together to give metals the properties we have described?

In metals, atoms give up their outer electrons to form a 'sea' of relatively free electrons, which are constantly moving. As the atoms have given up some of their negatively charged electrons they become positively charged. The negatively charged sea of electrons is attracted very strongly by these atoms (Figure 6.4, overleaf). The structure is known as a **giant structure** because billions of metal atoms are held together in this way.

117

Figure 6.4 The bonding in metals is due to strong attraction between the giant structure of metal atoms and the negative free electrons

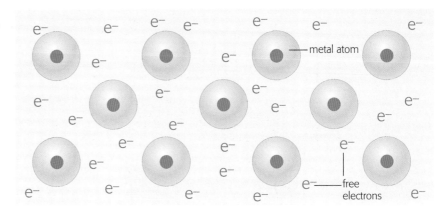

This form of bonding is called **metallic bonding** and it allows us to explain the properties of metals.

▶ Most metals are solids with high melting points. This is because the metal has a giant structure of atoms held together by the relatively free electrons. Remember, in a solid the particles (in this case metal atoms) are fixed in place. When a metal melts, the metal atoms become free to move. The stronger the attraction between the metal atoms and the sea of free electrons, the higher the melting point of the metal. This strong attraction also explains why metals usually have high boiling points. When liquid metal boils the metal atoms have to escape from the attraction of the sea of electrons to become widely separated in a gas.

▶ The hardness and high density of metals are also caused by the attraction of the sea of free electrons to the metal atoms. This holds the metal atoms close together.

▶ Metals are good conductors of electricity because electrons in the sea are free to move. When one end of the metal is made positive and the other end is made negative, the electrons will move towards the positive end and this flow of charged electrons is the electricity being conducted. More electrons arrive at the negative end from the power pack to replace those that flow out.

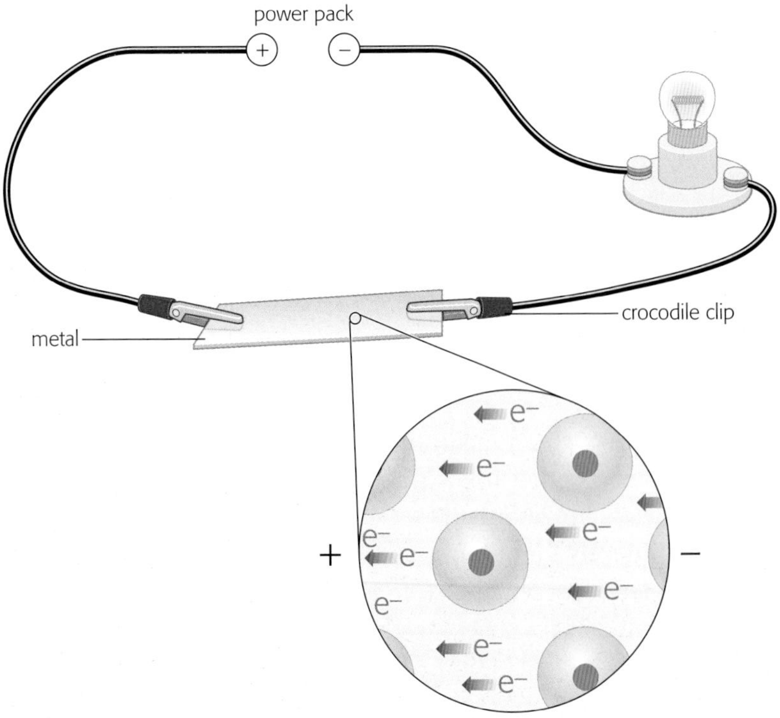

Figure 6.5 The electrons are free to move. When one end of the metal is made positive, the negative electrons will flow towards it causing an electric current to flow. As the electrons flow out more arrive at the negative end

How well a substance conducts heat or electricity is called its **conductivity**. Metals have good conductivity, whereas nearly all non-metals have poor conductivity.

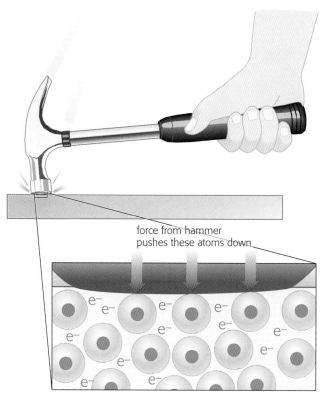

Figure 6.6 The force from the hammer causes some atoms to move out of place but the attraction of the sea of electrons keeps the metal structure together

force from hammer pushes these atoms down

▶ The sea of electrons will also transfer heat energy from one electron to another, making metals good conductors of heat. It is because the electrons are free to move that the energy is transferred so quickly. Non-metallic substances are poor conductors of heat energy because only the vibrating atoms, which are fixed in place, transfer energy.

▶ The sea of electrons also makes metals shiny.

▶ Metals can be hammered into shape (are malleable) because the atoms in a metal move when they are hit but they are still held together by their attraction for the sea of electrons (Figure 6.6). This also explains why metals can be drawn into wires (are ductile).

Alloying: changing the properties of metals

An **alloy** is a mixture of a metal with another element – usually another metal. At the beginning of this section we looked at one alloy, nitinol, which is a mixture of nickel and titanium. Alloying changes the properties of these two metals because neither nickel on its own, nor titanium on its own, will remember shapes the way that the alloy nitinol does.

Let's take another example. Aluminium is a very good metal to use in aircraft manufacture because of its low density. However, aluminium on its own does not have the strength needed to withstand the stresses and strains of flying. When it is alloyed to other metals such as copper and magnesium it becomes stronger (Figure 6.7).

Duralumin is an aluminium alloy, made of 94% aluminium, 4% copper and 1% magnesium. The alloy still has the low density of aluminium but it is much stronger.

Figure 6.7 The European Airbus A380 is the largest passenger plane ever built and can carry up to 840 passengers. Aluminium alloys are essential to its structure

So how does alloying change the properties of metals? Look at the metal in Figure 6.8. The layers of metal atoms can slide over one another when a force is applied. However, in an alloy, different-sized atoms can prevent the layers sliding over one another, making the structure much stronger (Figure 6.9).

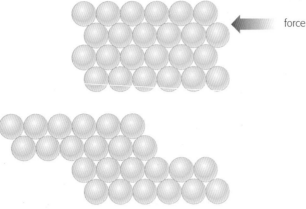

force

force

Figure 6.9 In an alloy, larger metal atoms prevent the layers sliding over one another as easily as in a pure metal

Figure 6.8 Layers of atoms can easily slide over one another in a pure metal

How much gold is in gold jewellery?

The gold in jewellery is almost never pure gold because gold is a very soft metal. Instead, gold is alloyed to other metals such as copper and silver. You only need to think of the wear that a gold wedding ring gets if it is worn for many years to understand just how hard and strong a gold alloy needs to be.

So how do you know how much gold is in the jewellery you are buying or wearing? The proportion of gold in the alloy is measured in carats. 24 carat gold is pure gold. Many wedding rings are made from 18 carat gold. This means there are $\frac{18}{24}$th of gold in the alloy, which is $\frac{3}{4}$ or 75%. The other metals that are mixed with the gold change its colour (Table 6.1).

Table 6.1 The different colours of 18 carat gold

Colour	Gold (%)	Silver (%)	Copper (%)
green-yellow	75	25	0
pale yellow	75	16	9
yellow	75	12.5	12.5

If you have gold jewellery made from 9 carat gold then there is only $\frac{9}{24}$th of it in the alloy, which is only 37.5%. 9 carat gold is harder wearing. However, if the rest of the alloy is made up from copper the gold may tarnish to a greenish colour, and if the rest of the alloy is silver it may tarnish to black.

Figure 6.10 This gold wedding ring needs to be hard enough and strong enough to withstand the knocks it receives in all types of jobs

Summary

- Physical properties are those properties that do not involve any chemical change, such as melting point, hardness and electrical conductivity.
- The physical properties of metals are:
  - high melting points and boiling points
  - hardness and high density
  - shiny
  - good conductors of heat and electricity
  - malleable (can be hammered into shape)
  - ductile (can be drawn into wires).
- Metallic bonding explains the physical properties of metals. The metallic structure consists of a giant structure of metal atoms surrounded by relatively free electrons. The strong attraction between the atoms and the electron sea gives high melting points and boiling points and makes most metals hard and dense. The free negatively charged electrons can move towards a positive charge, which is why metals are good conductors of electricity. Good heat conduction is also explained by the free electrons, which transfer heat energy from one to another very quickly.
- An alloy is a mixture of a metal element with another element, usually another metal.
- Alloying changes the properties of metals because different sized atoms are inserted into the metal structure. For example, larger atoms can prevent layers of metal atoms sliding over each other, giving the alloy greater strength and hardness.
- Aluminium is made stronger by alloying it to copper and a little magnesium.
- Gold alloys are used to make jewellery: 24 carat gold is pure gold, 18 carat gold is 75% gold mixed with 25% of other metals such as copper and silver.

Questions

6.1 a Give *five* physical properties of metals.

    b Draw a diagram to show metallic bonding.

    c Use the diagram you have drawn in part **b** to explain the properties you have described in part **a**.

6.2 a What is an alloy?

    b Why is gold jewellery not usually made from 24 carat gold?

    c What is the percentage of gold in a 12 carat gold necklace?

6.3 Alloying changes the properties of metals. Explain, using diagrams, how copper added to aluminium can make the resulting alloy stronger than aluminium.

6.4 Brass is the alloy used to make musical instruments such as the horn and the trumpet. Use the internet to research the following:

    a the mixture of metals in the brass alloy

    b why brass is more suitable for making musical instruments than the metals that make up the alloy.

B The Periodic Table and the structure of atoms

At first sight the Periodic Table arranges elements according to their atomic masses. It is only when you look more closely that some elements do not fit this pattern. In 1869, Dmitri Mendeleev, a Russian chemistry professor, put the 62 elements so far discovered on Earth in order of atomic mass. When he had done this he tried to group elements with similar properties together. He was successful with some but others just would not fit his grouping pattern.

This is where Mendeleev's creative insight proved crucial. He realised that some elements could not be arranged according to their atomic mass because they would not fit into the groups he was devising. He simply swapped their order. If you look at a Periodic Table you will notice that cobalt and nickel are two of the elements he swapped. He also realised that some elements must be missing and were yet to be discovered. He put spaces in his arrangement and predicted the properties of some of these elements, and in most cases he was proved correct. Once chemists knew what they were looking for it was much easier to find them.

A good example is the element germanium. Mendeleev predicted that there must be an element with properties similar to silicon in the same group. He named this element 'eka-silicon'. It was discovered 17 years later by a German chemist, Clemens Winkler, in a newly found mineral from a mine. It is named 'germanium' after his native land.

Figure 6.11 The work of Dmitri Mendeleev (1834–1907) led to many new elements being discovered

● A closer look at the structure of atoms

It would be hard to underestimate just how important the Periodic Table is to chemists. From it we can see patterns and predict properties. When Mendeleev first devised it he tried putting all the elements in order of their atomic masses. As we have seen, this worked for most of the 62 elements known at the time, but some just would not fit into this pattern. We now know that the order in the Periodic Table is linked to the structure of the atom, not its mass. However, in 1869 an atom was thought of as one single particle – the smallest particle in the universe, from which everything else was made.

Almost 30 years after Mendeleev invented his Periodic Table, an English scientist, J.J. Thomson, discovered electrons while working at Cambridge University. Electrons are tiny particles that have hardly any mass and are negatively charged. A few years later, Ernest Rutherford, a New Zealander who had worked under Thomson, did some amazing experiments (see page 241) that showed most of the atom was really empty space, in the middle of which was a very small, positively charged nucleus. Electrons orbited this nucleus, a bit like planets around our Sun. Figure 6.12 shows the model of the atom proposed by Rutherford.

By 1919 Rutherford had discovered another particle, the proton. This was the particle that gave the nucleus its positive charge, and it was 1840 times heavier than the mass of the electron. He also

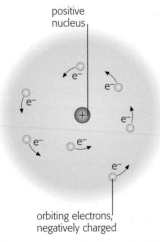

positive nucleus

orbiting electrons, negatively charged

Figure 6.12 Rutherford's model of the atom

predicted that there must be another particle in the nucleus, which would have no charge. Other scientists did not believe him, but James Chadwick, a member of his research team, found the neutron in 1932. Neutrons have the same mass as protons.

So we now have a model of the atom like that shown in Figure 6.13. Table 6.2 summarises the properties of the three particles that make up the atom.

> A **model** is a scientist's attempt to explain observations.

Figure 6.13 The model of the atom showing the structure of the nucleus

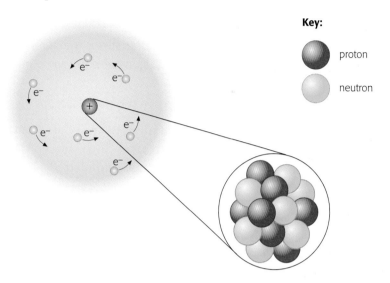

Key:

proton

neutron

Table 6.2 The particles in an atom

Particle	Relative mass	Relative charge	Location
proton	1	+1	nucleus
neutron	1	0	nucleus
electron	$\frac{1}{1840}$ (almost zero)	−1	orbiting the nucleus

Notice that the proton and the electron have equal but opposite charges, so in a neutral atom the number of protons and electrons must be equal. Also notice that the electron has hardly any mass compared to the proton and the neutron.

> An easy way to remember the charges on the particles is **p**roton is **p**ositive and **neutr**on is **neutr**al, so this leaves the electron, which must be negative.

Atomic number and the Periodic Table

We now know that the order of the elements in the Periodic Table is by **atomic number**. But what is atomic number?

Atomic number is the number of protons in an atom.

Atomic number has the symbol Z and is also known as the proton number. Once we know the atomic number of an element we also know:

- which element it is, because only atoms of the same element have the same atomic number
- where the element is in the Periodic Table – remember that elements are arranged in the Periodic Table according to their atomic number
- the number of electrons in an atom of the element – atoms have no charge so the number of electrons must equal the number of protons.

Worked example 1

The atomic number of an element is 6.
a What is the identity of the element?
b How many protons and electrons does it have?

a Look at the Periodic Table on page 131. You do not have to count far into the Periodic Table to find the sixth element. It is carbon.
b The atomic number is 6 so there must be 6 protons. Remember, atomic number is the number of protons. The number of electrons is 6 because there is the same number of protons as electrons.

Mass number

Almost all the mass of an atom is in its nucleus. Electrons hardly have any mass. If we add up the number of protons and neutrons we have the **mass number**.

Mass number is the total number of protons and neutrons in the atom.

mass number (A) = number of protons (Z) + number of neutrons

Chemists summarise the information about an atom in this way.

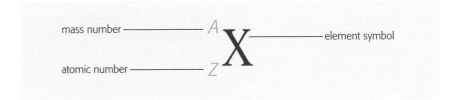

It is the atomic number that tells you what the element is.

Worked example 2

An atom of sodium has symbol notation $^{23}_{11}$Na. Work out the number of protons, electrons and neutrons in the atom.

Since the atomic number = 11, there are 11 protons.
There must also be 11 electrons because the atom is neutral.

mass number = number of protons + number of neutrons

number of neutrons = mass number − number of protons

number of neutrons = 23 − 11 = 12

How are the electrons arranged?

We know that the electrons orbit the nucleus. It was in 1913 that a Danish scientist, Niels Bohr, suggested that the electrons orbited the nucleus in shells. In his model, which we accept today, the first shell is nearest the nucleus and can only contain a maximum of two electrons. The next two shells will hold up to eight electrons each (Figure 6.14).

Figure 6.14 The Bohr model of an atom with the electrons in shells

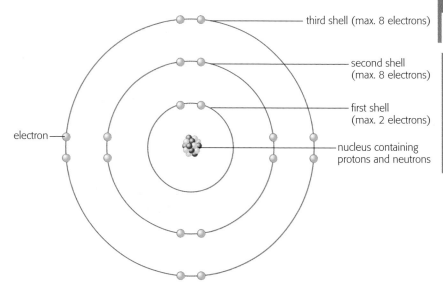

third shell (max. 8 electrons)

second shell (max. 8 electrons)

first shell (max. 2 electrons)

electron

nucleus containing protons and neutrons

We call the arrangement of electrons in the atom of an element its **electronic configuration**. In the worked example below we show two ways of representing electronic configurations. The first is using a shell diagram and the other is just using numbers of electrons in each shell, separated by commas.

Worked example 3

Work out the electron configuration of aluminium, $^{27}_{13}$Al. Show the number of protons and neutrons in the nucleus.

The atomic number is 13, so there are 13 protons and 13 electrons.

mass number = number of protons + number of neutrons

number of neutrons = mass number − number of protons
$$= 27 - 13 = 14$$

The electron configuration is shown in the **electron shell diagram** (Figure 6.15).

Figure 6.15 The electron shell diagram for aluminium

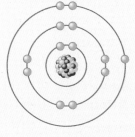

The shorthand way of writing this electron configuration is 2, 8, 3. The meaning of this shorthand is explained in Figure 6.16.

Figure 6.16 Electron configuration in shorthand

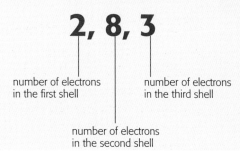

2, 8, 3

number of electrons in the first shell

number of electrons in the third shell

number of electrons in the second shell

125

Isotopes

We now know that the number of protons in the nucleus of a particular element is fixed. If the number of protons were to change then we would have a different element. However, this does not apply to the number of neutrons in the nucleus and this is where we find out about **isotopes**.

Isotopes have the same atomic number but different mass numbers.

This means that **isotopes have the same number of protons but different numbers of neutrons**.

Take carbon as an example. It has three isotopes:

$$^{12}_{6}C \qquad ^{13}_{6}C \qquad ^{14}_{6}C$$

There are 6 protons and 6 electrons in a carbon atom, because the atomic number is 6.

But we know that:

mass number = number of protons − number of neutrons

so

number of neutrons = mass number − number of protons

For $^{12}_{6}C$, the number of neutrons is $12 - 6 = 6$

For $^{13}_{6}C$, the number of neutrons is $13 - 6 = 7$

For $^{14}_{6}C$, the number of neutrons is $14 - 6 = 8$

> The word 'isotope' is based on the Greek word for *same place*. Isotopes have the same place in the Periodic Table because they have the same atomic number.

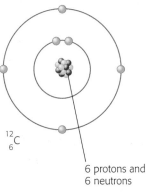

$^{12}_{6}C$

6 protons and 6 neutrons

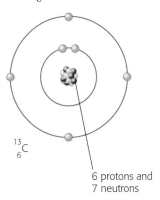

$^{13}_{6}C$

6 protons and 7 neutrons

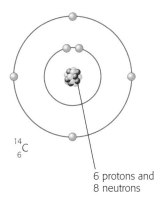

$^{14}_{6}C$

6 protons and 8 neutrons

Figure 6.17 The three isotopes of carbon

It is important to realise that the chemical properties of these three isotopes are identical. This is because it is only the electrons that take part in chemical reactions and the electrons have the same arrangement in all the isotopes. We shall find out more about this later in the chapter (page 130).

Let's consider another element, chlorine. This has two isotopes, as shown in Table 6.3.

Isotope	$^{35}_{17}Cl$	$^{37}_{17}Cl$
mass number, *A*	35	37
atomic number, *Z*	17	17
number of protons	17	17
number of electrons	17	17
number of neutrons	18	20

Table 6.3 The isotopes of chlorine

Relative atomic mass, A_r

Atoms are really very, very tiny. One full stop on this page will contain many millions of atoms. Because they are so tiny, their masses are also tiny. We measure the masses of the atoms on a scale called the **relative atomic mass scale** or the A_r **scale**. (The '**r**' stands for **r**elative.) The isotope carbon-12 ($^{12}_{6}C$) is used as the standard and is given a mass of 12.

As hydrogen is twelve times lighter than carbon-12, it has an A_r of 1. Magnesium has an A_r of 24 because its atoms are twice as heavy as those of carbon-12.

> We often write the mass number after the name of an element when we are referring to a particular isotope, for example, carbon-12.

> We first looked at relative atomic mass on page 107 when we were working out relative formula masses.

Element	Symbol	Relative atomic mass, A_r
hydrogen	H	1
carbon	C	12
nitrogen	N	14
oxygen	O	16
fluorine	F	19
sodium	Na	23
magnesium	Mg	24
aluminium	Al	27
sulphur	S	32
chlorine	Cl	35.5
potassium	K	39
calcium	Ca	40

Table 6.4 The approximate relative atomic masses of some elements

Table 6.4 gives the relative atomic masses of some of the elements with which you are familiar. From the table you will notice that chlorine has an A_r of 35.5. At first sight this seems very odd. Since protons and neutrons have a mass of 1 on the A_r scale, this would suggest that chlorine must contain only either half a proton or half a neutron, which is impossible. In fact, the relative atomic mass scale takes into account the average masses of all the isotopes and their abundance on Earth.

Chlorine has 75% of $^{35}_{17}Cl$ atoms and 25% of $^{37}_{17}Cl$ atoms. When you take the average of the masses of these isotopes and their abundance, you get an A_r of 35.5.

We can now define relative atomic mass.

The relative atomic mass of an element is the average mass of the atom compared to $\frac{1}{12}$ of the mass of an atom of carbon-12.

The 'average mass' takes into account all of its isotopes and their abundance.

Calculating relative atomic masses of elements

We can look more closely at how we can calculate the A_r of chlorine.

In an average sample of chlorine, there is 75% of $^{35}_{17}Cl$ atoms and 25% of $^{37}_{17}Cl$ atoms. This means that for every 100 atoms, 75 will have a relative mass of 35, and 25 will have a relative mass of 37.

We can now calculate the A_r.

$$A_r \text{ of chlorine} = \frac{(35 \times 75) + (37 \times 25)}{100} = \frac{3550}{100} = 35.5$$

Summary

- Mendeleev's construction of the Periodic Table was helped by two creative insights:
  - when elements did not fit into the pattern of increasing atomic mass he swapped the order of the elements to keep those with similar properties grouped together
  - he left gaps for the elements he thought had not yet been discovered.
- Atoms are arranged in order of their atomic number in the Periodic Table.
- The atom has a minute central nucleus, which is positively charged.
- The nucleus contains protons and neutrons.
- Protons have a relative mass of 1 and a relative charge of $+1$.
- Neutrons have a relative mass of 1 and have no charge.
- Electrons orbit the nucleus in shells and have almost zero relative mass and a relative charge of -1.
- The first electron shell can contain a maximum of two electrons.
- The second electron shell contains a maximum of eight electrons.
- The third electron shell contains a maximum of eight electrons.
- The arrangement of electrons in an atom is called the electronic configuration.
- Atomic number (Z) is the number of protons in an atom.
- Mass number (A) is the total number of protons and neutrons in the atom.
- Isotopes have the same atomic number but different mass numbers so they have the same numbers of protons but different numbers of neutrons.
- Relative atomic mass of an element is the average mass of the atom (taking into account all of its isotopes and their abundance) compared to $\frac{1}{12}$ of the mass of an atom of carbon-12.
- **H** It is possible to calculate the relative atomic mass once you know the masses of the isotopes and their percentage abundance.

Questions

6.5 a What is the relative mass and charge of a proton?

  b What is meant by *atomic number*?

  c What is the *mass number*?

  d An atom of potassium has this symbol notation, $^{39}_{19}K$. Work out how many protons, neutrons and electrons there are in this atom.

6.6 Draw the electronic configurations of the following elements:

  a magnesium, atomic number 12

  b fluorine, atomic number 9

  c chlorine, atomic number 17

  d neon, atomic number 10

  e potassium, atomic number 19. (Hint: you will have to start a fourth shell for this electronic configuration.)

6.7 a What is meant by the term *isotope*?

  b Bromine is an element which has two naturally occurring isotopes, $^{79}_{35}Br$ and $^{81}_{35}Br$. Draw a table similar to Table 6.3 (page 126) to show the mass number, atomic number, and numbers of protons, neutrons and electrons.

6.8 a What is meant by the term *relative atomic mass*?

b Explain why chlorine has a relative atomic mass of 35.5.

6.9 Calculate the relative atomic mass of magnesium using the information in the table below.

Isotope	Abundance (%)
^{24}Mg	80
^{25}Mg	10
^{26}Mg	10

C The Periodic Table and the electronic configurations of elements

Sir Humphry Davy was born in Cornwall in 1778. He became interested in chemistry and moved to Bristol to study the sciences. So successful was he that he published a book about his researches in 1800. He was then invited to become a lecturer at the newly formed Royal Institution at the age of 23. He started giving public lectures, which became extremely popular with London society. Two years later he became a Fellow of the Royal Society, which is still the most prestigious scientific organisation in the United Kingdom. However, his greatest contributions to chemistry were to be made in 1807 and 1808, for in these two years he discovered no less than six new chemical elements. So how did he do it?

In 1800, an Italian scientist, Alessandro Volta, invented the world's first battery. It was this invention that was going to lead Davy to discover these six elements. As with many scientific discoveries, it was Davy's creative insight that was to prove the key.

Volta's battery was composed of zinc and silver discs put one on top of the other in a pile (which is why it was known as a voltaic pile), with cardboard discs soaked in sodium chloride solution in between the discs. Davy thought that if the electric current was the result of combining these two elements, then perhaps an electric current could be used to decompose substances back into their elements.

Figure 6.18 Sir Humphry Davy (1778–1829)

He set about doing this with soda (sodium carbonate) and potash (potassium carbonate). He melted them first and then passed an electric current through them. Doing this he produced soft silvery metals, which quickly tarnished in air. He called these metals 'sodium' and 'potassium'. In the following year, he used this method to discover magnesium, calcium, strontium and barium.

Davy was knighted in 1818 and became President of the Royal Society in 1820. He had many achievements to his name, including the invention of a safety lamp for miners, but perhaps one of his greatest contributions was to encourage Michael Faraday to take up the sciences. You can read about Faraday on page 141.

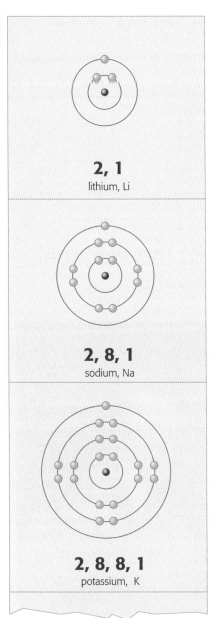

2, 1
lithium, Li

2, 8, 1
sodium, Na

2, 8, 8, 1
potassium, K

Figure 6.19 The first three Group 1 elements

2, 2
beryllium, Be

2, 8, 2
magnesium, Mg

2, 8, 8, 2
calcium, Ca

Figure 6.21 The electronic configurations of the first three Group 2 elements

The electronic configuration of the alkali metals

Sodium and potassium, metals discovered by Davy, were both put by Mendeleev into Group 1 of the Periodic Table. If you look at the electronic configurations of the first three members of Group 1 (Figure 6.19), can you notice a pattern?

All of the electronic configurations in Figure 6.19 have one electron in the outer shell. Although the elements below potassium have more complicated electronic configurations, they too have one electron in their outer shell.

This brings us to an important point. The only particles to take part in chemical reactions are the electrons.

This means that the way that the electrons are arranged in atoms – their electronic configurations – will affect the way each different element reacts. As we will see in the next section (page 134), it is only the electrons in the outer shell that are actually involved in chemical reactions.

As Group 1 is descended you should remember that the elements get more reactive. For example, lithium gently fizzes on the surface of water, while potassium reacts violently with water and the hydrogen gas produced in the reaction catches fire. This is related to the electronic configurations of the Group 1 elements. Each time you go down an element in the group, you will notice that another shell of electrons is added. This makes the outer negative electron further away from the attraction of the positive nucleus, so it becomes easier to lose in a chemical reaction.

Figure 6.20 Potassium is very reactive. Here it is reacting with water

The electronic configuration of Group 2 elements

By now you might be thinking that elements in Group 2 of the Periodic Table must have two electrons in their outer shell. If you were thinking this, then you would be correct! See Figure 6.21.

● The electronic configurations of the first 20 elements

Figure 6.22 The electronic configurations of the first 20 elements in the Periodic Table

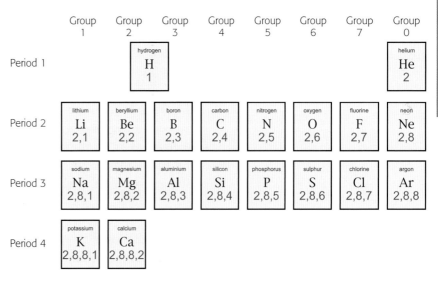

After the 20th element in the Periodic Table, the electronic configurations become more complicated. However, you should notice that with all the groups, the number of outer electrons is almost always the same as the group number. There are two exceptions to this, both in the first period. Hydrogen has one electron but it is not counted as a Group 1 element because it is a gas, not a solid metal like the other Group 1 elements. Helium in Group 0 has two electrons but this outer shell is a full shell, just like all the other Group 0 elements.

The other point to notice is that the number of shells corresponds to the number of the period. For example, in Period 1 the first shell is being filled and in Period 3 it is the third shell that is being filled.

● Electronic configurations in Group 7 and their reactivity

All the elements in Group 7 have seven electrons in their outer shell. But, unlike the alkali metals of Group 1, reactivity *decreases* as you go down the group. Fluorine, at the top of Group 7, is the most reactive member of the group. Why is this the case?

The members of Group 7 have almost full outer shells of electrons (see Figure 6.22 above). They only need one more electron to gain a full shell. Group 1 elements lose the one electron in their outer shells when they react. However, when Group 7 elements react they gain an electron to make a full outer shell. As the outer shell gets further away from the nucleus, the attraction for the extra electron needed for the halogen to react becomes weaker. This is why the reactivity decreases down Group 7.

Group 0 elements are also called the noble gases.

● Electronic configuration and the lack of reactivity of the noble gases

For many years after their discovery the noble gases were believed to be totally inert (unreactive) and so not form any compounds. We now know that under certain conditions some of them can be made to react. So why are they so unreactive? The answer again lies in their electronic configurations.

When an atom reacts its outer electrons must be involved. However, in the case of Group 0 elements they all have full shells (see Figure 6.22 on the previous page). The full shell is very stable and it takes a large amount of energy to change this electron configuration. This is why the noble gases are very unreactive.

Summary

- The number of outer electrons is connected to the position of an element in the Periodic Table. The outer shell that is being filled corresponds to the number of the period. The group number is the number of electrons in the outer shell (with the exception of hydrogen and helium).
- You need to know the electronic configurations of the first 20 elements.
- As Group 1 is descended the outer electron becomes easier to lose because it is further away from the attraction of the nucleus. This means that Group 1 elements get more reactive going down the group.
- Group 7 elements have seven electrons in their outer shells. In a chemical reaction they attract one more electron to make a full shell. As the group is descended the outer shell is further from the attraction of the nucleus so the extra electron is harder to attract. This explains why reactivity decreases going down the group.
- The noble gases of Group 0 are very unreactive because their outer electron shells are full.

Questions

6.10 Gallium has three electrons in its outer shell and it is filling its fourth shell.
    a What group is gallium in?
    b In what period can gallium be found?

6.11 Why does the reactivity of the alkali metals increase down the group?

6.12 Group 7 elements are known as the halogens.
    a How many electrons are in the outer shell of a halogen?
    b Explain why reactivity increases as you go up the group.

6.13 Group 0 elements are also called the noble gases.
    a Draw the electronic configurations of a helium atom and a neon atom.
    b Why are Group 0 elements so unreactive?

D Ionic bonding

Helium is the second most abundant element in the Universe, making up 7% of all matter. The most abundant element is hydrogen, which makes up another 92%. If helium is so abundant, why was it only isolated in 1895? The answer lies in the fact that it is not that abundant on Earth. It is also very unreactive and is a gas. Helium was not even discovered first on Earth; it was actually discovered in the Sun by two scientists in 1868. How was this

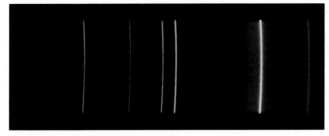

Figure 6.23 The lines that identify helium. Lockyer noticed the bright yellow one in his spectroscope

done? Pierre Janssen, a French astronomer, was observing an eclipse of the Sun in India in 1868 through a newly invented instrument called a spectroscope. In the same year Norman Lockyer, a British astronomer, also used a spectroscope to view the Sun. Robert Bunsen, of Bunsen burner fame, and Gustav Kirchhov had invented the spectroscope a few years earlier. A spectroscope splits up light into its visible spectrum of colours. If that light has travelled through atoms that have been subjected to a lot of energy then distinct lines are visible in the spectrum. This is a way of identifying elements, similar to fingerprinting. Lockyer noticed that there was a bright yellow line in the spectrum from the Sun that was not the same as any line from any known element on Earth. He proposed that a new element had been discovered. It is called helium from the Greek word for the Sun, *helios*. He was ridiculed at the time but William Ramsey, a Scottish chemist, discovered it on Earth a quarter of a century later. He found the gas trapped in a uranium ore.

Helium is not that abundant on Earth. In fact, supplies of it may run out within the next 50 years. This is because helium is produced by the radioactive decay of other elements deep in the Earth's crust. If it is not trapped in some way, the helium seeps into the atmosphere and once it gets there, it stays for about one million years before floating off to be lost in space.

Quite a lot of helium has been trapped in natural gas fields and natural gas can be up to 7% helium. The helium can be separated from natural gas when the natural gas is refined. Often, however, it costs too much for companies to do this and the helium is just lost into the atmosphere when the methane is burnt.

Helium is a truly amazing element, but does it matter if we run out of it? Under normal conditions of pressure it does not become a liquid until −269 °C (4 K), which is the lowest temperature at which any known substance liquefies. This is the key to some very important uses.

Figure 6.24 Liquid helium makes the electromagnets in this MRI scanner superconducting so that the scanner can image the body

- ⟩ Liquid helium is used to cool the wires of electromagnets in hospital MRI (magnetic resonance imaging) scanners so that they become superconducting. The MRI scanners are then used to produce brain and body images.
- ⟩ Liquid helium keeps hydrogen fuel and oxygen in the liquid state in space rockets. It is also used to cool nuclear reactors.
- ⟩ Because it is so unreactive, helium is used in arc welding to maintain an unreactive atmosphere around the weld.
- ⟩ Deep-sea divers avoid the bends by breathing a helium–oxygen mixture.
- ⟩ Helium is used in many lasers.
- ⟩ And, of course, it is used in the party balloons that float up to the ceiling if you let the string go!

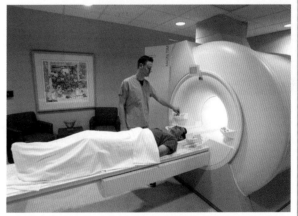

Figure 6.25 Helium is much less dense than the air, so keep a tight hold on these balloons!

● The bonding in sodium chloride

We now know that helium is so unreactive because its outer electron shell is full. All the noble gases have full outer shells. This is a very stable arrangement, so electrons cannot easily be lost or gained. Remember that it is the electrons in atoms that take part in chemical reactions, not the protons or the neutrons. If noble gas atoms hold on to their electrons and there is no space for them to accept more from other atoms, because they have full shells, they will not react.

The stable arrangement of a full electron shell can be achieved by other elements and this is the key to the formation of **ions**. An ion is an atom, or group of atoms, with a positive or negative charge. You have already met ions earlier in the course when we were looking at ordinary salt, sodium chloride. You may remember that if an electric current is passed through molten sodium chloride the sodium ions go to the negative electrode and the chloride ions go to the positive **electrode**.

So why do sodium and chlorine react together in the first place?

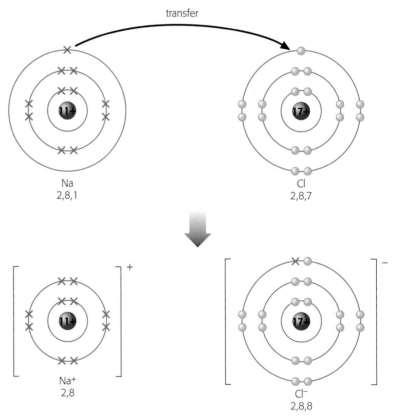

Figure 6.27 How sodium and chlorine react together

The easiest way for a sodium atom to achieve a full shell is for it to lose one electron. As there are still 11 protons in the nucleus the nuclear charge of 11+ stays the same. However, there are now only 10 electrons in the electron shells, with a combined charge of 10−, so the overall charge on the ion is 1+. We show that a sodium ion has a 1+ charge by writing it as Na⁺.

The **electrode** is the conductor, usually a rod, which conducts electric current into or out of the molten sodium chloride. You can read more about this on page 141.

Figure 6.26 When sodium reacts with chlorine the compound sodium chloride is formed

No matter which atom an electron belongs to, all electrons are the same. For convenience we show electrons as dots and crosses, so that we can see which electrons come from which atom. The diagrams are called **dot and cross diagrams**.

$$\begin{array}{l} 11 \text{ protons} = 11+ \\ 10 \text{ electrons} = \underline{10-} \\ \text{overall charge} = 1+ \end{array} \quad \mathbf{Na^+}$$

We refer to a chlor**ide** ion even though the element is called chlor**ine**.

17 protons = 17+
18 electrons = 18−
overall charge = 1−   **Cl**⁻

Now consider the chlorine atom, with seven electrons in its outer shell. The easiest way for it to achieve a full shell of eight is to gain one electron, and this is exactly what it does. Each chlorine atom takes an electron from a sodium atom. The protons don't move so the 17 protons give a charge on chlorine's nucleus of 17+. However, there are now 18 electrons, giving a charge of 18−. The overall charge on the chloride ion is 1− and we show this by writing it as Cl^-.

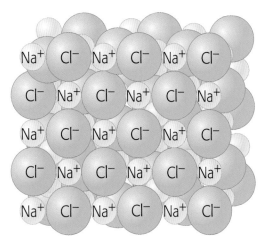

Figure 6.28 The oppositely charged ions attract each other strongly to form a giant structure of billions of ions

Ionic bonds are made by the transfer of electrons from one atom to another to form positive and negative ions. The oppositely charged sodium and chloride ions attract each other strongly and this attraction is called **ionic bonding**. Billions of ions are held together to make huge structures that we call **giant ionic structures**.

● Properties of giant ionic structures

We first met giant structures when we considered metals on page 117.

Now that we know sodium chloride has a giant ionic structure, we can explain some of its physical properties. All ionic compounds have giant ionic structures and they share these physical properties.

▷ They have a regular crystal shape. This is because the ions fit together in a regular way, giving differently shaped crystals depending on which ions are involved.

Figure 6.29 Shapes of ionic crystals: sodium chloride (left) and copper sulphate (right)

▷ They have high melting and boiling points. Oppositely charged ions attract each other strongly. For a solid to melt, the giant structure has to break down and allow the ions to move freely in a liquid (Figure 6.30, overleaf). This requires much heat energy, which is why the melting points of giant ionic structures, like sodium chloride, are high.

▷ They are able to conduct electricity when molten or in solution. A solid ionic compound cannot conduct electricity because its ions are fixed in place. When the solid structure (often called a **lattice**) breaks down the ions are free to move. This happens when the solid is melted and when it is dissolved in water. These ions can then travel to the positive or negative electrodes and this flow of charged particles causes the electric current to flow. See page 142 of the next section.

135

Figure 6.30
a In a solid, ions are fixed in position and can only vibrate.
b When the solid melts, the ions are free to move.
c When the solid dissolves, the ions are free to move in the solution.

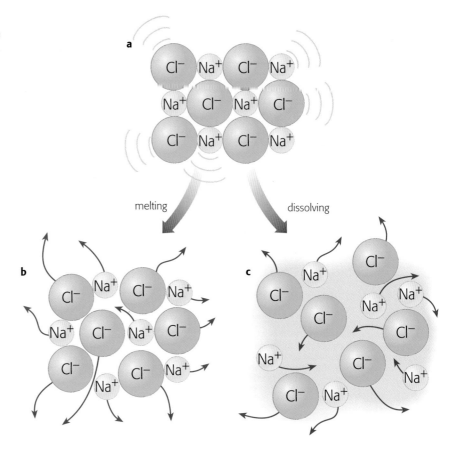

melting   dissolving

● Forming other ionic compounds

We have seen how one ionic compound, sodium chloride, is bonded. In the chemical reaction between sodium and chlorine there is a transfer of an electron from each of the sodium atoms to each of the chlorine atoms, to make oppositely charged ions. It has a **formula** of NaCl because there is one sodium ion produced for every chloride ion formed. The proportions of each ion are the same in the compound.

If, instead of sodium, we react magnesium with chlorine, we can predict which ions will be formed and the formula of the ionic compound.

Remember that magnesium (atomic number 12) is in Group 2 so we already know that it has two electrons in its outer shell. In the reaction it will lose these to form Mg^{2+} ions and achieve a full shell. This time two chlorine atoms are needed to pick up the electrons and gain complete shells to become Cl^- ions (Figure 6.31).

So the formula of the ionic compound magnesium chloride is $MgCl_2$. The strong attraction of the oppositely charged ions will give magnesium chloride a giant ionic structure.

As you can see, it is only the arrangement of the outer electrons that are changing, so chemists often leave out the inner shells in electronic configuration diagrams.

> The formula of a compound tells you which atoms or ions are present in each substance and in what proportions. We sometimes use the term **formula unit** for ionic compounds.

Figure 6.31 How magnesium and chlorine react together

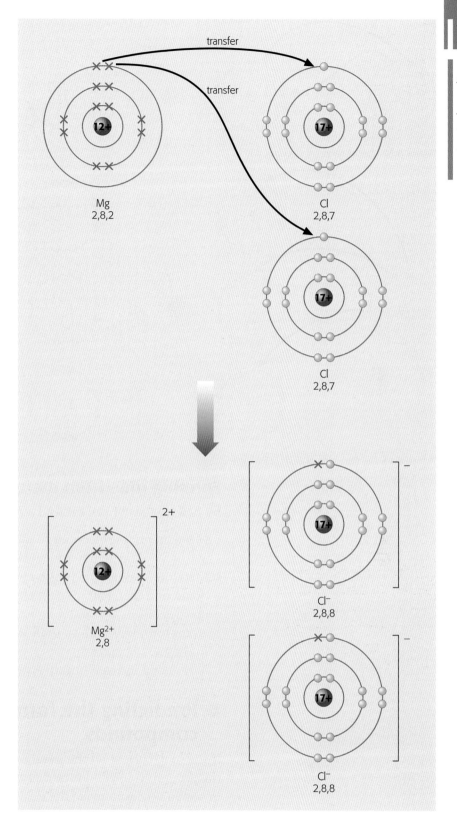

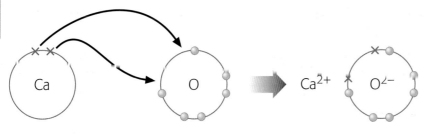

Figure 6.32 The formation of calcium oxide

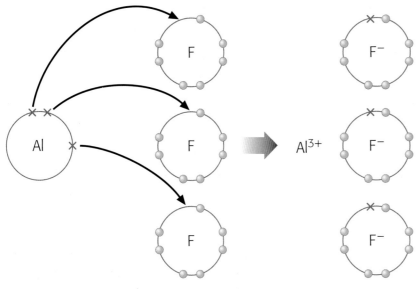

Consider the ionic compound, calcium oxide (Figure 6.32). Calcium is in Group 2 so it will have two electrons in its outer shell. Oxygen is in Group 6. Notice we have left out the inner shells.

Aluminium fluoride is another ionic compound (Figure 6.33). Aluminium is in Group 3 and fluorine is in Group 7. As you can see when aluminium and fluorine react together, the compound produced has the formula AlF_3.

Figure 6.33 The formation of aluminium fluoride

Forming ions from metal and non-metal atoms

By now you may have noticed a pattern emerging.

▸ Metal atoms lose electrons to form positive ions with charges of 1+, 2+ or 3+. You do not find metal ions with a charge greater than 3+.
▸ Metal ions are always positively charged.
▸ Some non-metal atoms gain electrons to form negative ions with charges of 1−, 2− and 3−, but never 4−. Not all non-metal atoms form ions and we shall learn about another type of bonding in the next chapter.
▸ Non-metal ions are negatively charged.

● Predicting the formula of ionic compounds

If you look back at all the ionic compounds we have considered in this section, you will notice that the oppositely charged ions combine in such a way as to make the compounds neutral. Ionic compounds are always neutral and this gives us a way to predict their formulae, so long as we know the charges on the ions that make them up.

Consider calcium chloride. We can predict its formula by knowing the charges on the ions.

Ionic compound: calcium chloride
Ions present: Ca^{2+} Cl^-
Balance the charges: one Ca^{2+} must be balanced by two Cl^-
Formula: $CaCl_2$

We can do this with other ionic compounds, using the information in Table 6.5.

Table 6.5 The charges on some common ions

Positive ions		Negative ions	
aluminium	Al^{3+}	bromide	Br^-
ammonium	NH_4^+	carbonate	CO_3^{2-}
calcium	Ca^{2+}	chloride	Cl^-
copper(II)	Cu^{2+}	fluoride	F^-
hydrogen	H^+	hydrogencarbonate	HCO_3^-
iron(II)	Fe^{2+}	hydroxide	OH^-
iron(III)	Fe^{3+}	iodide	I^-
lead	Pb^{2+}	nitrate	NO_3^-
magnesium	Mg^{2+}	phosphate	PO_4^{3-}
potassium	K^+	oxide	O^{2-}
silver	Ag^+	sulphate	SO_4^{2-}
sodium	Na^+	sulphide	S^{2-}
zinc	Zn^{2+}		

When working out the formula of sodium hydroxide you will notice that the hydroxide ion is not just one atom but is made of hydrogen and oxygen bonded together with the overall charge of $1-$.

Ionic compound: sodium hydroxide
Ions present: Na^+ OH^-
Balance the charges: one Na^+ is balanced by one OH^-
Formula: NaOH

The carbonate ion is CO_3^{2-}, which means in this ion there are three oxygen atoms bonded to one carbon atom, giving an overall charge on the ion of $2-$.

At this stage it is only necessary to know that ions containing more than one element do exist and that the charges can be used to work out the formulae of compounds that contain them.

Ionic compound: calcium carbonate
Ions present: Ca^{2+} CO_3^{2-}
Balance the charges: one Ca^{2+} must be balanced by one CO_3^{2-}
Formula: $CaCO_3$

The ending *-ate* in a compound usually tells you that oxygen is present in a compound. The ending *-ide* tells you that there are only two elements bonded together in the compound.

Some of the transition metals form ions with more than one charge. Compounds whose names begin iron(II) contain Fe^{2+} ions, where as those with names that start iron(III) contain Fe^{3+} ions.

Ionic compound: iron(II) nitrate
Ions present: Fe^{2+} NO_3^-
Balance the charges: one Fe^{2+} must be balanced by two NO_3^-
Formula: $Fe(NO_3)_2$

In this example the brackets around the nitrate ion are used to show clearly that there are two nitrate ions present.

Summary

- An ion is an atom, or group of atoms, with a positive or negative charge.
- Ions are formed when atoms lose or gain electrons.
- If an atom loses electrons it forms a positive ion.
- If an atom gains electrons it forms a negative ion.
- Ionic bonds are made by the transfer of electrons to form positive and negative ions.
- Ionic bonding is the strong attraction of positive and negative ions in a giant ionic structure.
- Giant ionic structures have a regular crystal shape because their ions are regularly arranged. They have high melting points and boiling points because of the strong attraction of oppositely charged ions in a giant structure. They conduct electricity when molten or in solution because the ions are then free to move to the positive and negative electrodes.
- Atoms usually achieve a noble gas electronic configuration in the formation of ions, which is a full outer shell.
- It is possible to predict the charges of some ions in their compounds if the group number of the element is known. Group 1 elements form 1+ ions, Group 2 elements form 2+ ions, Group 6 elements form 2− ions and Group 7 elements form 1− ions.
- Atoms and ions may be represented by dot and cross diagrams.
- Once the charges on the ions making up an ionic compound are known, the formula can be predicted.

Questions

6.14 a Draw the full electronic configurations of the lithium atom and the fluorine atom using dot and cross diagrams. (Hint: look at Figure 6.22 on page 131.)

b Show the formation of the ionic bond in lithium fluoride.

c What type of structure will lithium fluoride have in the solid?

d Predict, with reasons, *three* physical properties you would expect lithium fluoride to have.

6.15 Draw dot and cross diagrams, using only the outer shells, to show the formation of ions from atoms in:

a potassium chloride

b magnesium oxide

c sodium oxide

d calcium iodide.

You can find the electronic structures of most of these atoms in Figure 6.22 on page 131. Iodine is in Group 7.

6.16 Sensodyne toothpaste is manufactured for those people who have sensitive teeth. The active ingredient that helps to relieve the pain of sensitive teeth is the ionic compound strontium chloride.

a What is an ion?

b Strontium is a Group 2 element. What will the charge be on its ion?

c Predict the formula of strontium chloride.

6.17 When sodium forms an ion, its electronic structure is the same as the neon atom. Give *two* differences between an atom of neon and a sodium ion.

6.18 Predict the formulae of these ionic compounds, using the information about charges on ions found in Table 6.5 (page 139):

- **a** aluminium bromide
- **b** iron(II) sulphide
- **c** silver oxide
- **d** ammonium chloride
- **e** zinc fluoride
- **f** calcium nitrate
- **g** magnesium hydroxide
- **h** magnesium carbonate
- **i** iron(III) bromide
- **j** lead iodide.

E Electrolysis of ionic compounds

Michael Faraday was the son of a blacksmith. At the age of 13, he left his home in Yorkshire to seek work in London where he became apprenticed to a bookbinder. Through reading the books he bound, he began to develop an interest in chemistry and electricity. He built himself a battery like the one invented by Volta (see page 129), using halfpennies, and was soon experimenting with the electricity he produced.

Faraday was given tickets to attend a series of lectures at the Royal Institution delivered by the famous chemist Humphry Davy (see page 129). Faraday made detailed notes, added some excellent illustrations and bound

Figure 6.34 It was Michael Faraday (1791–1867) who first began the Royal Institution's Christmas Lectures for Young People, which are now televised every Christmas. This is a drawing of one of Faraday's Christmas Lectures, given in 1855. Prince Edward, later to become King Edward VII, is seated on the left of his father, Prince Albert, in the front row

them into a book, which he presented to Davy. Davy, recognising Faraday's talents, installed him as a laboratory assistant at the Royal Institution. Faraday was aged 21. His research work was so fruitful that within 12 years he was appointed Professor of Chemistry at the Royal Institution.

Faraday was one of the most influential scientists who has ever lived. His discoveries and achievements are vast and include the invention of the first electric motor and the dynamo. Of particular importance to this section of your course, he was the first person to try and understand the process of electrolysis. (Davy had used electrolysis to discover elements such as sodium, potassium and calcium.) He invented the word 'electrode' for the conducting rods dipping into molten compounds or solutions and he predicted that charged particles were present in the compounds that conducted. He called these particles 'ions'.

Potassium, sodium and calcium are at the top of the Reactivity Series. Other less reactive elements, such as zinc, iron and lead, can be extracted from their metal oxides by reacting them with carbon.

The electron was discovered by J.J. Thomson in 1897.

What happens during electrolysis?

Electrolysis is the splitting of a substance using electricity. Humphry Davy was the first to use electrolysis to split compounds up and he discovered reactive elements that could not be extracted from their compounds in any other way. This is because the ions they form are particularly stable.

It was Faraday who helped people understand the process of electrolysis. He realised that the compounds that conducted electricity when molten and in solution contained charged particles, which he called 'ions'. These charged ions are attracted to the oppositely charged electrodes, so that negative ions go to the positive electrode and positive ions go to the negative electrode (Figure 6.35). Here the ions lose their charge and form neutral atoms. We sometimes say they have been **discharged**. Faraday worked all this out 70 years before the electron was discovered.

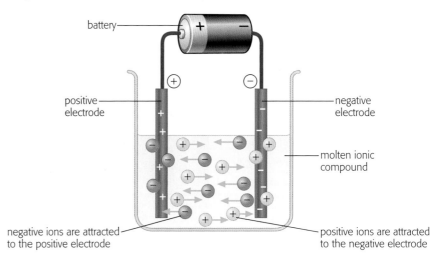

Figure 6.35 During electrolysis the ions move to the oppositely charged electrodes

Explaining electrolysis

We can explain what happens during electrolysis in more detail now that we know electrons are involved. The electric current from the battery, or d.c. power pack, is a flow of electrons from the negative terminal to the positive terminal (see *GCSE Science* page 177). Electrolysis only works with **direct current (d.c.)**. This means the electrons are flowing in one direction only.

However, it is not electrons that flow through molten salt. Let's consider the electrolysis of molten sodium chloride. Na^+ ions are attracted to the negative electrode and here they each pick up an electron (Figure 6.36). They lose their $1+$ charge and become neutral sodium atoms.

We can represent this using a **half equation**. Half equations show the loss or gain of electrons from atoms and ions. They represent *half* the reaction that is going on during electrolysis. They are balanced in much the same way as the balanced formulae equations you have met so far in the course, only this time the charges on each side of the equation must also balance.

$$Na^+(l) + e^- \rightarrow Na(s)$$

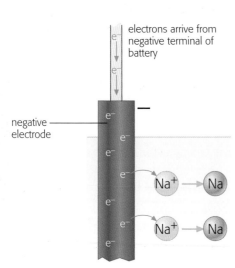

Figure 6.36 The electrons at the negative electrode are picked up by the positively charged sodium ions that have been attracted to the electrode. The sodium ions are discharged and form sodium atoms

H

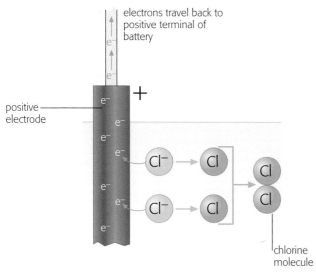

electrons travel back to positive terminal of battery

positive electrode

chlorine molecule

Figure 6.37 The chloride ion discharges at the positive electrode by releasing its extra electron, which travels back to the positive terminal of the battery. The chlorine atoms combine to make chlorine molecules

Note we have used state symbols (l) for molten, or liquid, and (s) for the solid sodium that is produced. 'e$^-$' is the symbol for an electron, showing its negative charge.

At the positive electrode the negatively charged chloride ions arrive and lose their one extra electron so that they form neutral chlorine atoms (Figure 6.37).

$$Cl^-(l) \rightarrow Cl(g) + e^-$$

In this case chlorine atoms combine immediately to form chlorine molecules (Cl_2), so we write the balanced half equation like this:

$$2Cl^-(l) \rightarrow Cl_2(g) + 2e^-$$

Notice that not only do the number of chlorine atoms balance but the charges are the same on both sides. The state symbol for gas is (g).

The flow of the electric current in the circuit is completed by the flow of the charged ions between the electrodes.

● Predicting the products of electrolysis for other molten binary salts

Once you understand the principle of what happens in electrolysis, it is possible to predict the products of other binary salts. A **binary salt** is a metal compound that can be made from an acid and which contains the ions of two different elements. For example, sodium chloride is a binary salt because it contains sodium ions bonded to chloride ions. It can be made by neutralising hydrochloric acid with sodium hydroxide.

Because metal ions are always positively charged they will always be attracted to the negative electrode, while non-metal ions will always go the positive electrode because they are negatively charged.

The products of the electrolysis of copper bromide

Copper bromide has the formula $CuBr_2$. Copper ions are Cu^{2+} and bromide ions are Br^-.

▶ **At the negative electrode**
Copper ions are attracted and copper will be discharged. The electrode reaction is:

$$Cu^{2+}(l) + 2e^- \rightarrow Cu(s)$$

▶ **At the positive electrode**
Bromide ions are negatively charged and will be attracted and discharged. The electrode reaction is:

$$2Br^-(l) \rightarrow Br_2 + 2e^-$$

Binary salts always end in *-ide* because this ending tells you that only two elements bond together in the compound.

The products of the electrolysis of lead iodide

Lead iodide has the formula PbI_2. Lead ions are Pb^{2+} and iodide ions are I^-.

▸ **At the negative electrode**
Lead ions are attracted and lead will be discharged.
The electrode reaction is:

$$Pb^{2+}(l) + 2e^- \rightarrow Pb(s)$$

▸ **At the positive electrode**
Iodide ions are negatively charged and will be attracted and discharged, so iodine is formed.
The electrode reaction is:

$$2I^-(l) \rightarrow I_2(g) + 2e^-$$

Summary

- Electrolysis is the splitting of a substance using electricity. During electrolysis ions move towards oppositely charged electrodes, so positive ions move to the negatively charged electrode and negative ions move to the positively charged electrode.
- Metal ions are always attracted to the negative electrode because they are positively charged, so metals are produced at this electrode.
- Non-metal ions are always discharged at the positive electrode.
- Binary salts are metal salts that contain the ions of only two elements, e.g. aluminium chloride.
- You will need to predict the products of electrolysis of binary salts and give their electrode reactions.
- Half equations are used to describe the reaction occurring at each electrode. In a balanced half equation the number of atoms of each element and the total charge must be the same on both sides.

Questions

6.19 a Explain what is meant by the terms *electrolysis*, *electrode* and *ion*.
   b Explain why, during the electrolysis of potassium chloride, the potassium ion K^+ travels to the negative electrode.

6.20 Predict the products of electrolysis of the following binary salts. In each case give the half equations for the electrode reactions.
   a potassium chloride
   b copper(II) chloride
   c lead bromide
   d magnesium iodide
   e sodium bromide
   You can find out the charges on the ions in these compounds by looking at Table 6.5 on page 139.

7 Chemical structures

A New forms of carbon

The best optical microscope can be used to view objects down to the size of 250 nm. (1 nanometre, abbreviation 'nm', is one millionth of a millimetre.) Individual atoms are much smaller than this, so is it possible that we can view them? The answer to this lies in the invention of the scanning probe microscope (SPM). The first SPM was invented in 1981 by Heinrich Rohrer and Gerd Binning, while working at IBM's research laboratory in Zurich, Switzerland. It earned them the Nobel Prize for Physics in 1986. (You can read more about Nobel Prizes on page 170.)

The SPM works by probing the surface of a substance. No surface is really flat. The atoms stick out like bumps. A 1 mm length of surface may contain about 3 million atoms sticking out. The first SPM had a very fine conducting tip which came very close to the bumpy surface, allowing electrons to jump from the tip (Figure 7.1). As it moved over the individual atoms it would become nearer or further away, depending on whether it was scanning the top of the bump or the bottom. This changed the number of electrons that were able to 'tunnel' into the surface and altered the electric current flowing back to be detected. A computer processed the changes in current to give a visual image of the surface, allowing the atoms to be 'seen' for the very first time. This first SPM was called the 'scanning tunnelling microscope'.

Within a few years the design had been adapted to include a wide range of different types of SPM. The 'atomic force microscope' probes the surface using a tip that literally brushes the atoms and rises and falls with the shape of them. Laser beams measure how much the tip goes up and down, giving another very powerful way of imaging atoms.

SPMs have enabled the nanotechnology revolution to take off because now scientists can actually move atoms around. Figure 7.3 shows you one of the first attempts at this, done (in 1989), as you could probably guess, at an IBM laboratory!

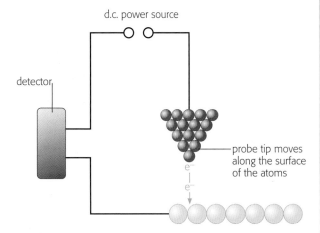

Figure 7.1 How the scanning probe microscope (SPM) works. A voltage is applied and the current changes depending on how far the probe tip is from the surface as it moves over it. This enables a three-dimensional image of the surface atoms to be made

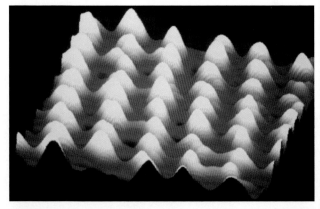

Figure 7.2 An image of surface atoms from an SPM

Figure 7.3 The scanning tunnelling microscope was the first device to be used to move individual atoms around. Each of these letters is only 5 nm from top to bottom and the blue dots making them up are xenon atoms.

● An amazing discovery

Many scientific discoveries have happened by chance. In other words, luck has had an important part to play. It may be a particular observation that is unusual or a result that wasn't predicted. When your experiment has appeared to go wrong and not given you the expected result you have probably started all over again and said 'it must have gone wrong'. However, sometimes it is the unusual results that can lead to the most amazing discoveries, and this is often how science has advanced.

Let's go back to the 1980s. A British research chemist, Harry Kroto, working at Sussex University, was investigating molecules found in outer space, not on Earth. Through using the techniques of spectroscopy (see page 133) it has been possible to discover molecules that do exist on Earth. Of particular interest to Kroto were long-chain carbon molecules, and he became more and more interested about where these carbon chain molecules were formed. He predicted that they might be made in the outer atmosphere of giant red stars. But how could he prove his prediction?

At this point (1984) he found out that a group of researchers at Rice University in Texas, led by Richard Smalley, had built a machine that could recreate the conditions of the outer atmosphere of these stars. They used high-powered laser beams to blast atoms from the solid into the vapour. At the time, they were doing this to create different molecules but had not thought about using it on carbon atoms. Kroto suggested that they might try, and eventually they agreed to vaporise **graphite** in their apparatus. Graphite is one form of the element carbon and contains only carbon atoms in its structure.

As soon as the American scientists and Kroto had the graphite under laser beam fire, Kroto's predicted carbon chains started to form. However, they noticed something very unusual. There appeared to be a carbon molecule with a relative molecular mass of 720. That meant that the formula of this molecule must be C_{60}. At first they just could not believe it, but every time they repeated the experiment this molecule appeared. It also seemed to be particularly stable. However, it was only ever there in minute quantities. They guessed that the stability of the C_{60} molecule must be because of its structure, but how do you arrange 60 carbon atoms into a stable molecule?

The idea began to form that C_{60} must be a cage-like structure of carbon atoms. This was a turning point. Harry Kroto remembered visiting a very famous exhibition held in Montreal, Canada, called Expo 67. Here one of the exhibits was a building designed by the architect and engineer Robert Buckminster Fuller. It was called a geodesic dome. Harry recalls: 'I had actually been inside this remarkable structure at that time and remembered pushing my small son in his pram along the ramps and up the escalators, high

> Remember: carbon is one of the very few non-metal elements to be able to form chains with itself (see page 82).

Figure 7.4 The structure of Buckminster Fuller's famous geodesic dome is repeated at the atomic level in C_{60}

up among the exhibition stands and close to the delicate network of struts from which the edifice is primarily constructed'.

Kroto also remembered making up a cardboard model of the night sky for his son from hexagons and pentagons. This was enough for Richard Smalley, who quickly constructed a paper model of the C_{60} molecule made of 20 hexagons and 12 pentagons. They named the molecule **buckminsterfullerene** in honour of Robert Buckminster Fuller and his visionary building. These molecules are also known as 'buckyballs' because a football has exactly the same design of pentagons and hexagons.

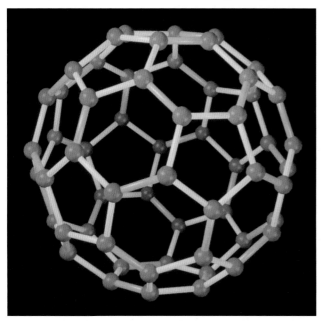

Figure 7.5 A model of the C_{60} molecule, buckminsterfullerene. There is a carbon atom at each point of the hexagons and pentagons

Figure 7.6 This football is also a model of buckminsterfullerene

Kroto, Smalley and their team published a paper about the C_{60} molecule in the scientific journal *Nature*. The paper caused a sensation. After all, carbon chemistry had been investigated for more than a century and only two forms of carbon were known, **graphite** and **diamond**. We shall look in more detail at the structure and properties of diamond and graphite on page 151.

Not all scientists believed that Harry Kroto had, by accident, discovered a new form of carbon. The next stage was to make buckminsterfullerene in larger quantities so that its chemistry could be investigated and its existence proved. Kroto set about doing this at Sussex University, but it was to take him 5 years and in the end he would not be credited with its production. He was narrowly beaten to this, as we shall see.

Another chance discovery

We now need to look at the second chance discovery in the buckminsterfullerene story. In 1983 Donald Huffman, an American scientist, and Wolfgang Krätschmer, a German colleague, had been experimenting by electrically heating graphite rods. They hoped to see if they could work out the way that carbon soot forms in interstellar space. They had some odd results but had dismissed these as contamination from oil in the apparatus. In 1988 they came back to this research and started to wonder if the results they had obtained might be due to the C_{60} molecule discovered by Kroto and his colleagues. It wasn't long before they realised that they were. They set about producing buckminsterfullerene in bulk and within 2 years they had succeeded, using much the same method of electrically heating graphite rods but this time in an inert atmosphere of helium. They sent their paper to the journal *Nature* in 1990.

When a paper is sent to a scientific journal, another eminent scientist in that area of science always reviews it. So who else would receive this paper but Harry Kroto. Days before this, he and his team at Sussex had succeeded in isolating enough C_{60} to work on. Both Huffman and Krätschmer and the Sussex team had dissolved the molecule in an organic solvent to produce a red solution from which crystals of buckminsterfullerene could be obtained. However, the honour of being the first to produce buckminsterfullerene in large quantities went to Huffman and Krätschmer.

Yet more fullerenes are discovered

The first fullerene may have been the molecule C_{60}, but heating graphite by electricity also produced an even bigger molecule C_{70}. Later, C_{72} and C_{84} were discovered and now many fullerenes are known, containing from 32 to 960 carbon atoms. All of these carbon molecules are collectively called the fullerenes. They are all hollow closed structures that contain 12 pentagons of carbon but with differing numbers of hexagons (Figure 7.8). They are counted as a third form of carbon, alongside diamond and graphite.

The above story is an example of serendipity in science. 'Serendipity' means happy chance. Louis Pasteur, the famous 19th century French scientist, said 'chance favours the prepared mind'. In other words, there may be luck in scientific discoveries but it is a great scientist that recognises the implications of a happy chance.

Harry Kroto, Richard Smalley and Robert Curl were jointly awarded the Nobel Prize for Chemistry in 1996 for their discovery of the fullerenes. You may well ask where Robert Curl featured in the buckminsterfullerene tale. He introduced Kroto to Smalley and also worked alongside them as they made their discoveries. Harry Kroto received another high honour as he was also knighted in 1996.

Let's leave the last words to Sir Harry: 'It doesn't matter how good a scientist you are, the likelihood of a discovery like that is like winning the pools.'

Figure 7.7 Sir Harry Kroto, holding a model of buckminsterfullerene in his left hand, along with other fullerenes he has discovered. The buckminsterfullerene molecule is really only 1 nm in size

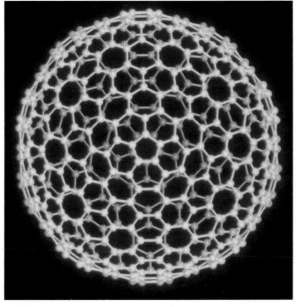

Figure 7.8 The giant fullerene C_{540}

● Nanotubes

Harry Kroto and Richard Smalley began to think about what would happen when you made fullerenes that were very large. They wondered if the molecules might be cylinders rather than balls. Their question was answered in 1991, in Japan, when Sumio Iijima reported that the method used to produce C_{60} and other fullerenes also produced cage-like cylinders of carbon. The first ones to be produced were multi-walled **carbon nanotubes** made up of several cylinders of carbon atoms, one inside the other. Now it is possible to make single-walled carbon nanotubes.

> **Carbon nanotubes** are so-called because they are made up of only carbon atoms and their diameter is about 1 nanometre (50 000 times thinner than a human hair). Their length may be measured in micrometres. (1000 micrometres = 1 millimetre)

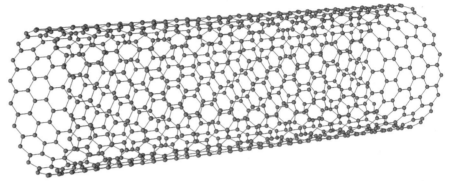

Figure 7.9 a A multi-walled carbon nanotube, discovered by Sumio Iijima in 1991

b A single-walled nanotube, also made up from carbon atoms

● Uses of fullerenes and nanotubes

Clearly, whatever fullerenes and nanotubes are used for must be related to their properties. It is now possible to produce fullerenes and nanotubes in reasonable quantities and this means that there is much research into their properties.

Uses of fullerenes

▶ The fullerene structure is strong and can withstand high pressures and high temperatures. The structures might act like tiny ball bearings, lubricating surfaces.

▶ Drug molecules could be placed inside fullerenes, allowing them to act as drug delivery vehicles inside the body. It may soon be possible to target cancer drugs directly at cancer cells using fullerenes.

▶ In the solid, C_{60} molecules pack together, leaving holes that can be filled by metal atoms, which gives some very interesting properties. For example, when rubidium atoms fill these holes the substance can become superconducting below 28 K (below −245 °C). Although this is very cold, further research has already raised the temperature at which these metal salts become superconducting to 40 K (−233 °C) by using caesium in the compound Cs_3C_{60}. This holds out the possibility of very small lightweight motors and electromagnets.

> A **superconductor** has zero resistance so no energy is lost when an electric current flows through it. Normally, materials only become superconducting at *very* low temperatures (see Figure 6.24, page 133, where liquid helium, at 4 K (−269 °C), is used to cool a superconducting magnet). For a superconductor to be a successful commercial product, the target temperature is 77 K (−196 °C).

Uses of nanotubes

The potential uses of carbon nanotubes may be even more exciting than the uses of fullerenes. For a start they are incredibly strong. Richard Smalley, who worked with Harry Kroto, is now a leading researcher into nanotubes and he reckons a nanotube is the strongest

149

Composite materials are made up from more than one component. Carbon fibre is a composite of plastic and fibres of carbon that are much wider than nanotubes.

substance in the Universe. Nanotubes are believed to have between 50 to 100 times the strength of steel of the same diameter when the ends are pulled to breaking point. This incredible strength is already finding its way into composite materials. By encasing nanotubes in plastic the composite material is much stronger than carbon fibre, offering a very strong, very light material that is already being used in car bumpers.

However, the nanotube could revolutionise our lives through its use in electronics in a way it is difficult to imagine. Some nanotubes can conduct electricity just like metal wires, giving them future uses in the electronics industry. For example, they could improve the performance of flat panel display devices and make the tiniest circuits imaginable. Others uses are as semiconductors, which will only conduct an electric current in one direction. Semiconductors are essential in many electronic components but perhaps their most important use is in transistors. Every year, the size of microprocessors for computers gets smaller, enabling more and more powerful computers to be made. However, at some stage soon, it won't be possible to get these circuits any smaller and so the development of the computer could stop. This is where nanotubes come in. Nanotube wires and nanotube transistors could allow circuits to be built that use single molecules as the electronic components.

Summary

- Buckminster fullerene was discovered by chance when Harry Kroto suggested that firing laser beams at graphite might produce carbon chains. Chance discoveries are often very important in science.
- Buckminster fullerene is named after the architect/engineer whose geodesic dome has a similar construction to the football-like C_{60} molecule.
- Another chance discovery enabled Buckminster fullerene to be produced in larger quantities.
- Many fullerenes have now been discovered.
- Fullerenes and carbon nanotubes are forms of carbon.
- Diamond and graphite are other forms of carbon.
- Once the properties of nanotubes and fullerenes were known, uses for them could begin to be developed.
- Fullerenes may be used for lubrication, in the way that ball bearings are. They could also deliver drugs in the body and may find applications in electronics.
- Nanotubes can be conductors, like metals, or semiconductors. They could be used to further miniaturise electronic circuits in computers down to the level of single molecules.

Questions

7.1 a When Harry Kroto suggested to Richard Smalley that they should fire laser beams at graphite, what did he expect to happen?

b What was the formula of the molecule that they discovered?

c What two geometric shapes make up Buckminster fullerene?

d Explain why graphite and fullerenes are different forms of carbon.

7.2 Carbon nanotubes can be encased in plastic to make a composite material.

  a What is a composite material?

  b What properties of nanotubes will make this composite so useful?

7.3 a Give *two* properties of nanotubes that could make them very useful in electronics.

  b Why could nanotubes be very important to the development of more powerful computers?

7.4 a A fullerene has a relative formula mass of 864. What is its formula?

  b Fullerenes have some very interesting properties. Give *one* property and explain how this could be used.

B Giant covalent structures and simple molecular structures

Diamond is the most valuable and prized gemstone in the world, yet it is made from a very common element, carbon.

In nature, diamonds are thought to have formed 200 kilometres below the Earth's surface, where carbon atoms were subjected to tremendous temperatures and pressures over millions or even billions of years. Due to volcanic activity they rose nearer the surface and may well have been shot out of volcanoes during eruptions. It is not surprising that large diamonds are very rare.

For more than 200 years scientists have been trying to synthesise diamonds from graphite, the common form of carbon. By attempting to recreate the conditions far below the Earth's surface they hoped to break the very strong bonds between the carbon atoms in graphite and rearrange them into a diamond structure. A team in Sweden succeeded in doing this in 1953, by squeezing graphite in a press that produced 83 000 times more pressure than the Earth's atmosphere, together with a temperature of 2000 °C. However, they kept their discovery a secret so a year later scientists working for General Electric (GE) in the USA were credited with making the first artificial diamonds. GE's process lay in using pressure of 60 000 atmospheres, a temperature of 2500 °C and a compound of iron that helped to catalyse (speed up) the process.

The diamonds produced industrially were very small, gritty and unattractive but they immediately found uses where diamond's great hardness was required, such as drill tips. However, they were hardly a threat to diamond mines producing their very expensive natural diamonds. What may be more of a threat is a much newer process called chemical vapour deposition (CVD). CVD does not need very high pressures and the carbon atoms come from methane (CH_4), not graphite. A low-grade diamond acts as a seed crystal. Methane and hydrogen are introduced at low pressure and bombarded by microwaves. The hydrogen breaks into atoms and this helps methane form carbon atoms. These carbon atoms then start bonding to the seed diamonds, causing them to grow. Some quite large diamonds have been produced using this method and one day they may be impossible to tell from the natural diamonds that took millions of years to form.

Figure 7.10 This diamond in the Royal Sceptre is called the 'Star of Africa'. It was cut from the largest diamond ever found

Figure 7.11 These diamonds have been made industrially

● The properties of diamond and graphite

Diamond and graphite are both forms of carbon. They are made up of only carbon atoms, yet they could not be more different in some of their physical properties. Diamond is the hardest substance known. It is also the stiffest and least compressible, which is quite a contrast to graphite, which is slippery and layers of it break off easily enough to leave carbon atoms marking a piece of paper. This is why graphite is used in pencil leads and as a lubricant. Diamond does not conduct electricity but is an excellent conductor of heat energy (much better than metals) so it is used to conduct away the heat energy produced in tiny electrical circuits. Graphite is a good conductor of electricity. Diamond melts at 3550 °C and graphite does not even melt as its solid structure goes straight to a gas at 3727 °C. To explain the properties of diamond and graphite we must look at their structures.

The structure of diamond

If you look at the structure of diamond (Figure 7.12) you will notice that each carbon atom is bonded to four other carbon atoms by strong **covalent bonds**. We first met covalent bonds in Chapter 5 (page 83) and we will look in more detail at how these bonds are formed on page 156 of the next section. Covalent bonds are strong – just as strong as the ionic bonds that we considered in Chapter 6 (page 134). We call structures where all the millions of atoms are bonded together in a big three-dimensional, interlocking arrangement **giant covalent structures**. Giant covalent structures have high melting points and boiling points because all the strong bonds must be broken to melt them. In the case of diamond all the strong covalent bonds between the carbon atoms must be broken. Diamond is the hardest known natural substance because of its strongly bonded giant covalent structure and this is also why it cannot be compressed. It does not conduct electricity because there are no charged particles, such as electrons or ions, free to move.

The structure of graphite

When a substance changes from solid to gas, without passing through a liquid stage, we say that it **sublimes**.

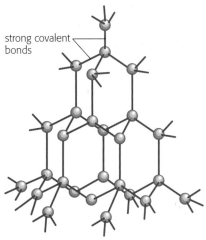

strong covalent bonds

Figure 7.12 The giant covalent structure of diamond

We have already met some giant structures – giant ionic structures (page 134) and the giant structure of metals (page 117). In the case of metals it is the free electrons that allow them to conduct in the solid.

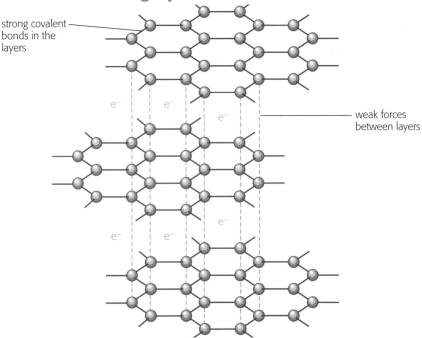

strong covalent bonds in the layers

weak forces between layers

Figure 7.13 The giant covalent structure of graphite

Because graphite has a giant covalent structure we would expect it to melt and boil at high temperatures. In fact the solid changes straight to a gas, but at the very high temperature of 3727 °C, when the covalent bonds between the carbon atoms start to break.

The structure of graphite gives some clues as to why it is so slippery. Although each carbon atom within a layer is held by covalent bonds there are only weak forces between the layers, allowing them to move over each other.

Why can graphite conduct electricity? Each carbon atom is held by only three bonds and this leaves a free electron that is able to move.

● Simple molecular structures

We have already seen that covalent bonds are strong bonds. Giant structures have high melting points and boiling points because millions of covalent bonds have to be broken. However, many covalently bonded substances have **simple molecular structures** made up of individual molecules. The molecules stay intact when these substances melt because there are strong covalent bonds *between the atoms* in the molecules. However, the forces *between the molecules* are weak forces and some of these break to allow molecules to move about in the liquid state. When the liquid boils all the intermolecular forces are overcome so that the molecules can separate and a gas forms.

> Carbon has four electrons in its outer shell. It uses one electron for each covalent bond it forms. In diamond there are four covalent bonds for each carbon atom, so there are no free electrons. In graphite there are only three covalent bonds, leaving one electron free to conduct.

> Forces of attraction between molecules are called **intermolecular forces**.

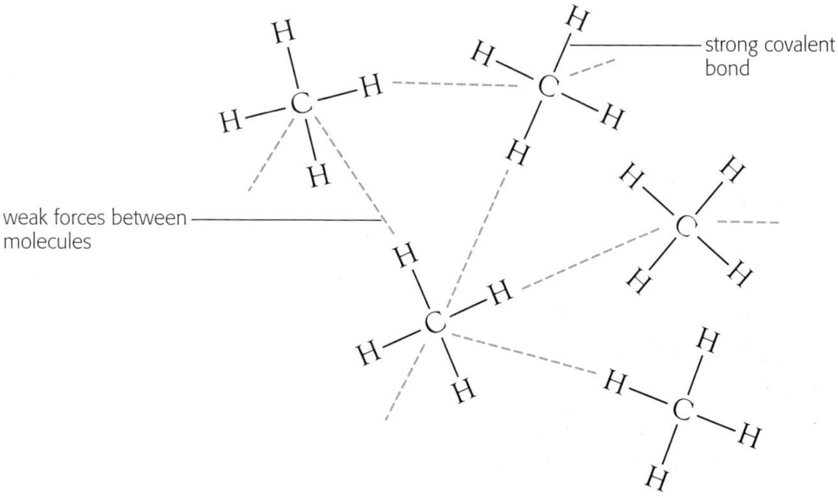

Figure 7.14 When methane is solid, the molecules are held in a lattice by weak intermolecular forces

strong covalent bond

weak forces between molecules

Methane is an example of a simple molecular structure. Weak intermolecular forces hold methane molecules together in the solid. At the melting point of −182 °C the methane molecules are able to move over one another, forming a liquid. The melting point is very low because the intermolecular forces are very weak. Some of the intermolecular forces remain, so that methane molecules do not separate completely until the boiling point of −161 °C is reached.

If you look at Table 7.1 on the next page, you can see a major difference between giant covalent structures and simple covalent molecular ones by comparing the melting points and boiling points.

> Remember that −182 °C is a lower temperature than −161 °C.

Giant covalent structure			Simple molecular structure		
Substance	Melting point (°C)	Boiling point (°C)	Substance	Melting point (°C)	Boiling point (°C)
diamond	3550	4827	ammonia	−78	−33
silicon	1410	2687	sulphur	119	445
silicon dioxide (sand)	1703	2230	water	0	100

Table 7.1 Comparing the properties of giant covalent structures and simple molecular structures

Another physical property that is characteristic of simple molecular structures is that they don't conduct electricity. This is because there are no free electrons or ions that can move and carry charge.

Explaining the melting points and boiling points of the halogens

Property	Fluorine, F₂	Chlorine, Cl₂	Bromine, Br₂	Iodine, I₂
physical state	yellow gas	green gas	brown liquid	black solid
melting point, °C	−223	−101	−7	114
boiling point, °C	−188	−34	59	183

Table 7.2 Properties of the halogens

If you look at Table 7.2 you will notice that the melting and boiling points of the Group 7 elements (the halogens) are all low, so immediately you can predict that they will have simple molecular structures. But you will also notice that the melting and boiling points increase as you go down Group 7, and the reason for this lies in the strength of the intermolecular forces of attraction. Fluorine has the weakest intermolecular forces so it melts and boils at the lowest temperatures. The forces between chlorine molecules must be greater than those between fluorine molecules because the melting and boiling points of chlorine are higher, even though chlorine is still a gas at room temperature. Bromine is a liquid at room temperature because the intermolecular forces are enough to keep the bromine molecules very close together. Iodine is a solid at room temperature so the intermolecular forces must be even stronger, keeping the iodine molecules in fixed positions in a lattice.

We also know that the halogens will not conduct because there are no free electrons or ions to carry charge.

a chlorine

b bromine

c iodine

Figure 7.15 The halogens

Summary

- Diamond and graphite have giant covalent structures because millions of carbon atoms are covalently bonded together in a big three-dimensional, interlocking arrangement.
- Giant covalent structures have high melting points and boiling points because all the strong covalent bonds need to broken before the substance can melt.
- Diamond is the hardest substance known because of the strong covalent bonds holding all the carbon atoms together in a giant structure. Diamonds are used in drill bits. Graphite is slippery because its giant structure is in layers that have weak forces between them. This makes graphite a good lubricant.
- Diamond does not conduct electricity because all of its electrons are used in the covalent bonds and there are no free electrons available. In graphite carbon has free electrons and so can conduct electricity.
- Metals are also giant structuress with free electrons that allow them to conduct electricity.
- Simple covalent molecular substances have weak forces of attraction between molecules, called intermolecular forces. This means that they have low melting points and boiling points because these forces don't need much energy to break them. There are no free electrons and no free ions so they do not conduct electricity.
- The melting points and boiling points of the halogens increase going down Group 7 because the intermolecular forces of attraction get stronger.

Questions

7.5 Diamond and graphite have some very different physical properties. Use their structures to explain these differences.

7.6 a Explain what is meant by the term *giant covalent structure*.

b Look at this table of substances A–D; they all have covalent bonds in their structures.

Substance	Melting point, °C	Boiling point, °C
A	−30	174
B	2300	2550
C	44	280
D	−259	−253

  i What is the physical state of each substance at room temperature (25 °C)?

  ii Identify which is a giant covalent structure.

  iii What is the name given to the type of structure that the other substances have?

c Identify *two* other types of giant structure that you have learnt about on this course.

7.7 Butane is a gas at room temperature.

a Predict its structure.

b Explain why butane is a non-conductor as a solid, liquid and gas.

7.8 Explain, using the concept of intermolecular forces, why the boiling points of the halogens increase down Group 7.

C Sharing electrons: the covalent bond

Dorothy Hodgkin is the only female British scientist to win a Nobel Prize. She won the 1964 Chemistry Prize for her work in determining the structure of several biologically important molecules by using X-rays.

Dorothy Hodgkin was born in 1910 and her life spanned much of the 20th century. While at school she nearly missed out on studying chemistry as it was regarded as a 'boy's subject'. She persuaded the headmaster to let her join the class and went on to study chemistry at Oxford University. In her fourth year at university she joined a group who were using X-rays to work out the structures of crystals. X-rays have wavelengths very similar to the spacing of atoms in molecules and if the molecules are regularly arranged in crystals they diffract (bend and scatter) X-rays to form a pattern that can be picked up as a series dots on a photographic plate (Figure 7.17). The technique is known as X-ray crystallography.

In 1945 she worked out the three-dimensional structure of penicillin before chemists had even agreed what its formula was. She was one of the first people to use a computer to help process X-ray images and in 1956, after 8 years of work, she unravelled the very complex structure of vitamin B-12. This molecule contains more than 90 atoms. Once the structure was known chemists could make it and use it to fight a disease called pernicious anaemia, which otherwise invariably causes death.

In 1969 she achieved a lifetime ambition to determine the structure of insulin. This had taken her 30 years. The molecule contains over 800 atoms.

Figure 7.16 Dorothy Hodgkin (1910–1994)

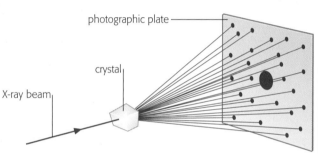

Figure 7.17 The pattern of dots that are produced after X-rays have passed through the crystal can be used to work out the structure of the molecules

● Forming a covalent bond

Many of the chemicals we come across in our daily lives are covalent compounds and this means they have covalent bonds holding their atoms together. It may be the plastic bag you use for your shopping, nearly all the food we eat, or many of the compounds that keep you alive and make up your body. So how is a covalent bond formed?

In Chapter 6 (page 132) we learnt that noble gases have a very stable arrangement of electrons because their outer electron shells are full. When ions are formed electrons are transferred from one atom to another to achieve the stability of a full electron shell. It is metal atoms that lose electrons and non-metal atoms that gain them.

But what about methane, CH_4, which only has non-metal atoms? Carbon and hydrogen can't both gain electrons, can they? Well they can if they *share* some of each other's electrons and this allows them to both achieve a full electron shell.

Carbon is in Group 4 so has four outer electrons; hydrogen has an atomic number of 1, so has one electron.

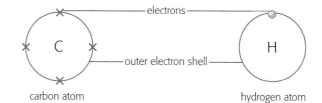

Figure 7.18 Hydrogen needs one more electron; carbon needs four more electrons to make a full shell

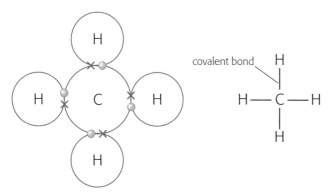

Figure 7.19 A covalently bonded methane molecule

Simple molecules are small molecules with only a few atoms covalently bonded together.

Hydrogen can get a full shell by gaining one electron, while carbon needs a total of eight electrons to achieve a stable noble gas structure. By sharing electrons both can achieve a full shell (Figure 7.19).

All electrons are the same, but for convenience we show electrons as either dots or crosses so that we can see which electrons come from which atom. These are **dot and cross diagrams**. A shared pair of electrons between two atoms is a **covalent bond**. Covalent bonds are drawn as single lines.

A covalent bond holds two atoms together because each atom has a positive nucleus and these attract the shared pair of electrons. The covalent bonds holding the carbon atoms together in the giant structures of diamond and graphite are formed in the same way. Each covalent bond is a shared pair of electrons.

Using dot and cross diagrams

Let's now look at drawing more molecules using dot and cross diagrams. Remember: a covalent bond is a shared pair of electrons and atoms achieve a full shell when covalent bonds form.

In the hydrogen molecule, H_2, both hydrogen atoms gain a full shell of two electrons by sharing each other's electron.

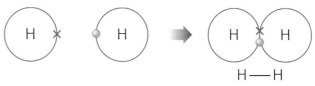

Figure 7.20 Formation of a covalently bonded hydrogen molecule

For the chlorine molecule shown in Figure 7.21 we will draw out all the electron shells. Chlorine has an atomic number of 17, so it has 17 electrons with an electronic configuration of 2, 8, 7.

Figure 7.21 Formation of a covalently bonded chlorine molecule

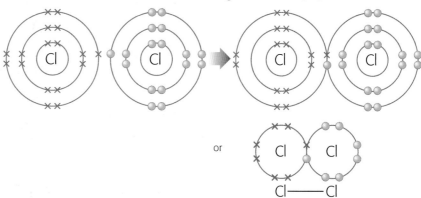

The only electrons that take part in bonding are the outer electrons, so we often just show the outer shells when drawing dot and cross diagrams (see the lower part of Figure 7.21).

Let's now consider hydrogen chloride. We can draw out the full electronic configuration or the dot and cross diagram just showing the outer shells (right).

H

Figure 7.22 A covalently bonded molecule of hydrogen chloride

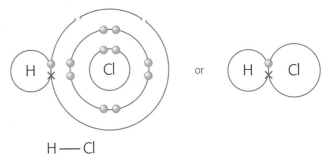

H — Cl

The formula of water is H_2O. The oxygen atom in the water molecule is in Group 6 and so has six outer electrons.

Figure 7.23 Formation of a covalently bonded molecule of water

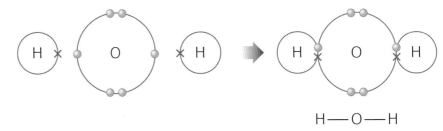

H — O — H

Double covalent bonds

We met double bonds in Chapter 5 when we looked at ethene (see page 86).

Oxygen has an atomic number of eight, so its full electronic configuration is 2, 6. To get a full outer shell it must share two of its electrons with another oxygen atom. This produces two covalent bonds, which we call a double bond. We also find double bonds in carbon dioxide.

Figure 7.24 Covalently bonded molecules of oxygen and carbon dioxide. Note that in the case of carbon dioxide we show only the outer electrons

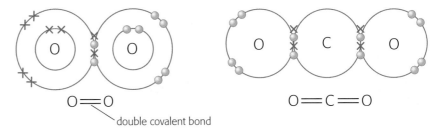

O = O
double covalent bond

O = C = O

● Representing molecules in three dimensions

The shape of a molecule is very important as it can affect the properties of the molecule. The tastes of different foods depend on the shapes of the molecules that make them up. The molecules fit into receptor sites in the mouth and these are connected by nerves to the brain, where they are interpreted as taste sensations.

It is often quite difficult to visualise three-dimensional shapes when you draw atoms and molecules in two dimensions on a flat sheet of paper. If you look back to Chapter 5 (pages 83 and 87) you can see that we have shown some ball and stick models, and you may have built some of these models yourself.

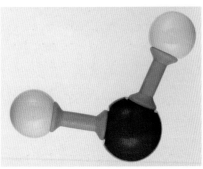

Figure 7.25 Ball and stick models of molecules show atoms and the way they are bonded. They also give an idea of the shape of the molecule. This is a model of a water molecule, H_2O

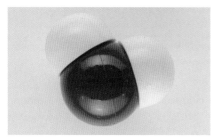

Figure 7.26 This space-filling model of the water molecule shows the shape of the water molecule more clearly

Another way of representing molecules is to show the atoms in the molecules but without showing the covalent bonds. These models are known as space-filling models (Figure 7.26). In these models the relative sizes of the atoms are accurately shown, as are their arrangements in three dimensions, i.e. the way the molecule is arranged in space.

The three-dimensional models for water are very simple to draw and to make. Now consider the structure of a molecule of vitamin B-12 (Figure 7.27). Remember that it took Dorothy Hodgkin 8 years to work out this structure (see page 156).

If you were drawing the structure of vitamin B-12 in two dimensions it would be difficult to do, it would take you a long time and still would not give you a clear picture of the shape of the molecule. This is where computers have revolutionised our understanding of the shapes of molecules. Software packages can allow chemists to create the shapes of molecules in three dimensions so that they can see if they will react with other molecules, or if their shapes prevent a reaction. Do these software packages show what molecules really look like? The answer is 'no', but they do simulate molecular shapes accurately. They are *representations* of what a molecule looks like.

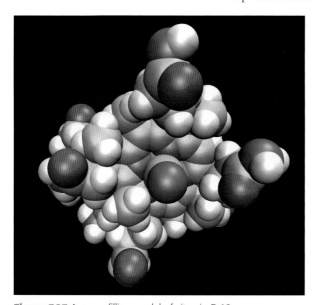

Figure 7.27 A space-filling model of vitamin B-12

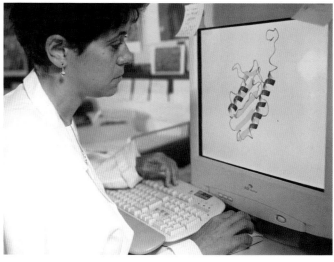

Figure 7.28 Research chemists used to spend hours, or even days, trying to represent molecular shapes on paper. Nowadays, software packages can clarify our understanding very quickly

Summary

- A covalent bond is a shared pair of electrons between two atoms. By sharing electrons each atom gains the stability of a full electron shell.
- Dot and cross diagrams help us to see how covalent bonds are formed in molecules.
- You will need to be able to draw dot and cross diagrams for simple molecules such as hydrogen (H_2), hydrogen chloride (HCl), water (H_2O) and carbon dioxide (CO_2).
- When two pairs of electrons are shared between two atoms this is a double covalent bond. They are formed in molecules such as carbon dioxide, oxygen and ethene.
- Computer software packages can simulate molecules in three dimensions, helping to clarify our understanding of their shapes.

Sharing electrons: the covalent bond

159

Questions

7.9 Water is called a simple molecule, while diamond has a giant structure. Both substances have covalent bonds in their structure.

    a Explain what is meant by the terms *simple molecule* and *giant structure*. (Hint: you will need to look back at the previous section for the answer to this part of the question.)

    b How does a covalent bond form?

7.10 Draw dot and cross diagrams, showing full electron configurations, for these molecules:

    a fluorine (F_2) (F = atomic number 9)

    b methane (CH_4)

    c hydrogen fluoride (HF).

7.11 Using only the outer electrons, draw a dot and cross diagram to show how nitrogen (N_2) contains a triple covalent bond. Nitrogen is in Group 5.

7.12 Why has simulation software clarified our understanding of the shapes of molecules?

D Conventional medicine versus complementary medicine

Jacques Benveniste, a respected French scientist, appeared to make a remarkable discovery in the 1980s. He was working with white blood cells that are part of the human immune system. These cells react to certain substances that cause allergies. When he used very dilute solutions of these substances the blood cells still showed their allergic reactions. He went on diluting and diluting the solutions until there were probably no molecules of the substances that caused the allergies left. Yet still the blood cells seemed to show an allergic response. Benveniste claimed that water had a 'memory' of the molecules that caused the allergic reaction even when they were no longer present.

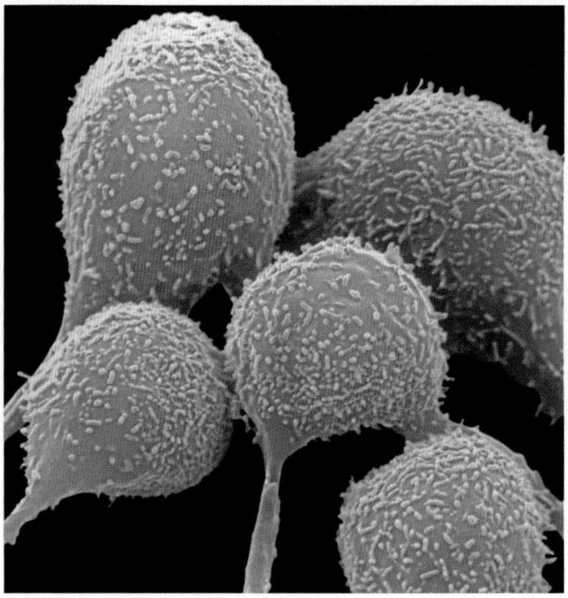

    After years of trying, Benveniste persuaded *Nature*, a highly respected scientific journal, to publish his results. The editor only agreed with the condition that Benveniste open his laboratory to independent referees who would check his methods to see that they were valid. On the team of three referees was a magician, James Randi, who went to great lengths to ensure the researchers could not know which test tubes contained the very dilute solutions and which were pure water. This time the experiment was inconclusive and Benveniste lost his research funding and the respect of the vast majority of scientists.

Figure 7.29 Benveniste claimed that these white blood cells appeared to show an allergic reaction even when mixed with very dilute solutions of substances known to cause allergies

● Homeopathy: does it work?

What made Benveniste's work so interesting was that it might provide evidence that **homeopathic** medicines are effective. Homeopathy is an alternative form of medicine to conventional medicine. It is often called a **complementary medicine**.

Complementary medicine is the collective name given to many different forms of treatment of illnesses that do not rely on the high technology of conventional medicines, usually involving chemicals called drugs. People often turn to complementary medicine when they have long-term illnesses that have not been cured by the drugs of conventional medicine. Acupuncture, chiropractic and herbal medicines are other forms of complementary medicine. What complementary medicines have in common is they treat the whole person, not just the symptoms of the disease.

Homeopathy has its roots in Ancient Greece but the ideas were revived about 200 years ago. The basic principle underpinning homeopathy is that 'like cures like'. What this means is that chemicals that produce the symptoms of the disease are given in very small quantities to stimulate the body's natural defences. The idea is that homeopathic remedies will encourage the body to heal itself. This is in complete contrast to conventional medicine, where the drug given has the opposite effect and is supposed to remove the symptoms. People that practise homeopathy are called homeopaths.

Scientists find the ideas behind homeopathy difficult to accept because the solutions of the remedies are so dilute that they are almost pure water. For a scientist to accept that homeopathy does provide an effective treatment it must be subjected to trials that compare the solutions to dummy solutions, usually pure water. Dummy solutions that contain no trace of the chemical used to treat the illness are called **placebos**. People sometimes start to get better even if they are given a dummy drug because they *believe* that the dummy drug will help them. This is called the **placebo effect**. In any clinical trial of a drug that a pharmaceutical company wants to sell to doctors, the actual drug must be compared to a placebo. Usually neither the patient nor the doctor knows if they are using the dummy drug. In this way scientists hope to eliminate the placebo effect.

In 2002 the *Lancet*, a highly respected medical journal, published a review of over 100 separate studies about homeopathy. It came to the conclusion that there was no evidence that homeopathic cures were any more effective than placebos. In a damning statement it said that doctors should be honest with patients about their 'lack of benefit'. At about the same time, James Randi, the magician mentioned in the opening box opposite, offered $1 million to anyone who could prove that homeopathy really worked. To date no one has claimed the money.

Despite this, interest in homeopathy continues to grow. Many people in this country firmly believe that it has cured them of all sorts of ailments, ranging from hay fever to the most terrible eczema, and the National Health Service has paid for many of these treatments. There are even five NHS homeopathic hospitals. In their defence, homeopaths say that every individual is different and because they treat each individual differently it is impossible for scientists to claim that there is no effect.

Figure 7.30 The magician James Randi has offered $1 million if anyone can prove that homeopathy works

In a recent study carried out at the homeopathic hospital in Bristol, 70% of 6500 patients with chronic diseases reported an improvement in their condition.

The row will continue to rumble on because there appears to be no mechanism by which homeopathic remedies can work. Many scientists would find it much easier to believe that homeopathic remedies were effective if a mechanism could be found. However, very recent studies into the effects first noted by Benveniste are providing some evidence that perhaps water does have a 'memory' of the molecules that were dissolved in it. Huge numbers of scientists will take much convincing that this is the case.

You can read more about clinical trials in Chapter 5 (page 102).

● Are chemical-based therapies effective?

Before a drug can be licensed for use on patients, it must go through a number of important stages. The last of these stages is called **clinical trials**. In Phase 2 of clinical trials, after the drug has been tested on healthy volunteers to check there are no dangerous side-effects, it is given to people who are suffering from the particular illness the drug is supposed to cure. In these trials patients are randomly put into two groups. The first group actually receives the drug while the other group is a control group, and it receives a placebo. Remember that a placebo is a dummy drug. It will look exactly the same as the medicine containing the actual drug but it won't really contain anything that will assist in curing the disease. The reason for this is to eliminate the placebo effect, when patients who think they are receiving a drug that will help cure them can start to feel better and lose some of their symptoms even if they are taking a placebo. Usually the doctors administering the drug will not know if patients are receiving the drug or a placebo. Following the trials, the results are analysed to see if the chemical-based therapy is effective.

Pharmaceutical companies invest many millions of pounds in getting their particular chemical-based therapy to this stage. If the drug is now shown to be ineffective then they will lose all the money they have put into research because no one will buy the drug. This puts a great deal of pressure on the clinical trials and sometimes results may be withheld.

One of the tragic cases of withholding information from a clinical trial happened in the 1980s. Following a heart attack the rhythm of the heart becomes erratic. The drug Lorcainide was developed to restore the proper rhythm of the heart. On admission to hospital 95 patients were randomly assigned to two groups. One group received the Lorcainide and one group received the placebo. The evidence strongly suggested that patients in the Lorcainide group had been given an effective treatment. However, what went unreported was the fact that there were nine deaths in the Lorcainide group but only one death in the placebo group. Had this information been available it is possible that 80 000 people who died in the USA after being given the drug would have survived to live out far longer lives.

Trial	Number of patients	Average number of days of illness		Reduction in illness days
		Placebo	Relenza	
1	455	6.5	5.0	1.5
2	777	6.0	5.5	0.5
3	356	7.5	5.0	2.5
overall	1588	6.0	5.0	1.0

Table 7.3 Results of clinical trials of Relenza

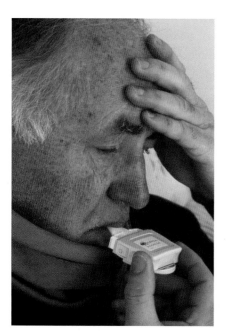

Figure 7.31 Relenza is a powder that is inhaled by spraying it into the mouth

You can now do question 7.15 on the next page, which considers the effectiveness of Relenza in preventing complications that arise during a flu illness.

Assessing the effectiveness of Relenza

Relenza is a chemical-based therapy that treats flu (influenza). It works by stopping the flu virus reproducing itself. Table 7.3 shows the results of three clinical trials. As you can see from the table, the number of days of illness is reduced by taking Relenza. However, the NHS does not pay for treatment of flu with Relenza unless patients are in a high-risk category such as those older than 65 and those with heart, kidney or lung infections. The reasons for the NHS decision are the following.

▸ People with bad colds may appear to have flu. Relenza is only effective against flu viruses. It is impossible to diagnose whether a patient has flu or a bad cold without doing laboratory tests to identify the virus. By the time the test is done it is too late for Relenza to be effective.
▸ If Relenza is not taken within 2 days of the onset of flu symptoms then the virus has multiplied so much that Relenza does not shorten the period of illness.
▸ If people suspecting they have flu all go to the doctor in the first 2 days of their illness then GPs could be overwhelmed.
▸ The cost of 5 days of treatment with Relenza is approximately £25. During a normal year 500 000 people suffer from flu. The cost to the NHS would be £12.5 million a year. However, a severe epidemic could cost the NHS over £100 million.
▸ The reduction in the period of illness is only 1 day on average so the cost does not justify the expense.

Summary

- Homeopathy is the treatment of illnesses by using very dilute quantities of substances that produce the same symptoms.
- Scientists find it difficult to accept that homeopathic remedies are effective because the solutions are so dilute they are almost pure water.
- Many people claim that homeopathic remedies are effective and that they have had relief from symptoms they have suffered for many years.
- When scientists test the effectiveness of chemical-based therapies in clinical trials one group is given the drug and another group is given a placebo. A placebo is a dummy drug.
- The placebo effect is the observation that even a dummy drug can make people feel better if they believe it is the real drug.

Questions

7.13 Many people believe that homeopathic medicines have cured them or made them feel much better than conventional medicines have.

  a What does the term *homeopathic* mean?

  b What is *conventional medicine*?

  c Why do many scientists find the effectiveness of homeopathic remedies difficult to accept?

7.14 Homeopathy is one form of complementary medicine. Use the internet to find out about the effectiveness of acupuncture or chiropractic.

7.15 The table below shows the results of a clinical trial using Relenza and a placebo. The complications were infections of the lung such as bronchitis and pneumonia, which increase the risk of death.

Analysis	Number of patients suffering complications:	
	treated with placebo	**treated with Relenza**
all patients with flu	152 out of 558	119 out of 609
patients at high risk	46 out of 117	26 out of 99

  a What is meant by the term *placebo*?

  b Why do clinical trials usually use placebos?

  c **i** Work out the percentage of patients that had complications during their illness in the placebo groups and Relenza groups for all patients with flu.

    ii Do the same calculation for the high-risk patients.

    iii Why do you think patients in the high-risk group have their treatment paid for by the NHS?

8 How fast? How furious?

A Reactions and energy

We are used to ready meals; all the supermarkets sell them. You don't have to peel the potatoes or slice the vegetables and the actual cooking has been done for you. All that you have to do is heat the meal up in an oven or microwave. Could things be any easier? The answer is 'Yes'. You can now buy some ready meals in containers that will even heat your food when you want to eat it. Sounds impossible? The army and the emergency services have been using self-heat meals for a very long time. When someone is cut off, perhaps by a mud slide or avalanche, the self-heat can of food is a real lifesaver.

So how do these self-heat cans work? Many chemical reactions give off heat. For example, one such reaction is that between quicklime (calcium oxide) and water. These two chemicals are kept separate from the food and also separate from each other. When you press a button at the bottom of the can the quicklime and water mix and this releases enough heat energy to cook the food or heat a cup of coffee.

Although the cost of the actual self-heat container makes it an expensive meal or drink, its sheer convenience on a long drive or while on a long walk, when you are away from kettles and cookers, means there is a market that food companies are keen to satisfy.

Figure 8.1 This can heats up the food inside it using a chemical reaction that gives out heat energy

● Exothermic and endothermic reactions

> One way to remember this is to remember that heat **ex**its in **ex**othermic reactions.

Reactions that give out heat energy are called **exothermic reactions**. These reactions raise the **temperature** of the surroundings. Temperature is just a measure of the amount of heat energy – the higher the temperature the hotter the surroundings.

The reaction between quicklime and water used in some self-heat cans is just one example of an exothermic reaction. The heat energy given out raises the temperature of the food in the can, making the contents very hot. In fact, most chemical reactions are exothermic. A very common exothermic reaction is the burning of fuels, whether it is natural gas (methane) combusting with oxygen on a stove, or the many thousands of reactions that produce intense heat in a house fire.

methane + oxygen → carbon dioxide + water

$$CH_4(g) + 2O_2(g) → CO_2(g) + 2H_2O(l)$$

Figure 8.2 Methane (natural gas) is reacting with oxygen to give out enough heat energy to fry an egg

Figure 8.3 In this fire there are hundreds of different exothermic reactions contributing to the intense heat

Endothermic reactions

> To remember that endothermic reactions involve heat energy being taken in, the first two letters give the clue: heat **en**ters in **en**dothermic reactions.

Endothermic reactions are reactions that take in heat energy. The heat energy is taken in from the surroundings and so the surroundings cool down and the temperature decreases.

Endothermic reactions are used in cold packs that treat sports injuries. Cold packs are usually made using a tough plastic bag that is filled with ammonium nitrate crystals and also a smaller bag of water. The bag containing the water is made of thin plastic that is easily broken. To make the pack work it is punched or squeezed, bursting

the inner bag. The water is released and dissolves the ammonium nitrate. This process takes in heat energy from the surroundings, in this case the contents of the bag and the part of the body it is pushed against. When applied to a sports person who has sustained an injury the coldness reduces swelling and eases the pain.

Figure 8.4 This footballer has fallen awkwardly. The application of a cold pack will prevent swelling and probably allow him to continue with the game

● Breaking and making bonds

In any chemical reaction there is at least one reactant and one product:

reactants ➔ products

But when chemicals react why do they give out energy or take energy in? The answer lies in what happens in a chemical reaction. Let's consider the reaction of methane and oxygen:

> The formulae equation is balanced because the number of atoms in the reactant molecules equals the number of atoms in the product molecules. This is true of all chemical reactions, because atoms cannot be created or destroyed in chemical reactions.

methane + oxygen ➔ carbon dioxide + water

$$CH_4(g) + 2O_2(g) \rightarrow CO_2(g) + 2H_2O(l)$$

To make the reactants turn into products, atoms must change places when the new substances are made. To do this the bonds in the reactant molecules must first be broken. This takes in energy.

Bond breaking is endothermic.

Then new bonds are made between the atoms when the product molecules are formed. This gives out energy.

Bond making is exothermic.

Figure 8.5 Breaking and making bonds during the reaction of methane and oxygen

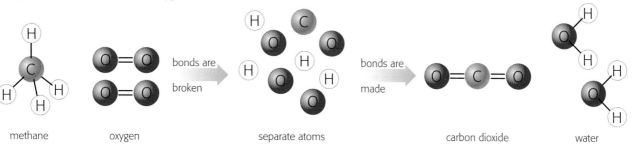

Energy level diagrams

It takes less energy to break the bonds in methane than is released when the bonds are formed in carbon dioxide and water. This is why heat is given out. We can show this more clearly on an energy level diagram (Figure 8.6). Notice that the energy level of the products is lower than the energy level of the reactants. This is because in exothermic reactions energy is lost as heat energy. This heat energy warms the surroundings.

Figure 8.6 An energy level diagram showing that energy is taken in when bonds are broken and released when bonds are formed

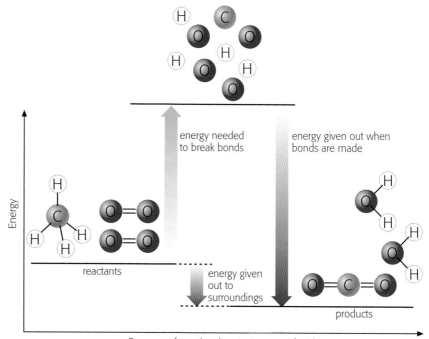

Energy level diagrams are different for endothermic reactions (Figure 8.7, overleaf). Heat energy is taken in so the energy level of the products is higher than the energy level of the reactants. Since the heat energy is taken in from the surroundings, the surroundings cool down.

167

Figure 8.7 An energy level diagram for an endothermic reaction. More energy is taken in when the bonds of the reactants are broken than is given out when the bonds of the products form

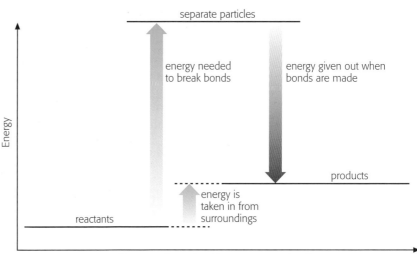

Reactants may be covalently bonded molecules or they could be ionic compounds. In this energy level diagram we have used the term 'particles' because when bonds are broken these particles could be atoms or ions.

Figure 8.8 The principle that propels a firework upwards also propels the Space Shuttle into space

You can read about the invention of dynamite in the opening box of the next section.

Rockets and explosions

The gunpowder packed into the tube at the top of a firework rocket contains two fuels, sulphur and charcoal (a form of carbon). These substances are mixed with potassium nitrate, which provides the oxygen to burn the fuels. When the fuse is lit and the flame reaches the reaction mixture, the reaction is very fast, producing the gases sulphur dioxide and carbon dioxide as well as other gases. It is also a highly exothermic reaction. This means that the gases produced are heated up and expand. Because the reaction is so rapid the force from the expanding gases propels the rocket upwards.

Gunpowder is a very reactive mixture but it doesn't explode at room temperature. The reason is that, before it can explode, some of the bonds in the reactants have to be broken and this requires energy. Once the reaction begins then the energy that is released from the new bonds being made is enough to continue the reaction.

Explosions are very fast reactions that produce large volumes of hot gases very quickly from small volumes of solid or liquid reactants. It is the sudden increase in volume that is the explosion. The expanding gases produce a huge force that can demolish anything in their path.

Summary

- Exothermic reactions give out heat energy and endothermic reactions take in heat energy.
- Exothermic reactions are accompanied by an increase in temperature, and endothermic reactions by a decrease in temperature.
- Natural gas combusting in air is an exothermic reaction. Ammonium nitrate dissolving in water is an endothermic process.
- For a reaction to occur atoms in the reactants are re-arranged to make products. The bonds of the reactants must first be broken. Bond breaking is endothermic. This separates the particles, such as atoms, bonded in the reactants.
- To form products in a reaction bonds are made between particles such as atoms. Bond making is exothermic.

Questions

8.1 Zinc reacts with sulphuric acid to give off hydrogen and produce zinc sulphate. If this reaction takes place in a test tube the test tube becomes very warm.

    a Explain, using the information above, how you know that the reaction between zinc and sulphuric acid is exothermic.

    b Write a word equation and a balanced formulae equation for this reaction.

        Formulae: sulphuric acid = H_2SO_4; zinc sulphate = $ZnSO_4$

8.2 When limestone (calcium carbonate) decomposes to make quicklime (calcium oxide) and carbon dioxide the reaction is endothermic.

    a What does the term *endothermic reaction* mean?

    Limestone is heated in a lime kiln to manufacture quicklime. Hot air is continually passed through the kiln or the reaction will stop.

    b **i** When bonds are broken in calcium carbonate, is energy taken in or given out?

        ii When bonds are made in calcium oxide and carbon dioxide, is energy taken in or given out?

        iii This is an endothermic reaction. Which process, bond making or bond breaking, is associated with the most energy given out or taken in?

        iv In view of your answer to part **iii**, explain why hot air is continuously pumped into the lime kiln.

8.3 Octane (C_8H_{18}) is one of the hydrocarbons used in petrol. If there is enough oxygen present in a car engine, octane burns to form carbon dioxide and water.

    a Write a word and balanced formulae equation for this reaction.

    b Why are all combustion reactions exothermic?

    c Draw an energy level diagram for this reaction.

8.4 A student dissolves ammonium nitrate in water and measures the temperature change. Read about cold packs on page 166 and predict what happens to the temperature during the experiment. Explain your reasoning.

B Rates of reaction

High explosives are very important chemicals. They have transformed the world by blasting out routes for roads, railways and canals. They are used to excavate the ground for the foundations of bridges and tall buildings. They are also used as weapons in war and terrorism.

Until about 160 years ago the only high explosive that had been made was gunpowder. The next two to be invented were nitrocellulose and nitroglycerine, in 1846. The problem with both was that they were unstable and would explode without warning. In 1863 Alfred Nobel, a member of an explosives manufacturing family, invented a detonator that would set off nitroglycerine. However, a year later his younger brother and four other workers were killed when the nitroglycerine they had made suddenly exploded. Alfred Nobel was determined that he would make nitroglycerine safe to handle. This he did, after 4 years of research, by inventing dynamite. Dynamite contains an inert solid surface on which nitroglycerine is absorbed. This makes the nitroglycerine safe to handle until a detonator sets it off.

A few years later Nobel invented another famous explosive, gelignite, which was even more powerful than dynamite. Gelignite also contains nitroglycerine, but this time mixed with nitrocellulose in a gel. Nobel set up manufacturing companies around the world and became very rich.

Alfred Nobel became convinced that he needed to invent an explosive so powerful that no one would dare use it and this would put an end to wars. In this he did not succeed but when he died he left his vast fortune to be used to set up five prizes to be awarded annually for outstanding contributions in the field of chemistry, physics, physiology or medicine, literature and peace. A sixth prize for economics was added in 1969. They are the world's highest awards and can only be given to people who are still living. Up to three people can share each prize. You can read about the award of some Nobel Prizes on pages 148 and 156.

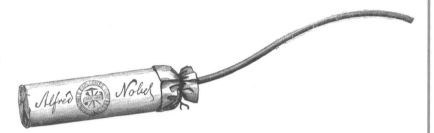

Figure 8.9 Alfred Nobel in his laboratory

Figure 8.10 This illustration was printed in a London magazine in 1884, advertising dynamite made by the Nobel Explosives Company in Scotland

● How fast is a reaction?

You have now seen and written many chemical equations, but these tell you nothing about how fast the reactions they represent are. The reactants in gunpowder react together very fast indeed, once some energy is supplied from a burning fuse. However, the chemical reaction of iron rusting is a very slow process, which is just as well or billions of structures that rely on iron and steel, such as cars, buildings and bridges, would very soon cease to exist.

Chemists use the term **rate of reaction** to describe how fast a reaction is going. This is how quickly reactants are changing into products. It is particularly important that industrial chemists know the rates of reactions that produce the chemicals they are manufacturing and how to increase these rates or slow them down. Mostly they want to increase reaction rates, as time in industry costs money. If it takes 1 day to manufacture 1 tonne of a particular chemical, it is going to be much more expensive than if the reaction can be made to take place in 1 hour. The manufacture of

Figure 8.11 The Titanic sank in 1912 yet, even after nearly a hundred years, it is still obviously a passenger ship. This is because the rusting reaction of the ship's hull is a slow reaction

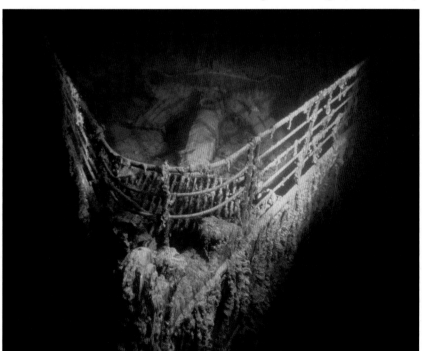

gelignite used to take a week until, during the Second World War, a British chemist came up with a way to speed up the rates of reactions that made it, so that the same amount of gelignite could be made in only 1 day. This was very important to the war effort. Sometimes, industrial chemists want to slow reactions down so that they do not go so fast that explosions occur.

Measuring the rate of reaction

The only way to find out the rate of a reaction is to carry out experiments. Marble chips (calcium carbonate) react with hydrochloric acid to give off carbon dioxide. The word and balanced formulae equation (with state symbols) for this reaction are:

calcium carbonate + hydrochloric acid → calcium chloride + water + carbon dioxide
$$CaCO_3(s) + 2HCl(aq) → CaCl_2(aq) + H_2O(l) + CO_2(g)$$

Another way of measuring the rate of reaction between calcium carbonate and hydrochloric acid is shown on page 178.

Since carbon dioxide is a gas, we can investigate the rate of this reaction by measuring the volume of gas that is given off at certain times from the start of the reaction. A convenient way of doing this is to use a gas syringe or a measuring cylinder.

Figure 8.12 a The volume of gas given off is being used to follow the rate of this reaction using a gas syringe

b Instead of using a gas syringe, a measuring cylinder can be used

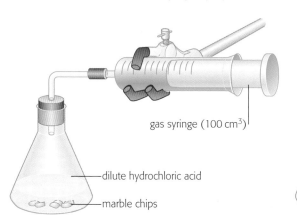

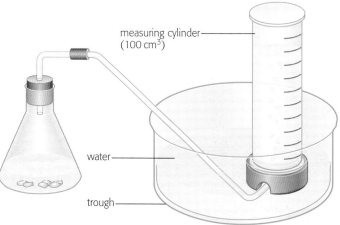

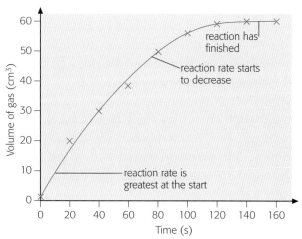

Figure 8.13 A graph showing the volume of gas collected during the reaction between marble chips and dilute hydrochloric acid

Plotting a graph of the results

If the volume of carbon dioxide is measured every 20 seconds until the reaction is over the results can be plotted and a graph drawn (Figure 8.13). The time interval can be any period of time that you choose. Here we have chosen 20 seconds; we could have chosen 10 seconds, which would have given more readings and helped determine the shape of the graph even more reliably.

Notice that not all the points lie on the line of the graph. There will be reasons why this experiment gives readings that are not totally reliable. We call the line a **line of best fit**.

Notice the following points about the graph in Figure 8.13 on the previous page.

- The graph is at its steepest at the beginning. The slope of the graph is called its **gradient** and is a measure of the rate of reaction. The steeper the gradient the higher the reaction rate. This graph tells you that the reaction is quickest at the start.
- The graph starts to get less steep. This tells you that the rate of reaction is getting less so the reaction is slowing down.
- Finally the graph goes horizontal. This means that the reaction has stopped because no more carbon dioxide is being formed. At the end, the rate of the reaction is zero.

Explaining what happens during a chemical reaction

We have seen that the rate of reaction is fast at first, but what is the explanation for this observation?

- At the beginning of the reaction, as the reactants are mixed together, the concentration of hydrochloric acid will be at its highest. Many hydrochloric acid particles can collide with calcium carbonate particles in the solid marble chips and it is these collisions that cause the reaction.
- As the hydrochloric acid reacts there are fewer hydrochloric particles left in the acid solution. This means there are fewer collisions with the calcium carbonate particles.
- When there are no more hydrochloric acid particles in the solution the reaction stops.

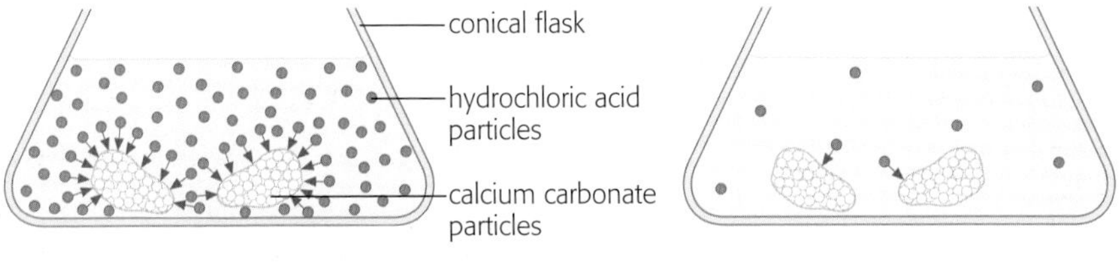

Figure 8.14 At first the concentration of hydrochloric acid particles is at its greatest so the reaction is at its fastest. When the reaction is nearly over the reaction rate falls because there are fewer hydrochloric acid particles in the solution to collide with calcium chloride particles

Start of reaction — conical flask — hydrochloric acid particles — calcium carbonate particles — Towards the end

The particles in hydrochloric acid and calcium carbonate are ions. You can read more about ions in Chapter 6 (page 134).

You can now see that for a reaction to happen the reactant particles must first collide. These particles can be molecules, ions or atoms. In the acid solution, the hydrochloric acid particles are constantly moving and so they collide with the solid particles at the surface of the marble chip and cause a reaction. Remember that for a reaction to happen bonds must be broken and it is the energy of the collision that breaks the bonds.

Not all collisions have enough energy for the bonds to break and these collisions cause no reaction. But the more concentrated the hydrochloric acid solution is, the more acid particles there are and therefore the more collisions there will be with enough energy to break bonds and cause a reaction.

● Collision theory

The **collision theory** is one way that chemists explain how reactions occur. We know that all substances are made up of particles. For a reaction to occur reactant particles must collide with sufficient energy for their bonds to break and this allows atoms to rearrange into product particles by making new bonds.

Remember that bond breaking is endothermic (takes in energy). This energy is supplied by the collision.

Figure 8.15 This shows the collision between two reactant particles that causes one bond to break and another one to be made

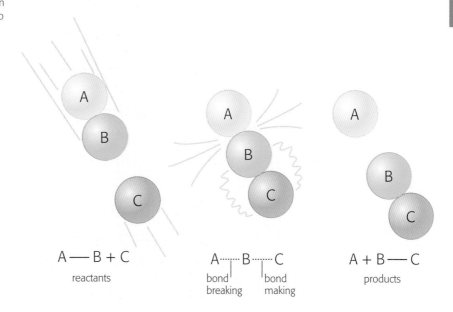

A — B + C
reactants

A⸳⸳⸳⸳B⸳⸳⸳⸳C
bond breaking | bond making

A + B — C
products

When there is a greater frequency of collisions the rate of reactants changing into products increases, so the rate of reaction increases. It is the same if the particles are given more energy by increasing the temperature. The particles will crash into each other harder. There will be more collision with sufficient energy to break bonds and so the rate of reaction will also increase.

Summary

- Rate of reaction tells you how fast reactants are changing into products. The rusting of iron has a very slow rate of reaction, while gunpowder reacts with oxygen with a very fast rate of reaction.
- The only way to find out the rate of reaction is to carry out an experiment.
- For reactions that produce gases the volume of gas produced can be measured every few seconds using a gas syringe or measuring cylinder.
- Graphs of results produced from experiments show that the rate of reaction is at its highest at the beginning of the reaction because the concentration of the reactants is at its highest. The reaction slows as reactants get used up in the reaction.
- For a reaction to occur, reactant particles must collide with sufficient energy for their bonds to break. This is called the collision theory.
- Increasing the frequency and energy of collisions increases the rate of reaction.

Questions

8.5 **a** Explain what is meant by the term *rate of reaction*.

   b Magnesium reacts with dilute sulphuric acid to produce magnesium sulphate and hydrogen gas.

   i Write word and balanced formulae equations for this reaction. Include state symbols.

   ii Draw and label the apparatus that a student could use to collect results about this rate of reaction.

   c A student carries out an experiment to follow the rate of reaction between magnesium and sulphuric acid. She measures the volume of hydrogen produced every minute from the start of the reaction at time 0 minutes. Her results are shown in the table.

Time (s)	0	1	2	3	4	5	6	7	8
Volume of hydrogen (cm³)	0	15	30	42	52	58	62	62	62

   i Plot these results on a graph. The volume of hydrogen goes on the vertical axis.

   ii Label the part of the graph where the reaction rate is highest.

   iii At what time does the reaction stop?

   iv Explain why the graph becomes horizontal.

8.6 **a** Explain what is meant by the term *collision theory*.

   b Use the collision theory to explain why a reaction slows down and eventually stops.

C Factors that affect rates of reaction

In the early hours of 22 December 1977 a grain silo near New Orleans exploded with terrifying force. Several more explosions ripped through other silos and within a few seconds there were 37 people dead and many of the buildings completely destroyed. If you try and set fire to individual pieces of grain you will find that it is not that easy, so what had caused the grain to explode?

   Grain is poured into the top of huge containers called silos, where it is stored before it is used. The grain silos in this particular facility were about 80 metres high. As the grain fell into the silos, grain dust filled the atmosphere. Grain only burns at its surface where it can react with oxygen in the air. If the grain is present as dust then it has an enormous surface area where oxygen can react. This makes the combustion reaction very, very fast and large

Figure 8.16 This devastating dust explosion near New Orleans occurred when grain dust in silos exploded with oxygen in the air, killing 37 people

volumes of hot gases are produced very quickly. It is the force of the expanding gases that makes an explosion.

   When grain dust is present, a spark is all that is required. The first explosion occurred on a grain elevator carrying the grain up to the top of the silo. This explosion caused more dust to rise in the silos and warehouses around it, causing yet more explosions. Unfortunately, one of the collapsing structures fell on a building full of employees.

   Grain dust is not the only dust that can explode. Coal miners have known about the dangers of coal dust explosions for centuries and even aluminium will combust explosively if it is in powder form. This shows that one of the factors which can increase the rate of a chemical reaction is the surface area of solid reactants.

● Controlling chemical reactions

Chemists control rates of reaction in industry by altering the conditions in which the reactions take place. The conditions they can change are temperature, concentration, surface area of solids and use of a catalyst. We shall look at each of these in turn.

Changing the temperature

We can look at food to see how we use temperature to control the rates of reaction.

▶ Putting food into a refrigerator or freezer can slow the reactions that lead to food spoiling, such as fats turning rancid.
▶ Cooking food by increasing its temperature causes reaction rates to increase and brings about the changes that we expect in cooked food.

It is the same in many industrial processes. Reactants are heated up so that the rate of reaction can be increased. This means that it takes less time to make a certain amount of product, which probably means it will be cheaper, since time in industry costs money.

> There is a balance to be struck between how much energy is used in an industrial process, which costs money and often uses fossil fuels, and the cost of the time it takes to make a particular chemical.

▶ **Explanation: temperature**

Increasing the temperature increases the rate of reaction for two reasons.

▶ Firstly, particles move around faster when heated, so they collide more often.
▶ Secondly, the particles have more energy and so hit each other harder.

The second reason is by far the most important when considering rates of reaction. Increasing the temperature by 10 °C only increases the number of collisions slightly, but the reaction rate doubles because of the increased energy of the collisions, meaning that more collisions will lead to a reaction.

▶ **An experiment to investigate the effect of temperature on the rate of reaction**

Sodium thiosulphate reacts with hydrochloric acid solution to produce a precipitate of sulphur. The balanced ionic equation is:

$$S_2O_3^{2-}(aq) + 2H^+(aq) \rightarrow S(s) + SO_2(g) + H_2O(l)$$

thiosulphate ion   hydrogen ions from
                              hydrochloric acid

The sulphur that is produced means that the reacting solution becomes more and more cloudy until it becomes opaque. This change can be observed by drawing a cross on a piece of paper that is placed underneath the reaction mixture. By looking down through the reaction mixture the cross eventually disappears. The time it takes for the cross to disappear can be used to measure the rate of reaction (Figure 8.17).

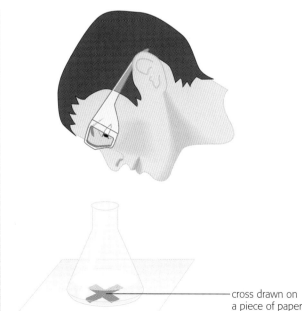

cross drawn on
a piece of paper

Figure 8.17 The cross on the piece of paper gradually disappears from view as the solution becomes more and more cloudy

175

There are a number of factors that must be kept constant when repeating this experiment at different temperatures. Think about these and then try to answer question 8.10 on page 183.

For safety, the thiosulphate solution is not heated above 50 °C, as above this temperature too much sulphur dioxide is produced.

To measure the rate of reaction at different temperatures, the sodium thiosulphate solution can be heated up or put into a refrigerator before the hydrochloric acid is added. The time taken for the cross to disappear becomes much less at higher temperatures, showing that increasing the temperature increases the reaction rate.

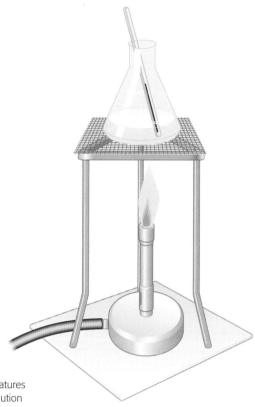

Figure 8.18 The sodium thiosulphate solution is warmed to different temperatures before adding the hydrochloric acid solution

NORMAL SOIL   HEAVY SOIL

2 Tablets   3 Tablets

See bottom of the pack for more details.

Figure 8.19 Increasing the concentration of washing powder chemicals in a washing machine increases the rate of reaction for removing stains

Changing the concentration

If you look at a container of washing powder you will notice that it recommends using more powder if clothes are heavily soiled. ('Soiled' means how dirty and stained they are.) Washing powder manufacturers understand that in an automatic washing machine the clothes are in contact with the washing powder solution for a fixed length of time before the rinse cycle starts and the chemicals are washed away. The dirtier the clothes, the faster you need your washing powder chemicals to work. By adding more powder or tablets you increase the concentration of the washing powder chemicals and this leads to a faster reaction.

▶ **Explanation: concentration**

Increasing the concentration of a reactant increases the rate of reaction. **Concentration** is a measure of the amount of chemical in a particular volume of solution. Hydrochloric acid can be used in different concentrations. The more concentrated the hydrochloric acid the more hydrochloric acid particles there are in a particular volume. The more particles there are the more collisions there will be that cause the hydrochloric acid particles to react with other particles. You can see this idea in Figure 8.14 (on page 172).

> **An experiment to investigate the effect of concentration on the rate of reaction**

Magnesium reacts with sulphuric acid. The equation is:

magnesium + sulphuric acid → magnesium sulphate + hydrogen

$$Mg(s) + H_2SO_4(aq) \rightarrow MgSO_4(aq) + H_2(g)$$

Figure 8.20 Both these test tubes contain magnesium ribbon and sulphuric acid. The test tube on the left is producing many more bubbles of hydrogen than the one on the right because the sulphuric acid solution is more concentrated in the left-hand test tube

The same volume of sulphuric acid is used with the same length of magnesium ribbon and the reaction takes place inside a test tube. Different concentrations of the sulphuric acid are used and, as you can see from Figure 8.20, the more concentrated the sulphuric acid the greater the rate of reaction. The reaction in the test tube on the left will be over much quicker than the reaction with the less concentrated sulphuric acid in the right-hand test tube.

Changing the surface area of a solid reactant

Think for a moment about cooking chips at home. You peel the potatoes and then cut them into strips before plunging them in hot oil and cooking them. The thicker the chips the longer they take to cook. As potatoes are cut up into thinner and thinner slices the surface area gets larger and larger. The larger the surface area the faster the rate of the cooking reactions in the potato.

It is exactly the same in the chemical industry and chemical laboratories. The larger the surface area of a solid reactant the faster the reaction rate will be. To get a larger surface area more surface must be exposed. This is done by cutting, chopping, grinding or crushing. An iron nail reacts very slowly with oxygen in the air, even if heated in a Bunsen burner flame. However, iron filings react very quickly in sparklers to shoot out golden sparks when the sparkler is lit.

In a reaction **surface area** is the amount of surface that is available for a reaction.

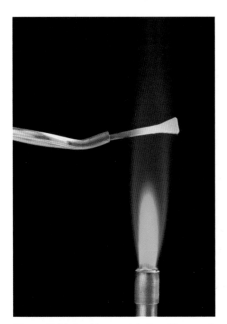

Figure 8.21 Sparklers contain iron filings and so have much more surface area than an iron nail. The iron nail can be heated by a Bunsen burner without appearing to react with the oxygen of the air but the iron filings in sparklers react very quickly

177

Explanation: surface area

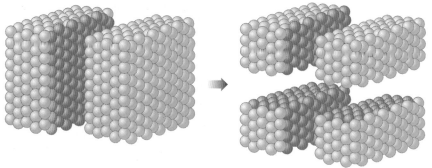

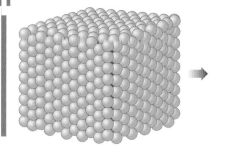

Figure 8.22 As the block of reactant is cut more and more times, more particles are exposed as the surface area increases

When a solid reactant is cut up or crushed, its surface area is increased. This means that more particles are exposed at the surface. The reaction with particles from another chemical only happens at the surface. The more surface that is exposed the more collisions there will be. Increasing the surface area of a solid reactant increases the rate of reaction.

An experiment to investigate the effect of surface area on the rate of reaction

When we looked at how we might measure a rate of reaction we used the reaction of dilute hydrochloric acid and marble chips as an example. Look back to page 171.

$$CaCO_3(s) + 2HCl(aq) \rightarrow CaCl_2(aq) + H_2O(l) + CO_2(g)$$

Measuring the volume of carbon dioxide is one way to follow the rate of this reaction. Another method is to measure the loss of mass due to carbon dioxide being given off (Figure 8.23).

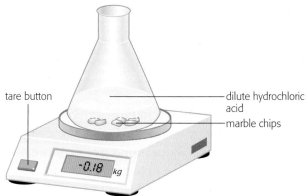

tare button — dilute hydrochloric acid
— marble chips

Figure 8.23 The mass lost during the reaction due to carbon dioxide being given off can be followed using a digital balance

- 10 g of large marble chips are placed in a conical flask and the **tare** button is pressed. The tare button zeros the balance.
- 20 cm³ of dilute hydrochloric acid is now added and the tare button pressed again. At the same time a stopwatch is started.

The loss of mass during the reaction is the mass of carbon dioxide produced. This can be plotted on a graph. The experiment is then repeated using 10 g of smaller marble chips and 20 cm³ of the same concentration of dilute hydrochloric acid.

Graphs of the results for reactions with differently sized marble chips can be plotted on the same axes, as in Figure 8.24. Notice that the smaller marble chips produce a steeper graph. This tells you that the rate of reaction is faster and the reason is that smaller marble chips have a larger surface area than the same mass of larger marble chips.

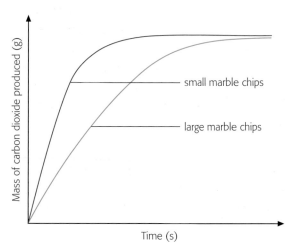

small marble chips

large marble chips

Mass of carbon dioxide produced (g)

Time (s)

Figure 8.24 Graph to show rate of reaction with different sized marble chips

Using a catalyst

A **catalyst** increases the rate of a chemical reaction but remains chemically unchanged at the end of the reaction. For example, car exhausts have catalysts inside them. One of these catalysts is platinum. Platinum increases the rate of reaction between carbon monoxide and oxygen because it is acting as a catalyst.

$$carbon\ monoxide + oxygen \xrightarrow{platinum} carbon\ dioxide$$

$$2CO(g) + O_2(g) \xrightarrow{Pt\ catalyst} 2CO_2(g)$$

Carbon monoxide is produced when petrol burns inside an engine without enough oxygen for complete combustion. Carbon monoxide is a highly toxic gas as it combines with haemoglobin in the blood and reduces the ability of blood to carry oxygen. In the UK, 90% of all carbon monoxide released into the atmosphere comes from vehicle exhaust emissions. Platinum speeds up the reaction that oxidises (adds oxygen to) carbon monoxide to make carbon dioxide, which is not toxic to humans.

In industry, catalysts are often used to speed up the manufacture of chemicals. Many transition metals and their compounds make good catalysts.

> When fuels burn without enough oxygen it is called **incomplete combustion**. You have met this term earlier in your course.

Enzymes

Enzymes are biological catalysts. They are responsible for the millions of reactions that are going on inside you as you read this sentence: reactions that digest your food, produce energy for your muscles to work, send signals to your brain and keep your body in a steady, stable state. Enzymes are incredibly efficient catalysts and work much faster than the catalysts found in manufacturing industry. They can catalyse the reactions of thousands of molecules each second. Enzymes are essential to the maintenance of life because they speed up vital chemical reactions that keep living things alive.

Unusually for catalysts one particular enzyme may only catalyse one particular reaction of the millions that are occurring inside living things. Another unusual feature is that when the temperature of enzyme-catalysed reactions increases too much, the enzymes stop working because their structure is destroyed. This usually happens above 40 °C. For industrial catalysts, increasing the temperature increases the rate of reaction of the catalyst. This is why running a very high temperature in your body when you are ill can be so dangerous. Your normal body temperature is 37.0 °C (98.6 °F) and your enzymes work very efficiently at this temperature. Much higher than this and they stop working.

Explanation: enzymes

Bonds must be broken for a reaction to occur. Remember that bond breaking requires energy. A catalyst makes it easier for bonds in the reactants to break and so collisions between particles do not require so much energy.

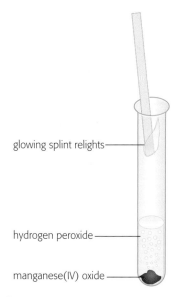

Figure 8.25 The glowing splint does not relight when it is held over a test tube of hydrogen peroxide, but as soon as the catalyst (manganese(IV) oxide) is added it relights

glowing splint relights

hydrogen peroxide

manganese(IV) oxide

> **An experiment to investigate the effect of a catalyst on the rate of reaction**

Hydrogen peroxide is a chemical that decomposes to form oxygen and water:

hydrogen peroxide → water + oxygen
$$2H_2O_2(aq) \rightarrow 2H_2O(l) + O_2(g)$$

Without a catalyst, hydrogen peroxide decomposes very slowly and the amount of oxygen released is difficult to detect. However, if you add a minute amount of manganese(IV) oxide the reaction rate is rapid and the oxygen can be detected easily using a glowing splint (Figure 8.25).

● Using a datalogger to investigate rates of reaction

When a reaction is happening we know that reactants are changing into products.

reactants → products

Suppose you wanted to investigate the reaction between magnesium and sulphuric acid:

magnesium + sulphuric acid → magnesium sulphate + hydrogen
$$Mg(s) + H_2SO_4(aq) \rightarrow MgSO_4(aq) + H_2(g)$$

The first thing to notice is that a gas is being given off. We could measure this using a gas syringe, just like we did on page 171, and check the syringe volume every 20 seconds. However, we could use a sensor to collect the data for us. The sensor could take readings at any time interval, for example every second. In this reaction we could use a position sensor (Figure 8.26), a pressure sensor (Figure 8.27) or a digital balance (Figure 8.28). The information from the sensor is captured by an interface box that stores and converts the data from the sensor into a digital signal, which can be read by a computer.

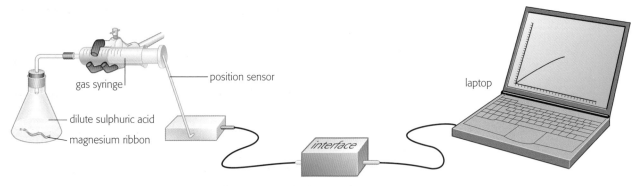

gas syringe

position sensor

laptop

dilute sulphuric acid

magnesium ribbon

interface

Figure 8.26 As the barrel of the syringe moves out the position sensor records this movement. The data passes to the interface box and then to the computer

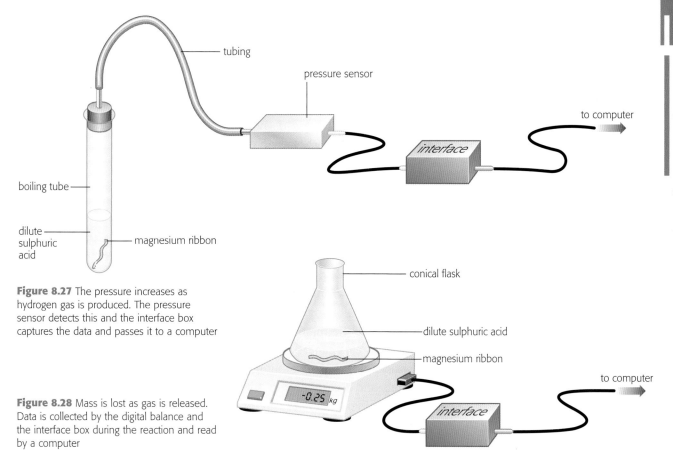

Figure 8.27 The pressure increases as hydrogen gas is produced. The pressure sensor detects this and the interface box captures the data and passes it to a computer

Figure 8.28 Mass is lost as gas is released. Data is collected by the digital balance and the interface box during the reaction and read by a computer

The datalogging process

We have seen three examples of datalogging and the process is the same for all of them. There is a sensor to measure the physical quantity, such as pressure or mass. There is usually some sort of interface that collects the data and converts it into digital signals that can be read by a computer. The interface can store data so it does not have to be connected to a computer immediately. Once connected to the computer the data is stored, often in a spreadsheet. Once the data is in the spreadsheet it can be manipulated to give graphs.

There are many advantages to using dataloggers to study rates of reaction.

▶ The readings are often more accurate than if a person takes the readings.
▶ Many more readings can be taken. This makes the readings more reliable.
▶ The experiment can be set up and left, leaving a person free to carry on with other work.
▶ The data can be stored in a spreadsheet software package on a computer and is easily manipulated to draw graphs and calculate rates of reaction.

Summary

- Increasing the temperature or the concentration or the surface area of a solid reactant can increase the rate of a reaction.
- Increasing the temperature increases the energy of the collisions between reactant particles so more collisions lead to a reaction. The frequency of collisions is also increased. This is why the reaction rate is increased.
- Increasing the concentration of a solution means there are more particles in a particular volume of a solution. If there are more particles there will be more collisions and this will lead to a faster reaction.
- If a solid is crushed, the lumps become smaller and smaller. This exposes more and more reactant particles at the surface. Increasing the surface area means there will be more collisions with other reactant particles and this increases the rate of reaction.
- Catalysts increase the rate of a chemical reaction but remain chemically unchanged at the end of the reaction.
- Enzymes are biological catalysts. They speed up reactions that are essential to the maintenance of life.
- Reaction rates can be followed using datalogging equipment. This consists of a sensor, an interface that converts the data to digital signals and a computer to enter the data into a spreadsheet. Once in a spreadsheet the data can be manipulated to produce graphs.

Questions

8.7 Zinc reacts with hydrochloric acid to give hydrogen and zinc chloride.

   a Write word and balanced formulae equations for this reaction. The formula of zinc chloride is $ZnCl_2$. Use state symbols.

   b Two test tubes are used. One has 10 cm^3 dilute hydrochloric acid at 20 °C and the other has the same volume and concentration of dilute hydrochloric acid at 40 °C. Large zinc granules are added to each at the same time. Which reaction will finish first? Give your reasons.

   c The experiment is repeated but this time the temperature of the hydrochloric acid solutions is kept the same but one test tube has zinc powder added to it instead of large zinc granules.
Which test tube will finish its reaction first – the one with zinc powder or the one with zinc granules? Explain your reasoning.

8.8 For each of the following changes (**a** to **c**) in the conditions of a reaction, explain what happens to the number of collisions and why.

   a Increasing the concentration of one of the reactants.

   b Cooling the reaction mixture down.

   c Using larger lumps of a solid reactant.

   d One of the changes in parts **a** to **c** causes the energy of the collisions to change. Which one of these will do this?

8.9 Biological washing powders and tablets contain enzymes. These enzymes work in reactions to do with food stains.

   a What is an enzyme?

   b Why must the water in the washing machine not be too hot if food stains are to be removed using biological washing powder?

   c Which will dissolve faster, the tablet or the powder? Give your reasons.

   d Using more washing powder or an extra tablet is important when clothes are heavily stained. Explain why.

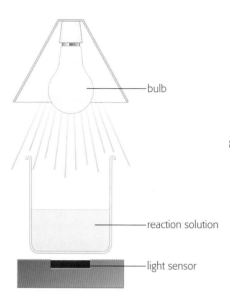

Figure 8.29 Using a light sensor

bulb

reaction solution

light sensor

8.10 Sodium thiosulphate reacts with hydrochloric acid solution to produce a precipitate of sulphur. Read about an experiment to investigate the effect of temperature on the rate of this reaction on page 175.

a When carrying out this experiment the only factor you want to change is the temperature. Why is changing only one factor so important?

b What factors would you need to keep the same?

c The same basic experiment can be used to investigate the effect of concentration on this reaction. Write an instruction sheet for a student in your class to carry out this investigation. Remember to say what must be kept the same.

8.11 A reaction forms a precipitate of sulphur. The reaction solution starts off colourless and transparent and slowly changes to contain a yellow precipitate. A light sensor can be used to investigate the rate of this reaction. The light sensor can be set up as shown in Figure 8.29.

a Explain how the data can be captured and a graph of the results drawn on a computer. You should use a diagram in your explanation.

b Give *three* advantages of using datalogging equipment to investigate the rate of a reaction.

D Reversible reactions and equilibrium

If you have ever visited an ancient cave formed in limestone rock you will have almost certainly seen the spectacular sight of stalactites that hang down from the roof and the stalagmites that rise up from the floor. Often these structures have taken thousands or even millions of years to form. But what are they and how are they made?

Although the stalactites and stalagmites look like icicles they are not made of water but limestone (calcium carbonate, $CaCO_3$). As water from rainfall seeps down through the ground above the cave it dissolves carbon dioxide. This

Figure 8.30 The magnificent stalactites and stalagmites shown here are limestone structures formed by a reversible reaction between limestone, water and carbon dioxide

makes the water acidic. When this water passes through limestone rock it reacts with it to give a solution of calcium ions (Ca^{2+}) and hydrogencarbonate ions (HCO_3^-).

$$CaCO_3(s) + H_2O(l) + CO_2(g) \rightarrow Ca^{2+}(aq) + 2HCO_3^-(aq)$$

When the water starts to drip through the cave roof this reaction reverses and limestone is made again.

$$Ca^{2+}(aq) + 2HCO_3^-(aq) \rightarrow CaCO_3(s) + H_2O(l) + CO_2(g)$$

This is a very slow process. Drips that stay on the ceiling make the limestone for stalactites. When they fall to the floor stalagmites build up.

Figure 8.31 The reaction between magnesium and oxygen is irreversible

Some apparently irreversible reactions are reversible but to such a small extent that we still call them irreversible.

Figure 8.33 The reaction can be reversed by adding the water back to the anhydrous copper sulphate

● Reactions that go both ways

When you burn magnesium oxide in the laboratory, a brilliant white flame is produced and a white powder of magnesium oxide forms. Once the reaction has taken place it is impossible, in a laboratory, to get the reaction to go back again. We call this type of reaction **irreversible**. The single-headed arrow used in a chemical equation shows that the reaction only goes in one direction, from reactant to products.

Reversible reactions

You may remember heating blue copper sulphate crystals and turning them into a white powder.

The blue copper sulphate crystals have water molecules bonded in them and are called hydrated copper sulphate (copper sulphate-5-water). When the water is removed by heating we get anhydrous copper sulphate and water.

Figure 8.32 Hydrated copper sulphate crystals being heated to form anhydrous copper sulphate and water

$$\text{copper sulphate-5-water} \xrightarrow{\text{heat}} \text{copper sulphate} + \text{water}$$
$$CuSO_4.5H_2O(s) \quad \rightarrow \quad CuSO_4(s) \quad + 5H_2O(l)$$

Adding water to the anhydrous copper sulphate to re-form hydrated copper sulphate can reverse this reaction (Figure 8.33).

$$\text{copper sulphate} + \quad \text{water} \rightarrow \text{copper sulphate-5-water}$$
$$CuSO_4(s) \quad + 5H_2O(l) \rightarrow \quad CuSO_4.5H_2O(s)$$

This is an example of a **reversible reaction**. In a reversible reaction products can be made to react to form the reactants again.

We can show that a reaction is reversible by using this sign in the equation, $\rightleftharpoons$:

$$CuSO_4.5H_2O(s) \rightleftharpoons CuSO_4(s) + 5H_2O(l)$$

The reaction that forms stalagmites and stalactites, as discussed in the opening box on page 183, is also a reversible reaction:

$$CaCO_3(s) + H_2O(l) + CO_2(g) \rightleftharpoons Ca^{2+}(aq) + 2HCO_3^-(aq)$$

● Reactions in equilibrium

The word '**equilibrium**' tells you that something is in a state of balance. You could think of a seesaw, where two people sit on it and it stays balanced. In a chemical reaction we can also have an equilibrium, where the reactants and the products are both present and their amounts (and concentrations) do not change. For an equilibrium to form the reaction must be reversible. It must also take place in a **closed system**. This means that nothing can escape from the reaction mixture. Sealing a reaction mixture in a bottle is one way of allowing an equilibrium to form.

The reaction between hydrogen and iodine is reversible. If the gases are sealed in a glass container and heated to 450 °C (Figure 8.34) eventually an equilibrium mixture is formed:

hydrogen + iodine $\rightleftharpoons$ hydrogen iodide
$$H_2(g) \;+\; I_2(g) \;\rightleftharpoons\; 2HI(g)$$

Figure 8.34 The sealed glass bulb on the left shows the reaction at the beginning. The sealed glass bulb on the right has reached equilibrium. There will be no further change in the concentration of each of the three particles in the mixture but the reaction continues in both directions at the same rate

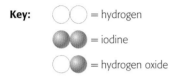

Key:
= hydrogen
= iodine
= hydrogen oxide

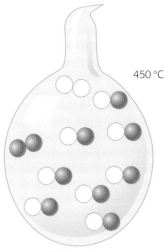

glass is sealed

450 °C   450 °C

sealed glass container

At the start

At equilibrium the amount of each different particle stays the same

Once the equilibrium mixture has formed, the concentration of each chemical in the equilibrium does not change. But this does not mean that the reaction has stopped. The equilibrium is a **dynamic equilibrium** where both the forward and reverse reactions are occurring, but they are both occurring at the same rate.

reactants $\xrightleftharpoons[\text{rate of reverse reaction}]{\text{rate of forward reaction}}$ products

rate of forward reaction = rate of reverse reaction

Think of running up a down escalator. If you want to stay in the same place your rate of progress going up must match the rate of the escalator going down.

● Changing the position of equilibrium

The position of equilibrium tells you whether there are more products or reactants in the equilibrium mixture.

▷ If the position of the equilibrium lies to the right then there are more products than reactants. The concentration of the products will be much higher than the reactants.
▷ If the equilibrium lies to the left there will be a higher concentration of reactants than products.

Industrial chemists are very interested in what changes they can make in reaction conditions so they can alter the position of an equilibrium in order to make more products. More than a century ago a French chemist called Henri Le Chatelier came up with a famous principle.

The position of equilibrium changes to minimise the effect of any change in conditions of a reaction.

This principle, called Le Chatelier's Principle, works for any reaction that reaches equilibrium. Let's look at what happens to the position of equilibrium when we change the conditions of temperature, pressure and concentration.

Changing the temperature

If the temperature is changed how can the effect of this change be minimised? The answer depends on whether the reaction is exothermic or endothermic. Let's first look at exothermic reactions.

For example, the formation of ammonia (NH_3) from nitrogen and hydrogen is exothermic. This means the forward reaction of the equilibrium gives out heat energy:

$$N_2(g) + 3H_2(g) \rightleftharpoons 2NH_3(g)$$

Increasing the temperature increases the energy of the reaction so the equilibrium will shift to take energy in. Since the reverse reaction is endothermic the equilibrium shifts to the left and the concentration of products falls. To get the most product the temperature needs to fall. This way the equilibrium will shift to produce more energy and so move to the right, producing more ammonia.

Now we'll look at endothermic reactions. These take in heat energy in the forward direction. For example, the reaction between nitrogen and oxygen to form nitrogen monoxide is endothermic:

$$N_2(g) + O_2(g) \rightleftharpoons 2NO(g)$$

If the temperature is increased, this increases the heat energy. The equilibrium position will shift to the right to remove this energy because this is the endothermic direction and so the change is minimised. If the temperature is lowered the equilibrium position will shift to the left because in this direction heat energy is produced, so again minimising the change.

Changing the pressure

Changing the pressure only has an effect on reactions involving gases. Let's look again at the production of ammonia:

$$N_2(g) + 3H_2(g) \rightleftharpoons 2NH_3(g)$$

The pressure depends on the number of molecules hitting a particular area. As you can see there are four reactant molecules (three hydrogen and one nitrogen) and two product molecules (two ammonia). If the pressure is increased the equilibrium position will shift to the right because this is the side with fewest molecules. Moving the equilibrium position to the right will reduce the pressure and minimise the increase in pressure.

Let's look at another reaction:

$$N_2(g) + O_2(g) \rightleftharpoons 2NO(g)$$

Pressure has no effect on the equilibrium position because there are two molecules on both sides.

The following reaction makes hydrogen from methane and steam:

$$CH_4(g) + H_2O(g) \rightleftharpoons CO(g) + 3H_2(g)$$

This time there are more molecules on the right. Increasing pressure means that the equilibrium position will shift to reduce the pressure and so move to the left.

Remember: heat energy is given out in an exothermic reaction when reactants change to products. In the reverse direction, the reaction must be endothermic.

Increasing the temperature shifts the equilibrium position to the side of the reaction that is endothermic.

Changing the concentration

Altering the concentration needs to be considered when the reaction takes place in solution.

$$A + B \rightleftharpoons C + D$$

If the concentration of A or B is increased then the equilibrium will shift to the right to minimise this increase. In a similar way, increasing the concentration of C or D will shift the equilibrium to the left.

Summary

- In a reversible reaction products can be made to form reactants again.
- Reversible reactions are represented by $\rightleftharpoons$.
- In a dynamic equilibrium both the forward and reverse reactions are occurring at the same rate.
- If the position of the equilibrium lies to the right then there are more products than reactants.
- The position of equilibrium changes to minimise the effect of any change in conditions of a reaction.
- Increasing the temperature shifts the equilibrium position to the side of the reaction that is endothermic, thus taking in energy.
- Decreasing the temperature shifts the equilibrium position in the exothermic direction, thus releasing energy.
- For a gaseous reaction, increasing the pressure shifts the position of equilibrium in the direction that has fewer numbers of gas molecules because this reduces the pressure.
- Decreasing the pressure shifts the equilibrium position in the direction that has most numbers of gas molecules, thus increasing the pressure.
- Increasing the concentration of a reactant shifts the position of equilibrium to the right to reduce the concentration again. Increasing the product concentration will shift the equilibrium position to the left.

Questions

8.12 Explain what is meant by *reversible reaction* and *dynamic equilibrium*.

8.13 Ammonium chloride (NH_4Cl) will decompose into ammonia (NH_3) and hydrogen chloride (HCl) gas on heating. When the ammonia and hydrogen chloride gases cool, ammonium chloride is re-formed.

   a Write word and balanced formulae equations showing this as a reversible reaction.

   b If this reaction was heated to a constant temperature in a closed system, what would happen?

8.14 The following reaction is an important reaction in the production of sulphuric acid. It is exothermic.

$$2SO_2(g) + O_2(g) \rightleftharpoons 2SO_3(g)$$

How would the position of equilibrium be changed by:

   a increasing the temperature

   b increasing the pressure?

Explain your reasoning.

E Feeding the world

At the beginning of the 20th century the shortage that was most concerning people was not the oil shortage but a shortage of nitrogen compounds. This may seem a very strange statement since nitrogen is all around us in the air. However, nitrogen gas found in the air is very unreactive. A nitrogen molecule contains two nitrogen atoms held together by a triple covalent bond. It takes a lot of energy to break this triple bond and start a reaction with nitrogen. Lightning will do it, to make nitrogen oxides, and enzymes in bacteria in the roots of some plants, such as peas and clover, will also do it to produce ammonium ions and nitrate ions.

Figure 8.35 The energy from this lightning bolt will produce nitrogen compounds

Nitrogen compounds are essential for plants to grow. Every time a crop is harvested it takes its nitrogen compounds with it. Farmers add nitrogen compounds back to the soil in the form of fertilisers. As we shall see, this may be from manure or compost, called organic fertilisers, or from artificial fertilisers that have been manufactured. One hundred years ago extra fertiliser to feed the expanding populations of North America and Europe came from Peru, where there were bird droppings metres deep, and from sodium nitrate found in the deserts of Chile.

Unfortunately, there is another use for nitrogen compounds, in making explosives such as TNT, gunpowder, nitroglycerine and gelignite. Although there are many peaceful uses for explosives, the First World War was approaching and Germany realised that the British Navy could stop supplies of sodium nitrate from Chile reaching Germany. This made it very important to make nitrogen compounds directly from nitrogen in the air.

Figure 8.36 Bacteria in the roots of certain plants, such as these pea plants, will make ammonium ions and nitrate ions

It was Fritz Haber who succeeded in doing this in his laboratory in Germany in 1909, producing 100 g of ammonia (NH_3) from nitrogen and hydrogen. It took Carl Bosch, a chemical engineer, 4 years to scale the production up into an industrial plant producing 30 tonnes a day. Ammonia is used to make nitric acid, which is a starting material for making nitrates and explosives.

Haber won the Nobel Prize for Chemistry in 1918. Although his process, called the **Haber process**, enabled Germany to make weapons of war, it has also allowed many millions more people to be fed during the 20th century who would otherwise have starved.

When it is applied to farming, the term **organic** is associated with natural processes or living things.

● Organic farming versus intensive farming

If you go back to the beginning of the 20th century, most of the chemicals which are regularly used in agriculture today, to kill weeds, kill pests and fertilise crops, just did not exist. There was no mention of **organic farming** because organic farming was the only type of farming that was possible. So what is organic farming? It is growing crops and raising animals for food with the minimum use of manufactured chemicals. Such manufactured chemicals include herbicides (weedkillers), pesticides and fertilisers.

Intensive farming aims to produce large yields from small areas. This has only been possible with the chemicals that allow crops to be grown on the same field year after year (artificial fertilisers and pesticides) and allows animals to be reared closer together, often indoors (medicines to prevent diseases and hormones to speed up growth). Hedgerows have also been removed to make huge fields from small ones, making planting, crop spraying and harvesting easier and therefore more efficient.

Figure 8.37 This huge field grows wheat year after year. This is only possible using artificial fertilisers that replace the nitrogen compounds and other nutrients removed when the crop is harvested

Fertilisers are chemicals that are added to the soil to increase plant growth and so increase crop yield. Nitrogen compounds are essential for healthy plant growth and most fertilisers contain them. Fertilisers dissolve in soil water and enter the plants via the roots. Until Fritz Haber invented his process for making ammonia from nitrogen and hydrogen there were no artificial fertilisers. **Artificial fertilisers** are manufactured by the chemical industry and an important component of these is nitrogen compounds; for example ammonium salts, such as ammonium nitrate (NH_4NO_3) and ammonium sulphate $((NH_4)_2SO_4)$, contain nitrogen. Artificial fertilisers have allowed many millions more people to be fed than if they had not been used. We shall return to this point later.

Figure 8.38 Artificial fertiliser is being added to this field to replace nitrogen compounds and other nutrients

Figure 8.39 This farmer is adding manure to his soil in a process known as muck spreading

Before artificial fertilisers were used there were only **organic fertilisers**. These fertilisers are obtained from rotted organic matter. This might be compost, which is rotted plant material, or manure, which is rotted animal waste. This is not the only way of getting nitrogen compounds into the soil. As you may have read in the box opposite, thunderstorms provide enough energy to split nitrogen molecules (N_2) and allow a reaction with oxygen. The other route nitrogen can get into the soil is via bacteria in the root nodules of certain vegetables. These bacteria have enzymes which can make nitrates and ammonium compounds directly from nitrogen in the air (see page 51).

For centuries farmers have used a system of crop rotation to put back into the soil the nitrogen and other nutrients that harvesting removes. This could be by growing vegetables such as peas and clover one year, which put nitrogen compounds into the soil, then next year planting a crop that requires these nutrients from the soil, such as wheat or potatoes. Each year different crops are grown in the same field. This is crop rotation and it has other advantages because it prevents the build up of pests and diseases that can occur if just one crop is grown on the same field year after year.

Which is best – artificial or organic fertiliser?

There has been debate amongst scientists, farmers and the general public for the last 50 years about whether to use artificial fertilisers or rely only on organic fertilisers.

Here are the advantages of artificial fertilisers:

- they boost crop yields, so more crops are harvested from a particular area – making food cheaper
- they allow the same crop to be grown year after year on the same fields
- they have allowed millions more people to grow up without starving.

However, there are problems with artificial fertilisers.

- The same crop grown in the same field year after year allows the build up of pests and diseases which attack this particular crop. The soil structure can also be damaged by constantly ploughing the same field year after year.
- Artificial fertilisers do not appear to allow as much variety of life in the soils that they fertilise. This means that natural predators of insects and other pests may not survive in the soil, meaning that pesticides need to be used instead.
- Organic matter rotting in the soil retains nitrogen compounds better, keeping them near the roots of plants. Artificial fertilisers do not contain organic matter and are much more easily washed away from the roots.
- It takes a lot of energy to make artificial fertilisers and this usually comes from fossil fuels. Chemicals in oil and natural gas are used to make the hydrogen that is the starting point of ammonia manufacture. Fuels are used to transport the artificial fertiliser to where it will be used. Organic fertilisers are often made on or near the farm where they are used, so less fossil fuel is used to make or transport them.

The case against artificial fertilisers is controversial. There is some scientific evidence to suggest that soil farmed organically contains much more biodiversity (different forms of life), which is important to soil fertility.

● The Haber process for manufacturing ammonia

The manufacture of ammonia needs nitrogen and hydrogen. The reaction is reversible and so may reach a dynamic equilibrium.

$$N_2(g) + 3H_2(g) \rightleftharpoons 2NH_3(g)$$

Air is 79% nitrogen; the fractional distillation of liquid air is used to obtain nitrogen. Hydrogen is made from natural gas (methane).

Conditions used in the Haber process

In the previous section we saw that the position of an equilibrium could be altered by changing the conditions of a reaction. The position of equilibrium changes to minimise the effect of any change. Now let's apply this to the Haber process.

> **Temperature**

The Haber process reaction is exothermic, so heat is given out when ammonia is produced. To shift the equilibrium position to the right, and so increase the yield of ammonia, we need to lower the temperature. However, too low a temperature means that the rate of reaction is too slow, which is not economic, as the reaction takes far too long.

A compromise temperature is used so less ammonia is made but the rate is high enough to be economic. This temperature is **450 °C**.

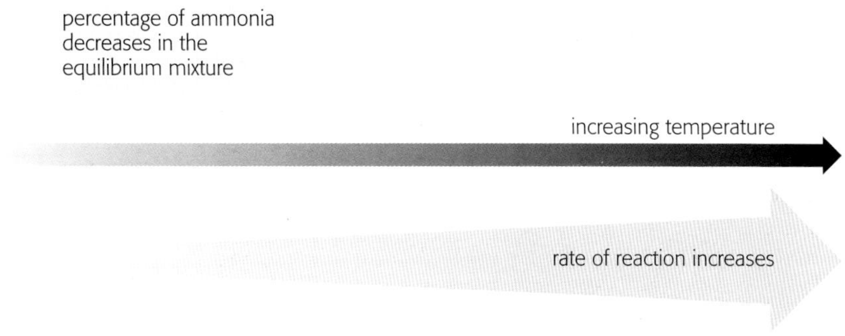

> A dynamic equilibrium is reached when the rate of the forward reaction equals the rate of the reverse reaction. See page 185.

> By reducing the temperature the equilibrium position shifts to the right so that more energy is released, so the effect of the change in temperature is minimised.

percentage of ammonia decreases in the equilibrium mixture

increasing temperature

rate of reaction increases

Figure 8.40 The effect on the Haber process of increasing the temperature

> **Pressure**

This is a gaseous reaction, so increasing the pressure shifts the position of equilibrium to the right because this is the direction that has fewer numbers of gas molecules. Increasing the pressure also increases the rate of reaction.

However, increasing the pressure means that thicker walled pipes will be need to be used to preveent them from exploding and this adds considerably to the expense of making ammonia. A compromise pressure of **200 atmospheres** is used that gives a reasonable yield of ammonia at a reasonable rate.

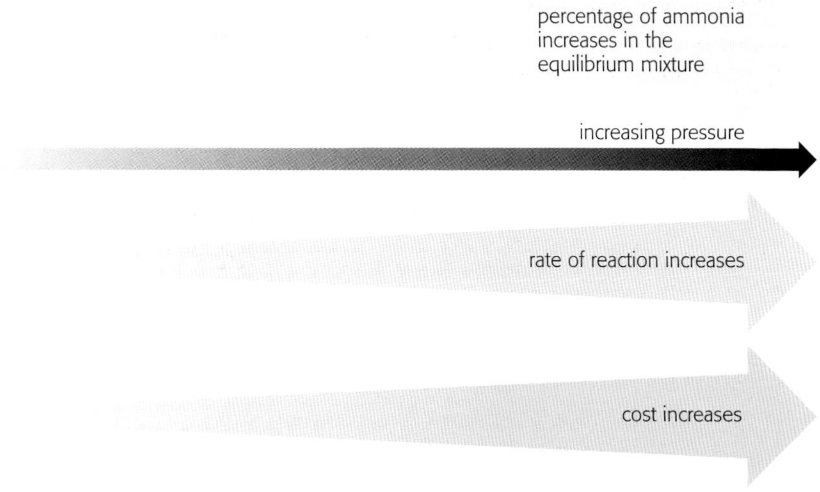

> If the pressure is increased the equilibrium position shifts to reduce the pressure, which in this case is to the right.

percentage of ammonia increases in the equilibrium mixture

increasing pressure

rate of reaction increases

cost increases

Figure 8.41 The effect on the Haber process of increasing the pressure

H

⟩ Using a catalyst

A catalyst speeds up the rate of reaction so more ammonia is produced in a shorter time. The catalyst speeds up the reaction in both directions in a dynamic equilibrium so it does not affect the equilibrium position. Small lumps of iron are used as these have a larger surface area than large lumps.

The yield

Under the conditions shown the yield is only about 10%. However, the unreacted nitrogen and hydrogen pass through the process again.

$$N_2(g) + 3H_2(g) \xrightleftharpoons[]{\text{450 °C, 200 atm pressure, Fe catalyst}} 2NH_3(g)$$

Some ammonia plants will use different conditions. It is a case of balancing the economics of using a high pressure and a high temperature against slower rates and higher yields.

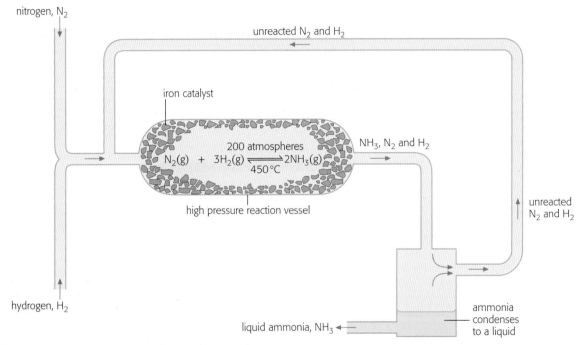

Figure 8.42 The Haber process for the production of ammonia

Summary

- Nitrogen is an essential element for plant growth. Plants take it in through their roots in compounds that dissolve in water in the soil.
- Nitrogen is a very unreactive element and does not readily form compounds.
- Artificial fertilisers are manufactured by the chemical industry. They have allowed millions more humans to be fed who would otherwise have starved.
- Organic fertilisers are obtained from rotted organic matter (compost or manure).
- Organic farming does not require the use of artificial fertilisers. The yields per area of field are lower but fossil fuels are not used to make artificial fertilisers and energy from fossil fuels is not used to transport them to farms.
- Crop rotation is also used in organic farming so that some crops that put back nutrients into the soil are grown. Also pests and diseases do not build up to such an extent.

- Artificial fertilisers produce higher yields and the same area of land can be used year after year.
- The production of ammonia in the Haber process is a reversible reaction, which may reach dynamic equilibrium:

$$N_2(g) + 3H_2(g) \rightleftharpoons 2NH_3(g)$$

- The conditions for this reaction are 450 °C, 200 atmospheres pressure and an iron catalyst.
- The Haber process is exothermic. Too high a temperature and the equilibrium position is too far to the left and the yield is too low. Too low a temperature and the reaction rate is too slow even though the equilibrium position is well over to the right. A compromise temperature of 450 °C is used.
- The forward reaction of the Haber process produces fewer molecules, so increasing the pressure shifts the position of the equilibrium to the right and increases the reaction rate. A pressure of 200 atmospheres is often used.
- An iron catalyst is used to increase the rate of reaction.

Questions

8.15 a Explain what the terms *artificial fertiliser* and *organic fertiliser* mean.
    b Give *three* positive reasons for using artificial fertilisers and *three* arguments against their use.

8.16 a Write the equation for the Haber process.
    b Explain how this reaction can reach a dynamic equilibrium.
    c What raw materials are used to manufacture ammonia?
    d At a constant temperature of 400 °C the following pressures produced different percentages of ammonia in the equilibrium mixture.

Pressure (atmospheres)	Percentage ammonia in equilibrium mixture
25	8
100	23
200	40
300	50
400	58

        i Use the table to decide what happens to the percentage of ammonia in the equilibrium mixture when the pressure is increased.
        ii Using your understanding of how pressure can affect equilibrium position, explain the results in the table.
    e The Haber process reaction is exothermic. If the temperature was increased to 500 °C what would you predict would happen to the percentages of ammonia in the table in part **d**? Explain your answer.

Physics

9 As fast as you can!

A Speed and velocity

Speed kills – every motorist knows that. And yet, many motorists are happy to break the speed limit. Young drivers are among the worst offenders. They learn to drive quickly and pass their test. Then they may go crazy, driving at high speeds in built-up areas, endangering the lives of their passengers and of pedestrians.

Why is this? Perhaps it's because speed is thrilling. It gives the young driver a chance to take a risk, and to show off to his or her friends. Perhaps it's just because the new driver likes the sensation of rushing around, getting quickly from place to place without thinking of the possible risks to others.

Residents often become frustrated when their roads are used as race tracks. The police can help them by supplying a speed camera to monitor the speeds of passing vehicles. If the evidence shows that the speed limit is being regularly broken, the police then take over and prosecute the offenders. They may install permanent speed cameras to record speeding motorists.

Figure 9.1 Speeding may be fun, but it is also risky. Perhaps it is fun *because* it is risky?

Figure 9.2 There is more than a camera in the box. Electronic circuits detect the van as it passes, calculate its speed and record it on the photograph

● Measuring speed

Speed cameras work in two different ways.

The roadway in front of a fixed camera (Figure 9.2) has two detector strips. An electronic circuit in the camera box detects a vehicle as it passes over one strip and then the other, and measures the short time interval taken. It then uses the distance between the strips to calculate the speed of the vehicle. A photograph records the car's registration number.

Hand-held speed 'guns' send out radio waves which reflect back from the moving vehicle. The gun detects the reflected waves and measures their frequency. The bigger the change in frequency, the faster the vehicle is moving.

In the lab

You can investigate the movement of a trolley in the lab using light gates (Figure 9.3). The trolley has an 'interrupt card' mounted on it; as it passes through the light gate, the infra-red beam is broken, and this is recorded by the datalogger. This can be used to find the **speed** of the trolley.

Suppose the card is 5 cm long, and the beam of the light gate is broken for 0.2 s. You should recall how to use this information to calculate the trolley's speed:

$$\text{average speed of trolley} = \frac{\text{distance}}{\text{time}} = \frac{5\,\text{cm}}{0.2\,\text{s}} = 25\,\text{cm/s}$$

We have to say 'average speed' because the trolley's speed may be changing as it moves past the light gate.

Figure 9.3 The card breaks the beam as the trolley passes through the light gate

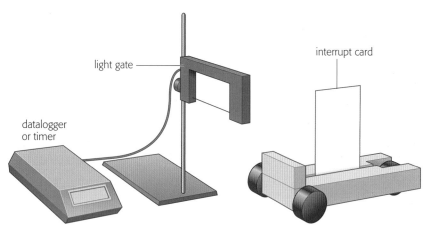

● A sense of direction

Occasionally, you may hear people talking about the *velocity* of an object, rather than its *speed*. In Science, the word *velocity* has a special meaning.

The **velocity** of an object is its speed in a particular direction.

So, to give the velocity of an object, we have to state two things: its speed, and the direction in which it is moving.

The map (Figure 9.4) shows an example. The green arrow represents a train travelling at 50 m/s from Bristol to London. Its velocity is 50 m/s due east.

Any quantity that has both **magnitude** (size) and direction is called a **vector** quantity. On diagrams, vector quantities are represented by arrows.

Here is another vector quantity. Look again at Figure 9.4, and suppose you drive from

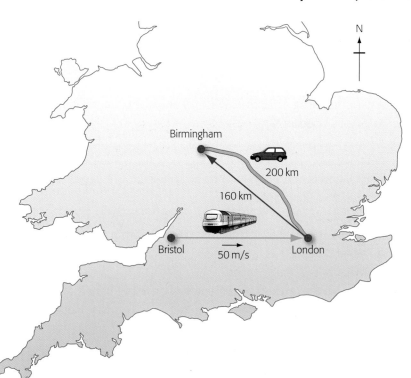

Figure 9.4 Velocity and displacement are vector quantities

London to Birmingham along the motorway. It takes you 2.5 hours, and the mileometer says you have travelled 200 km. Your average speed was 80 km/h. However, you measure the distance between London and Birmingham on the map and find that it is 160 km. Your **displacement** from London is just 160 km. Since displacement is a vector quantity, we have to give its direction: north-west from London. Figure 9.4 shows the difference between the distance you have travelled (blue route) and your displacement (red arrow).

Calculating average velocity

Here is the equation used to calculate average velocity:

$$\text{average velocity} = \frac{\text{displacement}}{\text{time}} \qquad v = \frac{s}{t}$$

So, for the journey to Birmingham:

$$\text{average velocity} = \frac{\text{displacement}}{\text{time}} = \frac{160}{2.5} = 64 \text{ km/h north-west}$$

Note that the average velocity in this example is less than the average speed. For the two to be the same, the motorway from London to Birmingham would have to be a straight line. Note also that we can only calculate the average velocity; your car would be going faster at some times, slower at others, and would also change direction along bends of the motorway.

> Note that we use the letter s to stand for displacement. Don't confuse it with s for seconds.

Summary

- A vector quantity has both magnitude and direction.
- Velocity is speed in a given direction.
- Average Velocity $= \dfrac{\text{displacement}}{\text{time}} \qquad v = \dfrac{s}{t}$

Questions

9.1 Which of the following are vector quantities?

   speed, displacement, distance, velocity

9.2 A car is travelling at 25 m/s. What other piece of information is needed to give its velocity?

9.3 A force is represented on a diagram by an arrow. This is because it has both size and direction. What type of quantity is a force?

9.4 A truck travels due north for 3 hours. In this time, it travels 210 km. What is its average velocity?

9.5 The Australian city of Perth has a rectangular street-plan (Figure 9.5, opposite). A taxi takes 10 minutes to travel from X to Y.
   a What distance has it travelled?
   b What is its average speed?
   c What is the taxi's displacement after travelling from X to Y? [Hint: you will need to measure the angle that XY makes with North.]
   d What is its average velocity in the direction XY?

Figure 9.5 Street plan for question 9.5

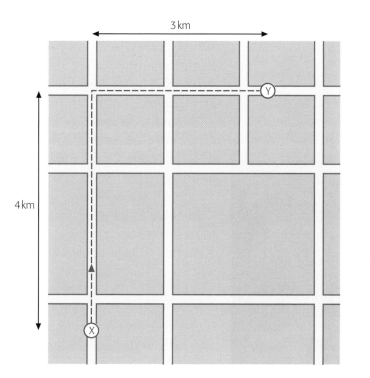

3 km

4 km

N

9.6 A car is travelling due west from Edinburgh to Glasgow with a velocity of 30 m/s.
  a What will its displacement be after 5 min (300 s)?
  b If its average velocity remains at 30 m/s, how long will it take to travel 27 km?

B Changing velocity

Many modern cars are fitted with air bags. In the event of an accident, the air bag suddenly inflates and prevents the driver from flying into the windscreen.

How does this work? The air bag has to detect a sudden change in velocity of the car; in particular, it must detect when the car suddenly comes to a halt. To do this, it uses a tiny device called an accelerometer. If the car stops suddenly because it has hit another object, its velocity changes to zero in a very short time. The accelerometer detects this and sends an electrical signal to the trigger of the air bag, which explodes outwards in a tiny fraction of a second.

The accelerometers used in cars are very tiny devices – they are among the first examples of nanotechnology to come into widespread use.

Figure 9.6 An air bag in operation. The black dot on the palm of the hand shows the tiny accelerometer used to detect the sudden slowing down of the car

● Acceleration

When a car starts off, its driver presses on the accelerator pedal. The harder he or she presses, the greater the force causing the car to speed up. The rate at which the car's velocity increases is called its **acceleration**.

You will sometimes see cars, especially sporty ones, advertised with information about how great their acceleration is. For example, '0 to 60 in 10 seconds' tells you that a car can reach 60 mph (miles per hour) in 10 s. That is, its speed increases by 6 mph every second. This is a measure of its acceleration.

In Science, we generally consider speeds and velocities measured in metres per second (m/s). A car that can accelerate from 0 to 30 m/s in 10 s has an acceleration of 3 m/s per second. This is usually written as 3 m/s^2 (metres per second squared).

Acceleration can be fun

If you have ever ridden in a rollercoaster (Figure 9.7), you will have experienced the thrill of acceleration. Moving at a steady speed is rather dull. But *changing* speed can be exciting. You may experience some big accelerations on a rollercoaster ride:

) speeding up down a slope – perhaps 5 m/s^2
) dropping vertically downwards – 10 m/s^2
) turning a sudden corner – 20 to 30 m/s^2.

The bigger the acceleration, the more you feel yourself thrown about, and the louder you scream.

Calculating acceleration

Any object whose velocity changes has an acceleration. Its acceleration depends on two things:

) the change in velocity
) the time taken.

The bigger the change in velocity and the shorter the time taken, the greater the acceleration. Here is the equation used to calculate acceleration:

$$\text{acceleration} = \frac{\text{change in velocity}}{\text{time taken}}$$

$$a = \frac{(v - u)}{t}$$

In symbols, we write $(v - u)$ for change in velocity, where u = initial velocity and v = final velocity.

Figure 9.7 Experiencing high acceleration

Remember, u for initial velocity comes before v in the alphabet.

Worked example

A car leaves a 30 mph speed limit and the driver accelerates. Its velocity increases from 10 m/s to 26 m/s in 20 s (Figure 9.8). What is its acceleration?

10 m/s   26 m/s

←————————————— 20 s —————————————→

Figure 9.8

It is easiest to do this calculation in two steps.

Step 1: Calculate the change in velocity.

change in velocity = final velocity − initial velocity
= 26 m/s − 10 m/s = 16 m/s

Step 2: Calculate the acceleration.

$$\text{acceleration} = \frac{\text{change in velocity}}{\text{time taken}}$$

$$= \frac{16 \text{ m/s}}{20 \text{ s}} = 0.8 \text{ m/s}^2$$

So the car's acceleration is 0.8 m/s²; its velocity increases by 0.8 m/s each second.

> Notice that, if the car was slowing down, its acceleration would be negative.

Changing direction

The Earth goes around the Sun at a steady speed (almost). Although it is not speeding up, its velocity is changing, because it is continually changing direction. The pull of the Sun's gravity is the force that makes it accelerate and keeps it in its orbit. Without this force, the Earth would move away in a straight line.

The same is true for a car travelling around a bend at a steady speed – it is accelerating because its velocity is changing direction all the time. On a rollercoaster, the highest accelerations are when the car you are travelling in goes round a tight bend at high speed.

● Velocity–time graphs

We can represent the motion of a moving object using a velocity–time graph. This shows how the magnitude of the object's velocity (its speed) changes as time passes. Figure 9.9 on the next page shows some examples.

Car A is moving with constant velocity; its graph is a horizontal straight line.

Car B is speeding up; its graph is a straight line, sloping upwards, showing that its velocity is increasing.

Car C has a greater acceleration than Car B; its graph is a steeper straight line.

Car D accelerates, and then continues at a steady speed.

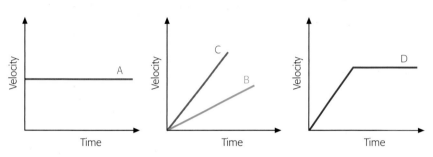

Figure 9.9 Velocity–time graphs for four cars. The steeper the slope of the line, the greater the car's acceleration

From these examples you should be able to see that the **gradient** (slope) of the velocity–time graph tells us how the car's velocity is changing. The steeper the gradient, the greater the acceleration. In fact the value of the gradient equals the value of the acceleration.

Worked example

Figure 9.10 represents the motion of the car in the previous worked example. It is travelling in a straight line, and its velocity increases from 10 m/s to 26 m/s in 20 s. To find its acceleration, we can calculate the gradient of the graph.

Step 1: Start by selecting two points on the line and drawing a right-angled triangle beneath the line.

Step 2: Then find the lengths of the two sides of the triangle, as shown.

Step 3: Calculate the gradient:

$$\text{acceleration} = \text{gradient} = \frac{8\,\text{m/s}}{10\,\text{s}} = 0.8\,\text{m/s}^2$$

Of course, we find the same result as before.

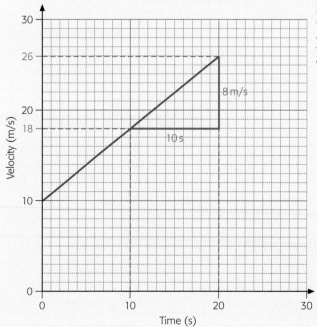

Figure 9.10 Calculating acceleration from the gradient of a velocity–time graph

Summary

- An object has an acceleration when its velocity (speed or direction) changes.

$$\text{acceleration} = \frac{\text{change in velocity}}{\text{time taken}} \qquad a = \frac{(v - u)}{t}$$

- For an object moving in a straight line, acceleration can be found from the gradient of a velocity–time graph.

Questions

9.7 Which of these two cars has the greater acceleration? (You can find the answer without calculating the acceleration.) Explain your answer.
  Car A accelerates from rest (0 m/s) to 20 m/s in 10 s.
  Car B accelerates from rest to 15 m/s in 12 s.

9.8 Jon and Jen are on a merry-go-round. It spins them round at a steady speed. Jon says, 'We are accelerating!' Jen says, 'No, we're not!' Who is right? Explain your answer.

9.9 Explain the meanings of the symbols in the equation $a = (v - u) / t$.

9.10 The graph (Figure 9.11) shows how the velocities of four cars changed.
  a Which car was travelling at a steady speed?
  b Which car was slowing down?
  c Two cars were speeding up. Which had the greater acceleration? Explain how you can tell.

9.11 A bus accelerates from 5 m/s to 13 m/s in 40 s. What is its acceleration?

9.12 The graph (Figure 9.12 below) represents the motion of a train.
  a How fast is the train moving after 50 s?
  b By how much does the train's velocity change during the first 50 s of its journey?
  c What is the train's acceleration during this time?

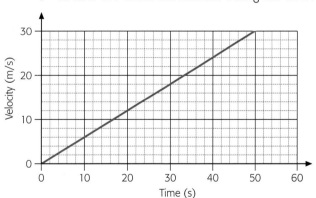

Figure 9.12

9.13 The table shows how the velocity of a car changed during a short journey.

Velocity (m/s)	0	8	16	22	28
Time (s)	0	10	20	30	40

  a Use the data to draw a velocity–time graph for the journey.
  Use the graph to calculate the car's acceleration:
  b during the first 20 s
  c during the last 20 s.

Figure 9.11

Velocity

Time

A
B
C
D

C Forces and motion

One of the most dramatic fairground rides is Oblivion, at Alton Towers. The riders in their car are held for several seconds above a vertical drop. Below is a smoke-filled pit into which they know they will plunge. Suddenly they drop. As the car disappears into the pit, the curved track breaks its fall so that it ends up moving horizontally. And within a few seconds of the drop, the car's brakes bring it to a sudden halt.

There are several forces at work here (Figure 9.14). The ride's excitement comes from the suddenly changing accelerations produced by these different forces.

Figure 9.13 The Oblivion ride at Alton Towers

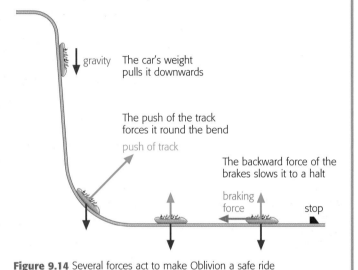

gravity The car's weight pulls it downwards

The push of the track forces it round the bend

push of track

The backward force of the brakes slows it to a halt

braking force stop

Figure 9.14 Several forces act to make Oblivion a safe ride

● Forces producing acceleration

As the Oblivion car drops (see box above), it speeds up – it accelerates. This is because there is only one force acting on it – its **weight**, caused by the pull of the Earth's gravity. Any falling object speeds up, although it isn't easy to see this happening. Figure 9.15 shows the pattern of motion of a falling ball.

The falling ball is shown at equal intervals of time. Each gap is bigger than the one before, showing that the ball is accelerating. The ball's acceleration is downwards, in the same direction as the force causing it.

Unbalanced forces

The falling ball accelerates because there is only one force acting on it. This force can be described as unbalanced. Now think about the Oblivion car as it comes to a halt. Its brakes provide the necessary force to make it come to rest. This is an unbalanced force pushing backwards on the car, so that it slows down.

You should recall that the forces on an object must be unbalanced if the object is to change its speed or its direction – in other words, to change its velocity.

▸ Balanced forces: the object remains at rest, or keeps moving at a steady speed in a straight line (constant velocity).
▸ Unbalanced forces: the object's speed and/or direction change.

Figure 9.15 As the ball falls, its weight causes it to accelerate

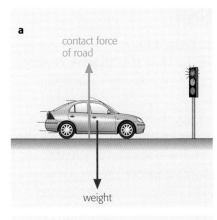

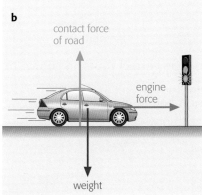

Figure 9.16
a Waiting at the lights, the forces on the car are balanced
b Three forces act on the car as it sets off from the lights

Resultant force

Here is an example to make this clear. A car is waiting at the traffic lights. Figure 9.16a shows the forces acting on the car. There are two:

- its weight acting downwards
- the contact force of the road pushing upwards.

These forces are equal in size but opposite in direction, so they cancel each other out. The forces on the car are balanced, so it remains stationary.

Now the lights change, and the driver presses on the accelerator. The engine provides the forward force needed to make the car accelerate forwards (Figure 9.16b). Now there is a third force acting on the car:

- the engine force acting to the right.

As before, the weight and the contact force cancel each other out. This leaves the force of the engine, which causes the car to accelerate to the right. We say that the car is acted on by a **resultant force** to the right. The resultant force has the same overall effect as all three forces combined, and the car accelerates in the direction of the resultant force.

Calculating resultant force

To decide whether an object will accelerate or not, you have to decide whether there is a resultant force acting on it. If there is a resultant force, it will accelerate in the direction of the force; otherwise the forces acting must be balanced, and the object will not accelerate.

Figure 9.17a shows the car when it is travelling fast. There is another force acting:

- air resistance acting to the left.

Is there a resultant force acting on the car? You can see that the vertical forces cancel out, as before. However, the horizontal forces do not cancel out, because the engine force is greater than the air resistance. So:

resultant force = 500 N − 300 N = 200 N to the right

Figure 9.17
a Here there is a resultant force to the right because the force of the engine is greater than the force of air resistance
b Now the brakes are applied and there is a resultant force to the left

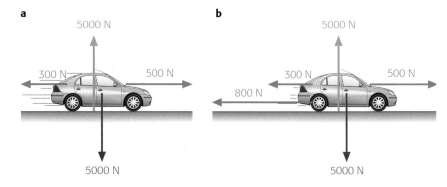

Figure 9.17b shows what happens when the brakes are applied. We can calculate the resultant of the three horizontal forces:

resultant force = 500 N − 300 N − 800 N = −600 N

So the resultant force on the car is 600 N to the left (the minus sign tells us the direction). You can see from the diagrams that it helps to draw longer force arrows for bigger forces.

● Calculating acceleration

Imagine throwing a tennis ball – perhaps in a PE lesson. The harder you throw it, the further it goes. That's because the bigger your force on the ball, the more it accelerates, and so the faster it is moving when it leaves your hand.

Now imagine throwing a medicine ball. Its mass is much greater than that of a tennis ball. Even with your greatest force, you will not be able to give it much acceleration, and it won't travel very far.

So the acceleration produced by a force depends on two factors: the size of the force, and the mass of the object being accelerated.

We can turn this idea into an equation relating force F, mass m and acceleration a:

force = mass × acceleration $\qquad\qquad F = ma$

For this equation to work, we must use the correct units, as shown in Table 9.1.

Note that you have met this equation before in a slightly different form, when calculating weight:

weight = mass × acceleration of free-fall $\qquad W = mg$

Quantity	Unit
force F	newton N
mass m	kilogram kg
acceleration a	metre per second squared m/s^2

Table 9.1 Quantities and units

Worked example

What force is needed to give a tennis ball of mass 0.2 kg an acceleration of 25 m/s^2?

Write down the equation and substitute the values:

force = mass × acceleration = 0.2 kg × 25 m/s^2 = 50 N

So the force needed is 50 N.

If the same force acts on a medicine ball of mass 20 kg, what acceleration will it produce?

This time, we must rearrange the equation:

$$\text{acceleration} = \frac{\text{force}}{\text{mass}} = \frac{50\,\text{N}}{20\,\text{kg}} = 2.5\,\text{m/s}^2$$

Repetitive calculations

Once we know an object's acceleration, we can work out how it will move. Here is a step-by-step technique for doing this:

A stone has mass 2 kg. It is dropped from a large height. It is acted on by a downward force of 20 N (this is its weight). Using $F = ma$, we know its acceleration is 10 m/s^2, so its velocity increases by 10 m/s every second.

Step 1: After 1 s, the stone will be moving at 10 m/s.

Step 2: During this 1 s, its average velocity will be 5 m/s (half way between 0 m/s and 10 m/s).

Step 3: During this 1 s, it will travel 5 m.

Step 4: Total distance travelled so far = 5 m.

Step 5 (= Step 1 again): After 2 s, the stone is travelling at 20 m/s.

Step 6 (= Step 2 again): During this second 1 s, its average velocity will be 15 m/s (half way between 10 m/s and 20 m/s).

Step 7 (= Step 3): Distance travelled during this 1 s = 15 m.

Step 8 (= Step 4): Total distance travelled so far = 5 m + 15 m = 20 m.

You could continue this calculation for many more seconds, but it is easier to use a spreadsheet. The advantage of a spreadsheet is that you can easily change factors, such as the mass or weight of the stone. You can also plot graphs automatically, as shown in Figure 9.18.

Figure 9.18 Using a spreadsheet to perform repetitive calculations: here we are calculating the motion of a falling stone

	A	B	C	D
1	time (s)	velocity (m/s)	extra distance (m)	total distance (m)
2	0	0	0	0
3	1	10	5	5
4	2	20	15	20
5	3	30	25	45
6	4	40	35	80
7	5	50	45	125

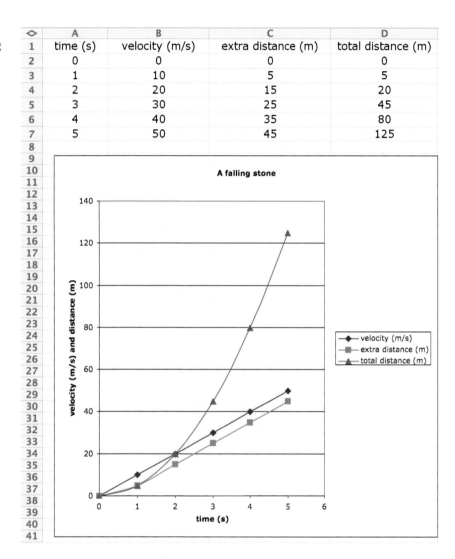

● Identifying forces

It is important to be able to identify all of the forces that act on an object. Only then can you work out the resultant force on the object, and then its acceleration. Figure 9.19 shows two examples.

Notice that each diagram is in two parts. On the right, we see the object of interest separated from its surroundings. This is to make sure that we consider only the forces acting *on the object*, and not the forces it is exerting on other objects. So, in Figure 9.19a, the girl is pressing down on the chair, but we do not show that force in the right-hand diagram, because it is not a force that acts on her. A diagram like this is called a free-body force diagram.

Figure 9.19 The diagrams on the right are free-body force diagrams

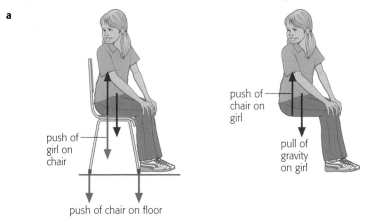

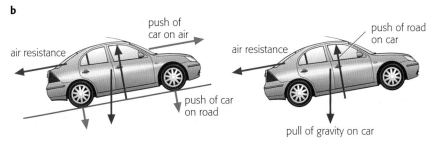

Action and reaction

Where do forces come from? They arise whenever two objects interact with each other. For example, when you stand on the floor, your feet press down on the floor (Figure 9.20a). At the same time, the floor presses upwards on your feet. (If you put your hand in between someone's feet and the floor, these two forces would crush your hand.)

Figure 9.20
a Action and reaction forces appear when you stand on the floor
b When your foot pushes backwards on the ground, the ground pushes forwards on your foot

These two forces appear at the same time (when your feet touch the floor), and disappear at the same time (when your feet leave the floor). They are described as **action** and **reaction** forces, because we imagine one force being a reaction to the other. In fact, this is a bit misleading, because we can't say which force is the action and which is the reaction – they appear at the same time.

There are two important rules about action and reaction forces:

▷ They are equal in size and opposite in direction.
▷ They act on different objects.

Because they act on different objects (for example, on your feet and on the floor), they can't cancel each other out. Only one of these forces would appear on a free-body diagram of your feet.

We make use of action and reaction forces all the time; for example, when we walk (Figure 9.20b). We can't push ourselves forwards. Instead, our feet push backwards on the ground (action force). This results in a forward force from the ground on our feet (reaction force), and it is this force which makes us move forwards.

There are many other examples of action and reaction forces.

If you hold two magnets close together, with opposite poles facing, you will feel the attractive forces between them. The two magnets attract each other with equal forces, in opposite directions – even if one magnet is stronger than the other.

The Moon is held in its orbit by the Earth's gravity. At the same time, the Moon's gravity pulls on the Earth with an equal and opposite force. This is the force that causes tides.

In the same way, the Earth pulls on you with a force that we call your weight. You pull on the Earth with an equal and opposite force. However, because the mass of the Earth is so great, you have very little effect on the Earth.

Figure 9.21 The Earth and the Moon pull on one another with equal and opposite forces

Summary

● The resultant force acting on an object has the same effect as all of the individual forces acting on it.
● If the resultant force on an object is zero, the body will remain at rest or continue to move at a constant speed in a straight line.
● If the resultant force on an object is not zero, the object will accelerate in the direction of the resultant force.

force = mass × acceleration $F = ma$

● A free-body force diagram shows only the forces that act on an object.
● When two objects interact, they exert equal and opposite forces on each other (action and reaction forces).

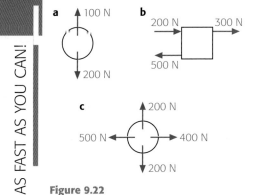

Figure 9.22

Questions

9.14 Calculate the resultant force in each of the examples shown in Figure 9.22. Remember to give both the magnitude and the direction of the resultant force.

9.15 For each of the objects in question 9.14, say whether it will accelerate, and, if so, give the direction of its acceleration.

9.16 What force is needed to give a car of mass 500 kg an acceleration of 4 m/s²?

9.17 Figure 9.23 shows a box on the ground. A boy is trying to push it along. The forces acting are marked.

Figure 9.23

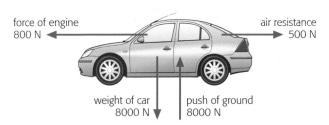

    a Which *three* pairs of forces are action and reaction forces?

    b Draw a free-body force diagram of the box.

    c The box starts to move. What can you say about the sizes of the horizontal forces acting on the box?

9.18 A force of 100 N acts on a ball of mass 4 kg. What is its acceleration?

9.19 The car in Figure 9.24 has a mass of 800 kg.

Figure 9.24

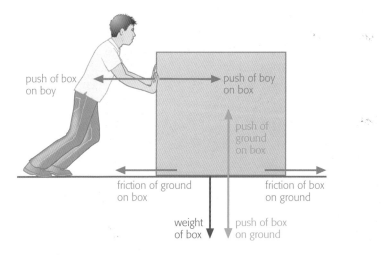

    a What is the resultant force acting on the car?

    b What is its acceleration?

9.20 Look again at Figure 9.14 on page 202, which shows the forces at work on the Oblivion ride.

    a Which force always acts on the car?

    b Which force causes the car to change direction along the curved part of the track?

    c At which point is there no resultant force on the car?

H

D Falling through the air

Parachuting is fun – at least, some people think so. Many charities organise sponsored parachute drops, and teenagers often take part.

You drop from the plane, and you accelerate faster. As you fall, you feel the air rushing past. The faster you go, the greater the rush of air. This tells you that air resistance is greater when an object is moving faster.

When your instructor tells you, you open your parachute. Suddenly, a much larger upward force is acting on you, and you slow down. There is a curious effect here, which you may have noticed in films of parachuting. Someone opens their parachute and they appear to be pulled upwards –

Figure 9.25 Free-fall parachutists open their parachutes when they are about 600 m above the Earth's surface

they disappear upwards, out of view. In fact, they don't move upwards. It's just that the photographer continues falling rapidly (until they open their parachute), so they overtake the person who has just opened their parachute.

air resistance

weight

Figure 9.26 A ball accelerates as it falls because its weight is greater than the force of air resistance

Figure 9.27 This jumping spider makes use of air resistance to leap safely through the air

● Forces and falling

When an object falls through the air, it is its weight that causes it to accelerate downwards. At the same time, there is an upward force acting on it, tending to slow it down. This is air **resistance**.

Figure 9.26 shows these two forces acting on a falling ball. The forces are unbalanced because the ball's weight is greater than the air resistance. This means that the ball will accelerate downwards.

Insects and spiders are small, so moving through air is difficult for them. Air resistance slows them down. However, they can make use of this. Many spiders, for example, can fall safely through the air thanks to their hairy legs, which they spread out like a natural parachute to make the most of air resistance (Figure 9.27).

Figure 9.28 A ball reaches terminal velocity when its weight is balanced by air resistance

Figure 9.29 A parachute has a large area, so the upward force of air resistance is greatly increased and the parachutist reaches the ground at a safe speed

Figure 9.31 A new land speed record was set by *Thrust SSC* (supersonic car), which achieved over 1227 km/h in 1997

Terminal velocity

Air resistance depends on two factors:

- the speed of the falling object – the faster it moves, the greater the resistance
- the area of the object – an object with a larger area experiences more resistance.

How does this affect the falling ball? As the ball falls faster, the air resistance increases. Eventually, the air resistance equals the weight of the ball; now the forces are balanced and the ball falls at a steady speed (Figure 9.28). It has reached **terminal velocity**.

For a falling person, terminal velocity is about 40 or 50 m/s; that's fast – about 100 mph. You are unlikely to survive if you hit the ground at that speed. An open parachute increases air resistance enormously, and terminal velocity reduces to about 10 m/s, a safe speed to land at. Figure 9.30 shows a velocity–time graph for a parachutist.

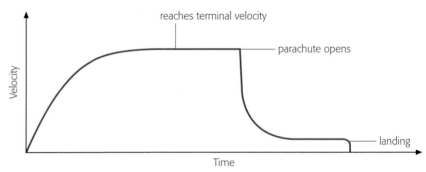

Figure 9.30 Velocity–time graph for a parachutist

Cars also have 'terminal velocity'. As a car travels along, it is acted on by air resistance. If the driver accelerates, air resistance increases. Eventually, the forward force of the engine is balanced by the backward force of air resistance, so the car cannot travel any faster. It has reached its top speed. To go faster, it must have either a more powerful engine (to increase the forward force) or a more streamlined shape (to reduce the backward force).

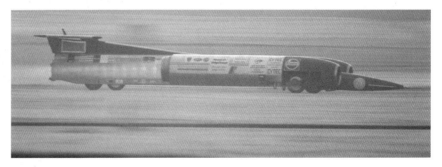

Summary

- A falling object is acted on by its weight and by air resistance.
- At first, these forces are unbalanced and the object accelerates downwards.
- Air resistance increases with speed, and eventually equals the object's weight. Now the object has reached terminal velocity.

Questions

9.21 **a** Which *two* forces act on an object when it is falling through the air?

   b Draw a free-body force diagram of a falling stone to show these forces.

   c Use your diagram to explain why the stone accelerates.

9.22 Explain why a parachutist falls more slowly when their parachute is opened than during the time of free-fall before they open their parachute.

9.23 Every car has a top speed, the greatest speed at which it can travel along a flat road. Car X has a top speed of 40 m/s; its engine provides a driving force of 5000 N.

   a Draw a free-body force diagram of Car X travelling at top speed.

   b Car Y is similar to Car X, but it is fitted with a more powerful engine, capable of providing a forward force of 6000 N. Draw a free-body force diagram for Car Y travelling at 40 m/s, with the engine providing its maximum force. Use your diagram to explain why Car Y has a higher top speed than Car X.

   c Car X could be given a more streamlined shape. Explain why this would give it a higher top speed. Illustrate your answer with a suitable force diagram.

E Taking chances

Car manufacturers have been discouraged from advertising their cars by claiming that they are fast, and that they have high acceleration. Today, motoring adverts have more emphasis on car safety and, to make sure that their claims are fair, the European New Car Assessment Programme performs standard tests on all new cars.

Figures 9.32a and b show the results of tests on a Renault Clio. The car is crashed at a standard speed (40 mph, 64 kph) into a barrier. Sensors record the forces which act on the car and on the dummy driver and passenger. You can see that the air bags have inflated. Technicians will be looking to see whether the driver's head hit the windscreen or dashboard – that is why the dummies' heads have red and green blobs of paint on them.

Dummy pedestrians are also used in test impacts with cars. This is vital, because a driver may feel very safe inside the car, and this can lead them to drive with less attention to the safety of other road users.

Figure 9.32 a A Renault Clio undergoes a head-on impact test

b You can see the electrical leads to the various sensors within the driver dummy

● Feeling safe, being safe

There are many features built into new cars to increase the safety of the driver and passengers. It is impossible to make car travel perfectly safe, but the numbers of deaths on UK roads have been decreasing for several decades, despite the great increase in road travel.

Some of the safety features in cars are:

- **safety belts (and harnesses for babies)** These reduce the risk that the passenger will be thrown about in the car (or out of the car) in the event of an impact. The idea is that the wearer is brought to a halt in a controlled way, so that they are less likely to hit the windscreen or the seat in front.
- **crumple zones** The front and back sections of the car are designed to collapse on impact, absorbing the energy of the impact. The occupants of the car are protected in the strong, rigid passenger compartment (Figure 9.33).
- **air bags** As we saw on page 197, these detect sudden large accelerations and inflate to protect the driver or passengers during a crash.

There is a problem with all of these safety measures. If a driver feels safer, he or she may drive faster and take greater risks. This increases the chances of an accident happening, and so the driver is no safer than if they were driving a car with fewer safety features.

Figure 9.33 The crumple zones of a car are designed to take the worst of an impact while the occupants are protected within the passenger compartment

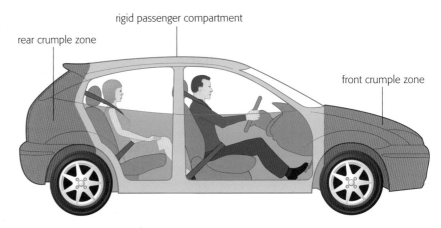

rigid passenger compartment

rear crumple zone

front crumple zone

● Momentum

In an impact, the damage is likely to be greater if the moving object has high velocity and high mass – it is much harder to stop a large object moving quickly than a small one moving slowly. It is useful to think about the **momentum** of a moving object, which takes account of both mass and velocity:

momentum = mass × velocity

Any moving object has momentum.

Worked example

What is the momentum of a car of mass 600 kg moving at 20 m/s?

momentum = mass × velocity
= 600 kg × 20 m/s = 12 000 kg m/s

Notice that the units of momentum are kg m/s (kilogramme metre per second).

Absorbing momentum

When a moving object comes to a halt, its momentum is reduced to zero. But the momentum cannot disappear – it must be passed on to the surroundings. So in a car crash, for example, the momentum of the occupants must be passed on to the car and the surroundings while causing as little harm to the occupants as possible.

This is the role of the different safety features we have listed above. Seat belts and air bags ensure that the driver's momentum is reduced fairly gently to zero. The crumple zones collapse, ensuring that the car's momentum is reduced to zero as slowly as possible, rather than suddenly. Then the force on the car and its occupants is minimised. The cars used in theme park rides are similarly designed to ensure that, in the event of an impact, a rider's momentum is absorbed gradually, bringing them to a safe halt (Figure 9.34).

Figure 9.34 Padded safety harnesses ensure that, if the ride comes to a rapid halt, the riders' momentum is absorbed safely

● Stopping safely

The Highway Code gives advice on safe driving. In particular, it advises drivers on the distance their car may travel when coming to a halt. Drivers often imagine that they will be able to stop in a distance of a few metres if they see a hazard on the road ahead, but this is not so. Figure 9.35 on the next page shows the shortest stopping distances at different speeds.

You can see that the **stopping distance** is divided into two parts:

▶ First, the driver must recognise the need to stop, and apply the brakes. This takes about two-thirds of a second. The distance travelled in this time is the thinking distance.

▶ Next, the driver must apply the brakes and come safely to a halt. Excessive braking causes the car to skid. The distance travelled as the car slows to a halt is the braking distance.

stopping distance = thinking distance + braking distance

213

Figure 9.35 Stopping distances, from *The Highway Code*

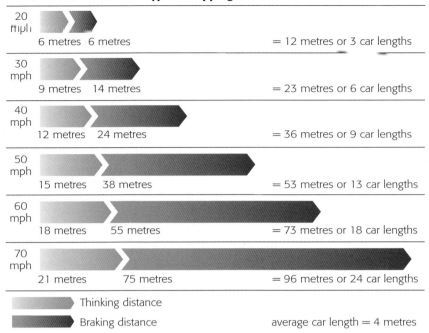

Typical stopping distances

Speed	Thinking distance	Braking distance	Total
20 mph	6 metres	6 metres	= 12 metres or 3 car lengths
30 mph	9 metres	14 metres	= 23 metres or 6 car lengths
40 mph	12 metres	24 metres	= 36 metres or 9 car lengths
50 mph	15 metres	38 metres	= 53 metres or 13 car lengths
60 mph	18 metres	55 metres	= 73 metres or 18 car lengths
70 mph	21 metres	75 metres	= 96 metres or 24 car lengths

Thinking distance
Braking distance   average car length = 4 metres

Here is how to understand the chart of stopping distances:

‣ The thinking distance is greater at higher speeds. During the two-thirds of a second it takes the driver to react, the car travels farther at higher speeds – twice as far at twice the speed.

‣ The braking distance is much greater at higher speeds. The driver applies the brakes; it takes twice as long to stop the car at twice the speed, and because the car is going faster, it travels four times as far in twice the time.

So drivers need to be aware that travelling at high speeds is much riskier. 'Tail-gating', when one car is only a metre or two behind the one in front, is exceedingly dangerous, because the driver of the rear car won't have enough time to react if the car in front brakes suddenly.

Staying safe

Hundreds of children die on the UK's roads each year, and thousands are seriously injured. Drivers need to react quickly when a child runs out into the road, but some drivers have slower reactions than others. A driver who is drunk or under the influence of drugs is likely to react slowly, and this increases the thinking distance. Elderly drivers may also have slower than average reactions.

Braking distance may be affected by the condition of the car. If the brakes are faulty, the braking force they provide may not be sufficient to stop the car in the distance shown in Figure 9.35. Similarly, if the road is wet or icy, the brakes will be less effective and so braking distance is increased.

Figure 9.36 Will the car stop in time? Evidence shows that far fewer fatalities occur when drivers limit their speed in towns to 20 mph

● Comparing risks

Each year, about 3300 people die on the UK's roads. Table 9.2 shows the different groups of people who are involved. You can see that many more car users than motorcyclists die in accidents. Does this mean that motorcycling is safer than travelling by car? Of course not. There are many cars on the road and relatively few motorcycles. We need another way to compare the risks of travelling in different ways.

Table 9.3 shows one way of doing this. It shows the number of deaths that result from one billion kilometres of travel. Now the risks are much easier to compare, and you can see that motorcycling is about 40 times as dangerous as travelling by car.

Table 9.2 Numbers of road deaths in a typical year

Road user	Deaths per year
pedestrians	750
cyclists	130
motorcyclists	600
car users	1700
bus/van/truck users	120

Table 9.3 Numbers of road deaths per billion kilometres travelled

Mode of transport	Deaths per billion passenger km
air	0.02
rail	0.9
water	0.3
car	2.8
motorcycle	112
pedal cycle	41
pedestrian	49

We take risks every day. It is risky crossing the road, eating chicken from the take-away or having a swim in the pool. As you go through life, your experience helps you to assess and reduce these risks – perhaps you had a narrow escape when crossing the main road, so now you always use the crossing.

We can reduce the risks that we take, but we have to accept some risks in our lives. What risks do we tend to avoid?

After a train crash has made headlines, many people avoid the railways and use their cars instead. Table 9.3 above shows that this doesn't make sense – the risk is much less when travelling by train than by car. In fact, fewer people have died on the UK's railways in their 180-year history than in one average year on the roads. Perhaps people feel in control when they are driving, but feel that the risk of using other forms of transport is out of their control.

You may be nervous about walking around town late at night. However, some people such as policemen and shift-workers have to do this every day, and they learn to accept the risk, which is not always as high as you might think. When you have become familiar with a risk, it is easier to accept it.

Summary

- Cars and other vehicles have many safety features designed to reduce the risk to occupants in the event of a collision.
- Vehicle safety features are designed to absorb passengers' momentum safely on impact.

    momentum = mass × velocity

- The stopping distance of a vehicle depends on the driver's reaction time, the speed of the vehicle, and the state of the vehicle and the road.
- We are more likely to accept risks when they are familiar to us, and when we feel free to accept them voluntarily.

Questions

9.24 We can think of the stopping distance of a car as being made up of thinking distance and braking distance:

    stopping distance = thinking distance + braking distance

   a What happens during the thinking distance?

   b Explain why the thinking distance is greater when a car is travelling faster.

   c In normal conditions, a car travelling at 30 mph should stop in 23 m. Imagine a driver who has had alcohol to drink, and a road that is icy. He is travelling at 30 mph. Explain how these *two* factors will lead to the stopping distance of his car being considerably greater than 23 m.

9.25 Many modern cars have crumple zones at the front and rear.

   a In what types of accident can these help to protect the occupants of the car?

   b Explain how they reduce the hazard to the occupants.

9.26 Jenny is fed up with walking to school. She would rather cycle. Her mother says that cycling is dangerous. Jenny says that walking is also dangerous, and her mother should take her in the car.

   a Study the data in Table 9.3, and comment on the statements made by Jenny and her mother.

   b Suggest how Jenny could reduce the risk of a serious accident when she is cycling.

9.27 An athlete of mass 40 kg is running at 15 m/s. Calculate her momentum.

9.28 Explain why drivers should travel more slowly than usual when the road is dry but there are patches of fog around. In your answer, refer to the equation:

    stopping distance = thinking distance + braking distance

9.29 Many people are nervous when they board an aircraft, but they do not worry about travelling by car. Are their concerns supported by the data in Table 9.3? Suggest reasons why people may be more nervous about air travel than car travel.

10 Roller coasters and relativity

A Doing work

How does a roller coaster work? You get in near the top of the ride. Then the car is pulled to the very top, and released. After that, the car simply travels down–up–down until it reaches the end. The brakes bring it safely to a halt.

What forces are at work here? A strong force is needed to pull the loaded car to the top of the ride. Then gravity takes over, as the car swoops downwards. Finally, the brakes provide the force needed to stop the car.

Forces cause acceleration (a change in velocity). As the car runs downhill, it goes faster. If the track takes it upwards again, you will feel it slowing down. At the lowest point, the car may be moving very fast, so a big braking force is needed to change its velocity to zero.

Figure 10.1 Every roller coaster ride needs a force to drag the car to the highest point. After that, gravity takes over

Roller coaster design is a specialised skill. The designer must know how the forces acting on the car (gravity, the push of the track, friction) will alter its motion, and so ensure that the ride is both thrilling and safe.

● Pulling and pushing

Imagine lifting a heavy object above your head (Figure 10.2a). You need to provide a big upward **force**. It is the same if you push a heavy object up a slope; gravity is pulling the object downwards, so you have to push hard to move it upwards (Figure 10.2b). If you are sliding something up a slope, the force of friction between the object and the slope will oppose that motion, so your force will need to be big enough to overcome that, too.

Figure 10.2 a You do work when you lift a heavy object, or **b** when you push a heavy load up a slope

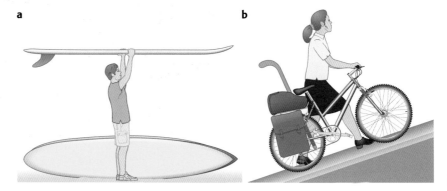

a

b

When a force moves like this, we say that the force is doing work. The word 'work' here has a specialised, scientific meaning. There must be a force acting, and the force must move. So, if you sit and think hard about your science homework, you are not doing any work (in the scientific sense), because you aren't providing a force. Similarly, once you have lifted a heavy object above your head, if you hold it there you are doing no work. You are providing a force (to hold up the object) but the force is not moving.

Doing work and transferring energy

If you spend the day lifting heavy boxes, you will soon get tired. You run out of energy. By lifting the boxes, you are transferring energy from your body to the boxes.

How do we know that a box has more energy when it has been lifted upwards? Simple: let go of the box and it will fall on your toes. That should convince you that the box has more energy when it is lifted up.

So, when a force does work, it **transfers energy**.

▸ The upward force of a weightlifter transfers energy to the weights, making them go higher.
▸ The forward force of a car engine transfers energy to the car, making it go faster.
▸ The electrical push of a battery transfers energy to a lamp, making the lamp glow.

These are all examples of forces doing work and transferring energy. The amount of work done by each force is equal to the amount of energy transferred.

work done = energy transferred

Calculating work done

The amount of work done by a force depends on two things:

▸ the size of the force
▸ the distance moved by the force.

The bigger the force and the further it moves, the more work is done. We can write this as an equation:

work done = force × distance moved in the direction of the force
$$W = F \times s$$

Note that we use the letter s for distance, or displacement, here. Don't confuse it with s for seconds.

Figure 10.3 shows why we have to say *in the direction of the force*. The car is starting off; there are three forces at work, but only one is doing work. The car moves in the direction of the engine force, so that is the force which does work. It transfers energy to the car, which makes it go faster.

The other two forces are vertical. The car doesn't move upwards or downwards, so neither of these forces does any work. If the car was moving downhill, the force of gravity would do work, because the car would be moving in the direction of that force.

Figure 10.3 In this situation, only the engine force is doing work

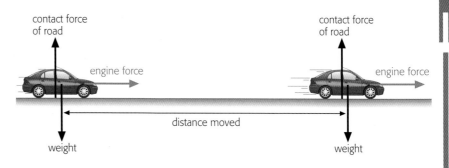

Worked example

The weightlifters in Figure 10.4 are having a competition. How much work does each do?

Figure 10.4

Notice that the unit of work done is the joule, J – the same as the unit of energy.

Weightlifter A: work done = force × distance moved
= 500 N × 2.0 m = 1000 J

Weightlifter B: work done = force × distance moved
= 800 N × 1.4 m = 1120 J

So, although A lifts his weights higher, B does more work than A.

● Working fast

When a force does work, it transfers energy. The faster it does work, the greater is the **power**.

You have already met the idea of power, in connection with the transfer of energy in electric circuits.

$$\text{power} = \frac{\text{work done}}{\text{time taken}} \qquad\qquad P = \frac{W}{t}$$

Power is measured in watts (W) and kilowatts (kW). A power of 1 watt means that energy is transferred at a rate of 1 joule per second, so a 60 W lamp transfers 60 J of energy each second.

Take care! We use the symbol W for work done and W for watts.

Worked example

A car engine does 3 000 000 J of work in 1 minute (60 s). What is its power?

$$\text{power} = \frac{\text{work done}}{\text{time taken}}$$

$$= \frac{3\,000\,000\,\text{J}}{60\,\text{s}} = 50\,000\,\text{W}$$

So the car engine's power is 50 000 W or 50 kW.

Summary

● Work is done and energy is transferred when a force moves through a distance:

work done = force × distance moved in the direction of the force
$$W = F \times s$$

● The energy transferred is equal to the work done.
● Power is the rate at which work is done:

$$\text{power} = \frac{\text{work done}}{\text{time taken}} \qquad P = \frac{W}{t}$$

Questions

10.1 A girl lifts a ball, which weighs 4 N, from the ground to a height of 2 m.
  a How much work has she done?
  b How much energy has she transferred to the ball?

10.2 An electric motor transfers 3600 J of energy in 30 s. What is its power?

10.3 A car's brakes provide a force of 800 N. They bring the car to a halt in a distance of 75 m.
  a How much work do the brakes do?
  b If the car stops in 10 s, what is the power?

10.4 A crane raises a load of bricks 20 m off the ground. It does 12 000 J of work. What lifting force does the crane provide?

10.5 A motor has a power of 200 W. How long will it take to transfer 5000 J of energy?

B How much energy?

Isaac Newton was the greatest physicist of his day. He worked out how forces affect motion – including the ideas you have studied about how a resultant force causes an object to accelerate – as well as how gravity keeps the planets in their orbits. But he had no idea about energy.

You have probably heard about energy in many different lessons. You may have heard about energy when you were in primary school. The idea of energy probably seems quite familiar to you. You may remember that energy comes in different forms – kinetic, potential,

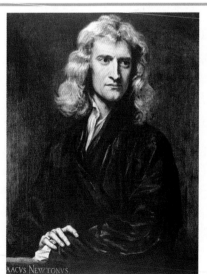

Figure 10.5 Isaac Newton (1642–1727), who knew nothing about energy

Figure 10.6 James Joule (1818–1889), a scientist from Lancashire who helped sort out the idea of energy

electrical, and so on – and that energy can be changed from one form to another. However, these ideas weren't understood until more than a century after Newton died.

Scientists realised that a hot object had more of 'something' than a cold one. A moving object had more of 'something' than a stationary one, and a battery stored 'something' which could be used to light a lamp or turn a motor. However, it took a long time to realise that these were all the same thing, what we now call 'energy'.

The key is the idea of doing work. When a force does work, it can make something move (give it kinetic energy), it can lift something up (give it potential energy), it can heat something up (give it heat energy), and so on. James Joule, whose name is used as the unit of energy, did some important experiments to show that the more work a force did, the greater the heating effect it had.

The idea of energy comes up in all branches of science, and in other subjects. It has proved such a successful idea that we cannot now picture science without it. And that makes it seem all the remarkable that Isaac Newton could achieve so much, without knowing anything about the idea of energy.

We shouldn't forget that it took a long time, with lots of arguments and false leads, to come up with the scientific idea of energy as we use it today.

● Calculating energy

It is useful to know about different forms of energy, such as potential energy, kinetic energy and electrical energy. We can use them to *describe* changes that are occurring. However, it is much more useful to be able to *calculate* energy changes. Then we can answer questions such as:

How fast will a roller coaster move?
How high will a rocket go?
How hot will the water in a kettle become?
How long will a battery last?

We will look at equations for calculating three different forms of energy.

Gravitational potential energy

If you lift an object up, you give it **gravitational potential energy** (GPE). The heavier it is and the higher you lift it, the more GPE you give it (see Figure 10.7). Here is the equation we use to calculate GPE:

gravitational potential energy = mass × acceleration of free-fall × change in height
$$GPE = m \times g \times h$$

The acceleration of free-fall, symbol g, is the acceleration any object has when it is allowed to fall freely. It is about 10 m/s^2 close to the surface of the Earth.

> Note that **potential energy** (PE) means any kind of stored energy. A raised object has gravitational PE; a stretched rubber band has elastic PE; the chemical energy of a battery or fuel could be described as chemical PE.

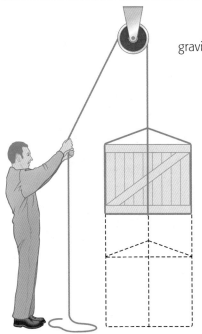

Figure 10.7 An object's GPE increases as it is lifted higher

Worked example

The crate in Figure 10.7 has a mass of 200 kg. It is raised 6 m off the ground. By how much does its GPE increase?

GPE = mass × acceleration of free-fall × change in height
= 200 kg × 10 m/s^2 × 6 m = 12 000 J

So the person pulling the crate upwards has transferred 12 000 J of energy to it.

Kinetic energy

A moving object has kinetic energy (KE). The greater its mass and the greater its velocity, the more KE it has. The equation is:

$$\text{kinetic energy} = \tfrac{1}{2}\,\text{mass} \times (\text{velocity})^2$$
$$KE = \tfrac{1}{2}mv^2$$

Worked example

A runner of mass 60 kg is moving at 10 m/s. What is her kinetic energy?

$$\text{kinetic energy} = \tfrac{1}{2}\,\text{mass} \times (\text{velocity})^2$$
$$= \tfrac{1}{2} \times 60\,\text{kg} \times (10\,\text{m/s})^2$$
$$= 30 \times 100 = 3000\,\text{J}$$

Take care with calculations like this! Start by squaring the velocity, and then multiply by $\tfrac{1}{2} \times$ mass.

Electrical energy transfers

Electricity is a useful way of transferring energy from place to place. For example, we use electric motors in many different places. These transform **electrical energy** into movement.

The electrical energy used by a motor depends on:

▶ the **voltage** across it
▶ the **current** flowing through it
▶ and the time for which it operates.

> You should recognise these symbols; don't forget that I stands for current.

$$\text{electrical energy} = \text{voltage} \times \text{current} \times \text{time}$$
$$E = V \times I \times t$$

Where does this equation for electrical energy come from? You should recall from *GCSE Science* (page 203) the equation for electrical power:

$$\text{power} = \text{current} \times \text{voltage}$$

Since power = energy/time, when power is multiplied by time we get energy.

Worked example

A hairdryer operates from the 230 V mains supply. When it is on maximum heat, a current of 2 A flows through it. How much electric energy does the dryer use in 3 minutes?

$$\text{electrical energy} = \text{voltage} \times \text{current} \times \text{time}$$
$$= 230\,\text{V} \times 2\,\text{A} \times 180\,\text{s} = 82\,800\,\text{J}$$

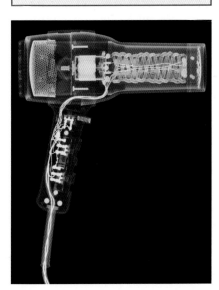

Figure 10.8 This hairdryer uses electrical energy for its heater and for the motor which drives its fan

Summary

- We can calculate amounts of energy:

gravitational potential energy = mass × acceleration of free-fall × change in height

$$\text{GPE} = m \times g \times h$$

- kinetic energy = $\frac{1}{2}$ mass × (velocity)^2

$$\text{KE} = \frac{1}{2}mv^2$$

- electrical energy = voltage × current × time

$$\text{E} = V \times I \times t$$

Questions

10.6 Copy and complete the table, to show the different quantities used in calculating energy changes, together with their symbols and units.

Quantity	Symbol	Unit
energy	E	
mass		kg
acceleration of free-fall		
	h	
velocity		
voltage		
	I	
	t	

10.7 A sky-rocket of mass 0.1 kg rises 500 m into the air. By how much does its gravitational potential energy increase?

10.8 What is the kinetic energy of a toy car of mass 0.4 kg moving at 6 m/s?

10.9 A 1.5 V battery supplies a current of 0.4 A to a torch bulb for 300 s. How much energy is transferred in this time?

10.10 A rock of mass 2 kg is balanced on the top of a cliff, 40 m above the sea. It falls and lands on a lower ledge, 15 m above the sea. By how much has its GPE changed? Has it increased or decreased?

10.11 A car of mass 400 kg has 20 000 J of kinetic energy. What is its speed?

10.12 An electric heater is connected to a 200 V supply. A current of 4 A flows through it. How long will it take to supply 1 000 000 J of energy?

C Energy is conserved

If you rub your hands together, the force of friction does work and your hands get warm. Heat energy has been produced. James Joule investigated the connection between the amount of work done and the amount of heat produced.

In 1847, Joule married Amelia Grimes and they went to Chamonix, in the Alps, for their honeymoon. He took a large thermometer to test his ideas. The couple visited a high waterfall. Joule realised that, when water drops down a waterfall, gravity is doing work on it, and this would raise the temperature of the water. Today we would say that the water at the top of the fall has gravitational potential energy; at the foot, this energy has been transformed to heat energy. Joule predicted that, for a waterfall 778 feet high, the temperature of the water would rise by 1 degree Fahrenheit. (Those were the units he worked in.)

water has gravitational potential energy

kinetic energy increasing

water gains heat energy

Figure 10.9 Gravity does work to make the water fall, and the temperature of the water rises slightly

So Joule measured the temperature of the water at the top of the waterfall, and at the foot. Sadly, his results were inconclusive. The fall wasn't high enough, there was a lot of spray at the foot, and his thermometer wasn't sensitive enough to measure the small rise in temperature.

Later though, through other experiments, Joule showed that you always get the same amount of heat for a given amount of work.

● Conservation of energy

James Joule was one of the first scientists to develop the idea of **conservation of energy**. The principle of conservation of energy says:

Although energy can change from one form to another, the total amount of energy remains constant.

Here are some examples:

▶ An electric heater is supplied with electrical energy. For every joule of electrical energy supplied to the heater, we get one joule of heat energy out of it.
▶ A car is travelling along the road – it has kinetic energy. The driver brakes so that the car comes to a halt. The brakes work by friction, so they get hot. The amount of heat energy produced is equal to the car's initial kinetic energy.
▶ A skier comes down a slope (Figure 10.10). At the top, she has gravitational potential energy; at the foot, her GPE has been

converted to KE. (In practice, there will have been some friction between her skis and the snow, so some energy will have become heat energy.)

Figure 10.10 As the skier comes downhill, GPE is transformed to KE (and some heat energy)

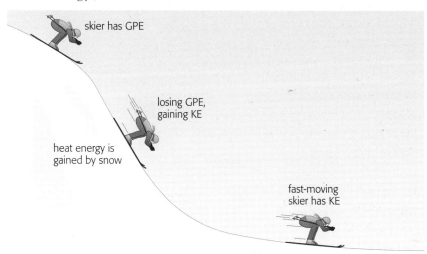

skier has GPE

losing GPE, gaining KE

heat energy is gained by snow

fast-moving skier has KE

▶ Electrical energy is supplied to a light bulb. The bulb produces light and heat. From the energy diagram (Figure 10.11), you can see that energy is conserved.

Figure 10.11 This Sankey diagram represents the fact that energy is conserved when a light bulb transforms electrical energy to heat and light

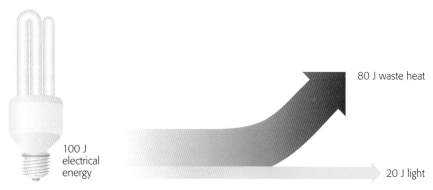

80 J waste heat

100 J electrical energy

20 J light

Energy calculations

Because we are able to calculate the values of different forms of energy, we can solve many different scientific problems. The worked examples which follow are simple examples, but the same ideas can be applied in many more complicated situations.

> If it says 'smooth' in a problem, it means there is no friction.

Worked example 1

A boy of mass 40 kg slides down a smooth playground slide (Figure 10.12). The slide is 5 m high. At the foot of the slide, the boy is moving at 10 m/s. Show that energy is conserved.

At the top of the slide, the boy has GPE. At the foot, he has KE. To show that energy is conserved, we have to show that these two quantities are equal.

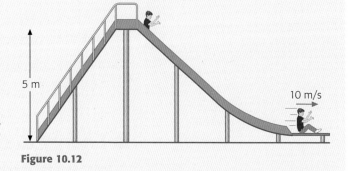

5 m

10 m/s

Figure 10.12

At top of slide: GPE = $m \times g \times h$ = 40 × 10 × 5 = 2000 J

At foot of slide: KE = $\frac{1}{2}mv^2$ = $\frac{1}{2}$ × 40 × 10² = 1/2 × 40 × 100 = 2000 J

Because the GPE at the top equals the KE at the foot, we can conclude that energy is conserved in this example.

Worked example 2

A roller coaster car, together with its passengers, has a mass of 800 kg. It starts off 40 m above the ground. It runs downhill, gradually picking up speed. At the lowest point of its ride, it is moving at 20 m/s. How much energy has it lost due to friction?

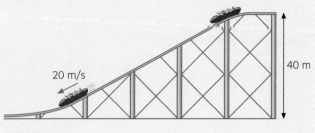

Figure 10.13

As the car runs downhill (Figure 10.13), GPE is being converted to KE and heat (because of friction). Using the principle of conservation of energy, we can write:

GPE at start = KE at end + heat energy

We can calculate the car's GPE and KE:

$GPE = m \times g \times h = 800 \times 10 \times 40 = 320\,000\,J$

$KE = \frac{1}{2}mv^2 = \frac{1}{2} \times 800 \times 20^2 = \frac{1}{2} \times 800 \times 400 = 160\,000\,J$

Now we can calculate the energy which has been lost as heat:

heat energy lost = 320 000 − 160 000 = 160 000 J

So the car has lost 160 000 J of energy as heat (half of its original energy).

H Worked example 3

A boy of mass 40 kg slides down a smooth playground slide. The slide is 5 m high. How fast is the boy moving at the foot of the slide?

Yes, this is the same situation as in Worked example 1, but here we are showing how to work out the speed of the boy at the foot of the slide. Using the principle of conservation of energy, we can write:

GPE at start = KE at end

At top of slide: $GPE = m \times g \times h = 40 \times 10 \times 5 = 2000\,J$

At foot of slide: $KE = \frac{1}{2}mv^2 = 2000\,J$

We know $m = 40$ kg, so:

$$\frac{1}{2} \times 40 \times v^2 = 2000$$
$$20v^2 = 2000$$
$$v^2 = 100$$
$$\text{and so } v = \sqrt{100} = 10\,m/s$$

So the boy is moving at 10 m/s when he reaches the foot of the slide. This agrees with the information in Worked example 1.

● Energy and roller coasters

A roller coaster makes use of gravitational potential energy. Once the car has been dragged up to the start of the ride, it runs down-up-down under the influence of gravity (Figure 10.14).

- As the car runs downhill, GPE is decreasing and KE is increasing.
- As the car runs back uphill, GPE is increasing and KE is decreasing.

Throughout the ride, the car's energy (GPE + KE) remains constant, apart from the effects of friction.

▶ Friction with the track and the air (air resistance) will reduce the car's total energy. This means that the car can never run back up to its original height.
▶ Friction in the brakes is used to reduce the car's energy so that it slows down, particularly at the end of the run.

In both cases, the friction results in heat energy being produced and escaping from the car.

Figure 10.14 Energy changes along a roller coaster ride

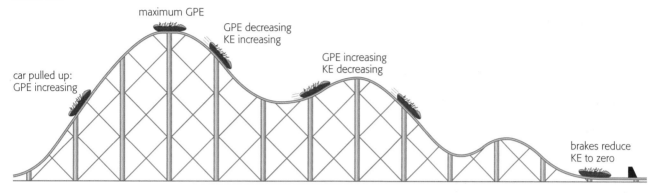

maximum GPE

GPE decreasing KE increasing

GPE increasing KE decreasing

car pulled up: GPE increasing

brakes reduce KE to zero

Thinking of forces

We can also think about the roller coaster ride in terms of forces and the work that they do.

▶ As the car runs downhill, the force of gravity is doing work. This makes it speed up.
▶ As the car runs back uphill, the car is doing work against gravity, and it slows down.

The car changes direction, as well as moving up and down. The track guides the car, and gives it the necessary push to make it change direction. If the car turns to the left, there must be a force to the left. If the car's **speed** remains constant, its kinetic energy has not changed, so the force has done no work. However, the car's **velocity** has changed (because it has changed direction).

Recall that velocity is a vector quantity, with both magnitude and direction.

● Circular motion

The people on the fairground ride in Figure 10.15 are going around in a circle. They are going at a **constant speed** (so the KE is constant) and at a steady height (so the GPE is constant).

However, there is something which *is* changing – their velocity. Because the direction in which they are moving is continually changing, their velocity is continually changing, too.

This means that the people on the ride are accelerating – any change in velocity is an **acceleration**.

Figure 10.15 The people on this ride are travelling around in a circle. This means that they have an acceleration, which is directed towards the centre of the circle

H

227

Recall that, if there is no resultant force acting on an object, it will carry on moving at a steady speed in a straight line.

Force and motion

It takes a force to cause an acceleration, so we know there must be a **resultant force** acting on the people on the ride.

When you were younger, you probably had a ride on a roundabout in the park. As it whirls you round (Figure 10.16a), you have to hold on tight. You can feel it pulling on your arms. That is the force that keeps you going around in a circle. If you let go, you fly off in a straight line (Figure 10.16b) – there is no force to keep you moving around.

Figure 10.16 a Hold on tight…
b …or you will fly off

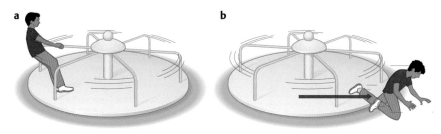

Whenever an object is moving in a circle, it should be possible to find the force which is keeping it moving in a circle. Figure 10.17 shows four examples.

Figure 10.17 What is the force that keeps these things moving in a circle?

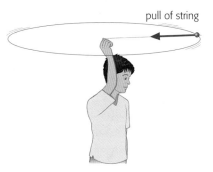

Whirl a conker around your head on the end of a string. The tension in the string pulls on the conker, holding it in its circular path.

A speed skater follows a curved track. She leans into the bend, so that her blades press outwards (action force). The frictional push of the ice (reaction force) pushes her inwards.

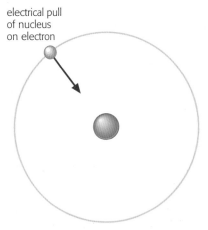

In an atom, an electron (negative charge) orbits the nucleus (positive charge). The electrostatic attraction between them holds the electron in its orbit.

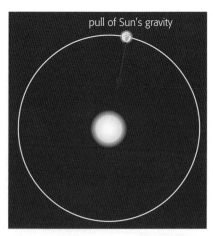

The Earth orbits around the Sun. The Sun's gravity holds the Earth in its orbit.

Notice that in all four examples the force acts towards the centre of the circle.

H

The word 'centripetal' means 'towards the centre'.

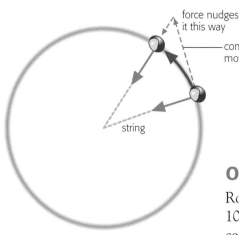

Figure 10.18 You can think of the centripetal force 'nudging' the moving object to keep it on its circular path

Figure 10.19 On a corkscrew section of a roller coaster ride, the car is following a circular path. It must be travelling sufficiently fast if it is to stay on the track

Centripetal forces

To keep an object moving in a circle, there must be a resultant force acting towards the centre of the circle. Such a force is described as a 'centripetal' force. A centripetal force can be caused by gravity, by friction, by pushing or pulling, by electrostatic attraction, or by any other type of force.

Figure 10.18 shows one way to think of this. The conker wants to continue in a straight line, but it is being pulled on by the string. As it deflects to the left, the force keeps pulling on it. This makes it move further round to the left, and so on.

Over the top

Roller coasters often have loop or spiral sections of track (Figure 10.19). The car presses on the track, and the track presses back on the car. It is this reaction force that makes the car follow the curve of the track. If the car is going fast enough, it can turn completely upside down. When they are upside down, the passengers may feel as if they are about to fall out – but there's no need to worry! Even without safety harnesses, they would stay in the car. (To convince yourself of this, imagine whirling a bucket of water around in a vertical circle. If you whirl it fast enough, it will go all the way round without losing any water. But whirl it too slowly and you will get wet.)

Summary

- The principle of conservation of energy says that energy can be changed from one form to another, but the total amount remains constant.
- This fact can be used to solve a wide range of problems.
- The energy of a roller coaster car changes from GPE to KE and back again as it moves downhill and then uphill.
- An object moving in a circle is accelerating; we know this because the direction of its velocity is changing.
- If an object is to follow a circular path, it must be acted on by a resultant force which is directed towards the centre of the circle.

Figure 10.20

Questions

10.13 A fairground swing-boat swings freely back and forth. A person sitting at the end of the boat swings downwards through a vertical distance of 10 m. At the lowest point, this passenger is moving at 14.1 m/s. The passenger has a mass of 50 kg.

    a Calculate the GPE of this person when at the highest point of the ride.

    b Calculate the person's KE at the lowest point.

    c Do your calculations support the idea that energy is conserved in this situation?

10.14 At a skate park, skaters can ride up and down on a curved track. Ben, a champion roller blader, starts at point A (Figure 10.21). He skates down the slope to B, and continues to C and D.

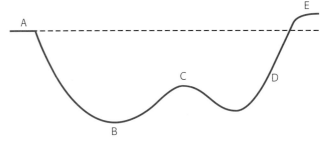

Figure 10.21

    a How does his speed change as he moves down the slope towards B?

    b How does his speed change after point B?

    c How does his gravitational potential energy (GPE) change as he moves down the slope towards B? How does his kinetic energy (KE) change?

    d Use the idea of conservation of energy to explain why even Ben cannot reach point E, which is higher than point A.

    e In fact Ben comes to a halt at point D, which is lower than point A. What does this tell you about how his total energy (GPE + KE) changes as he moves along the track from A to D?

10.15 A car of mass 600 kg is moving at 20 m/s. The driver sees a speed camera ahead and applies the brakes so that the car slows to 10 m/s.

    a Calculate the car's KE at 20 m/s, and at 10 m/s.

    b How much energy is lost as heat in the car's brakes as it slows down?

10.16 The toy car (mass 0.1 kg) in Figure 10.22 is pushed and released. At the foot of the slope, it is moving at 2 m/s. Assuming there is no friction, to what vertical height, *h*, will it rise up the slope?

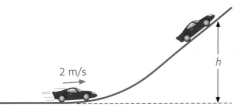

Figure 10.22

10.17 A torch bulb is connected to a 6 V battery. A current of 0.5 A flows in the circuit.

    a If the bulb is switched on for 5 minutes, how much energy is supplied to it in this time?

    b If the bulb is only 5% efficient in its production of light, how much energy is wasted as heat?

H

H

10.18 A racing car is travelling around a circular bend at a constant speed.
  a Explain how you know that it is accelerating.
  b What can you say about the resultant force acting on the car?

10.19 The Moon moves in a circular orbit around the Earth.
  a What force holds it in its orbit?
  b Draw a diagram to show the Moon at *three* different points around its orbit. Add force arrows to show the resultant force acting on the Moon in each position.

D The theory of relativity

In 1905, Albert Einstein was a young man of 26, working in the Swiss patent office. As a student, he had been very interested in physics and maths, but had only studied the topics that really interested him. He preferred to sit in cafés, discussing ideas about space and time, rather than studying other topics, which his tutors thought were important. He didn't achieve a very good pass in his exams, and his girlfriend failed completely.

So he had to find work as a patent clerk. In his spare time, he developed his own ideas, and he stunned the scientific world by publishing three papers on important topics, all in the same year, 1905.

- In one paper, he showed how to calculate the size and number of molecules in a gas.
- In a second paper, he explained how light can cause an electric current to flow from a piece of metal (the photoelectric effect), by thinking of light behaving as particles, not waves.
- And the third paper contained his first **theory of relativity**, which explained how things behave when their speed approaches the speed of light.

Physicists were astonished because, at that time, it was generally believed that existing theories could explain more or less every observation. Collisions of particles, the motion of the planets, electric circuits, sound and light – all of these had been explained. Now here was a young author, who didn't even have a proper scientific job, showing that there were great areas of physics that had yet to be properly understood. His creative imagination, rather than experimental skills, led to brilliant new theories.

Figure 10.23 Albert Einstein in 1905

● Special relativity

What is Einstein's theory of relativity all about? Here is one way to think about it. Imagine sitting in a train at a station, waiting to leave. Through the window, you look at the train at the next platform. It pulls gradually away – but you cannot tell whether it is your train or the other train that is moving – you can only tell that they are moving *relative* to one another.

Here is another situation to think of. When you look at the stars in the night sky, you are seeing them as they were, some time in the past. This is because light takes time to reach us – in the case of distant stars, it may take millions or billions of years. Now look at

231

the stars in Figure 10.24. Stars A and B are far distant from the Earth. Suppose an observer on the Earth sees star A explode – a supernova. Some weeks later, star B explodes. The observer believes that star A exploded first. But what would observers on planet Zeta see? To them, star B explodes before star A.

Looking from the outside, you might think that you could say that it was 'really' star A which exploded first. However, Einstein said that we cannot step outside the Universe like this, and so we cannot say which event happened first, the explosion of star A or star B. The order of events depends on where we are *relative to* what we are observing. This is the basis of his 'special' theory of relativity.

Figure 10.24 Stars A and B explode as supernovas – but which exploded first?

Consequences of the theory

These ideas may give you an inkling of what Einstein's special theory of relativity was about. Einstein realised that the speed of light is of the utmost importance in science. Light (as well as other forms of electromagnetic radiation) brings us information about what is happening around us. It travels very fast, but it is not instantaneous. In our everyday lives, this difference is insignificant. But when we think about space, the Universe and fast-moving sub-atomic particles, it becomes very important.

Einstein showed how to modify Newton's theories of force and motion to take account of the speed of light. There are some striking consequences. For example, it is impossible to accelerate an object until it reaches the speed of light.

In the giant particle accelerator at CERN, Geneva (Figure 10.25), electrons whiz round an underground tunnel at very high speed. The faster they go, the heavier they get, and the harder it is to make them go even faster.

It's the accelerator that's giant, not the particles.

Figure 10.25 The giant particle accelerator at CERN is underground; the circle marks the track of its tunnel

Why is this? A force is needed to accelerate the electrons. The force does work, and transfers energy to the electrons. Their KE increases. Einstein said that this means their mass also increases. This is what his famous equation $E = mc^2$ means – an object with mass m has energy E equal to its mass multiplied by the square of the speed of light (c). When you increase an object's energy, you increase its mass. So, as the electrons are accelerated, they are given energy and this increases their mass. The equation $F = ma$ tells us that the greater their mass, the harder it is to accelerate them.

Einstein's theory has some other weird consequences. For example, as an object approaches the speed of light, it gets shorter (Figure 10.26). So a spacecraft travelling close to the speed of light would become very short. It wouldn't matter to the people inside the spacecraft, because they would be shortened, too. Everything would look normal to them, but to an outside observer, the spacecraft would look as if it had been squashed. Again, it all depends on where the observer is, relative to the moving object.

Yet another consequence of relativity is that time runs more slowly as you approach the speed of light. Imagine a trip to a nearby star. If you could travel almost as fast as light, you might get there in a few years. But when you came back, you would find that everyone on Earth was much older, because their clocks had been running faster than yours.

At present, we don't have the technology to make spacecraft fly so fast, but we can make sub-atomic particles move at over 99% of the speed of light, and all of Einstein's predictions have been shown to be correct.

● All in Albert's mind

Einstein was not a great experimenter. He was a great thinker. His theories of relativity came from thinking about some basic ideas – the high speed of light, for example. He presented his ideas in the form of 'thought experiments', in which he posed 'What if…?' questions, and worked out the consequences.

Here is an example. Imagine that you are far out in space, a long way from Earth. You are inside a spacecraft, floating around, because there is no gravity. Now the spacecraft accelerates. You find yourself pressed down to the floor of the spacecraft (Figure 10.27). It is as if you were back on Earth, where gravity holds you to the floor. Einstein realised that this shows that you cannot tell whether gravity is acting on you or you are accelerating.

On a roller coaster moving at 30 m/s, your mass increases – but only by 0.000 01%.

Figure 10.26 According to Einstein's theory of relativity, moving objects get shorter as they approach the speed of light

Figure 10.27 In an accelerating spacecraft, you feel as though you are acted on by gravity. But when the rocket motors are turned off, the effect disappears and you experience weightlessness. Future spacecraft may create artificial gravity by rotating, so that the occupants are constantly accelerating

233

Einstein was able to work out the consequences of this, and these ideas became his second ('general') theory of relativity, which explained how gravity affects space.

Although Einstein didn't carry out experiments, he did have to keep in touch with the results of other people's work, and his theories led other people to carry out experiments to check his ideas.

Not so popular

Albert Einstein's ideas seemed weird when he published them, and they still seem odd today, because they don't fit with our everyday experience. If we moved around at close to the speed of light, no doubt we would take them for granted.

Einstein's ideas showed that Newton's theories of motion, which had held good for over three centuries, were incorrect (although they work perfectly well in most everyday situations).

Many scientific theories, particularly those which overturn long-established theories, are reluctantly accepted. Other scientists do not want to give up the ideas they have struggled to learn; it is sometimes said that a new theory has to wait until all the old scientists have died before it becomes accepted.

● Testing Einstein

Any new theory must be tested, especially one based on thought experiments. Einstein's theories of relativity have been tested many times, and have stood the test of time.

In one test, scientists carried very precise atomic clocks around the world on airliners. After their journey, the clocks were found to be a fraction of a second behind those which had remained on the ground – showing that, as predicted by Einstein, moving clocks run slow.

In another test, the rate of decay of sub-atomic particles arriving from space (called cosmic rays) was measured. The particles decayed much more slowly than the same particles in a lab on Earth, because they were moving very fast.

Today, we make regular use of technology that depends on Einstein's ideas being right. The GPS system (Figure 10.28), used by 'satnav' systems in cars, calculates your position using Einstein's equations. Without relativity, the system would get the wrong answer and you wouldn't know where you were!

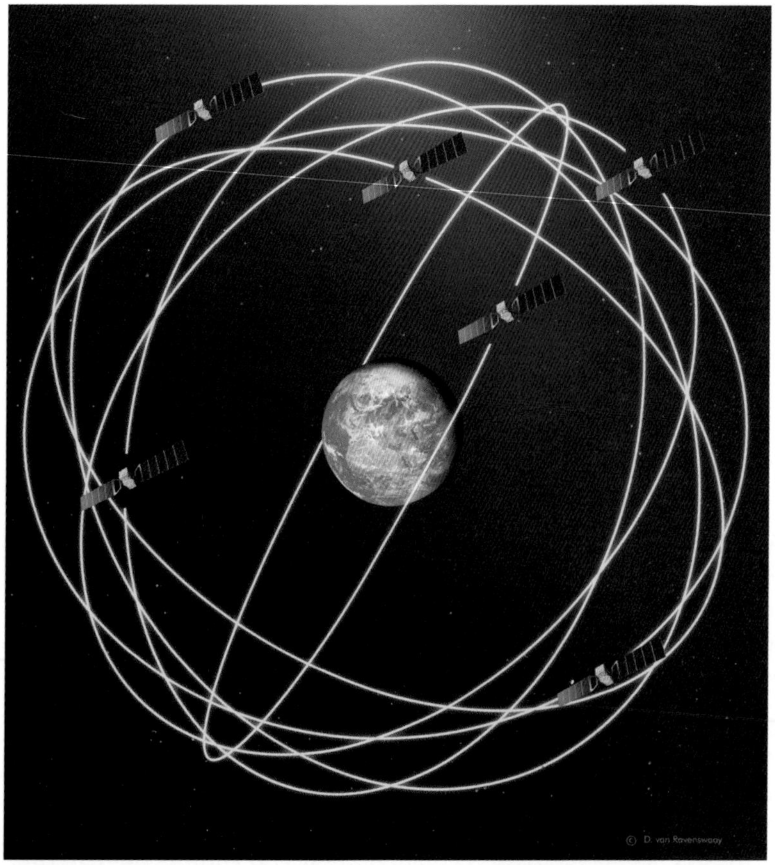

Figure 10.28 GPS (global positioning system) relies on fast-moving satellites, orbiting the Earth. Because of the speed of the satellites, Einstein's theories of relativity must be taken into account

Summary

- Some theories, such as Einstein's theories of relativity, are a result of a creative imagination devising 'thought experiments' and working out the consequences.
- A new theory may not be readily accepted by other scientists, especially when it overturns existing, successful theories.

H
- Einstein's theories of relativity have been tested experimentally in many different ways, with successful outcomes.

Questions

10.20 Scientists are often reluctant to accept a new theory, especially when it overturns an existing theory.

   a Suggest some reasons for their reluctance.

   b Before it becomes accepted, a new theory must be tested. How can a theory be tested?

H **10.21** Einstein's theories of relativity have been tested in many ways.

   a Why is it important for theories like these to be tested?

   b The predictions of Einstein's theories have been tested successfully many times. Does this mean that the theories are correct?

11 Putting radiation to use

A Invisible – but useful

In 1991, a small supermarket in Chicago, USA, started selling irradiated strawberries. These were perfectly ordinary strawberries that had been exposed to gamma radiation from a radioactive source. The irradiated strawberries soon began to outsell non-irradiated strawberries. Why was this?

The shop's customers knew that strawberries usually go mouldy and rot in a few days. They discovered that irradiated strawberries keep their good condition for several days longer.

Gamma radiation is used to damage the cells of microscopic mould organisms which are usually present on the fruit. The cells cannot divide, and so the mould dies. Sales of irradiated strawberries and other fruit increased rapidly in Chicago and neighbouring areas. In the UK, it is

Figure 11.1 These strawberries were photographed several days after picking. The ones on the left have been irradiated using gamma radiation

legal to irradiate and sell fruits such as strawberries, but very little irradiated food is sold here. (You would know if you were buying it, because it has to be clearly labelled.) Consumers in the UK have been very reluctant to accept irradiated food, and supermarkets haven't thought it worthwhile to repeat the Chicago experiment.

● Alpha, beta, gamma

The gamma radiation used for irradiating food is produced by a radioactive substance called cobalt-60. The people who work with it have to be very careful not to expose themselves to the radiation, because it could damage their cells in the same way that it damages the cells of microorganisms that contaminate food.

There are three different types of radiation produced by radioactive substances. You have probably heard their names:

alpha (α), beta (β), gamma (γ)

We picture the different types of radiation in different ways:

▶ alpha radiation consists of **alpha particles**
▶ beta radiation consists of **beta particles**
▶ gamma radiation is a form of electromagnetic radiation, travelling as **gamma rays**.

Radioactivity – the emission of radiation from a radioactive substance – was discovered in 1896. Since then, radioactive substances and the radiation they produce have been found to have many uses. The three different types of radiation have different uses.

Gamma rays and X-rays

What is the difference between gamma rays and X-rays? You have already learned a bit about X-rays. Gamma rays are a form of electromagnetic radiation, similar to X-rays but more energetic. The difference is in how they are produced. Gamma rays are emitted by radioactive substances.

X-rays are not emitted from radioactive substances. They are produced when fast-moving electrons crash into a metal target. The electrons' energy is released as X-rays. This is what happens in a hospital X-ray machine.

> Some very energetic gamma rays reach Earth from space: they form part of the cosmic radiation.

● Radiation spreading out

We need to distinguish two things: the radioactive substances themselves, and the radiation they produce. Figure 11.2 shows how the radiation from a piece of radioactive material spreads out in all directions. If an object is placed in the path of the radiation, some radiation may pass right through it. The rest is absorbed.

The radiation from a radioactive material can be very 'penetrating' – it can pass right through some materials. Other materials will absorb all or some of the energy of the radiation.

> This should remind you of what you have learned previously about X-rays. They can pass through the human body, but they are partly absorbed as they pass through. They are absorbed more strongly by bones than by flesh.

Absorption

You may have a useful piece of radioactive material in your home – in a smoke alarm. A smoke detector makes use of a substance called americium-241, which gives out alpha radiation. Here's how it works (Figure 11.3b).

Inside the smoke alarm, there is the source of radiation. A small hole lets out a thin beam of radiation. The beam is directed towards the detector. This is an electronic device which detects the alpha radiation. The detector is connected to a circuit which includes the alarm siren.

Normally, the radiation travels through the air to the detector, and this tells the detector that there is no smoke in the air. The siren is silent.

However, in the case of a fire, smoke fills the gap between the source and the detector. Now the radiation cannot penetrate the smoke – the smoke absorbs the alpha radiation. No radiation reaches the detector, which notices the change and sets off the siren.

A smoke alarm works because alpha radiation is very easily absorbed – it is even absorbed by air. Just 5 cm of air is enough to completely absorb alpha radiation.

Figure 11.2 Radiation from radioactive materials spreads out in all directions. It may be absorbed by the materials it passes through

Figure 11.3
a A smoke alarm – a wise safety precaution in your home

b Inside a smoke alarm. The black object holds the radioactive source; the detector is hidden underneath. The siren is lower left

Irradiation of food

Food is irradiated using gamma radiation, which is very penetrating. As it passes through the food, some of the radiation is absorbed. Its energy destroys the cells of microorganisms which could damage the food or cause food poisoning to whoever eats it.

It is important to realise that the irradiated food doesn't itself become radioactive. The radiation is *emitted* by a radioactive substance, but when it is *absorbed*, its energy ends up simply warming up the absorber.

Consumers tend to be suspicious of irradiated food. They think the food may be unsafe, or that it will be less nutritious. To some people, it seems as though the food industry is 'meddling with nature'. However, Government advisers have found no evidence that there is any hazard to consumers.

Food that has been irradiated can last for a very long time. This is important for astronauts, who may be on an extended space flight. They find irradiated fresh food more pleasant to eat than tinned food.

Some hospital patients are given irradiated food. This happens if their immune system has become very weak. Any slight infection could prove fatal; irradiated food can be guaranteed to carry no harmful microorganisms.

Figure 11.4 This child has a weak immune system. He is kept in a 'bubble' with purified air, and his meals are of irradiated food

Sterilising medical equipment

Medical equipment such as scalpels and syringes can be irradiated in the same way as food, to make them sterile. (Sterile means that they carry no harmful microorganisms.) Some everyday items, including tampons, are treated in the same way.

When a syringe is sterilised, it is first sealed in its plastic wrapper. Then it is irradiated with gamma radiation, which can pass through the wrapper and destroy any living cells that are contaminating the syringe. Because it is safely wrapped up, the nurse or doctor who uses the syringe can be sure that it is sterile when it is unwrapped.

Penetration

Alpha radiation is used in smoke alarms because it is easily absorbed by smoke in the air. Gamma radiation would be no use for this, because it would pass straight through the smoke, almost unaffected. This tells us that different types of radiation have different abilities to penetrate (pass through) matter. This is summarised in Figure 11.5.

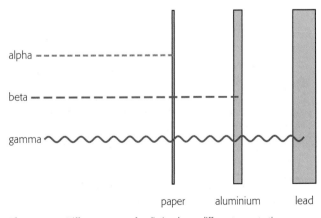

Figure 11.5 Different types of radiation have different penetrating powers

▸ Alpha radiation is absorbed by a few centimetres of air, or a thin sheet of paper.

▸ Beta radiation is more penetrating. It is absorbed by a thin sheet of metal, such as aluminium.

▸ Gamma radiation is the most penetrating. It takes a few centimetres of a dense metal such as lead to absorb gamma radiation.

People who work with radiation need to know about this. Those working with gamma radiation, for example, may need to wear lead-lined aprons to stop the radiation from penetrating their clothes.

● Ionising radiation

Alpha, beta and gamma radiations are sometimes known as **ionising radiation**. X-rays also cause ionisation. What does this mean?

Picture some radiation travelling through the air (Figure 11.6). Radiation carries energy. As it travels through the air, it collides with the atoms and molecules of the air. Its energy may be enough to alter these atoms and molecules, leaving them electrically charged. An electrically charged atom is called an ion. So any type of radiation which creates ions is called ionising radiation.

Ionisation explains how radiation can kill living cells. If radiation strikes the DNA of a cell, the DNA may be broken and unable to repair itself. Then the cell cannot divide and it will die.

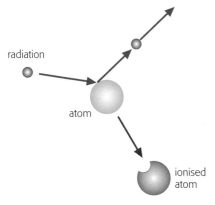

Figure 11.6 When radiation collides with atoms, it can alter them so that they become electrically charged ions

Comparing ionising radiations

- Alpha particles are slow and heavy. They cause a lot of ionisation as they bombard their way through a material; they have the greatest ionising effect.
- Beta particles are faster and lighter. They create fewer ions as they whiz along.
- Gamma rays and X-rays are less ionising still. That is why they can pass so easily through solid materials, and why they are difficult to absorb.

So the radiation that has the greatest ability to cause ionisation is the most easily absorbed – its energy is used up in creating the ions. Figure 11.7 compares the different types of ionising radiation, their abilities to penetrate and to ionise.

Figure 11.7 More ionisation means easier absorption

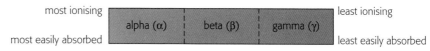

most ionising / least ionising / most easily absorbed / alpha (α) / beta (β) / gamma (γ) / least easily absorbed

Medical uses of ionising radiation

Medical physicists work with all types of radiation. They choose the best type of radiation for each job.

A patient may have a tumour (cancer) inside their body. It may be possible to see the tumour in an X-ray photograph or scan. X-rays or gamma rays are suitable for this imaging purpose because they can pass straight through the patient's body, to the detector on the other side. They are selectively absorbed by different tissues, and so create a 'shadow' picture.

An alternative way of detecting cancerous tissue is to inject a radioactive 'tracer' into the patient. This is a substance that can travel around in the patient's bloodstream; when it reaches the tumour, it sticks to the cancerous cells. A detector outside the patient's body detects gamma rays coming from the radioactive tracer, and this shows up where the tumour is. Figure 11.8 shows the results of such a scan.

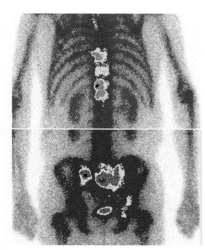

Figure 11.8 This patient has bone cancer, shown up using a radioactive tracer. Gamma radiation is strongest where the scan is green, showing that this is where the cancerous tissue is located

239

Radiation can also be used to treat cancer. Gamma radiation or powerful X-rays may be directed into the patient's body to destroy the cancer cells. For skin cancer, beta radiation can be used, because it will only affect skin cells, and will not penetrate further into the body. In this way, healthy cells are unaffected.

Summary

- Alpha, beta and gamma radiation are emitted from radioactive substances.
- Alpha, beta, gamma and X-radiation are all forms of ionising radiation.
- Alpha and beta radiations travel as particles.
- Gamma rays and X-rays are both energetic electromagnetic radiation, but they are produced in different ways.
- Alpha radiation has the greatest ionising effect; it is the most easily absorbed.
- Gamma radiation is the most penetrating.
- Understanding the properties of ionising radiations allows us to put them to many different uses.

Questions

11.1 a Name *four* types of ionising radiation.
   b Which *three* of these are produced by radioactive materials?
   c Which *two* of these travel as particles?
   d How do the other types travel?

11.2 X-rays and gamma rays are similar to each other. The difference is in how they are produced.
   a Which type is produced using an electron-beam machine?
   b What is the source of the other type of radiation?

11.3 Powerful gamma radiation can be used to destroy tumour cells inside a patient's body. This is risky, because the patient's healthy cells might also be damaged, and this could cause a new cancer to develop. Figure 11.9 shows one way in which this hazard is reduced. The source of radiation moves around the patient's body; as it moves, it is always directed at the tumour. Explain how this helps to reduce the risk to the patient, while helping to destroy the tumour.

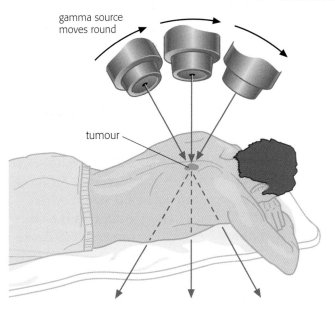

gamma source moves round

tumour

Figure 11.9

B Inside the atom

Ernest Rutherford was a scientist from New Zealand who came to work in the UK, roughly a hundred years ago. He made a startling discovery when he and his colleagues were investigating alpha radiation. Here is what they did.

They directed a beam of alpha particles at a thin gold foil. The foil was only a few atoms thick, and Rutherford guessed that most of the alpha particles would pass straight through. A few would be deflected off their straight path.

His prediction was partly correct – most of the alpha radiation went straight through the foil. However, he surprised everyone by showing that some alpha particles were reflected back towards the source. It was as if there was something small and hard in the foil, which the alpha particles were bouncing off.

Rutherford deduced that there was a tiny nucleus in the centre of each atom. Today, we know for sure that he was right. The atomic nucleus is very small compared to the amount of space in an atom, so most alpha particles failed to score a direct hit. But a few headed close in to a nucleus. The atomic nucleus has a positive electrical charge, and so do alpha particles, and since positive charges repel each other, these alpha particles were reflected back towards their source.

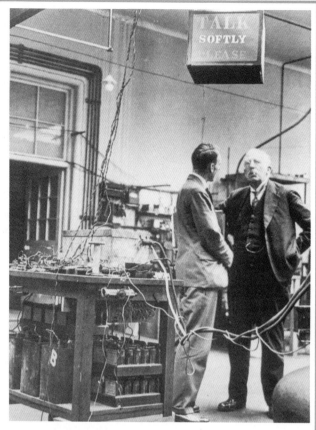

Figure 11.10 Ernest Rutherford (on the right) in a lab at Cambridge University in the 1920s. He was famous for his loud voice; its vibrations could interfere with delicate experiments – hence the notice above his head

Figure 11.11 In this standard picture of an atom, electrons orbit around the nucleus

● Protons, neutrons, electrons

Ernest Rutherford showed that every **atom** has a tiny **nucleus** at its centre. Figure 11.11 shows how we picture an atom today.

▸ At the centre is the nucleus. Around it orbit a number of **electrons**.
▸ The nucleus is made up of two types of particles, **protons** and **neutrons**.

Look back to Table 6.2 on page 123 to see the properties of these particles that make up an atom.

Representing an atomic nucleus

There are many different types of atom. As you will know from your studies of Chemistry, there are hydrogen atoms, carbon atoms, oxygen atoms, and so on. What is the difference?

▸ The commonest type of hydrogen atom has just 1 proton in its nucleus, with 1 electron in orbit.
▸ The commonest type of carbon atom has 6 protons and 6 neutrons in its nucleus, with 6 electrons in orbit.
▸ The commonest type of oxygen atom has 8 protons and 8 neutrons in its nucleus, with 8 electrons in orbit.

So you can see that different numbers of protons, neutrons and electrons give different types of atom. We can show this simply using symbols. The atomic nuclei described above are represented by letters and numbers as shown in Figure 11.12.

Figure 11.12 Some atomic nuclei and their symbols

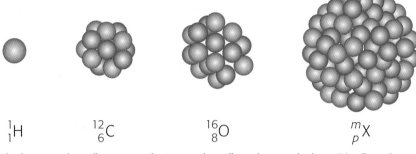

$^{1}_{1}H$ $^{12}_{6}C$ $^{16}_{8}O$ $^{m}_{p}X$

The lower number tells us the number of protons (p) in the nucleus

The top number tells us the number of protons plus neutrons (m)

The letter (X) tells us the chemical element

Isotopes

Every element has a variety of atoms. You may know from your Chemistry work (see page 126 of Chapter 6) that these symbols represent three different forms of carbon atom:

$^{12}_{6}C$ $^{13}_{6}C$ $^{14}_{6}C$

These are all atoms of carbon, but we say that they are different **isotopes** of carbon. You can see that the lower number is the same for each isotope, but the upper number is different.

▸ The lower number is called the **proton number** (or **atomic number**), because it shows the number of protons in the nucleus of the atom.
▸ The upper number is called the **nucleon number** (or **mass number**), because it shows the number of protons and neutrons (together known as nucleons) in the nucleus of the atom.

So isotopes of an element have the same number of protons, but different numbers of neutrons (see Figure 6.17, page 126). If we take an atom of $^{12}_{6}C$ and add a neutron, we get $^{13}_{6}C$. This is still an atom of carbon (because it has 6 protons), but it is a different isotope of carbon.

Out of the nucleus

Understanding the structure of atoms helps us to understand radioactivity. Where do alpha, beta and gamma radiations come from?

Most of the atoms around us are stable. This means that they do not undergo radioactive decay. However, a few are unstable; in order to become stable, they emit radiation of one type or another. This radiation comes from the nucleus of the atom.

Figure 11.13 shows how this works. An unstable nucleus emits *either* an alpha particle *or* a beta particle. It may *also* emit a gamma ray. These emissions cause a change in the structure of the atomic nucleus. The atom may now be stable; but if it is still unstable, it will emit some more ionising radiation until eventually it becomes stable.

The process of radioactive decay is described as random. This is because we cannot predict when an individual atom will decay. An

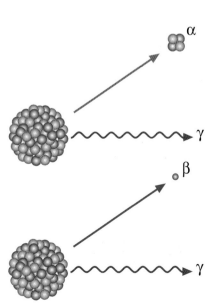

Figure 11.13 Unstable nuclei like these emit ionising radiation when they decay. They become more stable as a result

atom that is highly unstable is likely to decay in a very short interval of time, but we cannot predict exactly when it will decay. You can 'hear' the randomness of radioactivity as follows. Place a Geiger counter next to a weak radioactive source. Switch on, and listen to the clicks or beeps. You will hear that they are irregular – they don't come at equal intervals of time. You may hear nothing for a second or two, and then there may be three or four clicks in the next second.

Summary

- The nucleus of an atom is made up of protons and neutrons; electrons orbit the nucleus.
- An atomic nucleus can be represented like this: $_p^m X$, where p is the number of protons and m is the number of protons + neutrons.
- Isotopes of an element have the same proton number (atomic number), but different nucleon numbers (mass numbers). This is because their atoms have different numbers of neutrons.
- Radioactive atoms have unstable nuclei, which decay by emitting ionising radiation in a random process.

Questions

11.4 **a** Which particles are found in the nucleus of an atom?
   b Which particles orbit the nucleus?

11.5 A particular atom of nitrogen (symbol N) has 7 protons and 7 neutrons in its nucleus.
   a How many particles are there altogether in its nucleus?
   b Write down the symbol for this nucleus in the form $_p^m X$.

11.6 A particular atom of hydrogen has this symbol for its nucleus: $_1^3 H$.
   a How many protons are there in this nucleus?
   b How many particles are there altogether in this nucleus?
   c How many neutrons are there in this nucleus?

11.7 Two isotopes of oxygen are represented by the following symbols:

$$_8^{16}O \qquad _8^{17}O$$

   a What are the atomic numbers of these nuclei?
   b What are the mass numbers of these nuclei?

11.8 Four nuclei are represented by the following symbols:

$$_{17}^{37}A \qquad _{18}^{37}B \qquad _{18}^{38}C \qquad _{19}^{39}D$$

   (The letters A, B, C, D are not their correct chemical symbols.)
   a Which two nuclei are isotopes of the same element? Explain how you can tell.
   b Copy and complete the table to show the particles which make up each of these nuclei.

Nucleus	$_{17}^{37}A$	$_{18}^{37}B$	$_{18}^{38}C$	$_{19}^{39}D$
number of protons				
number of neutrons				

C Radioactive decay

The Turin shroud (Figure 11.14) is an ancient relic. In the 1990s, scientists were given permission to perform some experiments on a small fragment of the cloth to find out how old it was. There were two theories. Many people believed that it was the shroud in which Christ's body was wrapped, after the crucifixion, almost 2000 years ago. Others believed that it was a more modern artefact, a medieval icon representing Christ.

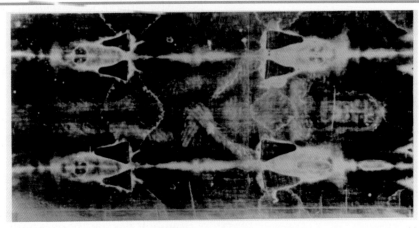

Figure 11.14 The Turin shroud – radiocarbon dating suggested that it was about 700 years old

To test these theories, the scientists used radiocarbon dating. They knew that the fabric was made from fibres containing carbon atoms. Some carbon atoms are radioactive and, as time passes, these gradually decay (emit radiation and become non-radioactive). By measuring the fraction of carbon atoms that are radioactive, it is possible to work out how old an object is. The older the object is, the smaller the number of radioactive carbon atoms which will remain.

In the end, the scientists deduced that the shroud was made in 1325±33 AD. In other words, it was only about 700 years old, not 2000. This didn't finally settle the argument; some people insisted that there were other reasons why the shroud might appear to be relatively recent. No doubt the debate will continue, despite the scientific evidence.

Notice that the scientists could not give a precise date for the shroud. The figure of ±33 years is an estimate of the uncertainty in the date.

Radioactive 'decay' is a way of describing the emission of radiation from a radioactive atom.

● Decaying away

Imagine starting an experiment with a sample of 1000 radioactive carbon atoms. After a while, one will decay, leaving 999 undecayed. Later, a second one will decay, leaving you with 998, then 997, and so on. What is the pattern of this decay?

Figure 11.15 shows the pattern. At first, the number of undecayed atoms decreases rapidly. Then the rate of decay gradually slows down. Because there are fewer and fewer undecayed atoms left, the rate of decay is less.

Every radioactive substance shows this same pattern, but some decay faster than others. In Figure 11.15, the red line represents the decay of a substance that decays more quickly than the substance shown by the blue line.

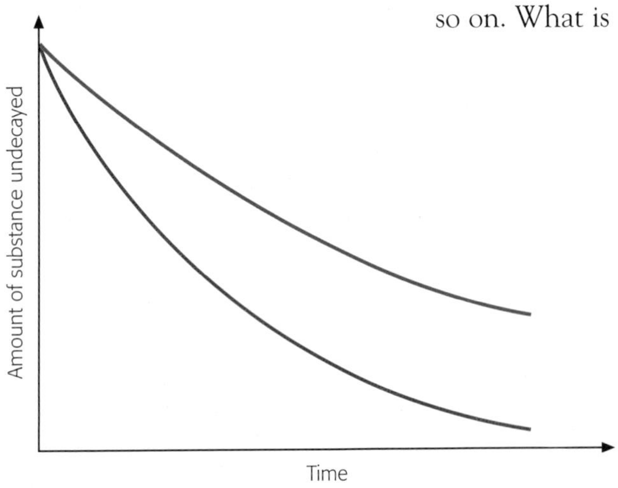

Amount of substance undecayed (vertical axis)

Time (horizontal axis)

Figure 11.15 All radioactive substances show this pattern of decay – fast at first, then gradually getting slower. Here, the red substance decays more quickly than the blue one

Three quantities show this same pattern of decay:

▶ the number of undecayed atoms in a sample
▶ the activity of a sample (the number of atoms which decay each second)
▶ the count rate (the number of decays detected each second by a Geiger counter).

Half-life

How can we describe this pattern of decay? What do we mean when we say that one substance decays faster than another? If you look at the curves in Figure 11.15, you will see that the amount of substance undecayed gets smaller and smaller, but it doesn't reach zero. So we can't say that the red substance has decayed away completely after a certain amount of time. We need a different way of expressing this.

Figure 11.16 shows how we do this. From this graph, you can see that the amount of substance decayed falls to half its original value after a certain amount of time, which we call the **half-life**. After the same amount of time again, one quarter will remain. After three half-lives, one-eighth remains, and so on.

To find the half-life of a substance from a graph like this:

▸ from half-way up the y-axis, draw across to the graph curve
▸ draw a vertical line down to the x-axis to find the time.

Each radioactive substance has its own characteristic half-life. The shorter the half-life, the more rapidly it decays, which means the greater the rate of radioactive emissions – or 'activity' – from the substance.

Figure 11.16 After one half-life, half of the original substance remains undecayed

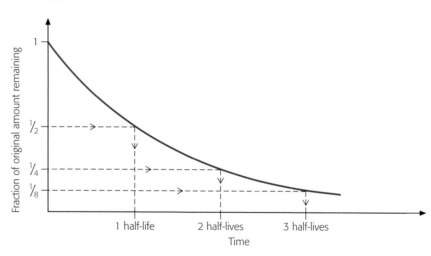

Worked example 1

A sample of radioactive material contains 800 undecayed atoms. How many will remain undecayed after 4 half-lives?

It is easiest to work through a calculation like this systematically.

After 1 half-life, 400 atoms will remain (800/2).

After 2 half-lives, 200 atoms will remain (400/2).

After 3 half-lives, 100 atoms will remain (200/2).

After 4 half-lives, 50 atoms will remain (100/2).

So 50 atoms will remain undecayed after 4 half-lives.

Worked example 2

A sample of radioactive material contains 1000 undecayed atoms. The half-life of the material is 8 years. How many atoms will remain undecayed after 24 years?

You may find it helps to use a table for this:

Time	Number of half-lives	Number of atoms undecayed
0	0	1000
8 years	1	500
16 years	2	250
24 years	3	125

So 125 atoms will remain undecayed after 24 years.

245

● Graphical representations

Imagine having 100 coins, representing 100 undecayed atoms. Toss each coin; remove the ones that come down 'heads' as these represent atoms which have decayed. You will have about 50 left. Toss them again, and remove the heads. Now you will have about 25 remaining. You could draw a graph showing how the number of atoms decreases after each toss: 100 – 50 – 25 – 12 and so on. The 'half-life' for this model of decay is one toss.

Computer software can do this much more efficiently – it will save you the bother of tossing all those coins. Figure 11.17 shows the output from one computer program.

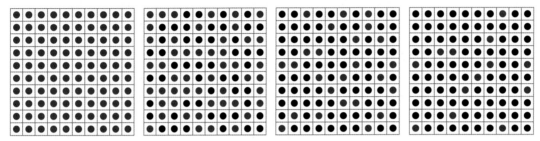 

Key
● undecayed atom
● decayed atom

Figure 11.17 This model of radioactive decay was generated using computer software

Each red circle represents an undecayed atom; there are 100 at the start. The computer looks at each circle in turn; if it represents an undecayed atom, it uses a random number generator to decide whether the atom decays. (For example, the program might say that, if the random number is between 0 and 6, the atom remains undecayed. If it is 7, 8 or 9, the atom decays.)

After each round, the program displays the atoms, red for undecayed, black for decayed. From Figure 11.17, you can see that the number of undecayed atoms decreases rapidly at first, then more slowly.

Software like this could provide a table of numbers instead of the diagrams. The table shows an example, and Figure 11.18 shows a graph of the data. The half-life of this computer-model 'decay' is about 35 s.

Software is useful for generating data like this. There is no need to toss coins or throw dice. It can display the results in different forms – charts, tables or graphs. And you can change the chance that an individual atom decays. (For a coin, the chance is always 50-50.)

Number of atoms	1000	820	670	550	450	370	300
Time (s)	0	10	20	30	40	50	60

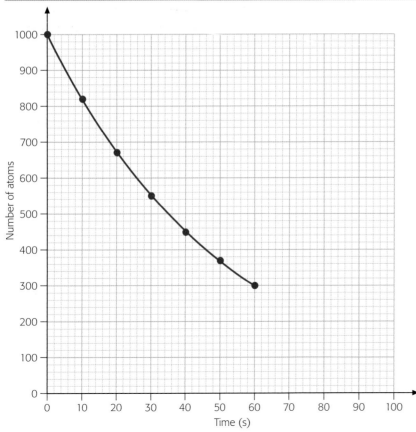

Figure 11.18 A graph based on decay data generated by computer software

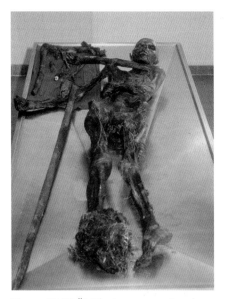

Figure 11.19 Ötzi the Iceman was found frozen in the Alps by two walkers. Radiocarbon dating showed that he died about 5300 years ago

● Dating

The example of the Turin shroud on page 244 showed how radiocarbon dating works. The half-life of radioactive carbon is 5730 years; this means that, after 5730 years, half of the radioactive carbon atoms will have decayed and half will remain. That makes it useful for dating things that are thousands of years old, such as the 'Iceman', discovered frozen in the Alps in 1991 (Figure 11.19).

Radioactive carbon is not the only radioactive substance used for such radioactive dating. The decay of radioactive potassium, for example, can be used to find out how many millions of years old a rock sample is.

Even the Earth itself has been dated using radioactive decay. Uranium decays very slowly, with a half-life of between 4 and 5 billion years. Measurements of uranium decay have shown that the Earth is about 4.5 billion years old.

These measurements (like most scientific measurements) are to some extent uncertain. We can't say that Ötzi the Iceman died *exactly* 5300 years ago. Why not? Firstly, we need to know the half-life of the radioactive substance very accurately, and that can be tricky. If the atoms decay very slowly, it is hard to work out when half have decayed. Secondly, the amount of a radioactive atom in a sample may be very small. The scientists who found the age of the Turin shroud were only allowed a small sample of the precious fabric. Since only about one carbon atom in a billion billion is radioactive, you can imagine that it is a difficult task to make accurate measurements of the fraction of carbon atoms that is radioactive.

Summary

- The rate of decay, or activity, of a radioactive substance decreases over a period of time, rapidly at first, and then gradually more slowly.
- The half-life of a radioactive substance is the time taken for half of its atoms to decay.
- Computer software can generate different graphical representations of radioactive decay.
- Radioactive decay can be used to date archaeological objects and rocks.

Questions

11.9 Look at the graph (Figure 11.20), which shows the decay of a radioactive substance.
  a How many atoms did it contain at the start?
  b How many atoms remained undecayed after 5 minutes?
  c What is the half-life of this substance?

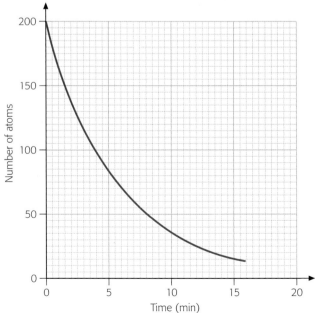

Figure 11.20 Radioactive decay curve

11.10 A sample of radioactive material contains 1600 undecayed atoms.
a How many of these atoms will remain undecayed after 3 half-lives?
b If the half-life of the substance is 40 days, how long will it take for the number of undecayed atoms to fall to 400?

11.11 In an experiment to find the half-life of a radioactive substance, a Geiger counter was used to measure its radioactivity. The table shows the results. Draw a graph to show this data, and use it to calculate the half-life of the substance.

Reading on Geiger counter (count rate per second)	900	740	600	490	400	330	270	220
Time (minutes)	0	20	40	60	80	100	120	140

D Learning to be careful

When radioactivity was discovered in 1896, it immediately caused a popular sensation – people were fascinated by radiation that could pass right through sheets of metal and even through the human body.

Intense radiation causes serious damage to body tissues. Milder doses cause inflammation, and some doctors suggested this could help to promote health by stimulating the body's immune system. Radioactive creams and drinks were sold, and even radioactive condoms. It is unlikely that these products ever did any good, and some people who used too much of them developed cancer.

Today, almost all scientists and doctors agree that it is wise to avoid unnecessary exposure to radiation from radioactive substances. However, there are clinics in the Alps where you can go and spend some time underground, in old mine workings, breathing in the radioactive air. Advertisements for these clinics claim that exposure to radon gas promotes health, and scientific studies have been published to support these claims.

Figure 11.21 An advert for a radioactive face cream from 1933, when such a use of radioactive elements was still believed to be beneficial

● Avoiding risks

Radium is a radioactive element. It can be used to make luminous paint – the energy released by its decay causes the paint to glow. In the 1920s and 30s, this paint was used on the hands of watches so that they would glow in the dark. Young women were employed to apply the paint. To get a fine point on their brushes, they would lick them. In doing this they transferred some radioactive material to their mouths, and many of them developed cancer of the jaw, and died as a result.

It took a while for this hazard to be understood. Cancer can take years to develop after exposure to radiation, and it is difficult to prove that something that happened a long time in the past is the direct cause of cancer. Also, employers are often reluctant to accept that their working practices are dangerous. Today, radioactive luminous paint is rarely used; other safer glow-in-the-dark materials are used in watches and clocks.

Most scientists who work with radiation now believe that any dose of radiation carries a small risk. The bigger the dose, the greater the risk – see Figure 11.22a. However, there is an alternative theory. Some scientists think that a very weak dose might be good for you, perhaps by stimulating the immune system – see Figure 11.22b. The evidence for this is not very good; a recent American report rejected the idea.

Scientific ideas often advance in this way. A new idea or discovery gets a lot of attention. Gradually the negative side, such as risks to health, become apparent. Alternative theories appear and have to be tested against the evidence. Just occasionally, an alternative idea can overthrow a long-established theory.

Figure 11.22 Two ideas about the effects of radiation. In **a**, the greater the dose, the greater the risk – even a small dose is hazardous. In **b**, small doses are health-giving

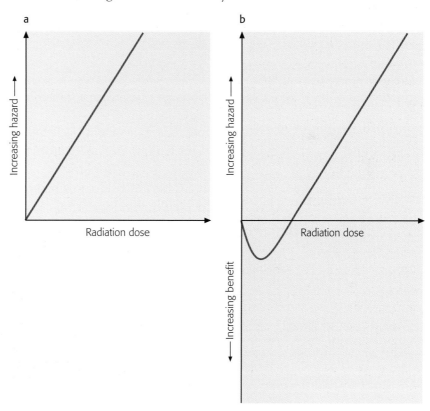

More radiation, more risk

So what can radiation do to you? Radiation damages cells and, if it damages the DNA in the cell nucleus, it can have serious consequences.

DNA controls the division of cells. If this goes out of control, a tumour (cancer) may develop.

If the DNA is in a sex cell (sperm or egg), the result may be a **mutation**. A baby may be born with damaged DNA, and then the child's development may be affected. The mutation will also be passed on to future generations.

Not all mutations are harmful. There is always a chance that a damaged gene may be beneficial.

Risks in the lab

The more we understand the hazards of radiation, the easier it is to take the necessary action to avoid harming ourselves. For example, there are rules about the safe handling of radioactive materials in school labs. We could say, 'No radioactive materials should be allowed in schools.' However, that would be throwing the baby out with the bathwater. It is better to use our understanding of radiation to work safely with radioactive materials and the radiation they produce.

Table 11.1 shows some sensible rules, and gives explanations for them. Figure 11.23 shows some radioactive sources of the types used in schools.

Table 11.1 Working safely with radioactive materials in school labs

Rule	Reason
No one under the age of 16 to handle radioactive materials	Teachers and over-16s can be relied on to behave responsibly
Radioactive sources to be locked away when not in use	Minimises the chances that people will be exposed to radiation accidentally
Radioactive sources to be stored in lead-lined boxes	Lead absorbs most radiation; some gamma radiation may get through
Radioactive sources to be handled with tongs	Reduces the chance that radioactive materials get onto the hands; keeps the source further from the body
Students remain at least 1 metre away from the source during an experiment	The further away you are, the weaker the radiation. Some is absorbed by air, and all radiation gets weaker as it spreads out

Figure 11.23 Radioactive sources must be handled and stored safely, to minimise the risk to students and teachers

In 1962, an accident occurred which had far-reaching consequences. Peter Parker, an American high-school student, attended a radioactivity demonstration. A spider was accidentally irradiated, and it bit Peter. He now had radioactive spider's blood in him, and he rapidly developed spidery characteristics. Like a spider, he could lift objects many times his own weight, and he could run up and down walls. He discovered how to spin webs and use them to trap his enemies. Peter Parker had become Spider-Man. Of course, this is fiction. But it illustrates the fears people may have if they do not have a scientific understanding of the hazards of radiation.

● Background radiation

We are all exposed to low levels of radiation all of the time. This is known as **background radiation**. Figure 11.24 shows where it comes from.

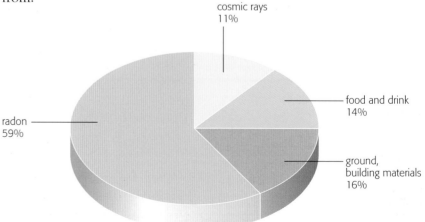

cosmic rays 11%

food and drink 14%

ground, building materials 16%

radon 59%

Figure 11.24 The different sources of background radiation

- Roughly half of background radiation comes from **radon gas** and other naturally occurring radioactive gases in the atmosphere. We breathe these in, and they irradiate us from the inside.
- Some radiation reaches us from radioactive substances in the ground and in the building materials around us.
- Our food and drink is also slightly radioactive. Because atoms from our food and drink become part of our bodies, we are radioactive too.
- Finally, a fraction of background radiation reaches us from space in the form of cosmic rays.

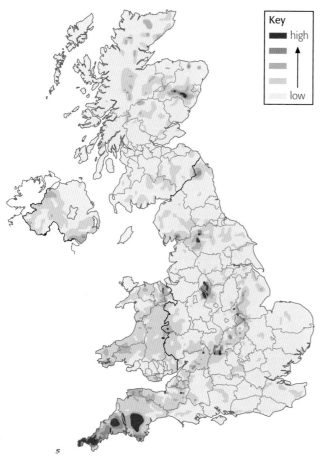

Key	
■	high
	low

Background radiation is ionising radiation. It can damage our cells, and so there is a small risk to human health. It is estimated that a few thousand deaths each year in the UK result from exposure to background radiation, particularly from radon gas.

Radon variations

The amount of radon gas in the air depends on where you live. The map in Figure 11.25 shows how this varies around the UK. Radon emerges from underground rocks; if these contain a lot of uranium, the amount of radon gas is likely to be high. Because the amount of radon in the air varies around the country, it follows that some people are exposed to higher amounts of background radiation.

Cornwall is a known radon 'hot-spot', and in some parts of the county people are advised to check the radon levels in their homes. It is advisable to keep windows open so that radon doesn't accumulate, and it may be necessary to fit a pump under the floorboards to remove any radon gas as it emerges from the ground.

Exposure to radon increases the risk of lung cancer. But the risk is much, much greater if people are also tobacco smokers.

Figure 11.25 How the amount of radon in the air varies around the UK
Source: www.defra.gov.uk/environment/statistics/

Cosmic rays

Astronauts in spacecraft are exposed to much higher levels of cosmic rays than people living on the Earth's surface. This is for two reasons.

Firstly, the Earth's atmosphere absorbs some of the energy of cosmic rays. Astronauts are above the Earth's atmosphere, so they do not have this protection. (People who live on high mountains are also exposed to higher levels of cosmic radiation.)

Secondly, cosmic rays are electrically charged particles, and so they are affected by the Earth's **magnetic field**. As they approach the Earth, they start to spiral off towards the poles. There, they strike the atmosphere, causing it to glow. That is the origin of the Aurora Borealis, or northern lights (Figure 11.26). It is thought that the Earth's magnetic field is gradually becoming weaker, so in the future people may be exposed to more cosmic radiation.

Figure 11.26 The Aurora Borealis is a spectacular light show, occasionally seen in the UK, but more often seen at high latitudes close to the North pole

Summary

- Our understanding of the risks of radiation has gradually developed over the last century.
- Ionising radiation can damage living tissue. Damage to the DNA of sex cells can result in mutations, which are passed on to the next generation.
- Radioactive sources used in school labs can be used safely because we understand how radiation behaves.
- We are all exposed to background radiation, from Earth and space.
- Background radiation varies around the UK mostly because the amount of radon gas in the air varies from place to place.
- The Earth's atmosphere and magnetic field help to protect us from the effects of cosmic rays.

Questions

11.12 a Why should radioactive sources used in a school lab be stored in a lead-lined box?

 b Why should the sources be handled using tongs?

11.13 Exposure to ionising radiation may result in radiation burns. It may also result in a mutation.

 a Which of these would only result from a high dose of radiation?

 b Can we be sure that a very small dose of radiation is safe?

11.14 As well as background radiation, we are all exposed to radiation from artificial (man-made) sources. Table 11.2 shows the different contributions to the average radiation dose of UK citizens.

Table 11.2 Sources of our radiation dose

Source of radiation	Fraction (%)
artificial sources (mostly medical)	13
radioactive gases	51
ground and buildings	14
food and drink	12
cosmic rays	10

Draw a bar chart to represent this information. Distinguish the *four* bars which represent natural background radiation.

11.15 Explain why the following people may be exposed to higher than average levels of radiation:

 a a pilot of a commercial aircraft

 b someone living in the Scottish Highlands (*two* reasons)

 c a hospital radiographer.

12 Power of the atom

A Nuclear fission

When radioactivity was newly discovered at the end of the 19th century, it was a great puzzle to scientists. A radioactive substance radiates energy all the time. Some radioactive substances actually feel warm to the touch. There is no chemical reaction going on – it is not like coal burning, for example. So where does this energy come from?

In the early part of the 20th century, when the structure of atoms was understood (see page 241), scientists guessed that the store of energy in radioactive atoms must be in the atomic nucleus. The amounts of energy being released were found to be much greater than the energy changes involved in chemical reactions. Radioactive atoms were remarkably concentrated stores of energy.

Albert Einstein, in his theory of special relativity published in 1905 (see page 231), had already predicted how to calculate the total amount of energy stored in an atom. Here is his famous equation for this:

$$E = mc^2$$

This equation says that, if you start with atoms of mass m, you can convert them entirely into energy E. The quantity that connects E and m is the square of the speed of light, c^2. Since c is a very big number ($c = 300\,000\,000$ m/s), it follows that a large amount of energy is released when only a small amount of mass is converted to energy. For example, if 1 gram (0.001 kg) of matter were converted to energy, the amount of energy released would be:

Figure 12.1 Albert Einstein in 1925. By this time, he was a well-established member of the physics community. His equation $E = mc^2$ showed how to calculate the energy released in radioactive decay – and in nuclear fission

$$E = 0.001 \times 300\,000\,000 \times 300\,000\,000 = 90\,000\,000\,000\,000 \text{ J}$$

That's a lot of joules of energy!

Careful measurements were made of the energy released from a given mass when a radioactive substance such as uranium decayed by emitting radiation. These results showed that Einstein's equation was right. This is one of the ways in which science makes progress. People develop new theories; the theories are used to make predictions, and the predictions are tested by observation and experiment. If the theory doesn't match the experimental results, the theory is likely to be scrapped. To be accepted, a scientific theory needs mountains of evidence to support it.

When uranium decays by emitting radiation, only a tiny fraction of its mass is converted to energy. In the 1930s, scientists discovered a way of releasing much more of the energy stored in uranium – by nuclear fission. This paved the way for nuclear power stations – and nuclear bombs.

● Splitting uranium atoms

Uranium atoms are among the heaviest atoms known – uranium is element number 92 in the Periodic Table. Each uranium atom is a concentrated store of energy.

Uranium is a **radioactive** substance, but its atoms decay only very, very slowly. So how can we speed this up, and get out more of the energy which the atoms store? A clue came from an experiment by a German scientist, Otto Hahn. He bombarded uranium with **neutrons**; he was surprised to find that much lighter atoms of barium were produced, and guessed that the neutrons might be splitting the uranium atoms. However, he couldn't bring himself to believe it. In 1938, his idea was proved correct by an Austrian scientist, Lise Meitner, and her nephew Otto Frisch. Figure 12.2 shows their idea.

Figure 12.2 The process of nuclear fission

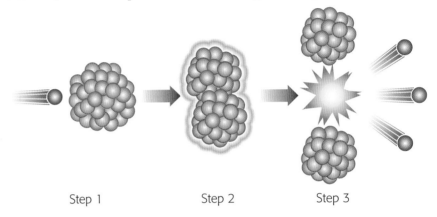

Step 1   Step 2   Step 3

Step 1: Uranium atoms are bombarded with neutrons.
Step 2: The **nucleus** of a uranium atom absorbs a neutron. It becomes highly unstable.
Step 3: The unstable nucleus splits in two, releasing two, three or four more neutrons and a lot of energy.

'Fission' means 'splitting'.

This is the process of nuclear **fission**. When the large nucleus splits in two, it forms two new **daughter nuclei**.

Each time a uranium nucleus is split in this way, some of the energy that was stored in the nucleus is released. The neutrons and the daughter nuclei fly apart at high speed (they have a lot of kinetic energy) and gamma rays are also released. This energy makes the lump of uranium get hotter.

Lise Meitner and Otto Frisch were able to show that this was happening by analysing the uranium after bombardment with neutrons. It contained atoms of elements with about half the mass of uranium atoms, such as barium, showing that the uranium atoms had indeed been split in two.

Chain reaction

Nuclear fission works best with a particular type of uranium atom, called uranium-235 (or U-235). It also works well with atoms of another element, plutonium-239 (Pu-239).

An important feature of nuclear fission was soon noticed by Otto Frisch. It takes just one neutron to split a uranium nucleus, but two or three neutrons are released in the process. If these neutrons go

Figure 12.3 Lise Meitner, one of the discoverers of nuclear fission. Many people feel that she should have shared Otto Hahn's 1944 Nobel Prize for the discovery

on to bombard and split more uranium nuclei, a **chain reaction** will be set up. This means you don't need to keep on firing neutrons at uranium nuclei – the process can provide its own supply of neutrons.

Figure 12.4 shows this in practice. A single neutron causes the first uranium atom to split. This releases three neutrons; two of these go on to split more nuclei, while one escapes. It only takes one neutron from each fission event to cause another fission event for the chain reaction to keep going, releasing a steady stream of energy.

Figure 12.4 A chain reaction in uranium

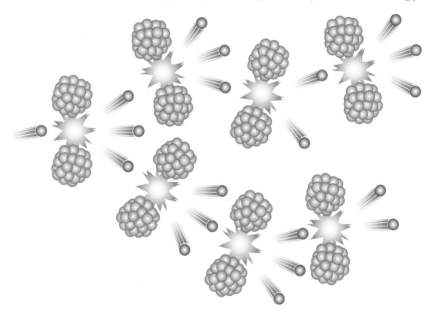

Using a chain reaction

Most nuclear power stations use uranium-235 as their fuel. (Some use plutonium-239.) A power station must produce a steady flow of energy, so the chain reaction must be kept under control.

A nuclear bomb is different. It is designed to release as much energy as possible in as short a time as possible. The chain reaction must go faster and faster. Here is what happens:

▸ A single neutron causes one uranium to split, releasing two or three more neutrons.
▸ Each of these neutrons goes on to split another U-235 nucleus. So now two or three split, releasing perhaps eight neutrons.
▸ Each of these goes on to split a U-235 nucleus, releasing perhaps 20 neutrons. And so on.

More and more neutrons fly around inside the uranium, causing more and more U-235 nuclei to split. Energy is released very rapidly, and the whole thing blows up. It only takes a fraction of a second to release the energy stored in the uranium in an explosion. This is much more powerful than any ordinary chemical bomb.

As well as producing a terrible fireball, a nuclear explosion also showers the surrounding area with the daughter products, which are usually highly radioactive and also chemically poisonous. Anyone exposed to these materials or the radiation they produce is at great risk.

Figure 12.5 A nuclear explosion – this photo shows a test explosion

Einstein's letter

At the end of the 1930s, war was brewing. Hitler was in power in Germany, and some of the scientists who had fled the country became concerned that Germany might develop a nuclear bomb, based on the newly discovered process of fission. They wanted to warn US President Roosevelt of this danger, so they persuaded Albert Einstein, then living in the USA, to write a letter to the president. In it, Einstein wrote:

'Some recent work ... leads me to believe that the element uranium may be turned into a new and important source of energy... It may become possible to set up a nuclear chain reaction in a large mass of uranium, by which vast amounts of power and large quantities of new radium-like elements would be generated.

'This new phenomenon would also lead to the construction of bombs of a new type. A single bomb, carried by boat and exploded in a port, might very well destroy the whole port together with some of the surrounding territory.'

The scientists had foreseen the possible consequences of their discoveries and felt it was their responsibility to inform the political authorities. Einstein's letter went on to ask for more money for American researchers. In response, the US Government set up the Los Alamos project, which developed the first nuclear weapons. Nazi Germany never managed to produce a nuclear bomb of its own.

Decay series

The daughter nuclei produced when a U-235 nucleus splits are unstable. They decay by emitting alpha, beta and gamma radiation. The nuclei which result from these decays are also unstable, and they decay. Eventually, after several decays, a stable nucleus results. A series of decays like this, from one unstable nucleus to another, is called a **decay series**.

Figure 12.6 shows one such decay series, starting with a daughter nucleus called barium-141. This has a half-life of just 18 minutes, so it decays quickly to become La-141, then Ce-141, and finally Pr-141, which is stable. A beta particle and a gamma ray are released at each stage in the series.

These substances are what is left over after a nuclear chain reaction. They make up the fall-out from a nuclear explosion, and they form the radioactive waste produced by a nuclear power station. You will learn more about this in the next section.

Figure 12.6 The decay series for one possible daughter nucleus, barium-141, produced when U-235 undergoes fission

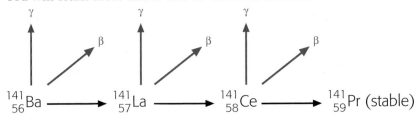

Summary

- Einstein's theories suggested that a great deal of energy is stored in matter.
- A lot of stored energy is released in the process of nuclear fission, when a nucleus of U-235 splits, to produce two daughter nuclei and two or more neutrons.
- A chain reaction results when these neutrons go on to cause further U-235 nuclei to split.
- **H** • The daughter nuclei are unstable, and decay from one element to another, forming a decay series.

Questions

12.1 A nucleus of uranium-235 may undergo nuclear fission.
  a Give one word which means the same as 'fission'.
  b What particle causes the U-235 nucleus to undergo fission?
  c What name is given to the two large particles which result?
  d What other particles are released, and how many of them?
  e What else is released?

12.2 Figure 12.7 shows how the number of free neutrons in a mass of uranium-235 changes with time. There are two lines on the graph.
  a Which line, A or B, represents how the number of neutrons in the reactor of a nuclear power station changes? Explain your choice.
  b What might the other line represent? Explain your answer.

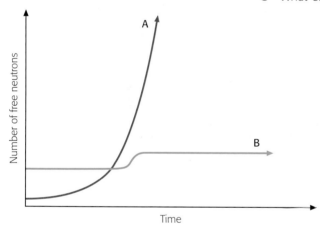

Figure 12.7

H **12.3** In 1945, at the end of the Second World War, two nuclear bombs were dropped on Japanese cities. One radioactive substance produced was strontium-90 (Sr-90).
  a Explain how such a substance is produced in a nuclear explosion. Study the table below, which shows information about the decay of Sr-90.

How Sr-90 decays	Sr-90 → Y-90 + β	half-life 28 years
How Y-90 decays	Y-90 → Zr-90 + β	half-life 58 days
Zr-90 is stable		

  b Why is there still today a lot of Sr-90 on the sites that were bombed?
  c Why is the amount of Zr-90 slowly increasing?
  d Why are the local people still at risk, more than 60 years after the bombs exploded?

B Nuclear power

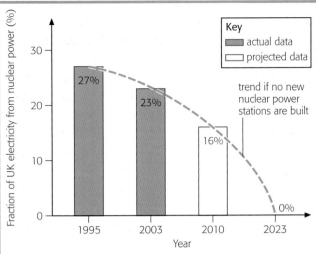

Figure 12.8 The nuclear contribution to the UK electricity supply is currently decreasing

Figure 12.9 Decommissioning a nuclear power station is an expensive business. It can go on for decades after the power station has finished producing electricity

The UK relies on nuclear power stations to supply about 20% of its electricity (Figure 12.8). Most of the existing nuclear power stations were built over 30 years ago and are now reaching the end of their working lives. This leads to two problems.

The first problem is, what is to be done with the disused power stations? They contain a lot of radioactive materials, which are hazardous to handle. In the decommissioning process, spent fuel and radioactive metal boilers are removed for careful disposal. Then the main buildings of the power station are demolished, leaving the most radioactive central part of the reactor building. This has to be left for decades before it can finally be dismantled.

Secondly, should the nuclear power stations be replaced by new ones? Many people would prefer to see renewable resources such as wind and solar power being used more, but these are costly and have other disadvantages. It would take thousands of wind turbines, for example, covering a large area of the countryside, to replace a single nuclear power station.

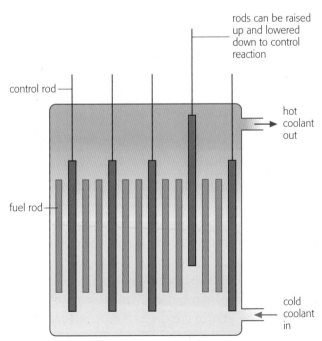

Figure 12.10 The core of a nuclear reactor, showing the fuel rods and control rods

● Chain reaction under control

Most nuclear power stations use uranium-235 as the fuel, in the form of fuel rods. These are contained in a **nuclear reactor** where their store of energy is released. Figure 12.10 shows the way in which the fuel rods are arranged in one type of reactor.

We have learnt that to release the energy stored in the uranium fuel, there must be a chain reaction going on. This must be controlled so that the energy release continues steadily. If it got out of control, the temperature inside the reactor could go shooting up, causing the materials inside to melt or catch fire, which would be disastrous.

In 1986, the operators of a nuclear power station at Chernobyl in the Ukraine ignored safety instructions and allowed their reactor to overheat. The resulting explosion and fire sprayed radioactive material over a large area and was responsible for many deaths – certainly hundreds, perhaps thousands.

The reactor couldn't blow up with the devastation on the scale of a nuclear bomb, because fuel rods are placed too far apart for things to go quite so seriously wrong.

So how is the chain reaction kept under control? Each time a U-235 nucleus splits, just one of the neutrons released must go on and cause a further U-235 to split. If fewer neutrons than this cause further fissions, the reaction will slow down and stop. If more than one neutron causes a further fission, the reaction will speed up and may go out of control.

This is where the control rods come in. They contain a material (usually boron) which is good at absorbing neutrons. To speed up the chain reaction, the control rods are gradually pulled upwards, out of the reactor core. This lets more neutrons fly around inside the core, causing more fission. To slow down the reaction, the rods are lowered slightly further into the core so that they absorb more of the neutrons. Fewer fission events then result, and the chain reaction slows down.

In an emergency, the control rods are designed to drop automatically into the core so that neutrons are rapidly absorbed and the chain reaction comes to a halt.

● Generating electricity

The core of a nuclear power station becomes hot – we say that **thermal energy** (heat) is released by fission of the uranium atoms in the fuel rods. How is this energy converted into electricity?

In most power stations, it is burning gas or coal which releases thermal energy.

The thermal energy from the core is used to heat water in a boiler (Figure 12.11). To do this, a fluid such as water or carbon dioxide is passed through the core in pipes, and then through the boiler.

Just as in a gas- or coal-fired power station, the water boils, producing steam at high pressure. This travels along pipes to the turbines, which are forced to spin round. The turbines turn the generators, which produce electricity. A large electric current flows, carrying **electrical energy**.

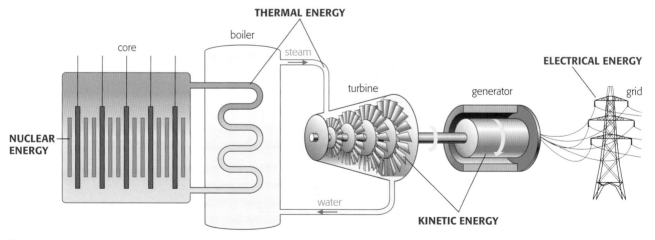

Figure 12.11 How thermal energy released in the reactor core is transferred to electrical energy

Cleaner power?

Nuclear power is not a renewable source of energy – once the uranium or plutonium fuel is used, it is described as 'spent' and it cannot be used again. However, it is sometimes claimed that nuclear power stations are 'greener' than fossil fuel power stations. These burn coal, oil or gas, releasing about half a kilogram of carbon dioxide (CO_2) for each kilowatt-hour of electricity produced. Carbon dioxide is the main greenhouse gas which is believed to be responsible for climate change.

Nuclear power stations (like the one shown in Figure 12.12) don't produce CO_2, but we should take into consideration CO_2 released in their construction. There is a lot of concrete in a power station, and concrete production is a major source of CO_2. On this score, nuclear fuels are better than fossil fuels, but they are not perfect.

Fossil fuel power stations also produce ash and soot, as well as polluting gases which cause acid rain. What comes out of a nuclear power station?

The biggest environmental hazard is radioactive waste. The daughter products of nuclear fission are highly radioactive; some remain radioactive for hundreds or thousands of years. The spent fuel rods must be handled with great care (Figure 12.13) and stored safely until they are harmless.

Figure 12.12 Sizewell B in Suffolk is one of the UK's more modern nuclear power stations. The reactor is housed under the white dome

Figure 12.13 This large flask containing radioactive waste from a nuclear power station is being lowered into a tank of cooling water. In the centre you can just see the technician who is operating the crane

Safe keeping

The radioactive waste from nuclear power stations remains radioactive for a long time. This is because fission results in some radioactive substances with very long half-lives, and so there is a big problem with keeping the waste safe – it must be stored safely for thousands of years.

How can this be done? Several methods have been suggested.

▶ Build an underground store where the waste can be monitored and guarded.
▶ Abandon the waste in a deep underground vault.
▶ Sink drums of waste in the deepest parts of the sea.
▶ Bury the waste beneath the seabed.
▶ Use a rocket to fire the waste into space.

All of these have their problems. The main worry is that we do not want the waste to escape into the environment. It could pollute water supplies or get into the food chain. (This has already happened in some areas.) So most people feel that the best solution is to keep the waste somewhere where it can be monitored, so that action can be taken if leaks appear. Since this may need to be done for centuries or even longer, the cost may be enormous.

A nuclear neighbour

Whenever there is a proposal to build a new nuclear power station, a planning inquiry is held to hear complaints from people who feel it may have a bad impact on the locality (Figure 12.14). What might their fears be?

The main concerns focus on the radioactive materials that are produced in the power station. There are fears that these may leak into the surroundings, creating a greater risk of cancer. Radioactive waste must be transported away from the site, and this could present another hazard.

Some people fear that a nuclear power station could be a target for terrorist action – the reactor might be bombed, releasing a lot of hazardous material.

Finally, a fire or explosion, as happened at Chernobyl, could devastate the area.

These are serious concerns, and the planners have to be sure that the power station will be secure and its operating procedures will be strictly followed. Once the power station is operating, regular checks are made to ensure that radioactive materials are not escaping into the environment (Figure 12.15).

A nuclear power station can bring advantages to a locality. It is likely to employ hundreds of people, so that means more local jobs. There will also be work during the construction phase, and during decommissioning at the end of the station's life. It may even have a visitors' centre and become a tourist attraction. However, it can be very difficult to convince sceptical members of the public that it will be safe for a power station to be built in their particular part of the country.

Figure 12.14 Protests in Slovakia against the construction of a nuclear power station

Figure 12.15 A scientist checking levels of radioactive substances in moss gathered from a hillside above a nuclear power station in France

Summary

- In a nuclear reactor, control rods which absorb neutrons are used to control the chain reaction.
- Thermal energy released in the reactor is used to boil water; the resulting high pressure steam turns turbines which turn generators to produce electrical energy.
- Nuclear power stations add little carbon dioxide to the atmosphere, but there are other environmental and social concerns.
- The hazardous radioactive waste produced by a nuclear power station is long-lived and so requires safe long-term storage or disposal.

Questions

12.4 What parts of a nuclear power station are described here?
  a Contains the fuel rods.
  b Lowered into position to slow down the chain reaction.
  c Carries thermal energy away from the fuel.
  d The place where steam is generated.
  e Caused to rotate by high-pressure steam.
  f Produce electricity when caused to rotate.

12.5 Copy and complete Figure 12.16, which shows the energy changes that occur in a nuclear power station.

Figure 12.16

12.6 In the core of a nuclear reactor, there are control rods between the fuel rods.
  a What particles must the control rods absorb?
  b If the control rods are raised out of the core, what happens to the chain reaction?
  c If the temperature in the core rises above a safe level, an automatic system drops the control rods into the core. Why is it important to have an automatic system like this?

12.7 a Why is the waste from nuclear power stations hazardous?
  b Why must the waste be stored for a long time?
  c Here are some ways in which the waste might be managed. For each one, give a reason why it might be unsatisfactory.
    i Build an underground store where the waste can be monitored and guarded.
    ii Abandon the waste in a deep underground vault.
    iii Sink drums of waste in the deepest parts of the sea.
    iv Use a rocket to fire the waste into space.

12.8 Make *two* lists, one of the possible benefits that a nuclear power station may bring to a locality, and another of the possible hazards it may bring.

C Nuclear fusion

In November 2006, construction of an experimental nuclear fusion reactor was started at Cadarache in the south of France. Nuclear fusion is an alternative to fission as a way of extracting energy from the nuclei of atoms. The new reactor is called the International Thermonuclear Experimental Reactor, or ITER, and it will cost about £7 billion.

This enormous cost explains why the project is international. The costs are being shared by the European Union, USA, Russia, China, Japan, India and South Korea. The project is so expensive that no single country (not even the USA) could afford to build it alone.

Figure 12.17 The construction site in Cadarache, the south of France, of the new International Thermonuclear Experimental Reactor, ITER

Increasingly, as scientific and engineering projects become bigger and more expensive, international cooperation becomes essential. In the past, European countries might have competed with each other and with the USA and Russia. With a project on the scale of ITER, international cooperation is the only way to raise sufficient funds. There is still competition, though, to be the country where the project is built. France was closely challenged by Japan to be the home of ITER.

> Another project on a similar scale is the International Space Station; many scientists feel that it has yet to justify the billions of pounds spent on it.

The aim is that ITER should lead the way to a new generation of cleaner power stations. However, we cannot be sure that ITER will be a success. The announcement that ITER would go ahead did not please everyone. A spokesperson for Greenpeace said, 'With 10 billion euros, we could build 10 000 MW offshore windfarms, delivering electricity for 7.5 million European households. Governments should not waste our money on a dangerous toy, which will never deliver any useful energy. Instead, they should invest in renewable energy which is abundantly available, not in 2080, but today.'

Figure 12.18 In the process of nuclear fusion, two hydrogen nuclei (at the top) collide to form a helium nucleus. A single neutron (blue) is also released

● Fusion or fission?

How does nuclear fusion differ from nuclear fission? In nuclear fission, the nuclei of large atoms (such as uranium) are split. This releases stored energy, because smaller atoms are more stable than big ones.

It turns out that medium-sized atoms are the most stable. So we can also release energy by joining (fusing) the nuclei of very small atoms, such as hydrogen. Figure 12.18 shows the idea of nuclear **fusion**.

Two hydrogen nuclei collide with each other and fuse together to form a helium nucleus, which is more stable. Energy is released and, as in a nuclear power station that uses uranium as its fuel, it should be possible to use this energy to generate electricity. Because fusion of hydrogen produces helium, a harmless, non-radioactive substance, a fusion power station should be a lot cleaner than one that uses fission. Fusion also has the advantage that its fuel (hydrogen) is freely available all around us – it is one of the components of water, so we should never run out.

The two hydrogen nuclei involved in the fusion reaction to produce helium are different isotopes (see page 242). You can see in Figure 12.18 that one has one neutron and the other has two neutrons. The most common isotope of hydrogen has no neutron.

Making fusion work

It is difficult to make nuclear fusion happen. The reason is that, if we try to squash two hydrogen nuclei together, they repel each other because they each have a positive electrical charge.

We know that nuclear fusion can work because it happens all the time, in the stars. The Sun, for example, is a giant ball of hot hydrogen and helium. The temperature in its core is about 14 million degrees, and the pressure is enormous. This means that the hydrogen nuclei, which form most of the Sun, have a lot of energy, so they are moving around very quickly. When two hydrogen nuclei collide, they are squashed together with great force, and this is enough to ensure that they fuse together. Energy is released, and this is the source of the Sun's energy.

So the problem for scientists trying to make fusion happen in a reactor is that they must heat up some hydrogen gas to a temperature of millions of degrees and keep it compressed to a high density. All known materials that could be used to contain the hydrogen melt at temperatures above 5000 °C, so that presents a problem!

One solution is to keep the hydrogen nuclei flowing around a circular path (Figure 12.19). Because they have positive electrical charge, they form an electric current. This hot, charged material can then be contained using electric and magnetic fields, so that it never touches the walls of its container.

You can imagine the difficulty and the expense of setting up such a fusion reactor. The aim is to get energy out, but a lot of energy must be put in to heat up the hydrogen gas. Experimental reactors like the one in Figure 12.19 have shown that fusion is possible, but it has proved very difficult to get out more energy than has been supplied in the first place. The ITER reactor is the first fusion reactor intended to actually supply electricity to the grid.

Figure 12.19 A technician carrying out checks inside an experimental fusion reactor near Oxford. When in use, the hot hydrogen gas travels around the central core; it is kept away from the walls by powerful magnetic fields

Cold fusion

Demand for energy is ever-increasing, but we are damaging the environment with our power stations. Many scientists would love to devise a truly clean source of energy. In March 1989, two scientists announced that they had done just that. Stanley Pons (from the USA) and Martin Fleischmann (from the UK) called a press conference to present their results. Their big claim was that they had discovered 'cold fusion'.

They had set out to find a way of squashing hydrogen atoms together so that they would fuse, without having to produce temperatures of millions of degrees. They knew that hydrogen gas would dissolve in some precious metals, so they experimented with rods of a metal called palladium. They used an electric current to encourage hydrogen to dissolve in the rods.

Pons and Fleischmann's measurements suggested that their experiment produced more energy than they originally put in, and they deduced that the hydrogen atoms were fusing together. To test their idea, they looked for neutrons coming out of their equipment. (Look at Figure 12.18 – you can see that a neutron is produced each time two nuclei fuse together.) Unfortunately, there were far fewer neutrons produced than would have been expected.

At the time, the two scientists were heavily criticised. They chose to present their results at a press conference; usually, scientists send their results in the form of a scientific paper to a journal, where it is reviewed by other scientists before it can be published. Pons and Fleischmann said that they were concerned that, with a new phenomenon like cold fusion, there was unlikely to be anyone who could give a fair review.

Another criticism came from physicists who said that their results could not be true; they did not fit with existing theories, and there was no good reason to change accepted ideas.

Figure 12.20 Martin Fleischmann (left) and Stanley Pons carrying out a cold fusion experiment in their lab in 1993

Subsequently, many attempts have been made to repeat the experiments. Some scientists claim to have obtained similar, or even better, results. Conferences are held, attended by scientists who 'believe' in cold fusion, without any 'non-believers' being prepared to come along.

If cold fusion is found to work, there would be a lot of money to be made from it, so tens of millions of pounds have been spent on experiments. However, it is still hard to say whether the effect truly exists.

This illustrates one aspect of how science works. When a revolutionary new idea comes along, it is not accepted automatically. It must be tested many times before it is regarded as a valid part of scientific knowledge – or it may fail the test and be rejected.

Summary

- Nuclear fusion may provide a new source of electricity for the 21st century.
- In nuclear fusion, small nuclei are fused (joined) together, releasing energy.
- Nuclear fusion is the energy source of stars.
- Nuclear fusion requires extremely high temperatures and densities, making it very difficult to use as a practical source of energy.
- The idea of cold fusion, like all new scientific theories, must undergo rigorous testing before it becomes accepted by the scientific community.

Questions

12.9 There are two ways to release energy from the nuclei of atoms:

nuclear fission   nuclear fusion

a Which of these involves joining two small atomic nuclei to form a single nucleus?

b In the other process, how is energy released?

12.10 When scientists have developed a new theory, they usually 'publish a scientific paper'.

a What is the purpose of this?

b Does this mean that their ideas have become part of accepted scientific knowledge?

H

12.11 a Explain why life on Earth is dependent on nuclear fusion.

b What conditions must be created if nuclear fusion is to occur?

c Why does this make it difficult to use nuclear fusion as a practical energy source on Earth?

D Static electricity

Have you ever wondered how Spider-Man can climb up walls? That's not really a question for science to answer, but scientists at the University of California have discovered how geckos can walk up the smoothest vertical surfaces (Figure 12.21). A gecko is a type of lizard. They have extraordinary feet (Figure 12.22), covered in millions of microscopically thin hairs. As the gecko places its foot on a surface, static electricity causes these hairs to stick to the surface. There is only a tiny force holding each hair to the surface, but all the forces added together are enough to hold the weight of the gecko.

Static electricity is the force you play with if you rub a balloon on your jumper and then stick it to a wall, or use it to attract your hair. It is also the effect you experience if you get an electric shock when getting out of a car. The car becomes charged up with static electricity as it drives along; when you touch the metal of the car body, the static electricity jumps on to you, causing a small electric current to flow through you, and that is what you experience as a shock.

Having understood how geckos climb walls, scientists at Manchester University have devised 'gecko tape'. This is a plastic tape, covered in synthetic hairs just two-thousandths of a millimetre long. The idea is that robots with gecko tape on their feet and hands will be able to move around in otherwise inaccessible places. So far, the tape is not strong enough to allow people to climb the walls.

Figure 12.21 Robert Full of the University of California, with one of the geckos his team studied to find why they are such agile climbers

Figure 12.22 The underside of a gecko's foot, which has ridges and fine hairs enabling it to cling to smooth surfaces

● Generating static electricity

When two different insulating materials (such as plastic, glass, or wool) are rubbed together, static electricity may be generated. We say that they have become 'charged up'.

Here are some typical observations (Figure 12.23) that we have to explain:

▶ Rub a polythene rod with a woollen cloth, so that they are charged.
▶ Hold the cloth near to the rod: they attract each other.
▶ Charge a second polythene rod and hold it close to the first one: they repel each other.

So **electrostatic** forces (forces between objects carrying static electricity) can be either attractive or repulsive.

Figure 12.23 Some basic observations of the effects of static electricity

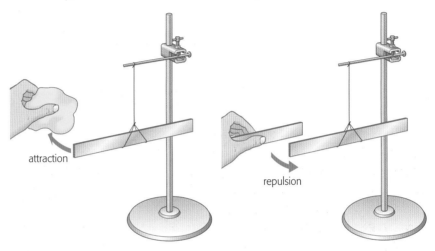

attraction

repulsion

▶ **First explanation**

The fact that sometimes we see **attraction**, sometimes **repulsion**, suggests that there are two types of electric charge. We call these positive and negative electric charge.

So, what happens when one material is rubbed against another? We say that one material gains a positive charge and the other gains a negative charge. In the example above, the woollen cloth becomes positively charged and the polythene rod becomes negatively charged.

The observation that the positive cloth and the negative rod attract one another suggests that:

opposite charges attract

In other words – positive and negative attract each other.

The observation that two negative rods repel each other suggests that:

like charges repel

In other words – positive repels positive, negative repels negative.

These are the rules which determine whether two charged objects will attract or repel one another.

▶ **Second explanation**

The 'opposites attract' explanation was devised in the 18th century, and it is correct. However, today we know more about static electricity and we can give a deeper explanation. It concerns electrons, those tiny particles which orbit around the nucleus of an atom (look back to Figure 11.11). Electrons have a negative charge.

Before they are rubbed together, the woollen cloth and the polythene rod are uncharged; they carry equal amounts of positive and negative charge. When they are rubbed together, the force of friction causes some electrons to be rubbed off the wool and on to the polythene (Figure 12.24). Now the polythene has extra electrons, so it has a negative charge. The wool has lost electrons, so it has a positive charge.

Note that the two materials must be insulators. If you rubbed a metal rod with a cloth, the electrons would be able to flow freely away through the rod, into your hand and so to Earth. (This would be an electric current.) For a metal object to hold its electrostatic charge, it would have to be insulated, for example, with a plastic handle.

The electrostatic force

The force of attraction between opposite charges is very important.

▶ It is the force that holds an atom together, as the negatively charged electrons are held in their orbits by the attraction of the positively charged nucleus.
▶ It is the force that binds atoms together to make molecules.
▶ It is the force that holds molecules together to make solid and liquid materials.

Without the electrostatic force, there would be none of the familiar materials around us, and there would be no us.

● Static hazards

You may have noticed tiny sparks which crackle when you take off items of clothing made from synthetic fibres. One fabric rubs against another and they become charged up. These sparks aren't serious, but bigger ones can be. A spark is an electric current, and static electricity generated by people walking across synthetic carpets can cause sparks big enough to damage a computer. Large computers are usually housed in rooms with flooring that has been sprayed with an electrically conducting substance, so that static charges flow away safely before they can build up to hazardous levels.

Electrical sparks can ignite fires. This can be a hazard, for example, when an aircraft is being refuelled using a pipe from a tanker (Figure 12.25). There is friction when fuel flows along the pipe, and this can cause static charge to build up. A spark could ignite a mixture of fuel vapour and air. To overcome this, the tanker and aircraft must be connected together using a metal cable before filling starts, so that any charge generated flows safely away to Earth. The same idea applies when the storage tanks at a petrol station are being filled from a tanker.

Lightning is a natural phenomenon caused by static electricity. Ice crystals and water droplets rub against one another as they move around in a thundercloud, and this generates vast amounts of static electricity, which jumps to Earth in the form of a lightning flash.

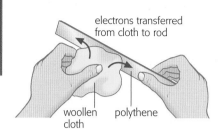

Figure 12.24 During charging up, electrons are transferred by the force of friction. The material that gains electrons gains a negative charge

Figure 12.25 Before refuelling starts, a cable is connected between the tanker and the aircraft to prevent charge building up and causing a spark

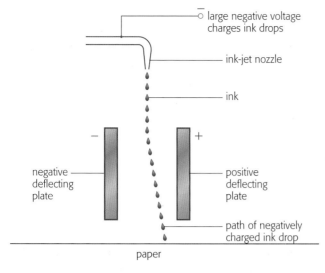

large negative voltage charges ink drops

ink-jet nozzle

ink

− negative deflecting plate

+ positive deflecting plate

path of negatively charged ink drop

paper

Figure 12.26 Using electrostatics in an ink-jet printer

Perspex	most positive
glass	
hair	
nylon	
wool	
silk	
polyester	
polythene	
PVC	
Teflon	most negative

Table 12.1 The Electrostatic Series

Using static electricity

Static electricity has its uses. For example, in fingerprinting, a fine powder is sprinkled on a suspect object. Static electricity holds the powder to the thin film of the fingerprint, revealing its presence.

Appliances such as photocopiers and ink-jet printers also use static electricity. In a printer, charged droplets of ink are guided to the paper using electrically charged plates. Negatively charged droplets are repelled by a negatively charged plate and attracted towards a positively charged plate (Figure 12.26). The drops of ink coming from the ink nozzle are deflected into the correct position on the paper, determined by electrical signals coming from the computer.

Summary

- When two different insulating materials are rubbed together, they may gain opposite electrical charges: positive and negative.
- Opposite charges attract, like charges repel.
- When electrons are transferred to an object, it gains a negative charge.
- Electrostatic charges can be hazardous, but they also have uses.

Questions

12.12 When a Perspex rod is rubbed with a woollen cloth, the rod gains a positive electrical charge.
  a What type of charge does the cloth gain?
  b If two Perspex rods are charged in this way, what force will act between them?
  c Use the idea of electron transfer to explain why the rod gains a positive charge.

12.13 Table 12.1 shows the Electrostatic Series. When two materials from the Series are rubbed together, the one higher up the list gains a positive electrostatic charge.
  a If a nylon rod is rubbed with a polyester cloth, what charge does the rod gain?
  b If a nylon rod and a polythene rod are rubbed with a silk cloth, will the rods attract or repel each other? Explain your answer.
  c Jane combs her hair with a PVC comb. After much combing, she finds that her hair stands on end, and that it is attracted by the comb. Using the idea of electron transfer, explain these observations.

12.14 a When a petrol tanker refills the metal storage tanks at a petrol station, there is a danger of explosion. Explain how an explosion might occur.
  b To avoid this hazard, the tanker and the tanks are first connected together using a metal cable. Explain how this helps to prevent an explosion occurring.

Acknowledgements

The following have supplied photographs or have given permission for copyright photographs or diagrams to be reproduced.

p.2 *t* © Bettmann/Corbis, *b* J.L.Carson, Custom Medical Stock Photo/Science Photo Library; **p.4** University of Edinburgh/Wellcome Library, Wellcome Trust; **p.6** Michael Abbey/ Science Photo Library; **p.7** Prof. David Hall/ Science Photo Library; **p.8** Cordelia Molloy/Science Photo Library; **p.15** *t* © Christophe Paucellier/Corbis, *b* Jussi Nukari/Rex Features; **p.16** Wellcome Photo Library; **p.23** *l* Rajesh Jantil/AFP/Getty Images, *r* Gregory Dimijian/ Science Photo Library; **p.26** Phototake Inc./Alamy; **p.28** *t* Prof. Miodrag Stojkovic/Science Photo Library, *bl* & *br* Eleanor Jones; **p.30** *l* © 1994–2006 Henri D.Grissino-Mayer, *r* © blickwinkel/Alamy; **p.31** Geoff Jones; **p.33** *t* & *br* Mary Jones, *bl* Geoff Jones; **p.34** *l* & *r* Geoff Jones; **p.35** NASC; **p.36** © Ed Young/Corbis; **p.38** *t* Corbis, *c* © John Potter/Alamy, *b* Dr Steve Harrison/LSU AgCenter; **p.42** © Andrew Brown, Ecoscene/Corbis; **p.43** *t* © Paul Doyle/Alamy, *c* © Richard Naude/Alamy, *bl* © Richard Hamilton Smith/Corbis, *br* Holt Studios International/Alamy, *bc* © Tobbe/Zefa/Corbis; **p.46** Dr Jeremy Burgess/ Science Photo Library; **p.48** Christian Darkin/Science Photo Library; **p.50** *t* © BIOS Gunther Michel/Still Pictures, *b* Nigel Dickinson/Still Pictures; **p.51** *t* Mark A.Klingler/Carnegie Museum of Natural History, *c* © Renee Lynn/Corbis; **p.53** *l* © Adam Woolfitt/Corbis, *r* Holt Studios International/Alamy; **p.54** Michael Marten/ Science Photo Library; **p.55** *l* Sean Sprague/Still Pictures, *r* Chris Jackson/Getty Images; **p.57** Sean Sprague/Still Pictures; **p.58** Fritz Polking/Still Pictures; **p.62** *t* Matthew Oldfield, Scubazoo/Science Photo Library, *b* Georgette Douwma/Science Photo Library; **p.63** © Andre Seale/Alamy; **p.64** *l* Visual&Written SL/Alamy, *r* © Lawson Wood/Corbis; **p.65** *c* © Robert Yin/Corbis, *l* © Amos Nachoum/Corbis; **p.66** © Stephen Frink Collection/Alamy; **p.67** *t* Hulton-Deutsch Collection/Corbis, *b* © Rick Price/Corbis; **p.69** *t* & *b* Geoff Jones; **p.70** © Michael & Patricia Fogden/Minden Pictures/FLPA; **p.71** © Howard Taylor/Alamy; **p.73** *l* © Phil Hurst/NHMPL, *r* Ed Reschke/Still Pictures; **p.74** Greg Shirah, NASA Goddard Space Flight Center Scientific Visualization Studio; **p.77** © David Tipling/Alamy; **p.78** *c* © Ashley Cooper/Alamy, *b* Geoff Jones; **p.79** Atmosphere Picture Library/Alamy; **p.80** Will & Deni McIntyre/Science Photo Library; **p.83** Martyn F.Chillmaid; **p.88** Andrew Lambert Photography/Science Photo Library; **p.90** Skyscan.co.uk/W.Cross/photographersdirect.com; **p.93** © Roger Ressmeyer/Corbis; **p.94** *t* The National Trust Photolibrary/Alamy, *b* Phototake Inc./Alamy; **p.95** © Pete Jenkins/Alamy; **p.96** Paul Thompson Images/Alamy; **p.98** Martyn F. Chillmaid; **p.103** Peter Menzel/Science Photo Library; **p.116** Cordis Endovascular, Division of Cordis Corporation; **p.117** *tl* istockphoto.com/Heiko Etzrodt, *tr* Sheila Terry/Science Photo Library, *cl* www.purestockX.com, *cr* Roger G.Howard Photography/photographersdirect.com; **p.119** Airbus S.A.S. 2006; **p.120** © Kimball Hall/Alamy; **p.122** Mary Evans Picture Library/Alamy; **p.129** Hulton Archive/Getty Images; **p.130** sciencephotos/Alamy; **p.133** *t* Dept of Physics, Imperial College/Science Photo Library, *c* Spencer Grant/Science Photo Library, *b* istockphoto.com/Ryan Poling; **p.134** Charles D.Winters/Science Photo Library; **p.135** *l* The Natural History Museum/Alamy, *r* Leslie Garland Picture Library/Alamy; **p.141** Popperfoto/Alamy; **p.145** *c* Philippe Plailly/Science Photo Library, *b* IBM Corporation, Research Division, Almaden Research Center; **p.146** © Rubens Abboud/Alamy; **p.147** *l* J.Bernholc et al., North Carolina State University/Science Photo Library, *r* istockphoto.com/Simon Askham; **p.148** *t* Geoff Tompkinson/ Science Photo Library, *b* Clive Freeman/Biosym Technologies/Science Photo Library; **p.151** *c* The Royal Collection © 2006 Her Majesty Queen Elizabeth II, *b* © Bisson Bernard/Corbis Sygma; **p.154** *l* & *r* Andrew Lambert Photography/Science Photo Library, *c* sciencephotos/Alamy; **p.156** Hulton-Deutsch Collection/Corbis; **p.158** Adam Hart-Davis/Science Photo Library; **p.159** *t* Adam Hart-Davis/Science Photo Library, *cl* Dr Tim Evans/Science Photo Library, *cr* Mauro Fermariello/Science Photo Library; **p.160** Visuals Unlimited/Corbis; **p.161** © Jeffery Allan Salter/Corbis; **p.163** BSIP, Auscape Ferrero/Science Photo Library; **p.165** Hotcan, Operational Support Limited; **p.166** *tl* istockphoto.com/Adam Kazmierski, *tr* © Danita Delimont/Alamy, *c* © Phil Degginger/Alamy; **p.168** © Philip Bramhill/Alamy; **p.170** *tl* & *tr* Mary Evans Picture Library/Alamy, *b* Sygma/Corbis; **p.174** Corbis; **p.176** James Jenkins Photography/photographersdirect.com; **p.177** *t* & *bl* Martyn F.Chillmaid, *br* ImageState/Alamy; **p.183** Hans Strand/Stone/Getty Images; **p.184** *tl* Charles D.Winters/Science Photo Library, *tr* & *cl* Martyn F.Chillmaid; **p.188** *t* © Jim Reed/Corbis, *c* AllOver Photography/Alamy; **p.189** *t* www.purestockX.com, *bl* Russ Munn/AGStockUSA/Science Photo Library, *br* Rick Miller/AGStockUSA/Science Photo Library; **p.194** *t* © Martyn Goddard/Corbis, *b* Michael Donne/Science Photo Library; **p.197** Peter Menzel/Science Photo Library; **p.198** © Rodolfo Arpia/Alamy; **p.202** Rui Vieira/PA/Empics; **p.205** David Sang; **p.207** Science Photo Library; **p.209** *t* © Chuck Bryan/epa/Corbis, *b* Satoshi Kuribayashi/OSF; **p.210** *cl* © Ron Dahiquist/SuperStock, *b* Cody Images/Science Photo Library; **p.211** *l* & *r* Euro NCAP; **p.213** © Michael Reynolds/epa/Corbis; **p.214** *t* © Crown copyright, reproduced under the terms of the Click-Use Licence, *b* Jim Varney/Science Photo Library; **p.217** © Oote Boe/Alamy; **p.220** *l* & *r* © Bettmann/Corbis; **p.222** Gusto/Science Photo Library; **p.224** Geoff Higgins/Photolibrary Group; **p.227** imagebroker/Alamy; **p.229** © Richard Cummins/Corbis; **p.230** Henry Westheim Photography/Alamy; **p.231** © Bettmann/Corbis; **p.232** CERN/Science Photo Library; **p.234** Detlev Van Ravenswaay/Science Photo Library; **p.236**, **p.237** *l* & *r* Cordelia Molloy/Science Photo Library; **p.238** BSIP, Laurent/Science Photo Library; **p.239** ISM/Science Photo Library; **p.241** Prof. Peter Fowler/Science Photo Library; **p.244** © 1978 Vernon Miller/Business Wire/Getty Images; **p.247** Vienna Report Agency/Sygma/Corbis; **p.248** Science Photo Library; **p.250** Philip Harris Education; **p.251** © Hinrich Bîsemann/dpa/Corbis; **p.253** General Photographic Agency/Getty Images; **p.254** Hahn-Meitner-Institut; **p.255** US Department of Energy/Science Photo Library; **p.258** British Nuclear Group Ltd; **p.260** *l* Skyscan/Science Photo Library, *r* Steve Allen/Science Photo Library; **p.261** © Paul Glendell/Alamy, *r* Pascal Goetgheluck/Science Photo Library; **p.263** *t* ITER, *b* Seymour/Science Photo Library; **p.264** Maximilian Stock Ltd/Science Photo Library; **p.265** Philippe Plailly/Eurelios/Science Photo Library; **p.266** *c* Peter Menzel/Science Photo Library, *b* Volker Steger/Science Photo Library; **p.268** EK Aviation/Alamy

t = top, *b* = bottom, *c* = centre, *l* = left, *r* = right

Every effort has been made to contact copyright holders but if any have been inadvertently overlooked the Publishers will be pleased to make the necessary arrangements at the earliest opportunity.

Index